HOME-LIFE

IN GERMANY.

BY

CHARLES LORING BRACE,
AUTHOR OF "HUNGARY IN 1851."

"We want a history of firesides."—WEBSTER.

NEW YORK:
CHARLES SCRIBNER, 145 NASSAU STREET.
1856.

PREFACE.

THERE are very many things we want to know about foreign countries, which we never do know from books. What people eat and what they drink, how they amuse themselves, what their habits are at home, what furniture they have, how their houses look, and above all, what the usual talk and tone of thought is, among the great middle classes of a country—these things are interesting, and are very hard to learn, except from travellers themselves.

WEBSTER, in almost his last great speech, said with reference to England, "there is still wanting, * * *, "a history which shall trace the progress of social life, in "the intercourse of man with man; the advance of arts, "the various changes in the habits and occupations of "individuals, and improvements in domestic life. We "still have not the means of learning * * * how our "ancestors in their houses, were fed, and lodged, and "clothed, and what were their daily employments. *We* "*want a history of firesides.* * * * We wish to see "more, and to know more, of the changes which took "place from age to age in the homes of England." * *

Of course, what I have given in this volume of the "Home-Life of Germany," can only be a suggestion for such a History of the Germans. My observations are merely the glimpses of a traveller, welcomed intimately in the homes of North and Middle Germany, during parts of two years. To the German, they will seem often superficial; still, they may be valuable hereafter, as the impressions of a stranger upon a subject of which so little is usually written or known—the internal social habits and thought of a leading civilized Nation. It will be seen that my facts and experiences are mostly gained from association with the middle classes. These—the men of business, the farmers, the merchants, the lawyers and scholars—are the influential portion of a People, who stamp especially its social character. It is their habits and manners we mean, when we speak of the social life of the Germans.

In view of this plan, I shall be pardoned if I have "cut" entirely guide-books, and the usual objects of interest to the tourist.

No one can understand even the modern domestic life of Germany, without knowing something of its Past. With intelligent men of foreign countries, there is usually the utmost vagueness of idea as to what Germany is, or what it has been; or what changes have brought it to its present form. I have accordingly devoted several chapters to Political and Theological History, as indispensable to a right understanding of my subject.

I have tried to give a true picture of German Home-Life, and all will, of course, draw their own conclusions. But I do not hesitate to confess that a definite purpose has been before me. It has seemed to me that in this universal greed for money, in this clangor and whirl of American life, in the wasteful habits everywhere growing up, and in the little heed given to quiet home enjoyment, or to the pleasures from Art and Beauty, a voice from those calm, genial old German homes, might be of good to us;—telling of a more simple, economical habit, of sunny and friendly hospitalities, of quiet cultured tastes, and of a Home-Life, whose affection and cheerfulness make the outside World as nothing in the comparison.

On but one subject, do I hesitate much at my conclusions. I earnestly wish they may be proved incorrect. I mean my remarks upon the German *religious character*. On those solemn and mysterious relations which bind man with his Maker, I would be the last to speak dogmatically. The expression of the religious Principle is not to be limited by any local or partial measure.

Still, the observations, sad as they are, which I have

stated, seemed to me true of the masses of the people. Our hope is, however, for Germany, that the darkest time of Unbelief has past, and that a day of purer Faith and Reason is dawning.

CHARLES LORING BRACE.

NEW YORK, *March*, 1853.

CONTENTS.

SOCIAL LIFE IN GERMANY.

CHAPTER I.

FROM LEITH TO HAMBURG.

I WAS leaning on the bulwarks of the steamer, watching the bold hills behind Edinburgh gradually sink away, and the long line of blue mountains, opposite to Leith, become more and more mellow in the distance, when I was interrupted by a pleasant voice, with

"The Nature is very fine on this coast!" I assented warmly, turned and found a man leaning on the fo'castle house, engaged like myself in watching the receding shore. From his language, though not his accent, a German, I judge—a gentleman evidently—tones refined and full—dress very simple, shaggy outside coat, rough vest, coarse gray pantaloons, but with a neat travelling cap, a fine shirt, and, as accidentally appeared, a handsome watch and chain—face closely shaven, like the English, and with well-cut features, still a *German* face. He has a pamphlet in his hand which he has been reading—very likely, some North-German gentleman, who has been on his travels in England, and is returning home by way of Hamburg.

We fall into conversation; and I ask him soon whether he has been long in Scotland?

"Oh no," he says, "only since three months in Scotland, but a year in England." He is not very communicative, until at length, I let fall incidentally, that I am an American.

"I am very glad," he says, "I thought you were an Englishman from your appearance, and I always am a little—eh?—*genirt*—how call you it?—embarrassed with an English traveller. You know how they are to strangers?"

I tell him that I like the Germans very much, that I have been on my travels for about a year, mostly on foot, and last year that I was on the Rhine, and was so much interested in South-Germany, that I determined to see something of the other parts, "and now I am going to Hamburg for that purpose."

This confidential account of my plans was enough, and he at once spoke as frankly with me. He had been a tutor in German to two young Scotch noblemen on the lakes, and teacher of this language in one of the English Universities; had graduated a short time before at Bonn, and his father was a distinguished scientific man, whose name I had often heard. His object in going to England was to perfect himself in English, and to earn money enough to continue his studies. He was now crossing to Berlin, to spend the winter there.

Such a companion was an especial windfall for me, but I was in somewhat of a perplexity. I had sent my luggage—carpet-bag and knapsack—down to the steamer in Leith, and had booked myself for the second cabin, for Hamburg, but on getting on to the boat, the second cabin proved to be filled up with casks and spare canvass, as they were not in the habit of taking second-cabin passengers on this line! So that the choice was left me, either of taking a first cabin passage at £2, with one or two dull, stiff-looking gentlemen, or of "roughing it" indiscriminately for three days with the sailors and engine-hands, at £1. A part of my plan, through my whole journey, had been to see the *undercrust* of Europe, as much as possible. So I chose the latter. But this appearance of my new German friend made a difference, and I told him the case and my perplexity. "So! Vortrefflich! excellent!" said he, "I came on board exactly in the same way. Now we will be comrades!" and we shook hands heartily over it, and at once sat down on a pile of canvass for a long chat.

"You see," said he, "a pound goes a great way in Germany—as far as three or four in England—and I thought I might as well save it here. It would carry me to all the concerts and theatres of the winter in Berlin. Besides, I should like to get acquainted with these fellows here!" and he pointed to the crew at work around us. This led on to various questionings and answerings about Germany and German habits.

"Would you like to have your wealthy friends know you travelled in this way?" I asked.

"Certainly," he answered, "I always travelled so, when I was a student, and half the Professors do it now. The truth is, there are not many circles in Germany, where poverty is a disgrace. It is not as it is in England; our higher classes are not ashamed of econo—what is your word?—money-saving. *Ach*—how glad I shall be to be back in the old Fatherland again, where one must not be always looking out, for—that for which we have no German word—the *Respectability!*"

He did not say it distinctly, but he had been much annoyed, I should gather, while a teacher in England, by the weight of *caste* above him; and he longed to be in a land again, where a man is taken for what he is worth, and not for what his grandfather was.

He was intending to spend the winter in Berlin, and I meant to be there in a few weeks. We engaged to meet, if possible. I then told him my more especial plan. I had seen enough of the usual sights of travel, and I wanted particularly now to see German society, to become acquainted with the *Home-life*. I thought an American could learn more from that, than from all other things in Europe. "As for your governments and your institutions, we have little to gain from studying those. Your Art, I hope to examine."

"*Ach!* and what beautiful! You know not our modern German Art. If you only could see Kaulbach and Cornelius!—but *pardon!* go on!"

"I want especially to see how you Germans live and talk at home, and I am going mostly with that object. Still my prospects do not seem very good, as I have only three letters to Hamburg!"

"*Es thut nichts!* It makes no difference! You need not the recommendation-letters. If you like the Germans, they will like you, and will pass you on from one to the other. Only, mein lièber Herr, is your mind fully made up for the *Sauerkraut*, and to renounce your English port?"

I laughed, and made him the earnest assurance that it was. "Ach! how you will our Germany enjoy! You are right. It is the *Home* which is the best thing with us. We know how to enjoy. Ah! when shall I see mine again, dear L——n! way off on the Rhine! the sunny Rhine land!" He was looking off to the South, where the waves were gilded under the setting sun. I said nothing.

After a pause we were soon again in pleasant conversation.

"What do you think it would cost a man by the year," said I, "in Berlin, living as we should want to live?"

"It is very different in different quarters of the city," he replied, "and the cost will so vary, as one shall understand the modes of the place. I shall take a room in one of the best streets, dress like other gentlemen, and have all our best pleasures—music, the art and the pleasantest society—all for about 300 *Shaler* ($225) a year. It would cost you or a stranger more. Berlin is more expensive, as—than the University-towns, or the cities in Southern Germany—Munich, for instance—I have lived there for 200 *Shaler*,—and such musique and theatres! But in general, living is very cheap in Germany."

Engaged in pleasant talk, we hardly noticed that the evening was coming on, until we remembered that there were sleeping-places to get for the night. Our first attempt was in the engine room, where we found some sociably-inclined firemen, who took us into their little cabin.

We were all soon on the best terms. The firemen brought out pipes, and N. (my German) sent for whiskey for them. I took a pipe, and we sat long chatting over our adventures.

At length I left my companion, stowed away in one of the dirty berths, and went forward and hired a *bunk* of one of the hands, in the little forecastle, and was soon sound asleep.

The next day there came on a hard storm—one of those tremendous gales which sweep often across the German Ocean. The waves poured over our bows in a constant stream, so that I was compelled to keep quietly in my berth all day. I am never sea-sick, and was well used to all possible rough quarters, but I thought my German friend would find his first experience in cheap travelling in English steamers, rather too much for him. He did come forth the next day, a most woe-begone, soiled, draggled-looking man. But he only laughed at his own miseries, and insisted that he had had "a grand time" with the boys below.

The contrast was most pleasant, when after the incessant tossing and rolling for three days, we entered the quiet river of the Elbe;

and a few hours later, came to anchor before the long, handsome quay of the city of Hamburg.

I said a hearty farewell to N., who was going up to Kiel to visit friends; we engaged where to meet in Berlin. My luggage was pitched into a boat, and in a few moments, I was being rowed quietly along through the still canals, overhung with trees, and under the fantastic warehouses of this quaint old city. A polite bow from the custom-house officer as we landed; my bags passed without examination; and behold me following the porter through the narrow streets of old Hamburg.

CHAPTER II.

HAMBURG, AND A GERMAN HOUSE.

October 9, 1850.

HAMBURG is a much more interesting city, in appearance, than I had any reason to suppose from the accounts of travels and guide books.

The contrast between "the old city" and the new, is very striking. The quiet antique alleys, like those of the Dutch cities, with canals and shade trees, and fantastic gables and rather anomalous statuary in the niches of the walls in one quarter, and in the other, the grand, new, bustling streets, built in the finest style of modern architecture, and opening out imposingly around the wide Basin of the Alster.

In May, of the year 1842, a great fire occurred here, which raged for four days, and reduced the finest part of the city to ashes. Over seventeen hundred houses were destroyed, and the flames were only checked by the skilful exertions of an English engineer, Mr. LINDLEY, of whom I shall have more to say hereafter. After the fire, the town was rebuilt under the direction of this gentleman, and in a very complete and splendid manner. The narrow, unhealthy alleys were widened; new streets laid out; the old stagnant ditches filled up, and some of the most imposing lines of buildings erected, which are to be seen in Europe. In fact, I know no city on the continent, whose business-streets make so fine an impression at first sight. Stone is very scarce here, so that nearly all the houses are built of brick, with a hard cement or stucco over it. Either the climate is more favorable, or it is a much better cement than with us,—certainly the stuccoed houses look far better than in our cities; and it has afforded an opportunity for something which is extremely needed in our country, that is, giving to each house its own peculiar ornament. One becomes so heartily tired of long rows of monotonous houses, exactly corresponding to each other, without an attempt at variety or character. Here I passed through streets of high, handsome houses, where they had all the advantage which ours have—and undoubtedly it is an advantage—of a succession of similar parallel lines of structure on the front, one above the other; but, besides, peculiar independent ornaments to each building. Every house had a character. Every man could show his own peculiar taste on the front of his home. And this cement gives a beautiful opportunity for all kinds of graceful moulding and ornament, and even for small statuary. The Hamburgers have improved it well.

I found the public walks, also, and gardens of the city, very pleasing. The old bastions are laid out into agreeable promenades, which were gay on this day with merry parties. At length, in the evening after my arrival, after much pleasant rambling about the city, I resolved to deliver one of my letters of introduction, and while away an hour or two. With some delay, I found the house; the servant carried up my card with the letter; a friendly, hearty voice bade me welcome in English, and I found myself in company with a genial old gentleman and two younger ones, engaged over a decanter of Teneriffe and a round of cold beef. A place was made for me at once, and we were all soon in animated conversation. They spoke English well, and were very much interested to hear anything of America, and especially of our recent extravagancies about Jenny Lind. *Punch* seemed the great authority about us, and they asked if "Barnum would really smoke at her concerts, as he is there pictured !"

After the supper was thoroughly disposed of, cigars were lighted without ceremony, and we spent a long evening in very pleasant talk.

They entered into my objects of seeing German life, rather than the usual sights, with much interest; and at the close, I had engaged to spend the next day with the old gentleman, and to submit myself entirely to his guidance. It was late in the evening when I groped my way to my hotel, very happy at the friendly welcome I had found so soon, in a German home.

OCTOBER —, 1850.

"There is certainly a kind of simplicity about these Germans, which one does not see in America," I thought to myself, as I sat in my friend's parlor, the next morning, in a comfortable house, looking out over the Alster. It was the house of a man of fortune, a retired merchant; yet the whole, though bearing tokens of a cultivated taste, showed a remarkable plainness. The parlor in which I sat—a high, handsome room, with prettily-painted ceiling and tasteful papering, had no carpet. The furniture was simple; there was no grand display of gilt and crimson anywhere; and it was evident very little had been laid out on mere splendor. Yet one could not but notice how carefully even very common implements had been chosen with reference to grace of form. The candle-stands, the shade-lamps, and even the pitcher, or the common vase, had something exceedingly graceful and almost classical in their shape. The designs of the music-holders, and of the table ornaments, caught the eye at once—every article seemed to have a meaning. The pictures on the walls or the table were not expensive—often mere sketches ; yet they were very pleasant to look at, and had not been placed there, evidently, merely because " pictures *must* be hung in every respectable parlor." The figures of the daguerreotypes showed the same traits ; not formidable ranks of stiff forms, but easy groups around some animal, or in some natural position. There were flowers, too, everywhere ; and especially that most graceful of all flower vessels, which I have seen alone in Germany, though I believe it came from Italy, called the " *Ampel.*" It is simply a half vase, very much like the old Grecian *lamp*, hung with cords from the ceiling, with some flowering vine in it, which twines and wreaths around it ; yet the beauty of it all can hardly be imagined. The only exception in this house to the general good taste, was the high white Berlin *stove*, looking like a porcelain tower with gilt battlements ; but possibly one who is accustomed to our quiet, sombre machines, must need a little discipline to get used to these gay articles.

While noticing all this, my friend came in and welcomed me cordially, as he had hardly expected I would be up early enough to accept his invitation to breakfast. " We keep much earlier hours," said he, " than you English. Business begins here at eight, where it would not in England till ten, and breakfast is even earlier than curs—usually at seven."

The breakfast was simply coffee and *Brödchen*—little bread-rolls —for which Hamburg is famous. The coffee was made at the table by the ladies, as it is in France, and sometimes with us, by pouring boiling water over the coffee and letting it drain for a few minutes in a machine for the purpose; the principal care being that it should drain slowly, through both a sieve and some tissue paper.

After breakfast, we went out to look at the garden. The house below—and I shall not fear to offend my friend by *particularising*, as the description would apply to two-thirds of the houses in Germany—resembles the upper part in its plainness of appearance. There are no carpets or matting on the stairway. On one side of the hall is a long dining-room, lined with portraits, with gilt moldings and tasteful papering, but the floor again, bare, though scrupulously neat. There are handsome curtains at the windows and a few substantial articles of furniture, but, altogether, it has a rather naked appearance, and probably serves as a dancing-room. The other side of the hall opens into a small room, looking out on the garden, and connected with a pleasant grapery, which is warmed from within, as grapes cannot be raised here without artificial heat. This room is used, perhaps, as a smoking or coffee-room—a cool, shaded room for the summer.

Like most of the buildings here, the house stands directly upon the street. The outer door is left unlocked, but the opening it stirs a bell, and the inner door is unfastened by a servant. The garden was tasteful and pleasant, with the fruits and flowers of a northern climate. It is singular that the apples here, as almost everywhere in Europe, are small and poor in flavor, compared to ours. My friend, like the English, considers our American pippins one of the rarest and most beautiful additions to a dessert-table.

The other parts of the house, so far as I saw them, had the same general air of simplicity and good taste. The bed-rooms are without carpets, too, at least in the summer.

Not having tried my friend's beds, I may claim without discourtesy, a traveller's privilege, in saying something here of *German beds.* The whole nation, with all their intellectual progress, have not made the first step in the philosophy of beds. And to one coming from England, Germany presents a most deplorable contrast. In England, the bed is considered almost a sacred spot. It is carefully and nicely made; it is curtained off from the world; and there are very few inns so poor, as not to have many ornaments and comforts about their beds. But in Germany, it does not seem to be considered a place where an important part of life is to be spent. It is only a narrow, open *lounge*—always too short for a long man, and too narrow for a restless one. The mattrass is a most light, flimsy affair, which is attempted to be counterbalanced by an immense hard pillow, reaching half way down the bed, so that one is obliged to lie at a half-sitting posture. And to crown all, for a coverlid, is a large, light feather-bed or pillow, which makes one intolerably warm under it, and leaves one very cold without it. These beds have been the subject of malediction with travellers, since Coleridge's feeling remarks on the subject, but they do not appear to have changed much, except in a few places on the Rhine, where the English have fairly *grumbled* them away.

The remainder of the morning my friend kindly devoted to showing me the principal sights of the town; and in the afternoon, I presented my other letters. One was to Mr. Lindley, the English engineer. Mr. L. is the last one to wish his name brought out in this conspicuous way, but I cannot forbear expressing my thanks for his many attentions to me, and my admiration for what he is accomplishing in Hamburg. A free-minded, untiring, hopeful man—one who believes that God's world is not quite a stagnant pool of wretchedness, but that something can be *done* to clear it and make it flow on again—and who is doing his part for this in a very thorough way. I had the pleasure of meeting him frequently, and the account of all his efforts in the city, his attempts to stop the progress of "the great fire" by the general blowing up of buildings; his struggles with the lower classes, who at first believed him almost a demoniac man, plotting the destruction of the city; his gigantic plans for rebuilding, and endeavors to inspire the Germans with something of the English practical spirit, would form an interesting history in itself.

He has just offered, I was told in private, $10,000 to the city corporation, if they would subscribe the rest, for building several large bath-houses for the poor, after the manner of the London houses. At his suggestion, and by his plan, some grand water-works have been erected, which supply the whole city with pure water, and the pipes from which can be used for the engines in every block, in case of another fire. He has constructed, too, an immense building and machinery, with a very high tower, for the gas-works—much of it contrived on new principles. He was superintending, while I was there, some new extensive docks, laid out by himself. One of the best quarters of the city, on the right bank of the Elbe, has been gained by him, from the marsh, by thorough drainage and by pumping out the water with a steam-engine, and filling in the space with the rubbish from the fire. Mr. Lindley has been the rebuilder of Hamburg; and all agree, that to his improvements a great change in the health of the poorest quarters, is due. The first feelings, as I said, towards him during the fire, by the lower classes, were of intense suspicion and hatred. Under his direction, some of the finest buildings in the city had been blown into the air. The crowd cried out that "the foreigner was trying to ruin Hamburg," and he hardly escaped with his life. But afterwards, as they saw the fire subsiding through these measures, and when later, they beheld his unceasing exertions to rebuild and improve the city, they began almost to idolize him. And now, by workmen and *Bürschen*, no man is better beloved than Mr. Lindley, the English engineer.

OCTOBER 18, 1850.

I went out to-day in company with one of my friends, to visit a wealthy gentleman, living in the outskirts of Hamburg. I preferred to walk, and was well repayed by the opportunity it gave me for examining the pleasant villas which surround the city. For some time, I wondered to myself what it was that gave so different an air to them all, from that of our country-seats. They were built not unlike them, of wood or stuccoed brick, in rectangular forms, or with slightly varied outline The grounds in general did not seem especially "foreign" in their designs. I concluded finally, the difference was in the universal tendency to make the most of the open air. The houses were all surrounded with pleasant balconies, opening into the sitting-rooms; there were porticoes, leafy boudoirs connecting with the inside; the gardens were full of arbors, and summer-houses and seats, where people were eating and drinking, as if it were as habitual there as within doors.

We found the family we would visit just sitting down to "lunch," and we were at once placed at the table. There was a little company accidentally assembled; and the lunch, though it was only eleven o'clock, presented itself as a rather formidable meal—steaks, bread-cakes, fish and claret, with a close of some beautiful grapes and pears from the gentleman's conservatories, and decanters of choice pale sherry. There was little form, though several servants were in waiting. The great topic of conversation was the war then going on in Schleswig-Holstein, against Denmark. All seemed to sympathise most deeply with the insurgents. I was somewhat surprised to notice, too, considerable conversation on religious subjects. My German is rather limited yet, and a very rapid conversation, where there is a confusion of voices, I find it difficult to follow; but I was struck with the earnest, practical tone of what was said. The subject seemed generally connected with something they called the "*Inner Mission*," which I did not at the time understand. My neighbors at the table were very polite. and very much was asked about America, where many of them seemed to have friends.

Our time, the remainder of the day till dinner, at five o'clock—for they would not hear of our returning till after we had dined with them—was spent in examining the very handsome estate of the gentleman, and in talking with the various friends who chanced to come in. As a considerable company of the neighbors had assembled, in part through invitation of the host, to compliment us, the dinner proved quite a formal affair. The ladies in full dress; a splendid dining-hall with flowers and lights; and a line of respectable-looking servants. I was curious to see what the arrangement of courses would be. Soup, as everywhere, the first—then a Rhine wine poured out to each one who would take it; the second course, boiled beef; next, fish with a red wine; then pigeons and Saxony larks, a little delicacy much valued here; pudding; and champagne served; and last of the solid courses, roast venison. The dessert was black bread and cheese, with port wine.

The especial enjoyment of the meal was evidently in the conversation, and there was little hard drinking. The ladies did not drink wine at all. The principal person at table, and one to whom all listened with marked attention, was a strong-featured, earnest-looking man, who, though he made a keen joke occasionally, was talking mostly of very serious matters. His voice was deep and fervid, and as he spoke some times of the social evils in Germany; of the wrongs of the poor; of the little hold which religion has upon them; and of the utter want through the nation of any practical piety, I could see from the deep stillness of the company, that they felt they were listening to great truths, uttered by an earnest man. He spoke of the "*Inner Mission*" again, as a means of reform.

I could not restrain my curiosity longer, and asked in a whisper of my next neighbor what this "*Inner Mission*" was, of which they were speaking so much. He answered with the enthusiasm which they all seemed to feel in regard to it, still his explanation had something of the German *vagueness*, and I only gathered that it was a grand Religious Institution, and that he himself was strongly "Evangelical" in his views. The gentleman who was speaking, he said, was a man well known through Germany—Herr Wichern. From this, we fell into something of a conversation on these matters.

He asked me whether I did not notice a very great contrast here in the observance of the Sabbath, to my own country. I had, I replied, and I had been wondering whether the people really held it as a religious day, only in a different outward mode from ours; or whether it was merely a day of amusement.

"There is not the least trace of religion in it," said he, "with the most of them. In the Protestant Church, which I attend, there are 20,000 members, and not 1200 of them ever come to the

Church. The lower classes drink beer and roll nine pins (*Kegel*) on that day, and the higher saunter about and go to dinner parties."

"I could hardly credit it," I said. "This was but a small part," he replied, "of what I would see, as I travelled more in Germany." I asked him, farther, whether he did not find a great want of sympathy in his peculiar views. "Yes, certainly, but, thank God! the darkest days for Germany in practical irreligion, are past!"

Our conversation was interrupted by the company rising, and each gentleman taking his lady again to the drawing-room. Here each bowed to the other, and said a few words, as if in salutation, all which of course I followed, with the exception of the "good wishes for the meal," which I did not well understand. A traveller's ignorance in these matters is always very charitably treated.

In regard to the *Inner Mission*, it may be well now to state, what I afterwards learned, especially as it is a movement which is even yet deeply influencing the religious condition of Germany. The name, *Innere Mission*, I will not attempt to translate, fcr it seems hardly to correspond to anything we have. It is not a Society, though the word sounds like it, nor a Brotherhood; but apparently it is an immense popular *movement* to meet the influence of Rationalism in Germany. The object is to call back the people from the abstract, mystical, skeptical tendencies which have distinguished them so long, and bring them to the practical good works of religion. They mean, as many of those engaged in the movement will tell you, to "*Englicise* Germany." They have found that religion has lost its practical hold of the people; that the churches are poorly attended; that spirituality has little connection with education; and that works of charity are shamefully neglected They design to change this. To go around and influence individually the lower classes; to introduce religious education in the schools; to bring together more to the churches, and to rëestablish family-worship in the houses; to form ragged schools and asylums, and places of reform for prostitutes; to establish temperance (*not* abstinence) societies in some communities; and to found sailors' homes in the seabord towns. The plan seems too great, and to embrace too wide a variety of objects, to be the plan of one movement. Yet so it is. And many who are joining in it look even higher than to these ends. They hope to change the relations of governments to one another, and gradually to make the State only one branch of this immense institution, the Church. The plan itself, perhaps, has something of what they are objecting to—the German Idealism. Yet I am bound to say, that thus far the results have been very practical. Institutions almost unknown before in Germany have arisen under its influence, for the poor and the unfortunate. Orphan asylums, vagrant schools, and "homes" for abandoned women have been erected by these faithful followers of the Inner Mission. Under its working, the attendance on churches and prayer-meetings, has widely improved. And if I can judge at all from the accounts of those interested in it, families have already felt the effects of it in a more hearty attempt to worship together, and in greater efforts for a useful religious life.

The King of Prussia—a man apparently very quick to feel any noble idea, and very uncertain sometimes in his action, and fitted to be anything better than a good *King*—has taken deep interest in many of these movements for forming charitable institutions, and has given very substantial aid.

The meetings of the "Missions" are held in various parts of Germany, and are some periodical, and others chance gatherings. Those connected with this enterprise are called the "Friends of the Inner

Mission," and can belong to any sect of Christendom; even prominent Roman Catholics have sometimes taken part in it. At the head of it all, holding the various strings which connect with its wide operations, the life and centre of the movement, is a man who in another age, and in other circumstances, would have been the *Loyola* of a religious society—HERR WICHERN. A man of indomitable energy, of high and enthusiastic nature, yet uniting with it in a combination not often seen in human nature, except in such characters as Ignatius Loyola, the shrewdness of a man of the world, and a thorough practical talent. By his efforts many of these charitable institutions have been formed through various parts of Germany, and he is now himself at the head of an immense charity or vagrant-school in Hamburg, of which I shall have more to say hereafter, conducted as it is on principles quite new in the management of such institutions. He is summoned constantly to different parts of the country on the work of this "Mission," and report says, has no little influence with the crowned heads of Germany. On the whole, the movement appears to be a grand one, and is certainly a tremendous protest against Rationalism; or, at least against the present religious condition of Germany, under the influence of Rationalism. "It is a second Reformation," some of those engaged in it will tell you, except that "it begins in the Church, and has the support of the Church." One might fear it would become in process of time, an immense religious society, controlling the populace everywhere, and liable to be used by ambitious men for bad purposes. But the day seems to have gone by for that, and we may hope for better things.

CHAPTER III.

SOCIAL LIFE IN HAMBURG.

HAMBURG is one of the wealthiest cities in Germany, in constant connection with England, and where English habits of luxury have penetrated. It is famous in the German States for the good dinners and the riches of its citizens. Yet there is throughout the middle classes—with a few inconsistencies—a simplicity and frugality, of which we know little in America. Money is made with more difficulty than with us, and is naturally not spent so freely. People talk of economy, as if it were a thing really to be considered. I find that merchants, in good business, not unfrequently retire on a fortune of $20,000 or $30,000. The gentlemen, too, travel in cheap conveyances, such as we Americans would never endure. I have scarcely seen carpets on the floors of a single house, except among a few of the wealthiest; and the furniture, in general, though tasteful, is not at all expensive. People are contented with mall means, and yet they make those means go a great way, in comfort and beauty.

I have said, there were some inconsistencies in this home-life of the Germans. With a most grateful and comfortable sense of all the hospitality I have received from them, I must be permitted to say, that in *eating*, and in a few of their habits, they are hardly consistent with their simple and ideal tendencies elsewhere.

The hours for rising in the city are much earlier, as I before remarked, than in England; usually in the middle classes half-past six or seven. The breakfast is always merely a cup of coffee and bread-cakes. After this slight meal, the gentlemen go to their business and the ladies to their household work; and I have been surprised to observe in the various families of my acquaintance how much the ladies do of housekeeping work, and even cooking. At eleven or twelve, those of the family who are at home, meet again for "lunch." This is a moderately substantial meal of cold meat, bread and butter, preserves and fruit, with some light wine like Burgundy or Claret. Then at three o'clock comes the dinner, *the* meal of the day of course. With many of the business men, the same custom prevails as in our large cities and in England, of having the dinner at five or six o'clock, after the business of the day. But three or four o'clock is the more general hour. The meal commences according to the world-wide custom, with soup; then succeed roast meat and vegetables, and then perhaps fish and various courses to the number, often, of five or six, each course however being only a small dish—and the remarkable thing about it all, being that the fruits come in, in the middle of the courses, and the roast meats just before the end. The dessert, according to an English custom, and one which does not prevail much in our country, is bread with butter, or cheese. The wines do not seem to be as varied, as in family dinners in England, being generally the light red wine, either of France or the Rhine, together with Teneriffe. The last dish is always a cup of strong black coffee. Of course, this arrangement of dinner differs somewhat in different families, and perhaps the order of courses is not strictly fixed; yet such a dinner would not be at all uncommon, and might be considered a fair sample of a good *family dinner.*

I have spoken of wine drinking—and it may not be out of place to mention my observations with respect to it here in Hamburg. Wines are cheap here, owing to the absence of all duties and the neighborhood of wine countries. Rhine wines are from 10d. to 1s. per bottle; common Burgundy from 8d. to 10d.; Bordeaux from 4d. to 8d.; and Champagne from 2s. to 4s. The people drink the lighter wines universally, yet the number of cases of intoxication is surprisingly small, and I never see men unduly excited by liquor at table, as I frequently have seen in Scotland, where the strong wines and whiskey are so much in use. The appearance of Hamburg, too, at night, is a wonderful contrast to that of Glasgow and Edinburg, where I have lately been, and the hideous rioting and drunkenness which disturb one in those cities, are seldom known here. These are facts which I cannot connect with any particular theory, but which are worth considering, as showing that there are countries where drinking is common, and yet where much truer ideas of *temperance* prevail, either than in rigid Scotland or in our own country. Whether the Scotch strictness in other matters drives men to extremes in this; or, what may be the reason, I cannot say. To one who would wish to look at all sides of the question of temperance, these facts will be worthy of attention.

The afternoon, among the Hamburgers, is devoted to exercise, walking and riding, and amusement—and the lady, who has been perhaps working in the kitchen, now escapes to pleasanter occupations. In some families we used to meet again at six, for tea, handed around without eatables—a custom probably derived from the English. The evening follows, and is spent either over whist or in pleasant conversation, or at concerts—and again at nine or ten o'clock, is another hearty cold supper, with meats and fruit and wine finished on the gentlemen's part by cigars, which are smoked here apparently as freely in the parlor or dining room as any where else.

Such an overflowing hospitality of good things, all day, is very pleasant, but how the Germans ever succeed in bearing up under it, is a matter of some surprise to the stranger. In fact, the nation seem generally most daring transgressors of all the rules of *dietetics*, and yet one cannot see, but that they are as healthy and work as hard as most other nations.

I have been very much amused in conversation with various people, at the popular impressions about America. They are all excellently well informed on the subject of our government and the character of the people; but their ideas of small matters are frequently taken altogether from the jokes circulating about us. *Punch's* "hits" and caricatures, and even the mere good-humored extravagancies of the "New York Herald," such as the loss of life attending on the rush for an "Extra Herald," are all believed with astonishing readiness. "Did our gentlemen sit at the opera, with their feet over the backs of the boxes?" some one inquired of me. I find it one of the hardest things to convince them that there is a difference between the North and the South; and that gentlemen do not carry bowie-knives about with them as they would tooth-picks, in the old States.

There is one subject I have found it best not to touch upon too much with many of the Hamburgers. It is the remarkable number of Prussian uniforms one sees every where in the city. I can scarcely go by a public building, without meeting the plain spiked helmet and blue coat; and not a day passes when I do not come upon companies of Prussian soldiers, drilling in the squares. When the Prussian troops returned from Holstein through Hamburg, a year or more ago, they were thought by the worthy democrats of that city, to have given up quite too easily the support of Liberalism, and in consequence were hooted at, and pelted by them. The City Senate and Bürgher Guard could do nothing against them, and it is generally supposed these foreign troops were privately invited in, for the sake of keeping down the ultra-republicans. At any rate—much as the citizens dislike the term—Hamburg, like the *free* city of Frankfort and independent Duchy of Baden, is under the *protection* of Prussia, and Prussian bayonets uphold the representative government!

October 20.

I was to-day at a dinner party, and in the evening after it, a very characteristic conversation took place. We were gathered around a table, looking at some spirited illustrations of the Bible. A young man with finely cut features and full moustache, whom from, his whole appearance, I took to be an artist, seemed much interested in them. His remarks upon them were very appropriate, and showed the deepest feeling for the beauty of outline, as well as the thought expressed. At length he dropped some depreciatory expression in regard to the facts thus illustrated. His words were at once taken up by a benevolent-looking old gentleman—a clergyman—who stood near, and then ensued a well-sustained discussion, the young man maintaining the *mythical* theory of the Bible, and the "Pastor" arguing the literal. The artist's points were well put, but on the whole, fairly met by the other. Yet it struck me that the younger disputant was far the most in earnest, and there was a half-sorrowful expression occasionally in his eye, which showed he had some other object than mere *talk*, in the discussion. The Pastor argued as if it was his business, and the young man as if he sought with whole soul for Truth. The conversation soon passed, in some way, to these struggles in Europe for liberty. Here the religious man had changed his ground. Hopeful before, when he met the sombre doubts of Immortality, he was now faith ess, gloomy, timid.

"Europe is not ready for freedom, and does not at heart want it," said he. "The people are wild with Socialism and Infidelity. They want license, indulgence. They have tried and failed enough in their efforts for Liberty. Have we not now a steady, Christian Government in North-Germany? A King on the throne of Prussia, known as an humble, faithful Christian? Why should we tempt Providence, by aiming at what God shows himself unwilling to give?"

"Mein Gott!" said the artist, almost with a burst of passion. "And is this Religion—to lie down as slaves always? The people are infidels, Herr Pastor, because the Church and Tyranny are bound together. Not a word of free noble sentiment against the oppressions of Germany ever comes from your pulpits! Look at Prussia, and see that accursed unconstitutional rule upheld by the priests of God! Yes, we have failed. We gained the victory and then trusted the princes—but so has every noble cause failed. We shall not trust so much again! The King of Prussia"—and by this time he had gained the attention of the whole room—"is perjured before God and men! He has publicly broken the oath he gave only two years ago. And what is going on now over poor Holstein, but another act of this same oppression?" His appeal to Holstein evidently aroused the sympathies of the whole company, and the preacher was almost silenced, though he could not restrain some allusions of contempt to the struggles in Hungary and South-Germany. I took up the cudgels here, and an animated debate followed, and desultory conversation, until at length we came to the subject of the German laws enforcing Confirmation, and the connection of Church and State.

"In our country," said I, "we find religion far better sustained by leaving it entirely to individual, voluntary support."

"It might be so with you," he replied, "but the system would not work here. By the laws of confirmation, every child must go through with a certain course of religious instruction under the Pastor. In this way, thousands of children are instructed, who would never otherwise come near a clergyman. I myself spend some two hours almost every day in the week, in such labor with the children of my parish. Besides, the certificates of baptism and confirmation are absolutely necessary for the numbering the population and proving their legitimacy."

"But," said I, "do you not find, where a religious confession is enjoined by law, that Religion becomes a matter of form, not of the heart? And does not the church pass into a mere instrument for upholding established authority? I should expect to find many, like this gentleman, considering orthodoxy and tyranny as very much bound together."

He was obliged to admit that these evils often did result, though counterbalanced, he thought, by the advantages.

I fell into a very interesting conversation, afterwards, with the artist, and I think he was surprised to meet any one with a distinct religious faith, yet sympathising in the great struggles of the day.

"Thank God!" I said to myself as I walked home, "it has not come to this yet in our country, that Religion and a dead Conservatism are the same thing. Young America is Religious America until now!"

CHAPTER IV.

A GERMAN LADY.

I HEARD much during this visit in Hamburg, of a remarkable lady, long resident in the city, and gratefully known through all Germany. As my friends described her, she seemed the Mrs. Fry of Germany—a woman who had visited the lowest prisons of the city for objects of charity, and to gather facts relative to prison-improvement; who had erected institutions for the abandoned and outcast of her own sex, and had thoroughly familiarized herself with the late establishments for reform in all the countries of Europe. They also represented that she was a woman of high cultivation and intelligence—a personal friend of the Queen of Denmark, and a correspondent of the first men in Germany, in talent and benevolence Her plans, too, were far more wide-reaching than for any temporary reforms. She aspired to raise the position of woman in social life throughout Germany, and to spread her own ideas, in the most efficient way, by education. With this purpose she had formed a school, they said, where fourteen or twenty scholars from the most influential families were instructed by herself *gratuitously*. It was one of the best schools in Germany, as Miss SIEVEKING—for that is her name—is very accomplished in modern languages and in all the higher branches of instruction.

Her plan was, to implant indirectly, during her intercourse, her own fervent religious convictions, and her ideas of woman's duties, in these pupils' minds. The first ladies in Hamburg were glad to commit their daughters to her; and the result was, that she had sent abroad, through Germany, accomplished women filled with the same purposes of practical usefulness.

I may say here, interrupting my narrative, that I afterwards met in various parts of Germany these ladies, and have found them every where leading the movements now in progress in Germany for spreading a purer and more practical piety. One I remember—a lady of rank—as the overseer of the "Hospital for women" in Berlin; another, the earnest and actively religious lady of the court-chaplain in the same city—Madame Snetlage—and others equally devoted with these, to works of reform.

Besides these labors, Miss Sieveking had organized a society of the ladies of Hamburg, whose objects should be thoroughly to investigate the condition of the poor through the whole city. The city was divided into small districts: each lady took one, went over it every few days, made note of those needing relief or work, or talked with those in sorrow, and carefully inquired as to those who had had no religious instruction. The reports thus made are read at each general meeting and measures there adopted for relief, unless the need is too pressing to allow of delay—the great principle being to give the people *work*, not alms.

I asked, in the course of our conversations, how this lady man aged to get money to support herself in so many gratuitous labors. They said, that originally she had owned some property, which she had now entirely spent for these objects, but that she lived in so simple a way that it was easy for her to get along on very little indeed; and now, when any rich Hamburger died, even if he had never given a penny in his life, he was sure to leave something to Miss S., as a kind of salve for his conscience.

I felt very desirous of knowing her—it is so seldom that a woman has the courage or ability to stand out from her sex, in a life worthy of a being of high powers; and of all countries in the world where it would be hard for a woman to act against the usages of society, for some great intellectual or benevolent purpose, Germany is the worst. The cry of "*emancipirt!*" (emancipated!) is worse than ever *blue-stocking* was with us, and is a sentence of death to any lady's success for evermore in society. All accounts, too, so agreed, that with this lady, rough work on the realities of life had not worn away refinement, or modesty, or good sense, that I anticipated much in meeting her.

I shall remember long my first interview with her, from a side-circumstance that occurred—one of those little blunders which a stranger may always make in first speaking a foreign language, and to which he must harden himself, if he would ever progress at all. In the course of our conversation, I inquired in regard to an "Appeal" she had been lately making—of which more presently—to the ladies of Germany; but by a slight change of *one* consonant, I had politely asked after the "uproar," she had been making among the ladies of Germany. She was too sensible to notice it, and the rest of the company preserved a courteous silence; the only effect being that the conversation soon turned into English, which I found she spoke very well.

I had expected in such a position to meet a very enthusiastic, ideal person. but was agreeably surprised to find her a sensible, practical woman, not particularly "exalted" with these ideas, but evidently carrying them out under a deep sense of Christian duty. An odd figure she was, too, at the elegant table where we were, with her simple, quaint dress, her little active form, and her keen blue eyes, moving so quickly when she spoke. She did not appropriate the conversation, though all listened with great respect when she spoke. I had much talk with her.

She told me of the difficulties she had had in starting benevolent institutions in Germany—how unused the people were to give, *in their lives*, for such objects; how little of the evangelical spirit, with which she had been so delighted in England, was to be found here. The ladies, too, at first could not be induced to come forward in practical efforts. No one was "good" here till she began to be *passé*, and the young ladies feared to rise above this public opinion. The name of "emanciprit" was worse than martyrdom. Some of the parents, too, objected in the beginning to their daughters entering her Asssociation for the Poor, because it might have a bad influence on their moral purity to see the worst classes. She thought it a good thing, on the contrary, for a young woman to see something of the dark sides of life. Besides, any modest ignorance of such subjects, she said, was altogether out of place on the part of the ladies, as every one knew they were entirely familiar in one way or another with them. She had found it very difficult, too, with the higher classes, to break down the unreasonable customs about fashionable work. Every lady of rank has come to think it an unchangeable duty to embroider, or do ornamental sewing, a certain number of hours each day. The best part of her time—hours which might be given to educating her mind or laboring for others, is spent in this useless way. "And worse than useless," said she, "for it is not economical, as the thimbles and needles and nicknacks for all this cost more than the profits, and work is taken away from poor women who need it." She remembered, she said, to have read very early in life a treatise on woman's duties, in which it was declared to be the "first duty of woman to sew and embroider." She could not see then, and had not been able since to discover, why it was the universal duty of every woman to sew, any more than for every man to cobble or to dig. She thought there was quite as much variety in women's capacities as in men's. She had at last been able to induce many ladies from the higher class to leave this baby-house occupation, and engage in real, benevolent work for the suffering; and it seemed to her now that there was more of practical, evangelical piety among the wealthier classes than any other.

I made in the conversation some remark about the institutions of reform in London, but found at once that she was far more thoroughly informed than myself about them, though I had visited them carefully. The "Schools for vagrant children" and the "Homes for reformed women" she had thoroughly examined, under the guidance of the most prominent nobleman of England, and she had already aided to found such institutions here. Still, she had not much hope for the reformation of these women, she said, unless families would consent to take them in and give them *work*. Merely living in a "home," hearing preaching, and having repentant thoughts, was not enough. They must have something in place of the intense excitement of their life—some steady, honorable labor.

I drew the conversation to her efforts, a few years ago, in the fearful year of the cholera. She described to me a few scenes, but she did not say—what the citizens of Hamburg will never forget—how heroic and untiring her labors were in that dreadful time of pestilence. She did not say, that when clergyman and friend and father had fled in terror from the dying-bed, she could be seen, hour after hour, entering the deserted houses, bringing medicine and aid and her kind words of Christian consolation to the sufferers; that when the magistrates of the city had almost abandoned the hospitals, she was there to regulate again, to encourage, to give her judicious counsel, and to collect food and medicine.

There is many a family in Hamburg, both of rich and poor, who will forget every friend and benefactor before they cease to remember that little, active, quaintly-dressed woman, with the keen, kind eye, who came so like an angel among them, in those terrible days of disease and death.

I had been very much interested in this conversation. The woman's benevolence was so evidently rational, and there was such a common-sense and almost sharpness of tone to her ideas, that you saw at once she was no mere enthusiast. As soon as possible afterwards, I obtained her "Appeal to the Women of Germany," and read it with great interest.

I will give some extracts from it, as the pamphlet has had considerable influence in Northern Germany.

"APPEAL TO THE CHRISTAIN WOMEN AND MAIDENS OF GERMANY.

"You have, during these last few years, often heard of the '*Emancipation of Woman*,' but for the most part in the antichristian sense of the Communists, and it is very natural that you have a certain repugnance to the word. Yet I believe it admits also a Christian interpretation, and I shall not fear therefore to use it." * * * Then follow her opinions as to the position of woman in modern society, and the accompanying passage: "After these explanations you will recognize, my dear sisters, that in that which I wish for our sex, my purpose is not at all directed to a removal of natural limitations, and those by God himself arranged. What I want is only a freedom from the reigning frivolity, and from the iron force-rule of fashion and a senseless propriety. Understand me, it is not my purpose to utter a sentence of condemnation upon every occupation of women with the thousand trifles, which belong to the decorations of life. It is not my meaning that they should raise themselves above every law of fashion and propriety. What I mean is this: the side-matters of life should not be made its head-matters; the toilet and needle-work and novel-reading should never be the principal occupation of woman, or that filling up the greatest part of her time."

She then alludes to those to whom this is especially addressed—"Those who in general have the good will to do their duties, but are not sure of the nature and extent of them; and who on this account often neglect the essential for the unessential, and, not accustomed to a regular activity, split up time and powers in such a manner, that a true enjoyment comes neither for themselves nor for others, not to say any lasting profit." * * * * * *

Her opinions of the sewing-work among the ladies of the wealthy classes, are given as I before expressed them: "I really believe that many a lady who places her highest glory in this—that nothing is ever sewn out of the house, or that she does all the needle-work of the house with her own hands—would do far better if she would give this work over to some poor sewing woman or tailoress, and thus be of real assistance to them, and at the same time buy, at so small expense, valuable time to herself, to be devoted either to the common interests of the family, or to their higher spiritual interests."

She then enumerates some of the objects to which she would call forth woman's activity, especially that of wives and mothers.

"A rational guidance of the housekeeping and attention to detail, where the limited circumstances of the husband demand it; if in a higher position, a supervision and oversight of accounts, with the duty always upon her of watching over the bodily and spiritual good of the servants;—*the education of her mind*, so that the wife can be something more to the husband than a mere housekeeper or plaything; so that she may be capable of sharing the interests of his profession, and of being to him a *helpmate* in the most beautiful sense of the word; so that her conversation can be a refreshment to him from his earnest business and cares, without drawing his spirit down to what is entirely vain and trifling; education of children in the nurture of the Lord; and finally, whenever the household circumstances allow it, a share in useful public labors, especially for the poor brethren and sisters."

One or two extracts more must suffice. This is characteristic:— "THE RIGHTS OF THE POOR. With careful consideration do I choose these words. I would produce in every Christian woman, mistress of a household, the conviction that, as such, she is under an obligation to give aid to the needy. In the oldest Christain churches, this was decidedly the ruling idea." Or this address to "The Unmarried." "To the last named, who come especially near me, since I belong to them, I would address a warning word of love. Oh, dear sisters, I know many a one among you who, freshly and joyfully, is working under God's visible blessing in His kingdom; but many another is also known to me, to whom such an activity is wanting, and it does not surprise me that such a one looks out sad and out-of-harmony (*verstimmt*) on the Life which has perhaps cheated her in its sweetest hopes. Is it so, thou dear, poor sister? Oh, take fresh courage! It is indeed a beautiful calling—the calling of wife and mother; but meanest thou the Lord has this *one* blessing only for those who serve him? I tell thee this blessing is as manifold as is the mode in which we can devote our powers to His honor in the service of others. Rest not till thou hast found such a life's calling. That this must of course be in the circle of the sick and the poor, is no way necessary. It is not there alone that there is need of the free labor of love. In all circles of human society, can a field for this be found, if only each one understand her own correct limitation and work.

"One thing only would I lay to thine heart, that in the forming thy life-plan thou shouldst not place the demands upon thee too low; that thy activity be as much as possible a regularly arranged one; and that thou subjectest thyself to a binding rule, and never, without absolute necessity, variest from it."

We close with this extract, in regard to woman's engaging in politics, which shows the same sensible tone, and gives us a glimpse at Germany. "In general, I believe that the natural capacities of woman's mind are as little favorable to the deeper study of politics as to that of mathematics. * * * Women here have no reason to lament that they see the entrance to the depths of politics closed to them. Alas! there are so many discords there, which it is so hard to bring in harmony with the feelings of a soul directed by the gospel-truth to a universal philantrophy! * * * * And to what end would her activity here be? To man, and to woman especially, in all efforts, there is ever a need to have a practical aim before the eyes, and here it must be entirely wanting."

CHAPTER V

EXCURSION TO THE DUCHIES.

My purpose had been, in visiting this part of Germany, to make an excursion into the Duchies of Schleswig and Holstein, both that I might see something of a country in a state of war, and because this is said to be one of the most truly *original* parts of Northern Europe. The people, as they are fond of boasting, are from the old, original Anglo-Saxon stock, from whose coasts came the wild freebooters that peopled England and gave to it and to America their most vigorous race.* The inhabitants please themselves now with tracing their resemblance to the English, and there is much attachment among them for that people; so that the position England has taken in their war with Denmark is peculiarly bitter to them. The country varies much in the capacities of its soil and its appearance. The central tracts running from Altona up as far as Flendsburg, are flat and sandy, and in some parts exceedingly boggy, with no very productive land. On the west of this, near

* It will be remembered that the *Juti*, and *Angli*, and *Frisi* who invaded England in the fifth century, and eventually conquered it, came from these various districts of Denmark.

the coast of the German ocean, is a wide strip of marshy country, but wherever recovered and drained, the best land in North Europe; while on the other side, all along the Baltic, and reaching in near the interior lakes, and embracing the small Duchy of Oldenburgh, is the pre-eminently fertile land of the Duchies; a country generally level and with springy soil, but highly cultivated, and containing in parts some of the richest pastures and best dairy farms in Europe.

Towards this part of Holstein I directed my journey, purposing to go farther into the northern and western districts, if I could obtain the requisite "permits," or if the country seemed sufficiently safe.

Encumbered with no luggage, and with only my knapsack and walking-stick, I took the omnibus for Altona, a very thriving commercial town, only some three miles down the Elbe from the city, and so connected by country-seats and numerous houses of refreshment that it seems almost another quarter of Hamburg. It is however, in fact, a prosperous rival in commerce to the larger city, and the citizens say, answers too well to its name "All-zu-nahe," "All-too-near." Before this war between the Duchies and Denmark, it was second only to Copenhagen in the Danish kingdom, both for population and commerce. It took sides strongly with the provinces against the king, and has suffered much during this unfortunate war. The inhabitants are mostly of German descent and speak the German language, so that they joined heartily in the universal movement for a nationality in Germany, and are bitterly reluctant to come again under the Danish rule. At Altona my plan was to take the cars for Neumünster, on the railroad which connects Hamburg with Kiel and the Baltic. The train was delayed somewhat, and I waited at the station.

A railroad depôt in North Europe is an entirely different affair from anything of the kind with us. The principal and peculiar trait which the stranger observes on entering it, is the remarkable adaptation of the building for eating and drinking. The whole structure may be as large as our best station-houses; but the best halls, the finest rooms are reserved for dining and lunching rooms. The waiting halls, the baggage-closets, the platforms are small, ill-furnished, or inconvenient, but wherever there is any eating to be done, you have convenience and even comfort.

I entered a large, handsome apartment that morning, filled with small tables, which even at that early hour (seven o'clock) were crowded with various parties, and ordered my glass of coffee and rolls. Every variety of class seemed to be gathered there at their *Frühstück* (breakfast). The common Holstein peasant women, with their neatly-fitting red boddices and sun-browned faces, eating the *Wurst* (a kind of sausage) and black bread. The men, their huge baskets by their side, drinking beer and smoking the long pipes. At other tables, soldiers playing cards, with interludes of sour wine and bread and butter; officers in dashing helmets reading their morning papers over bottles of Rhenish; travellers in great fur wrappers drinking coffee, and ladies sipping tea. All in one room; a cloud of tobacco-smoke rising over it all, and a confused noise coming forth of clinking beer glasses, German oaths, jangling sabres, and cheerful gossip.

On each side there appeared to be smaller breakfast rooms, where the more select parties met—usually officers of rank going to the Holstein camps. At the signal of a bell, we all arose and went through different doors marked with the numbers of the three different classes, to get our tickets. Each class had its own ticket-office, and there were officers stationed everywhere to prevent mistake. Scarcely any one, except a few foreign-looking travellers, went to the first-class office. I took a place in the third class.

In England, the great principle of rail-road arrangements as respects third class travelling, is to discourage it in every way possible. The "parliamentary trains" are always the slowest, the most uncomfortable, and the most uncertain and inconvenient in times of departure and connections, of all the trains. In Germany it is not so. The accommodations for the third class are very nearly equal to those of the second; and the time and speed is the same for all classes. After the tickets were bought, each of us who had heavy baggage went to another office, presented the luggage and the ticket, received a baggage receipt, and if the baggage was overweight, paid accordingly. At the end of the journey, the baggage is returned at the presentation of the receipt. These arrangements on all the German roads are remarkably thorough and faithful. I have travelled over thousands of miles on them, and never yet saw the slightest difficulty on any of them with the baggage of travellers. Nor, in fact, have I ever witnessed the smallest accident. The double tracks, the sentinels stationed every half-mile, and the very strict regulations for the companies, make any dangerous occurrence very improbable.

The cars, or "carriages," as the English say, I found differently arranged from our own. In place of one long apartment running through the whole car, there are several different compartments entered from the sides, and with seats extending from one door to the other. In the first class, the *coupès* or partitioned parts contained only two or four seats, each a cushioned arm-chair, as in our own cars, though not half so elegant. The divisions in the second and third classes can contain each some twelve or fourteen persons, sitting on two lines of seats facing each other. The third class seats have no cushion, and the second only a thin hair covering. Smoking was forbidden on these cars in notices, printed in some three or four different languages; and I should not exaggerate in saying, that there were no less than three or four different "nationalities," smoking all tobacco from the strongest "Virginia" to the mildest Hungarian, in every compartment of every car! The military-looking man, who at once demanded our passports and our tickets, kept a cigar smoking in one hand behind him while he took them with the other.

The only other thing which struck me as peculiarly foreign in the arrangements, was the locking every door, just before the trains started. There is no rail-road either on the continent, or in England, which will at all compete with the American roads in the convenience and elegance of the carriages. Even the "royal cars" have not that grace and airiness, and the conveniences attached which belong to our common cars; and the providing of a stove, or of an apartment for sickness in a rail-car is altogether unknown in Europe.

Our ride this day towards *Neumünster* was at first quite uninteresting—the country flat and dreary, and so like many of the sandy and boggy tracts along our rail-roads at home, that, sunk in my newspaper, I had quite forgotten I was in a strange land, until the "*Wohl bekommts!*"—"May it be well with thee!"—from a little girl opposite, at my sneeze, reminded me I was not at all in Yankee land. Farther on, the country became gradually more interesting. There were more cultivated farms, and various little villages, with the red-tiled roofs, and high-pointed gables. Pretty hedges, too, began to appear over the whole country, much like the English. They are raised on mounds, and many of them are of small beach trees. There were signs along the road of a country in a state of war Crowds of soldiers stood at the different stopping places, and filled up the cars, hastening on generally towards Rendsburgh, near which is the central camp of the army. They were young, and seemed in high spirits, and were apparently farmers and business men, drafted in to fill up the army, so much thinned by some of these late assaults. Many of them had almost the Prussian uniform, especially the round smooth helmet, with a spike in the top. Near one or two of the stations were hospitals, and the sight of men walking about with bandages, or limping on their crutches, and with weapons battered and worn, began to make War seem a reality. My car was occupied by the peasants for the most part, and I was much struck with their politeness to one another. Every clumsy *Bauer* that tumbled in with his bags, or that left the cars, wished us all "good morning," with the greatest ease and politeness; and the Kiel students, who came in with their jaunty caps and long pipes, bowed to the old apple women as they would have done to ladies.

At Neumünster I left the rail-road and struck off on foot eastward towards the "*Plöner See*," a large interior lake. It was reallly exhilarating to be travelling away on foot again—knapsack on my back and walking-stick in hand—with such perfect independence of vehicles and conveniences. I have traversed something of Europe in this way; and over an interesting country, I know no more exciting mode of journeying. There is a dash of adventure in it all the while. You meet strange comrades, see what books and travellers do not tell of much; and can have many a chat with common people in their own homes. There is so much less of the usual traveller's annoyance of cheating and bargaining. It is all so independent. I was, at this time, in very good condition for walking, having just "finished" the highlands of Scotland, and accordingly felt nothing to lessen the interest of the walk. There was something stimulating to my fancy in the idea of journeying over this old patriarchal country. I found much, too, all along the road new to me. The one-story farm-houses with their immensely high peaked red roofs; and the heavy thatched barns quite as handsomely built as the houses; the long green banks with the hedges upon them, and the huge wagons of wicker were all peculiar to this part of Europe. Occasionally, too, I passed a squad of the new recruits, or walked through a village where military drilling was going on. I feared some interruption, or insult with my foreign look, and travelling in this rather peculiar way, but there was never anything of the kind. And, I may say here with real thankfulness, that in all my wanderings and rough adventures in Europe, at least, on the Continent, I have never experienced from the lowest or highest classes anything but courtesy and kindness. The only annoyances I have suffered have been from *Governments.*

As I went on in my walk in Eastern Holstein, the country became more and more interesting. The beautiful lakes which mark this part of Europe began to appear. The banks were all skirted with trees to the water's edge, and were bright now with autumn coloring. The foliage is not so brilliantly tinted as with us, yet it has a soft, pleasant coloring, and the frequent mingling of the American wild vine, (*ampelopsis quinquefolia,*) throws in a vivid hue with striking effect. The waters were filled with pretty little fringed islands, and on every side stretched away cultivated fields, with hedges or graceful clumps of trees here and there. Over all was the soft, rich October light, so that the landscape left upon me an indescribable impression of gentleness and peacefulness. And in the quiet scene, I forgot that I was entering a land where every green valley and hill-side had just been stained by the blood of its best and bravest sons.

It was only till after night-fall, that I judged I must be near the estate of the gentleman I intended to visit.

As I could find nothing of it, I turned to a peasant's cottage knocked and entered a large room which extended the whole length of the house. It seemed a stable, as the cows were fastened on one side, though on the other, rooms opened into it. At the other end was a great fire burning, and an old woman tending it. When she heard me entering, she came forward, and in answer to my inquiry, delivered an unintelligible speech in *Platt Deutsch*, (Low German). I repeated, and she apparently understood me, while I could make nothing of what she said. We laughed at our difficulties; and she called a boy, who took my knapsack at her direction, and beckoned to me to follow him. I walked along after him, and after winding in the twilight through a long lane, and then through an avenue of old trees, we reached the house.

I had been growing gradually more and more timid at the idea of penetrating thus, a stranger with my limited German, into a family who probably knew nothing of English; but my fears were quickly removed by the friendly and almost primitive hospitality with which I was received, and I was soon in pleasant conversation with an excitable young politician, who had served awhile against the Danes, and who labored most earnestly to show me the wrongs heaped upon the Duchies by the accursed Denmark. Some pleasant ladies welcomed us to one of those bountiful German suppers which travellers only can fully appreciate, and I listened till a late hour, as the "*Politiker*" argued or fought his battles over and described how the Danes fled at Schleswig beyond all pursuit or trace, and how the canals and ramparts drove back the brave Holsteiners at Friedrichstadt; or while the sisters told their hopes and fears for their two brothers in the camp.

At the close of the evening, I was shown into a large "guest-chamber" on the ground floor, and was soon sound asleep on a genuine, old, patriarchal, Saxon bed.

CHAPTER VI.

A HOLSTEIN FARM.

The next morning, as soon as possible after breakfast, I started out with the son of my host, the young politician, to see the buildings and grounds on the estate. The house itself, like nearly all I have seen of the "proprietors" (*Guts besitzer*) here, is built of oak beams, filled in with bricks, similarly to the "timber houses" of England. It is only one story, but very long and with high pointed roof, covered with red tiles. Within, there are great numbers of those large rooms which the Germans appear to delight in. Here again, as everywhere, are the high porcelain stoves, and beside, heavy articles of oak furniture with brass ornaments, giving a most antique air to the rooms. There are the same marks which one finds in nearly all the German houses of a highly cultivated taste.

The buildings on most of these estates are arranged in the form of a parallelogram. Here, for instance, we passed down the court from the house under a fine avenue of lindens, with high roofed buildings on each side which had brick walls and windows, and looked like dwellings, but were only barns and cattle-stables, until we came forth under a gate-way, through a large granary at the end of the court. This farm, like most of those in Holstein, is principally a dairy farm, though having large fields of grain. I saw in the pastures some hundred and fifty cows, many of them crosses of the Ayrshire breed, with the old native *Angeln* stock. Agriculture is carried to a high degree of perfection in the Duchies. The whole system of "thorough draining," an improvement so little known even in our country, with its immense advantage to such a soil as this, has been understood and successfully practiced in Holstein nearly eight years.

We passed in our walk large fields, where wheat, oats and barley had been grown, and long stretches of turnips and carrots for cattle. Generally, however, in Holstein, these are not used for cattle-feed—the common fodder in winter being hay and corn-straw, with bran or oil cake. The barns and stables were all of brick, and were remarkably comfortable and substantial.

The horses were of good blood, and were the best I have seen out of England. The export of horses from Holstein is one of the most profitable branches of business.

Our path carried us by, also, some of the cottages of the *Bauer*, or peasants, who are tenants on this estate. They seemed many of them to be living in considerable comfort, though the barns looked better often than the houses. I observed here again that singular arrangement of houses which surprised me the first evening in the peasant's cottage. Large folding-doors at the end of the house open into the stable, and the rooms for the family are on one side, and entered from this. The high loft above is used for fodder and rubbish. Everything is kept so neatly that little inconvenience is experienced from this arrangement. The inside rooms are often quite tastefully ornamented.

My host, as I said before, is a landholder—with some 300 acres

These large estates of from 100 to 5,000 acres are now mostly farmed by tenants. They are reckoned by *Laing*, at 3,057. The land of the Duchies is generally occupied by small proprietors, corresponding to our American "farmers," on dairy farms supporting ten or fifteen cows. These farms, according to the same authority, number 125,150. Originally these estates all had the "Bauer" attached to them, as serfs; but within forty years, serfdom has been entirely done away, and the only remains of it are a kind of perpetual rent, (*Abgabe*), which a few of the Bauer are still obliged to pay, though they are considered owners of the land; somewhat as it is on part of the Patroon estates in New York, with the exception that these tenants are obliged to pay in money, and that their estates would be sold at auction, if they refused. Some of the Bauer are *bona fide* owners of the land, and hold large estates, with an income in some cases of $10,000 a year. Others are tenants, paying rent like the small farmers of England. In a population of 662,500 souls in the Duchies, there are 67,700 peasants who own a house and land; 17,480 who own a house alone; and 36,283 who are merely day-laborers.*

A great deal has been done in the Duchies, and indeed in all Germany, for the education of the lower classes. Every man is obliged to send his children to school, or he is exposed to a fine. Advancement in the army, attaining of the commonest state offices and even confirmation in the church is made dependent, in a greater or less degree, on the previous education. Yet I am bound to say, I am struck everywhere with the fact—a fact which all good men in Germany deeply feel—that the great *results* of education are not apparent in their lower classes. The peasants can write and read,

* Laing's Denmark.

and cast up accounts, but they never have been taught to *think*. There is very little active intelligence among them, very little which would fit them to support a system of self-government. When we talk of our grand system of schools and colleges at home, it may be worth while to remember that they are not by any means all the basis of our education. The American people has been passing through, and is passing still through, an education very different from what is gained from either books or lectures.

It is always hazardous, accounting for the condition of a whole people on one cause; but I would say, that if any one thing could be found which deadened all religious life, and along with it, all intellectual life in the peasantry of Germany, it is this making Religion and the developments of religion a subject of *Law*. Wherever I have been in Germany, the conversation has fallen very naturally on this "Confirmation-law;" and I have never yet heard any sound reason given for it. By this enactment, no man can attain to any civil office, no man can be a pedlar or a soldier, or even claim the protection of his country's law, without having first made a solemn confession of his faith and hope, and received confirmation from his pastor. The natural consequence is, that every Bauer comes to look upon the profession of his faith much as he does upon his drill and his tax-paying, as a task commanded by government, which he had better go through with quietly, and so save himself from fine. But the deep experience in religion, as an individual matter of the heart; the personal interest in the church and in the preacher; the consciousness of sympathy with those who have united voluntarily for good objects, he very seldom feels. In Holstein, and wherever I travel in Germany, I hear constant complaints of the very little interest taken by the lower classes in religion, and in the institutions of worship. They are honest and moral and industrious; but as to troubling their minds very much about the Being above them, or a future, that is quite another matter. They are content to go on, as their fathers have gone before them, to smoke their pipe and drink their coffee, go to church as little as possible, and then quietly and easily drop away from life.

It is a sad picture, perhaps one of the saddest to draw of any people. Yet, I am compelled to believe it is true.

Many of the Germans will defend this law on the ground that the great object of it, is *education;* to give the State everywhere educated servants, and that the religious confession is only a side matter. Others, with the usual tendency of the nation, will carry you back to the original "foundation-idea" of government, as including in it that of church and of education also.

Waiving this last argument here, as somewhat too remote in the mists of metaphysics, we may say, as far as mere education is concerned, or as far as the idea of religious life being generally a gradual development is included, we could not have so strong an objection to this system of the Germans. But the whole appearance of the law, and the general effect, is something entirely different from this. It is, in fact, compelling a man, by formidable punishments, to do that which of all acts of his life should be the freest and the truest—to make publicly a profession of religious belief and religious obligations; and the natural effects seem to me easily foreseen.

But to return to the Holstein farm, where I was walking around among the Bauer-houses and in the harvest fields. The morning was very pleasant, and my friend took me up to a hill from which I could get a good view of the neighboring country. It was a beautiful land. My eye passed over a wide landscape of gently-sloping hills, and smooth fields, and graceful clumps of beeches and elms, the whole mellowed by the soft tint which autumn-light throws over everything; while far in the distance we could just see the sparkle of the first of the lakes which vary so beautifully the surface of Eastern Holstein. There were green hedges everywhere, and the whole had the appearance of a quiet, peaceful English landscape. It was one of the last scenes which would remind one of fierce fight and bloodshed and war. Yet it is such quiet country-scenes as this all over Holstein, which have been trampled and wasted in this hotly-contested struggle. Every one of its features has had its influence in the war. The hedges which beautify the whole country of the Duchies, planted as they are upon high mounds, have almost entirely prevented the use of cavalry by either party, and have afforded excellent shelter for the rifleman. The low, level character of the land, and the frequency of lakes, has given the Danes their greatest defence—the inundations which they could cause around their works; while the gentle, easily-sloping hills, have prevented the opportunity everywhere for very strong defences, except in the cities.

My companion was a very intelligent person, and despite my imperfect German, we discussed everything about both America and the Duchies, which would interest either of us.

On our walk back to the house, we passed through a large garden, showing not by any means such careful cultivation as the fields.

In such a family, and with so many interesting objects around, a few days passed very pleasantly. The whole life here has something extremely generous, and almost oriental, about it. When we meet in the morning at "morning coffee," we all shake hands as if we had been to a distant country, and wish each other almost solemnly the morning salutations. Every one pays great deference to the father, a simple, dignified old man; and the *Bauer* come up constantly to the house as though they were members of the family, for his advice and assistance. And as I walked over the farm, I observed that every laborer and boy we met, took off his hat, and the master did the same. We meet again about eleven for the breakfast, a more formal meal. Here, as nearly everywhere in Germany where thanks are offered at all at a meal, it is done *in silence*—a much more impressive ceremony, than our hurried, careless form. It is very difficult for most persons to preserve *the life* in words so often repeated, or to invent new words for each occasion; but in these few moments of solemn stillness, thoughts can be breathed which are really prayer.

After this morning meal, comes the principal business of the day; and in this family, the ladies do the principal part of the housework. Again in the middle of the afternoon, we meet at the great meal of the day, the dinner. This is a long, social meal, with a strange variety of dishes, which I will not try to enumerate. After it is over, we all rise and shake hands, with the words, "*Gesegnet die Mahlzeit*," (blessed be the meal!) in a quite serious manner; then follows coffee in the sitting room, and in the beginning of the evening again, tea and biscuit; and at the end, another hearty supper of meats, &c.

In education and refinement, the whole family would compare favorably with the families of our best farmers at home. The father is very much like some of the English country gentlemen I have seen, in the genial, hospitable way he has; yet his politeness seems much more from the heart than theirs, and there is much less that is coarse and animal about him. He drinks the light wine, but does not seem to consider it at all a duty, that he should force every guest to drink till he is under the table. They were all well-read, and I was surprised to find that Cooper's novels had penetrated there, (in translation,) and that they were deeply interested in them. Of course they were thinking and talking mostly of the war; and, like nearly all I meet, they could not but acknowledge, how little object there was in it.

As one reads in the *Times* how England and Russia on one side, and Prussia on the other, stand looking down upon this little War of the Duchies, ready like sportsmen in the ring, to bet now on this side and now on that, and admiring complacently the "pluck" of the two combatants, one gets a very different idea of the struggle from what one does when among the parties. Here every man's heart and soul are in the war, as a struggle for independence from the hated Danes; and the issue assumes a terrible aspect to them, as they see that life and property will depend on it.

This family had two sons in the army; and as I saw that day the trembling anxiety of the mother for the news from the camp—and as I heard from the sisters, how in the battle of Idstedt, which was not very far from them, they listened all day to every boom of the cannon with beating hearts—and how happy the home was when the news came that their brothers were unhurt—I felt how terrible a thing, even on the smallest scale, this "*War*" is! My friend had served awhile in the army, and we had many conversations on this contest with Denmark. I have since seen many of the party of the Duchies, and have read quite thoroughly the documents and state papers issued in regard to the grounds of the war. Of the questions at issue, I shall have more to say hereafter.

But the melancholy thing about it all is—whichever side has the right—that all this loss of life, and bombarding of cities, and desolating of happy provinces, is *of no use* so far as the result is concerned. The destiny of Schleswig-Holstein will be decided by diplomatists far away; and the great powers of Europe, whichever side gain the victory, will settle the disputed question themselves.

CHAPTER VII.

HOLSTEIN AND THE CAMPS.

October, 1850.

I FELT as if parting from old friends, when after a few days' stay, I shook hands with each one of the family, and started off in my host's carriage for the neighboring town of EUTIN. The country all through this part of Holstein is very beautiful. I was constantly reminded of England, in the gently sloping hills and hedges, and level, carefully tilled fields. The farm houses, however, are not at all English; being, as I before mentioned, usually only of one story, with a high pointed roof, covered either with thatch or red tile. There are pretty lakes too, scattered all through the country —and groves, where sometimes on the estates of the large proprietors, the trees are grouped with a great deal of taste. Eutin, (pronounced *Oiteen*,) which we reached in a few hours, is the capital of the little Duchy of Oldenburgh—a province situated in the midst of the Duchies, but belonging to Oldenburgh. There is nothing, however, very remarkable about it; it being only the usual collection of red-roofed houses, with a modern castle, bearing a strong resemblance to one of our factories. The town and the province have thrived well through these neighboring wars; for they escape entirely the burdens which press upon the Duchies, while they find a far readier market for their produce.

I took up my quarters at once in the best inn—and a very pleasant specimen of a neat German inn, it was. A large, handsomely-furnished room with a fire; a boy kept in attendance; my meals sent up, and everything arranged in the most comfortable way—all, as I afterwards found, at the price of 87½ cents a day!

I spent a day or two in the place, and had the pleasure of attending, in company with some friends, a political meeting, summoned to collect subscriptions for Schleswig-Holstein. I was quite curious to see how they would conduct it. When I entered, the speaker and every one else, from the "Amtmann" (county-magistrate) downwards, were puffing at their cigars. The principal speaker of the day, however, denied himself this universal luxury; and, apparently not being much accustomed to extempore speaking, contented himself for sometime, with reading minutes of the great convention at Hanover for the Duchies, as well as various spirited appeals, issued by the Assembly. When he did address the meeting, it was in a very melancholy, drowsy tone, which would have been utterly irresistible to the heavy-looking farmers assembled, had it not been for the cigars. However, his appeal for the Holsteiners, on the ground of their longings for a share in the "German Nationality," evidently found an answer in the breasts of very many, and after the meeting, considerable enthusiasm was shown in the planning for collecting subscriptions.

One cannot readily imagine in America, how very little facility there is in Germany in *extempore* speaking. I was talking with a German lately about the Peace Congress in Frankfort, and I happened to ask him, why there were so few speakers from Germany there. He replied, he supposed it was from the little practice the Germans had in that kind of speaking. And I have found that very generally, they acknowledge their inferiority in it. Yet this nferiority must be only from want of practice; for in private, I have seldom heard men speak with more enthusiasm and readiness.

My time in Eutin, in spite of its being so uninteresting a place, passed very pleasantly. There were some army officers stationed there, and very social and intelligent fellows I found them. I know not how to express my pleasure, the more I see of Germany, in the social, kindly character of the people. It seems almost as if the usual selfishness of humanity were laid aside in some respects. When you ask a man the way in a city, half the time he will go around one or two squares to show you it. If you are in a hotel or any public place, and are in difficulty about your route, instead of the cold "its-none-of-my-business" look of an English company, you find every one taking an interest in the matter and ready to assist you. People do not shut themselves within themselves, as in our country or in England; and when a party meet in a diligence or boat, they are ready and expect to *talk* at once, and not seldom about their own private matters. One is surprised to find himself forming confidential friendships with acquaintances not twenty-four hours old; and as he looks back on a week, he wonders whither the caution and coldness which used to distinguish him have departed. And in friendly and almost patriarchal hospitality, the Germans, thus far, seem to me unequaled over the world.

From Eutin, we took the night diligence northward for Kiel, on the Baltic. There were four or five travellers, all muffled in those huge furs which I have never seen except here, waiting in the office of the *Eilwagen*. They wished me good evening as I entered —and we fell at once into pleasant talk. This was continued farther, after we had settled each into a comfortable corner of the diligence—I having called out an admiring exclamation of *praktisch!*

(practical !) by shutting up my hat (a spring hat) and putting it in my pocket, and drawing on a warm travelling cap. The conversation, as everywhere, was of War, and the chances for little Holstein. It was morning, when we were aroused by rattling into the gates of Kiel.

Kiel is the principal port and city of the Duchies, with a University which has been somewhat famous. It is all quiet and empty now, however. The war has pressed hard upon it. Business is nearly at stand-still; every class is weighed down by taxes, and the best of the population are away in the army. The University is closed, for the students are all soldiers; and altogether Kiel has very little reason to wish well to the war with Denmark.

Kiel, I met with Herr Bargum, the President of the Assembly of the States; a man of great power as a speaker, and one of their prominent statesmen. He kindly gave me the letters required to gain admission to the camps around Rendsburg. Though my opinion, before expressed, that this struggle is not a *constitutional struggle*, has not changed, still I am bound to say, that I find more among the party of the Duchies ready for constitutional changes, than I had expected. They argue and perhaps justly, that the great mass of the common people in the Duchies and in Germany, are not yet ready for freedom; that universal suffrage or a complete Republic would only result as it has in France; that the mass must first be more educated; must be accustomed more in small matters to self government, ere it will be safe to throw the interests of the country entirely into their hands. Accordingly, they are approaching this general freedom gradually. In this new constitution of Schleswig-Holstein, the Representative Assembly is composed, I think, of one hundred members. Fifty of these are chosen by universal suffrage; of the remainder twenty are chosen by the cities, twenty by the landed proprietors of a certain moderate revenue, and ten by the great proprietors, having a somewhat higher revenue. Perhaps in view of the existing circumstances of the country, no better arrangement of suffrage could be devised. It is due, however, to Denmark to say, that an equally liberal Constitution would probably have been allowed the Duchies, if they had been united to that kingdom.

In travelling from Kiel to Rendsburg, I passed through the middle districts of Holstein—and found here again, the wide tracts of level land which are the characteristic of this part of Europe. But in general, they were far less fertile in appearance and less cultivated, than the eastern parts of this province. As we approached Rendsburg, we were obliged to stop in one of the neighboring towns, through some arrangement of the trains. Everywhere the signs again of approach to a scene of war. Officers in handsome uniform filled the coffee-rooms; soldiers with well-worn, weather-beaten arms drinking in the beer-houses, and a band of Tyrolese Minstrels were singing with great spirit, a song about Schleswig-Holstein and its great deeds, to the air of the "*Marseillaise*," while the patriotic ditty of "*Schleswig-Holstein, meerumschlungen!*" (Schleswig-Holstein, sea-surrounded!) rung on every side. It was certainly not a little comical to see on the walls—close by the scene of the operations themselves—*Panoramas* advertised of the battles with the Danes, *Pictures* of the onslaught at "Schleswig," and of the terrible explosion of the Danish frigate at "Ekernfiorde"—here almost within sound of the cannon, in either battle!

Rendsburgh, of course, is under martial law. My pass was demanded in the Station House, and as I walked up, in the evening, towards the City walls, sentinels met me every few rods, and I passed through a guard at the gate. The town was completely filled with a large body of troops, and I had to try almost every hotel before I could find a place. At length, however, I chanced upon a hotel, where, the waiter said, two English gentlemen were quartered who might be willing to take me in. I was shown up to their rooms, stated my case, and was interrupted almost before I had begun, by their saying, at once, I was welcome to a share in their quarters, and that they were "right glad to meet any one who spoke something besides this d—d Dutch!"

Cigars and Bavarian beer were brought out, as I would drink nothing stronger, and we had a merry evening together. I found they were English army officers, who had been spending the summer salmon-fishing in Norway, of which they related marvellous stories in the sporting way. They had come here, on the strength of their military rank, to inspect the works.

The next morning I presented my letters, and rambled over the town. It must have been before the war a quiet shady, pleasant country town, now, it is full of bustle and noise. Large battalions of soldiers were exercising in the square; heavy artillery wagons thundering along the pavement, and the streets were crowded with every description of person and vehicle—dashing young officers on gay horses; peasants with baskets of vegetables on their heads; huge market wagons with provisions for the troops; little parties of soldiers with the smooth helmets running up to a spike in the top; and all the innumerable characters which a camp attracts.

Yet both that day and the next, despite the numbers crowded into the little city, I saw scarcely any outward signs of dissipation—and I am inclined to believe that many of the worst evils of war, in the ungovernable crimes it engenders, are escaped thus far in this War of the Duchies.

One of my acquaintances, by good luck, happened to be a soldier who was on furlough from another town, and he walked out of the gates to show me the route through the camps. Here again I had an instance of this German "*Gutmüthigkeit*," (good nature). All that I had expected, at the most, in my acquaintance, was some good advice about the best course among the many roads around the town. But, instead of that, he insisted on accompanying me, guided me everywhere, introduced me to his friends, and in all must have walked some fifteen or eighteen miles with me that day!

As we went out of the city, the first thing that struck the eye was the flat, unbroken country all around the walls. It is naturally a plain, and now every high tree and bush and hillock is "*rasirt*," (shaved off) as they say, to give free range to the cannon. About the town itself there are two ranges of solid brick and turf wall, with a wide moat before each. These moats are supplied with water from the Eider, and are used as canals. Farther on, some half mile from the walls, my companion pointed me out a range of "*Schanzen*," or forts, on various heights at a considerable distance from one another, encircling the city. The roads, as we went on, became worse and worse, from the heavy travel over them, and we were met constantly by various parties hurrying into Rendsburgh; the "*Dragoner*" splashing through the mud—the infantry officers riding in the large basket-like farm wagons; and the privates, with the short sword which they all wear, working their way like ourselves along the pavement. My friend, whose eye was quicker than mine in detecting distant military movements, would occasionally stop to show me, far off on the heights, some black mass, which only from its motion I could discern to be soldiers, or point out at a long distance on the plain, quick moving objects, which he said were the horse artillery in exercise.

The whole country was evidently filled with troops. In fact, there are about 4,000 men now in Rendsburgh, and some 10,000 in the works around it. We walked on in very pleasant conversation for some distance. Though a private soldier, this man was a highly educated person; had been a student in Kiel, when the war broke out, and having some influence in his native town, he had collected a company of recruits and joined the army. It must have been almost entirely from motives of patriotism, for he knew that, like the rest, he must go through his term of service as a private. He was evidently sick of the life of a common soldier, though he was too manly to complain. I saw that all the officers treated him in a very equal manner—and he says that all distinctions of rank among them, when not on duty, are very nearly lost. In him, and the many I saw, I was struck with the quiet determination manifested, to push the contest through. They all say, that the German recruits are rather chilled at the little high enthusiasm they find when they come on; they cannot understand the calm, settled resolve which the army feels.

The first encampment we found in a small village of Bauer-houses. The soldiers are quartered with the peasants. My friend, or the "Doctor," as they call him, had an acquaintance here, and we stopped at one of the houses to see him. He was a lieutenant, and occupied with his "Sub," one part of the house, while the farmer and his wife, and three cows and some horses, lived in the other. He had been a student, as well as his under-officer, and they received my companion most cordially. A huge mass of roast beef and potatoes was soon brought on, and without apology from them or us, we fell to most heartily; and lighting our cigars, we talked for a long time over the comparative merits of the American and Holstein equipments, and the general ills and jovialities of a soldier's life. They are all tired enough of the war, but they are fully confident they can beat the Danes. In fact, they have some reason to be confident; it is long since the Danes have ventured to meet them in open field. After passing through this encampment, I went in company with this officer and the "Doctor," on towards the outer works of the line, which has thus far been the separation between the Danish and Holstein armies.

If any one will look at the map, it will be seen that the boundary line between the Duchy of Holstein and Schleswig is the River Eider, and a Canal, connecting it with the Baltic. On this river is Rendsburgh, and it may be considered, for some distance at least, as the base line of the position of the Holstein army. The works around Rendsburgh, the centre of this line, reach some twenty miles, forming a very strong position. Where we were, on a high hill a short distance within the outer line, we had a fine view of it all. On the right, stretched away a beautiful lake, fringed with the bright colored woods. This, together with the Eider, formed the great cover of the right wing, though between it and the Eider, strong works had been thrown up. In front, was a smaller lake, so that any attack must be made either between these two lakes, or upon the left. The ground between them was well defended by "*Schanzen*," with palisades and deep ditches, perhaps the strongest works on the line; while the left part of the centre was secured naturally by a series of rocky heights, on all which, fortifications with bomb-proof block houses and the usual appurtenances had been placed. Far away on the left, could be seen the reflection of water, which was the overflowing of a branch of the Eider, and which, along with that river, effectually secured their left wing from attack. On all the fortified heights I observed telegraph poles, with arrangements for communicating at once to head quarters, the news of attack, either by day or night. These heights could be seen rising at various intervals through all the country, between the outer lines and the city. On the whole, it seemed a very strong position, not easily to be turned by the Danes, even if they felt disposed to attempt it, which they appear very far from doing.

The Danes themselves occupy a line reaching from Ekernfiorde on their left, to Friedrichstadt on the right, having Schleswig for the centre. The last attack had been made by the Holsteiners on the right on Friedrichstadt; and before that, on the left, so that many expected the next attempt to force their position, in the centre, on Schleswig. The probability is, that the Holstein General, Von Willisen, is waiting now for more recruits, which come in constantly from Germany, as well as for the approach of winter, which will give an opportunity to force the position of the Danes, where they are defended by the inundations. Though for my part, I do not see why this last would not be an advantage to one side as well as the other. The Danes would at least be cut off from the aid of their ships by the winter, which would be a great disadvantage to them. I notice the English papers dwell much on the sacred regard for treaties, apparent in the conduct of the Danish monarch, in thus carefully keeping himself within the boundaries of his ancestral duchy. Any one. however, who examines the position of the Holstein line may find some other fully as influential, though not quite so flattering, motives for this great self restraint.

The country, which stretched out on all sides around the hill where we were, was singularly mild and peaceful in its aspect. The flat, barren land around the city, had changed into a fertile and gently undulating country, with clumps of trees scattered over it, with that soft and pleasant outline, which everything wears under the autumn sunlight. The fortifications seemed only like fresh mounds in the distance, and the peasants were ploughing or sowing their barley, right under the mouths of the cannon. Before us lay the lakes with hardly a ripple on their surface, and far away, gleamed peacefully in the light, the waters of a branch of the Eider. It was not at all a scene of blood. It was difficult to realize, as one looked at it all, that it had so lately been trampled and stained in fierce fight. As I looked closer down, however, at the calm scene before us, I could gradually discern a long black line, moving through the valley, which soon resolved itself into smaller lines; then in front of us a dark object could be seen, moving towards the small lake, and extending itself into a line, and on the heights similar objects were stirring; and it needed no longer observation to ascertain that this whole "peaceful" country was filled with heavy masses of troops.

As we went down from the hill, we passed through a valley where there had been lately a battle with the Danes, and the blackened ruins of a farm house showed its effects. As we passed through the next range of fortifications, one of the Bauer houses appeared almost entirely surrounded by a "Schanze," (fort) and the chickens and sparrows were flying about among the cannon and breastworks.

The next encampment we visited, was far less comfortable than those nearer the city, the quarters being mud and log huts, with no flooring except straw. My companions had some acquaintance here, and we went into one of the huts. We found four officers quartered there, evidently doing their best to make their hard life a jovial one. They welcomed us very heartily; coffee and cigars were produced, and we talked over the rough table for a long time. They had all been students; one was a student of theology; and damp and cold as the low hut was, they managed to get a great deal of fun o ut of their wild life. Still, they and the privates have suffered much from the wet cold weather of late, and I should think were heartily tired of the war, though they may all be determined not to yield, in the contest. Very naturally their dislike to the Danes has not at all decreased by this two years fighting

We returned at night, and the heavy rumbling of cannon and the creak of wagons, sounded incessantly on the main road from the gates. It was the preparation for a night attack, expected from the Danes. I found on my return, the English officers still in the hotel. They had been treated very politely by the General—as the English are now—and had seen all the works, and though military men are rather critical in such matters, professed themselves entirely satisfied.

Thus ended my day in the Holstein camp; a passing glimpse into the interior of that struggle which has so agitated the North of Europe, and whose heart-burnings and bitter animosities, yet surviving, shall burst forth fearfully in another convulsion of Europe.

CHAPTER VIII.

THE DIFFICULTIES BETWEEN DENMARK AND THE DUCHIES.

It is now about six years since a member of the Danish "Assembly," then in session at Roeskilde, rose with the following motion: that "The States' Assembly propose that the King should solemnly declare Denmark, Schleswig-Holstein and Lauenburg a single indivisible kingdom, and that this indivisible kingdom, according to the Danish crown-law, should become the inheritance of the *female* posterity of Frederick III."

From this motion we may date the commencement of the present troubles between the Duchies and Denmark. It is true, before this time, since the year 1808 and the accession of Frederick VI. to the throne, Denmark had been accused of constantly encroaching on the Duchies, both in introducing the Danish language and in converting State-institutions into National; and a tendency to separation from the Danish crown had been given by the fact of Holstein's being included in the German confederacy. Still no very decided manifestations were made till this motion was put forward. The effect of it was stirring. Addresses poured in from every part of the Duchies to the "States," then meeting at Itsehoe, and a "Bill of Rights" was at once prepared by them, and sent to the king, containing the three great Articles, which lie, as they claim, at the basis of their political rights, and to support which, they have entered on this bloody war.

I. That the Duchies are Independent States.

II. That the male line rules in the Duchies.

III. That the Duchies, Schleswig and Holstein, are States united to one another.

From this time till the year 1846, there was no open hostility, except in the press, between the two parties, when there appeared what is called "The Open Letter" of the King of Denmark. As this is much referred to, in this dispute, and, in some degree, will determine the justice of the Holstein cause, it may be well to mention particularly some of the positions taken in it.

The Letter is addressed to his subjects, and after some preliminary remarks, the king states that he had placed this whole question of the Inheritance of the Duchies in the hands of an able committee, and that after a deliberate investigation, they had reported that the Duchy of Schleswig comes under the same law of inheritance by which the kingdom of Denmark is governed. But, that in regard to the Duchy of Holstein, there were certain parts where doubts existed as to their being included under the Danish law, and in consequence being necessarily assured to the royal line. Yet, the king continues, every effort will be given to do away with these objections, and to preserve the unity of the Danish State, and to unite under one sceptre, all these various divisions of the country, in such a manner that they shall never be separated. And he assures the people of Schleswig that in thus uniting that State with the Danish monarchy, it is not in the least his intention to encroach upon its independence, or to produce the slightest change in its close relations with the Duchy of Holstein.

There were not a few things in this letter which would naturally be exceedingly disagreeable and even alarming, to the people of the Duchies. In the first place, there appears to be in it a *recognizing* of the independence of the Duchies, as a matter of favor, while they had always claimed that their independence did not in the least depend on the will of their ruler. Then again, the laws of inheritance, which had always governed them, as they viewed it, were by this entirely annulled, and they were placed under a foreign law, and therefore under a foreign race. While the old laws, established by their fathers, were in force, they would fairly and justly abide by them, and remain connected with a foreign State; but when, in the natural course of events, these had become abrogated, they "wished under their own Dukes, to join in the movement for the unity of the great German Fatherland."

Beside this, the position taken by the King, that Holstein was not included under the same laws with Schleswig, seemed like an attempt to separate those two States,—a measure, which would be very alarming to all those in both, who believed that the prosperity and independence of the two Duchies depended on their union. Still less was the expression approved of, in which the King spoke of "preserving the unity of the Danish State,"—and of bringing under one government all these divisions of the country, (*Landestheile.*)

This letter and the "Remonstrances" succeeding it, were followed by an extended war of "Petitions," on the people's part, and "Declarations" on the king's, until it was finally made known publicly, that the king would receive no more bills or petitions from "The States," on the subject of the Laws of Inheritance. Many of these "Declarations" and "bills" are written with great eloquence, and show a people thoroughly aroused in the contest. They are interesting, many of them, from the great similarity in tone with those of our revolutionary patriots. The same elaborate respect to royal authority, while they are busily engaged in undermining it; the same charitable assumption, that it is the *ministers* who are thus conspiring against a loyal people, and that the king is only an unhappy tool. There are respects, however, in which they are widely different from the documents of our Revolutionary days, as I shall show afterwards. To the political student, these papers are interesting; they are not necessary to an understanding of the question now at issue.

After these "Declarations," came spirited appeals to the German Fatherland, which was now becoming deeply interested in the dispute. Even the "German League," or *Bund*, put forth a resolution favoring the cause of the Duchies; so that the result was another letter from the king, assuring the disaffected States of their independence and of his desire to preserve them in union. At this point, in the year 1848, affairs were changed somewhat by the death of the King, and by the accession to the throne of his successor, Frederick VII.

The first efforts of the new king were to pacify his subjects by the grant of that panacea for all evils—a "Constitution," to the whole kingdom. By this Constitution there was to be a "General Assembly" of the representatives both of Denmark and the Duchies, meeting alternately in the different countries; with such powers as would enable them to legislate on the various changes necessary in finance and other matters, throughout the kingdom; and it was assured that, by this new "Assembly," nothing would be changed of those laws which granted the meeting of provincial "States" or "Chambers" (*Stände*), or which secured the other right before mentioned, of the Duchies.

In addition to this, the king proposed a law for lightening the extremely strict supervision of the press, which had before existed in Holstein—and for entirely doing away in some cases with the censorship. None of these conciliatory measures appear to have given satisfaction; and a very bold address was presented from Al tona, demanding (1), the entire freedom of the press; (2), the freedom of holding any kind of meetings desired; and (3), the privilege of forming a citizen militia.

To this was added a demand for a new Constitution for the Duchies based on the freest democratic principle; the responsibility of the minister to *their* Assembly; the power of sending representatives to the German Confederacy; and the formation of new courts, on the principle of Jury Courts—(*Geschwornen gerichte.*)

Similar addresses—or addresses revolutionary in character—were presented by the higher classes, the prelates and nobles, as well as by the citizens. And it was apparent that the hostility to the government was very deep and wide spread. The first open outbreak occurred on the 24th of March, 1848, in Kiel, when the news arrived of the formation in Copenhagen of an ultra Danish ministry, and of the probability of their endeavoring to incorporate the Duchies by arms, in the Danish kingdom. A provisional government was at once formed in Kiel, the military enrolled—and the Duchies were proclaimed free, independent States. Movements of the same kind commenced throughout the two provinces, more especially in Holstein, which is more decidedly German in its character, and addresses were made to the throne, containing the same demands as those mentioned above. A letter appeared, too, of the King of Prussia, supporting these demands, at least as far as the independence and union of the Duchies was concerned.

This was the day of Revolutions, when the old monarchies of Europe threatened all to be swept away by the storm. The king wisely bowed to it, and in an answer to a Deputation of the

States, he said that, in view of all these circumstances, it was his intention to grant to Holstein, as an *independent member* of the German Confederacy, a Constitution based on the most liberal principles of suffrage; that he was ready to secure with this, the right of the freedom of the press, and the full power of forming a citizen militia; and that this province should, as soon as circumstances would allow, have its own separate finance. He should not be unfavorable, besides, to the formation of a powerful German parliament, representing the people, so much desired. But in regard to Schleswig, it was his duty to say, that he "had *neither the right, nor the power, nor the will*, to incorporate it in the German Confederacy." But, by a free constitution, and at the same time, by preserving its provincial institutions, he was resolved to attach it, unimpaired in its independence, to the Danish monarchy.

This is the last public document containing a statement of the points at issue, and may be considered as presenting the policy against which the Duchies are now contending. Many "Addresses" and "Proclamations" follow on both sides, which, though eloquent, throw no light on the question.

This answer of the king was made in March, 1848. In the following April, hostilities were in full progress. The events succeeding this, for the last two years, need not be related, though they will be interesting topics for history. The struggle of the Duchies with the crown; the marching in of the Prussian troops, and the terror they everywhere inspired to the Danes; the annoyance caused to Prussia by the blockade of her Baltic provinces, and the disagreements between her troops and their allies, all resulting finally in her leaving the Provinces to fight out the contest themselves—important events, but not especially affecting the merits of the contest, on one side or the other.

The great powers of Europe have taken a very deep interest in this war—much greater than its importance would seem to claim. And, perhaps to their own surprise, England, and France, and Russia, find themselves side by side in the support of a constitutional monarch, contending with his subjects; while the German people are glowing with an ardor we can hardly even imagine, to throw themselves into the struggle of their "brothers" with a foreign race; a race united with that Nation whose mighty power is already overshadowing their Eastern provinces. In regard to the English position in this contest, it is no easy matter to determine exactly its causes. Perhaps the ministry have considered that the entry to the Baltic would be much safer to the English, under the guard of a weak nation—their ally—than if placed in the power of the great German Confederacy,—and the old commercial jealousy may have concurred in depressing any efforts of Germany to make herself a maritime power. Then, if we come to minor causes, "*The Times*" may have *happened* to take that position and thus led the English mind; or that old English generosity may have arisen, at the sight of the *pluck* of the little Denmark against her formidable adversary, Prussia; or to come to the last reason, usual in such cases, the English government may have believed Denmark *right* in her position towards the Duchies. Still, so far as I had an opportunity to observe in England, there was very little understanding of the question, among either the people or the press.

Russia's course in the matter is very natural and very easily explained. It can never be for her interest, that any of the great rival powers—especially Germany—should hold the keys of the Baltic, and it is not improbable, as is frequently hinted, that some foot-hold in that part of the Northern seas may be the reward for the countenance, and, very probably, the more substantial aid, given to the kingdom of Denmark.

The statement which I have made of the various difficulties and disputes between the Duchies and Denmark for the last six years, I conceive to be a fair one, and certainly as favorable to those provinces as truth would allow. It has been gathered mostly from their own documents, and from conversation with men of their own party. When I came here, I supposed, in common with many of the liberal party in England, that this whole contest was a constitutional contest—a struggle of a free oppressed people for their rights, and for more liberal institutions. I found, that so it was regarded here by many, and I have been, not a few times, reminded by Germans of its great similarity to our own struggle for Independence. But, the more I examine it, the more I am inclined to the opinion, that it is not a constitutional contest at all.

The Holsteiners have as great a dread of "democratic progress" as the Danes. I know that German democrats and Hungarians are often refused admission into their ranks, that the institutions which they now uphold in their own provinces, are not as free as exist in Denmark. And it is only within a few days, I heard of men, still confined in the prisons of Altona by the Provincial Government, for *libelling* that king whom they have been so fiercely combating. In connection with this, should be noticed one of the inducements for making peace, presented by the members of the Peace Convention lately to the Danish Government, namely, that "a peace would release them from their obligations to foreign diplomacy, and give them an opportunity to develope their free institutions." Is this an inducement to be presented to a very conservative government.

It is to be observed in the history of this contest, that the hostility does not begin as in our Revolution, in a complaint of oppression and a demand for justice and freer institutions. It is only that these Duchies should be restored to that intensely loved but most mysterious and intangible Union—the German Fatherland; and that they should no longer exist as parts of a "*foreign State!*" in connection with which, it may be remarked, they had been for generations. It is not constitutions, nor better institutions, nor freer government which they want. Their forefathers had once formed a part of the glorious Fatherland, and this is enough! They *must* be members of that dazzling, incomprehensible Fraternity! Perhaps it is one-sided in me, but I must confess, I cannot but look upon these bloody struggles for such a visionary, impractical *idea*, as most foolish. It certainly is something as if the *Celtic Race* in all parts of the world should shake off the governments over them; fight and bleed, that they might carry out the beautiful idea of one great Irish or Gælic or Celtic Fatherland! I do not mean that the analogy holds in all respects. But this struggle for "German Unity" has something of that appearance to the uninitiated stranger.

Since the Revolutions of Europe began, (in 1848), one must allow that the insurgents have made truly constitutional demands on the Danish Government. But those demands will not be found in their official documents the great matters insisted on, and they do not seem the great points at issue. Besides, when the king does yield his full consent to all these, and still preserves his position in regard to the union of Schleswig to Denmark, there does not appear the least change in the feelings of the provinces. They are determined to be members of the Fatherland, and any other proposition is odious to them. And for my part, I fully believe, that if German sympathy and German aid do at length give the victory to these insurgent provinces, it will be seen to be no triumph of the liberal cause, and, that the institutions which the Duchies will form for themselves, will not equal in freedom those they might have had under the Danish Government.

Of the sad and gloomy close of this struggle, and of the prostration of the Duchies under the iron rule of Austria—events which occurred in the succeeding year—I shall have more to say in another portion of this volume.

CHAPTER IX.

HAMBURG AND THE RAUHE HAUS.

I WAS walking out one morning, after my return to Hamburg, to call upon my friend, the artist before mentioned, when I came suddenly on a sight rather remarkable in such a nineteenth-century city as this. A procession of Spanish cavaliers, apparently, was passing through the streets; just the same dark-haired men, with peaked sombreros, stiff white ruffs, short black cloaks and swords, as Velasquez or Rembrandt delighted to paint. They were following a coffin. It almost seemed as if I were looking at some touching tragedy among the exiled *hidalgos* of Spain.

My friend laughed when I told him my conceit, and assured me that the tragedy was all on the other side—as the family of every respectable Hamburger who died, had to pay ten dollars apiece for each of those *hidalgos*—and funerals frequently cost now some two hundred *Thaler*, ($150), much to the trouble of the afflicted families.

This gentleman was thinking much of emigrating to America. "Europe was no place for art for years to come. All Germany and the Continent might be in the full blaze of revolution, in a month, at any time. And now," said he. "in such disturbed times, there are few purchasers. Besides Hamburg is far too *material* a city for the encouragement of such a profession. People are wealthy and benevolent here, but there is no great inclination for these pursuits." It was too much a commercial city, he thought, and was inferior in intellectual tastes to most of the cities of Germany.

Like all who have studied the history of Hamburg, this gentleman considered its prosperity due to its long and steady adherence to *Free Trade.*

The success of this city alone, however, would be no test of the Protective question, as it is peculiarly a commercial Republic, and can have no great variety of interests to support. Still, it is a fact that the four cities in the Hanseatic League, Hamburg, Bremen, Lübeck, and Frankfort, did from the beginning adopt a most liberal Protective system, and that of all the cities of Germany, these have been the most prosperous.

"If Germany ever should become one united country," said this gentleman; "for which I most devoutly pray, Hamburg would be the most important point of all North Germany. It would be the outlet for all our commerce and naval enterprise. There is no situation like it. Here on one of the greatest rivers of Germany—connected by rail-roads with Prussia, Saxony, Austria, and Hanover; and with an excellent harbor, what might we not expect for it?"

This conversation and others of the same kind led me to examine more the commercial position of the city

The great currents of commerce on which Hamburg reached such prosperity have left it, and it is hardly probable that the days can come again when its fleets shall struggle equally, as once, even with those of Denmark. Within the last few years, however, its business and commerce have been steadily advancing; and especially since the raising of the Danish Armistice, (August, 1849), there has been a remarkable activity developed in the city. The number of vessels arriving at the port in 1849, is given at 3,459; of those sailing, 3,416. In 1850, the ships owned in the city are reckoned at 277, and the steam-ships, 9, with a tonnage of 82,053. The population of the city and its territory is 188,054. Naturally, with such capabilities of a great commercial growth, the inhabitants desire a free connection with the rest of Germany. Hamburg was one of the German States which urged vigorously a union of Germany in the Assembly, at Frankfort, in 1848, and which refused to recognise the old Diet established by Austria, in 1850. It sent, likewise, deputies to the Parliament assembled in 1850, by Prussia, at Erfurt, in her attempt to get up another "Union." Still, I gathered everywhere, the hope was that the United Germany would be a Free-Trade Germany, as the citizens are entirely convinced that the Austrian Protective system would ruin them.

There is great anxiety even yet with them, lest this late German Confederation, established by Austria, should force upon them a scale of protective duties. The contingent which Hamburg is obliged to furnish the German Confederation, when demanded, is 3,560 soldiers, and 7 cannons; and in money 4,083 *Thaler*, (about $3,000.)

OCTOBER 28, 1850.

THE ROUGH HOUSE.

I went out this morning to visit one of the Hamburg Institutions, which has interested me more than anything else in the city. And

I know of no similar institution, in any land, commenced on this plan, or carried on with such wonderful practical skill, and such wide-reaching benevolence. I see, however, that the French government have imitated it, in a grand school of the kind, established in *Met-trai.* I speak of the Hamburgh RAUHE HAUS, (Rough House), a large Vagrant School, established by Mr. Wichern, in 1833.

An omnibus ride of three miles carried me to its neighborhood, and after a walk through a pleasant wooded lane, I reached the place. The whole looked as little like the usual home for vagrants, as is possible. I saw no squads of boys walking demurely about, but looking as though the very devil was in them, if they could only let it out. There were no heavy-looking overseers, discoursing piously of the number whom Providence had committed to their charge—and thinking of their pockets. And there was not even the invariable home for forsaken children—the huge stone building, with one bare sunny court-yard. The idea seems to have been here, that to those who have no home of their own, as much as possible should be given of the home which God has prepared for all.

It was a large, open garden, full of trees and walks and flowers and beds for vegetables, while on each side stretched away green corn-fields. Among the trees there were some dozen plain, comfortable little wood-houses, like old-fashioned farm-houses, scattered about, and one quiet, shaded chapel. The boys visible outside, were busy cleaning the flower-beds, or working in the harvest field ; some also, repairing fences and buildings.

I walked up to the largest of the houses, and was directed pleasantly by a lad to Mr. Wichern's rooms. A little interlude occurred here very characteristic of our times.

Among the visitors who arrived just before me was dear old

Elihu Burritt, fresh from the Peace Congress, and on his way to Denmark, with two associates, to attempt to mediate between the Duchies and the King.

While we were all waiting in Mr. W.'s room, a conversation commenced between Wichern and Burritt on the subject of these peace efforts, which soon grew into a warm discussion. The one did not understand much German nor the other much English, yet there was such a natural eloquence in the two men, that, with the aid of a few interpretations thrown in by myself, they argued as well as if in the same language. I never saw a better contrast—the fine, mild, winning, thoughtful face of the American, as he spoke of the all-subduing power of Love, of the virtue that existeth in patience and forbearance and meekness, to hurl back the greatest violence; or pictured the time when havoc and war and hate should no more rage among men. And on the other side, the strong, marked, stern features of the German, denouncing in deep tones the oppression which was cursing Germany, and now soon to prostrate Holstein, and demanding how the injustice of the strong is to be met, but by the strong blow.

The name "Rough House" for this place originated, as Mr. W. informs me, seventeen years ago, when he took a little broken-down farm-house here to try if he could not start, on a new plan, a school for vagrant children. It were better called now—as some English traveller has already named it—the "Home among the Flowers." The great peculiarity of the plan is the dividing the children into families. In each of the little houses I visited is a family group of some twelve children, managed by a young man (an "overseer") with two assistants. The overseers are theological students, who have some way imbibed the idea that two or three years' practical labor among the helpless and forsaken is quite as good a preparation, for their duties, as preaching to admiring audiences or laying up a complete system of antiquated dogmas. The "assistants" are young men—farmers or mechanics of a religious turn, who intend to spend their lives in this kind of work. They are employed at first on the most common out-door labor; then are placed in the different workships to learn, and afterwards to direct; next are admitted to a care of the boys within the houses, and are taught by the overseers the various needed branches of education, and finally take a share with the Principal, in the general supervision of the Institution. After a four or six years' course here, they are sent abroad to preside or assist in similar institutions through Germany. They are mostly supported by voluntary contributions, or by their own labor. There are twenty-three here now. Mr. W. says that there is a great demand for them; and that they have been sent for even from Russia, for orphan asylums, houses of correction, ragged schools and the like; and that some are now preaching among the emigrants in America.

The matter of principal interest, of course, was the situation of the children. The first house we entered was a little wooden building among the flowers and the apple-trees. It was of only one story, with the exception of an attic chamber for the assistants. The first room was a long, clean one, where ten or twelve boys were sitting round a table, working at their slates, under the inspection of the students. Their time is divided off into so many hours for out-door work, so many for play and for study. This was the school-time. The lads were all clean, comfortable and cheerfully busy. When a wretched little vagrant from the gutter is sent in here, he is not at once thrown into a mass of boys, to work himself out to ruin or to goodness as he best can; to be kicked and cuffed; to grab what he can get, and to either teach others or learn from others. all the vile things which boys are certain to know. The little stranger is put with a few other new comers, into a separate house ("the novitiate house") where two or three young men have constant charge of him. He eats at their own table with his few comrades, and has enough. The overseers study his disposition, and set him either at a trade or at garden and farm-work, as he seems best fitted. He has his play, and playmates, and free fresh air, and friends to care for him, who hold it a labor of love, to do for the fatherless one, in a feeble manner, as Christ did for them.

He must work hard, but there is variety, and it is healthy work. After a time, he is introduced into one of the regular families, and there, in simple quarters, under kind care, he spends the five or six years. No wonder that it comes to be such a home to them all—and that the apprentices, whom the Rauhe Haus has sent out so plentifully through Germany, are so glad to come back, and work in the shops on the place.

Besides the room I have mentioned, there were in this house a sleeping room, a room for the sick, a little kitchen, and two bed-rooms for the students—all plain, but very neat.

After this, we went round to the various workshops—for shoe-making, tailoring, joinery, pattern-making, spinning, baking, etc.—in all these the boys w rking very handily. In addition, there were other buildings, where the boys, in company with workmen, were busy at book-binding, printing, stereotyping, and wood and stone engraving. A few were employed out of doors at the regular farm work. There was one good-sized building, where washing, ironing, and washing of dishes, and sewing work were done by the girls, for there must be some thirty or forty girls here. There is the same general arrangement for them as for the boys. They are usually taught all branches of housekeeping, and are expected to enter service. The boys are generally apprenticed to masters. And it is said, from the number of affiliated schools started by the students of this through Germany, and from its many friends, that no apprentices on their journeys, find a better reception than these from the Rauhe Haus. We found the chapel a quiet, tasteful building, just decorated by the boys for some festival which they wished to celebrate.

Perhaps the most remarkable feature about the whole institution, was the practical power displayed in it. It is so rare for a man, with the moral enthusiasm which would raise up the helpless and outcast from their degradation, to have, at the same time, the business talent for such a scheme as this. HERR WICHERN has shown that he unites both. His first step, after establishing a few of the "family groups" and common workshops, was to set up printing presses, where the boys could strike off, under the direction of a master workman, the tracts and little books needed in the school, and the Reports of the Rauhe Haus. They succeeded so well at this, that the works were enlarged, and now do a considerable external business, and go far towards supporting the other parts of the establishment. Many of the boys are apprenticed here, instead of being placed with masters.

In addition, a commercial agency (*Agentur*) has been formed to sell the various articles made by the boys. This is separate from the school, upon which its losses will not fall. The profits are to be devoted to meeting the general expenses for the children. Connected with it are the lithograph and stereotype shops, the wood-engraving and the book-binding. All these last have proved very successful, and the business done by the agency is quite extensive. It is expected that with the printing and the agency, the institution, expensive as it is, will in a few years support itself. Of course, all this complicated mass of detail needs a clear head to manage it—and for this management, Mr. Wichern appears to be the man. This, however, is only a small part of his labors. He is a powerful speaker, and has a great faculty of influencing any man with whom he is thrown in contact. He has pleaded the cause of his Vagrant Home well through Germany; and has gained liberal aid even from the princes. Of his labors for a wider object, I have already previously spoken. That I did not exaggerate, when I said this institution has not its counterpart in other countries must be apparent.

A "Home among the Flowers," where the vagrant—the child nourished amid filth and squalor—in the dark cellars of a great city, should at length see something of God's beautiful world; where among friends, in the midst of orchards and corn-fields, he could grow up, invigorated by healthful labor, to manhood—all this would seem alone more like the dream of a philanthropic French novelist, than the reality. But still farther, that this institution should have a system, almost Fourier-like, of "groups" and families, and yet be imbued with the simplest, truest spirit of the Christian religion; that it should send out not only skilled apprentices, saved from the prison and the alms-house, but educated young men to teach others, and to spread abroad the self-denying, Christian principles of the place—and most of all, that it should have existed seventeen years, and by its well-conducted industry, have almost supported itself, may fairly constitute it one of the wonders in benevolent effort. The friend of man, searching anxiously for what man has done for his suffering fellows, may look far in both continents before he finds an institution so benevolent, so practical, and so truly Christian, as the Hamburg ROUGH HOUSE.

CHAPTER X.

A BREAKFAST-TALK.

L——l, Duchy of Meklenburg Schwerin, Nov., 1850.

A LITTLE German country inn again! The tall white stove in one corner of the room; a well-stuffed, most uncomfortable German bed in another, and the floor, scrubbed and polished to the highest possible brightness which soap and water will give. I am seated at the table with the well-worn portfolio which has accompanied me in so many a tramp through Europe, and the little pocket inkstand, apparently contrived by the manufacturer with special reference to being knocked over. Thanks to the fates, *this* neat table-cloth, at least, remains unstained as yet! I have bid good bye to Hamburg, though it hardly seems yet, as if I had really parted from friends so warm and true; friends soon made, but not soon to be forgotten. You who wish really to know what a home is, must enter Germany as I did, a stranger; and then with the slightest introduction, be received as I was, at once into the midst of a kind-hearted family. You must see the mutual forbearance of all—the open, unconscious affection—the simple and cordial ways—the free respect for the old father, and the care for the amusements and plays of the children. You must see the generous, though plain hospitality—the unaffected friendliness towards all who enter—the sunny and confiding life through the whole family—and you must be as I was, a traveller, long away from all family influences, and tired with the incessant round of sights and the superficial life in picture galleries and museums, if you would understand how pleasant and satisfactory was this my reception into German Home-Life.

It seems to me that there is an element running through family-life here, of which we know little in America; but I reserve any very definite conclusions, until I see more of the Germans in the interior. I shall spend a day or two in this village, and then proceed at once to the central point of North-Germany—the old Prussian capital—Berlin. "*Ich bitte Sie.* I beg your pardon, sir; a gentleman for you! sir!" came forth in the midst of my meditations from an old servant, who had entered almost without my perceiving it.

I found my visitor was one of the acquaintances to whom I had presented letters of introduction the day before. "You must come right up, and take breakfast with us, and give the day to us!" said he. I met the invitation as freely as it was given, and only excused myself from taking up quarters in his house, by alleging the many letters I must write, and my wishing to be alone. In a few minutes I was seated in a snug little library, in a great arm-chair, with a coffee-cup in my hand. On another side, is the father, in a similar chair, his coffee on a book-stand beside him, and a long pipe in his mouth. The mother, a dignified lady, with one of the sweetest expressions of face I ever saw, sits at a little table in the midst of the room, making the coffee, or passing us a bread cake, and seeming as if she were trying to make the stranger forget he were among any other than his oldest friends, in which she succeeds very well.

The only other member of our coffee-party, is the gentleman who had come with me, a young lawyer from Schwerin, the capital of this little Duchy, the son of my friends. His breakfast, he says, is merely a cigar, a not uncommon custom here, as I observe. Here we are then, most pleasantly arranged for a morning chat! The conversation turns at first, on my own travels, my observations, and the contrasts I notice here to America. Then, as everywhere now in Germany, to the subject of most absorbing interest—politics. I asked the young lawyer, what the state of feeling towards the government was in this Duchy.

"Discontent, utter discontent! and we have reason."

I inquired for the particulars whether they were worse off than other German governments.

"Perhaps not," said he, "but look at our situation. Here we are, a little Principality,* with not more than 530,000 inhabitants, supporting a prince and expensive court. We are Germans and want to belong to Germany, and not be merely the providers for this duke. Our debt now is over ten millions of thalers, and the taxes come to some three millions and a half! How could we be contented?"

I saw I had stumbled upon a *Liberal*, and followed up the conversation eagerly.

"But the people have a constitutional government in the Duchy, have they not?" said I.

"Yes, the two Principalities of Mecklenburg, are under a common parliament, and a very old one, still the people do not take much part in the government. Our nobles and office-holders control everything."

I inquired about the aristocracy and whether the feudal relations still existed in Meklenburg.

* The Principality of *Meklenburg-Schwerin.*

"No," said he, "there are no serfs now, either in Prussia or in these Duchies; but we have an old nobility which weighs upon us. Our party, the Liberal, have just passed through a long struggle with the aristocracy. The noblemen have before always had everything under their thumbs, and have governed the Principality, when the parliament was not in session, by a most unconstitutional assembly of their own. We attacked them, and carried our point, and that accursed old "Committee" was abolished. But now they are getting the upper hand. They have appealed to the "Austrian Union" at Frankfort, and we shall have all the troops of the *Bund*, (Union) upon us, if we do not give in!"

"This comes from our divided Germany," said another gentleman, who had just entered. "If we had a real union—a German Fatherland, the people could protect themselves! But now, look at us! No German cares for Germany!"

"But do you think, dear Adolph," said the mother to the liberal young lawyer, "that we should be any the better for another revolution and bloody war?"

"Why not, mother? What could be worse than this? Look at poor Holstein! and Hesse! that old forger (*Hassenpflug*) will trample her down yet, and we shall have Austrian soldiers over every thing."

"Yes, my son, it looks dark, but God will not leave poor Germany, we know. And I do not believe He works through these violent outbreaks. Let us trust in Him, for we have tried the sword, and we must believe that the good time is not yet. Perhaps the people are yet in their sins too much, to be free; we must still——"

She was interrupted by a burst of feeling from the young man, "What, mother, wait! *Mein Gott!* Wait still longer! God made us to be *free men.* He never could have meant us to be a nation of slaves! I would rather have a war, than this grinding of tyranny day after day. Give us a revolution—anything! We had a glorious Germany once, and, by God's will, we can have it again!"

"Mein liebes kind, my son!" said she, and though I sympathised with the passionate son, I felt almost awed by the expression of earnestness, so loving, yet so deep, which settled on her face. "I started in life when the French movement for liberty was in full sweep. I threw myself into it, as all the young did around me, with all my heart. I would have died so gladly, then, to make my countrymen free.

"But this all fell to the ground, and nothing but infidelity was the fruit in France. I was all aroused too by the movements after the Conferences in '15, and I thought we were going to have a resurrection of Germany. But here bad passions, and want of trust in God, came in, and everything was worse than before. And then, when 1848 came, I had lost hope. I see that we must all be purified, and there must be more faith in God, and more true religion, before our German people are ready for Freedom.

"God knows, dear Adolphe, that I long and pray for happiness to poor Germany, but He must first prepare us! Perhaps we can never have a free government!"

"But it is not thoroughly tried, Mother! The kings promised and cheated us in 1812 and '15; and we were cheated again in '48. We trusted them too much. Look at that—King of Prussia!"

"Careful! Adolphe, be careful," said the father, looking anxiously round.

"I do not care, father; you know he was completely in the hands of the mob, and he swore to a Constitution and everything—

and *now!* That would not happen twice. The Germans are good-natured, but they know the princes now and woe to——"

"Let us not speak evil, my son, of those in authority. The King of Prussia is doing much for his people and the Church. It is not Liberty, dear Adolphe, which the mob wants; it is license and socialistic community of property, and the overthrow of the Church. See how it all succeeds now in France! Did we ever have a worse Despotism, than in your Republic there?"

"Still, mother," answered the young man, "there *can* be Revolutions which work well. The American Revolution, this gentleman will tell you, was not an infidel movement. They fought for freedom and built up a religious State. May not we too here?"

I ventured to put in a word here, and said something of our free institutions, and described the deep hold which religion has of the heart of the nation; and then asked, whether they ought to test these struggles by their success in France. The French character was certainly different from the German; and had been trained in another school.

The mother admitted our success in America, but they thought we had fresh materials and more room; and, especially, a basis in the old English Puritan religious character. "You have escaped much in the New World. Time only will show what will be the result from all these fearful wars and troubles in the Old. Where the Spirit of God is, there is Liberty."

I was intensely interested in this conversation at the time, though it is only a sample of what one hears everywhere in Germany. The pure-minded, the religious, the old on one side, who have seen too often the passionate hopes with which these struggles have begun, and the sad disappointments and lame conclusions; who recognise in the blind struggles for Liberty and these excesses and consequent defeats, the finger of God pointing out that the nations are unfitted for freedom. And the young, hopeful, enthusiastic on the other, who believe that there is a future of Liberty and Love for Humanity, and that they can do something to help it on; who see in every defeat, only another impulse to exertion; and who cannot think that tyranny is anything but an exception—an excrescence in God's world, to be cut off by the strong hand, and through many toils, if necessary.

One of the days which I spent here was a Sunday, and I was desirous to see how it would be observed. My friends had the charge of a boarding-school for young ladies. In the morning, the pupils met in a Bible-class, as they would in a similar establishment at home. There was more cheerfulness than is usual on this day with us; and, indeed, there was on all days more of an unconstrained, home-like aspect than I ever saw in an American boarding-school. About eleven o'clock, we all went out to the Lutheran Church. Here, however, there was nothing to remind of America. A gray, mediæavl church, very high and spacious, with a few seats placed in the centre of the transept; cold too and damp, with the voice of the clergyman barely audible under the lofty arches. The old, monkish preaching-desk—the images and paintings and stained windows—the chaunting by the clergyman, and the wax candles burning at the altar, almost made me think I was again in a Catholic cathedral. A great part of the audience were obliged to stand. The sermon was one of the usual sentimental, milk-and-water exhortations, of which the German clergy are so fond; and the hearers seemed especially sleepy, except during the music, which was very good, so that on the whole I did not get a very favorable impression of the religious privileges in this part of the Duchy of Mecklenburg

We met at dinner. As in all Christian countries, our Sabbath dinner was excellent; opening with red wine-soup, and terminating in the great delicacy of this Principality, a Meklenburg roast-goose. The conversation was very pleasant and cheerful, but mostly on religious or moral subjects. After it was over, the ladies went out to the Sunday-schools, and the gentlemen gathered in the drawing-room to their coffee. The talking, much more naturally too, than in most of our religious families, was serious in its tone.

There was another service in the afternoon in the same Lutheran church. At the close, all who felt inclined, started on a walk through the fine large park belonging to the Duke, and surrounding his palace—one of the finest palaces, by the way, in Europe, in the exterior.

A German never understands our mode of observing the Sabbath. It seems to him an utter change from the old idea of the day—a day set apart as a religious festival. He holds that to be gloomy, unsocial or averse to enjoying Nature on that day, is not only contrary to the old Jewish custom, which he does not consider binding, but opposed to the Christian event commemorated in it; an event beyond all others joyous to the believer. There is nothing with Germans who have visited England, which they look back upon with such such utter gloom and aversion, as the aspects they gained of the "English Sabbath," as they call it. One half of a city, with sour faces, shutting itself up in churches and houses on that day, and the other half, sunk in the lowest brutality.

Their object, as they will often tell you, is to make the day one of worship and practical benevolence, and at the same time, of religious sociality. They take long walks in the afternoon and evening, urging that it is unnatural to confine oneself to the house so closely a whole day; and that to a religious mind, nothing is so conducive to good thoughts, as a free movement among the beautiful things God has made.

This can be abused, they allow; but so can every privilege; and it may be doubted, say they, whether for the young any abuse is worse than the stupid, impatient hours they must have, if shut in the house through the long pleasant day. It is a time beyond all others, which they wish connected in their children's minds with pleasant, natural associations. These are the views of the religious community. The mass of Germans do not at all recognize the day as in any sense religious. Concerts, theatres, nine-pins, beer-drinking, and universal amusement and excess fill up the hours. A few of the women attend church service in the morning; the men seldom.

I have stood in German villages on the Sabbath, and as the memory of our New England homes came over me, I have felt almost sick at heart at the contrast. Here the workingmen sunken, degraded, with dull, sodden faces; dignified by little consciousness of an Immortality, and elevated by no share in an intelligent worship; almost without hope or aspiration, and spending the hours of a day, which God and man had given him for the elevation of his whole nature, in swilling beer, in dull games, and heavy sleep.

There, the man, intelligent; aroused; solemn—it may be gloomy sometimes—in memory of his Duty and his Destiny; his mind intensely active over the thoughts presented, and filled with infinite hopes; the day too formal often, but beautified with a few pure, calm hours, whose influence goes with him long in the whirl and excitement afterwards. "Thank God," I have said to myself, "the laborer with us has not forgotten that he is a man!"

I would never for a moment advocate any strict legal mode of observing the Sabbath; or any mode giving the impression that we are more bound to be religious on one day than on another.

The very idea of the day is, that it should be a time for free spiritual exercise; a change from usual pursuits, and a means necessary in the arrangements of society, for building up our piety. There may be hypocrisy, and formality, and a needless seriousness of manner on that day with us; still it will be long before any rational well-wisher to humanity would desire to see our New England Sabbath exchanged for the German Holiday.

CHAPTER XI.

WAR!

Berlin, Nov. 12, 1850.

BERLIN has been like a camp this past week; drilling and arming the recruits going on all the while; and the streets echoing, almost every hour of the day, to the tramp of companies, marching through the city to the railroad. All business is interrupted, for the workmen in almost every branch of employment are obliged to hurry off at once to their regiments. There is the greatest enthusiasm among all. Press and pulpit, the democrat and the royalist, alike sustain the war, and exhort all parties on, to uphold the honor of Prussia and the cause of constitutional liberty.

A war against Austria and her allies for poor Hesse-Cassel!

I have often laughed over the struggles of the Germans for the mysterious "Unity," and the incessant efforts for freedom, always ending in pamphlets and speech-making. But I shall not be inclined do so again. During the last two weeks, I have seen something of the deep German feeling on these matters. In our quiet, comfortable condition at home, where we vote at town-meetings, and choose a President, and come to look upon "liberty" much as we do on our breakfasts—as a very pleasant thing, but quite a matter of course—it is somewhat difficult to appreciate the intense feeling about it in foreign countries, and still more difficult, the feeling which exists in Prussia at the present time, as connected with German Unity and this war with Austria. But, if any one will imagine a despotic Power, pouring its masses of troops over our own land, not alone about to destroy our position among nations as an independent and self-protecting people, but with the Union to blot out the last hope of liberty in our part of the world, he will have some idea of the feeling of the Prussians, as they look at this mighty combination against them.

The patriot, who has been longing and laboring for liberty in Germany, sees in this attack of Austria, the breaking up of the Union, in which rested the great hope of constitutional changes; sees the advancement of the old "*Bundestag*" (Diet) with its hatred of free institutions, and its crushing of constitutional resistance; and Russia and Austria, the old arbitrary powers, fastening, hand in hand, their influence on Germany. All hope of carrying out the constitution in Hesse is gone; and Prussia, the representative in Germany of freer institutions, must take, henceforth, the position of a second-rate power.

The soldier—and in this feeling the majority of the people sympathize—sees the firm old state which he has loved so much, built up by the Great Frederick against overwhelming odds, sustained through many a reverse and powerful attack by a military organization hardly less stringent than the Lacedemonian, and by a military pride as high as was ever that of the Romans—he must see all this, at last, *disgraced.* The ignorant Austrian, and the beer-drinking, heavy Bavarian, are to give the law to his country.

Can we wonder at the excitement with which the news of the war was received throughout the land? Never, we believe, was the drafting for an army more cheerfully borne with. The law for "*mobilizing*" the army—that is for putting it on a war footing—required 200,000 men in twenty-four hours' time; yet in many districts, it is said, many more volunteers presented themselves than the regular number demanded.

Throughout the week previous there had been every appearance that the Ministry in the conference at Warsaw, intended to yield to the demands of Austria. The original order for *mobilizing* the army was countermanded. The official journal was peaceful in its tone, and the King was known to be for concessions. It cannot be imagined how deep the indignation and regret was at this, throughout the land. From every quarter, from conservative and constitutional journals, from soldiers and citizens, came the most heart-stirring appeals against this "disgrace" of Prussia—this bowing down to the arbitrary powers of Germany. And when, at last, the order came to fill up the army—that is, to prepare for war—there was a burst of joy throughout the kingdom. Thanks poured into the cabinet from every part. Not a newspaper which did not utter its congratulations over the step at last taken. And yet it was a joy tempered with serious forebodings in the minds of many. Prussia was entering upon a war, whose result no man could tell; a contest which might be as long and disastrous to German development as was the Thirty Years' War. It was against fearful odds also. There was Austria with an army of 120,000 men, many of them veterans in the campaigns of Italy and Hungary, right upon the borders of Hesse. There was Bavaria, with a body of 80,000 eager to pour themselves over Prussia. The other German states—unless perhaps Hanover—were either neutral or united with Austria. The colossal Power on the eastern frontier was an ally of Austria, and might at any moment take the opportunity to gain a foothold in Germany, by sending an immense army over Silesia.

England was averse, and France was reported even to have designs on the Prussian provinces on the Rhine.

Besides, it was felt Prussia was a country in the last degree unfitted to be *defended*. Open on every side, disjointed, with the enemy's forces between the two extremities, it could hope for nothing but in bold attacks.

Such was the feeling in Berlin, these last two weeks. Two more exciting weeks I have not passed in foreign lands. So many events in such quick succession. First the conferences in Warsaw, the countermanding the order for *mobilizing* the army, the resignation of Radowitz, the momentary withdrawing of the ministry; then war, with all its exciting preparations; and in the midst of all this turmoil, the quiet death of the brave old man* who was one of the chief actors, worried to his grave, some said, by these troubles in his country's affairs.

Such, as I have said, is the Prussian view of this war; but it is a view which I cannot at all take. I have talked about this contest often with my friends, and I feel deeply the hopes and desires which they connect with it, but I am compelled to believe they are deceived in the intentions with which it is carried on.

It is true, the old Bundestag is the enemy of constitutional changes; it is true, that in the Cassel affair, Prussia is on the side of the people against the arbitrary Curfürst, and that, as a nation, she is the representative of the constitutional party. Still I have no confidence whatever in the *Government*. They have crushed liberty in Baden; they have put down democratic efforts in Hamburg; they have cajoled the people into a constitution which is no constitution, and I do not see why they may not act consistently to their old character in Cassel, when the war is over.

* Count Brandenburgh, Prime Minister after the resignation of Radowitz.

At the head of this government is a most remarkable character—the present King of Prussia—on whom much of the results of the war will depend. Probably on no throne of Europe has there been for many years, so gifted a personage. In all the accomplishments which make the cultivated gentleman, in delicate taste for art, in a refined ear for music, in general scholarship, and in elegant address, he has no superior. Unlike the matter-of-fact character of most kings of the present day, he has a highly imaginative nature—given to *Phantasie*, as the Germans say—and quick often to move to noble impulses. But, as both friends and enemies confess, there is no dependence to be placed on his phantasies—and the enthusiasm of one day may altogether die away on the next. Still in all his political changes he has been true to one "ideal," an ideal formed long ago, and growing more real to him, till he forgets entirely the age in which he lives.

He believes in a State where no *written* constitution shall exist—where the king rules with a patriarchal authority, directly derived from God, and where different *classes* (*Mächte*) form the elements of government, restraining one another. This idea appears throughout his reign; under it, he has promised constitutional changes which he has never granted, deceived the people with constitutions where the true elements of liberty were gone, and has acted, whether fickle or false, again and again, with most disastrous influence on the liberties of Prussia. This idea comes forth again this very year, when he gives the Constitution of February; promising to observe this instrument, but with this condition always, that "*the King reigns;*" for "*he reigns by God's ordinance.*"

From such a man I do not believe Constitutional Freedom has anything to expect; and I cannot hope for favorable results from a war of which he has the guidance.

In my opinion, the government and the people have a different object, and the result will show either that the Cabinet will evade a war, which may strengthen the constitutional party, or that, when they have gained the victory in Cassel, they are no more desirous of granting constitutional privileges there than they have been in Heidelberg, or are now in Berlin.

Amid all this clangor of arms, and tumult, and passion of opposing nations, there is a plain, quiet, good-hearted man in one of the great cities of Germany, devoting his whole time and no small talents, in sending forth, through the German papers, *messages of Peace.* He has separated himself from his country, and even from those who sympathise with him, to do this. It is a work of labor, and of expense—for every article has to be paid for as if it were an advertisement. There is no honor in it; for the sneer, or the good-natured joke, is all that he gets in return. Yet through it all, in all this whirl and preparation of war around him, he works away; sending out, in faith, these little "*Olive Branches,*" as he calls them. Need I say, it is dear ELIHU BURRITT—the sturdy Yankee workman of former days—the kind-hearted, industrious *friend of man*, in these? If his voice be indeed so far beyond the age that none can hear it, one may still wish him God's blessing!

CHAPTER XII.

BERLIN.

In wandering about Berlin, I felt myself at once in an entirely different atmosphere from that in Hamburg. The books in the windows, the objects of art, the shops, and even the very *external* of the citizens were all changed. I had left commercial Germany for intellectual Germany. There were fewer marks of individual wealth—but far more of general taste and culture.

Berlin, as a whole, is not an agreeable city in appearance. Why any one should ever have chosen such a site for the Capital of a large kingdom ;—a place in the midst of a wide, sandy plain, with no beauty of scenery, unprovided with stone or building materials, and on the banks of a miserable little rivulet, is difficult to understand. The main street, (the Friedrichs strasse,) some two miles in length, is on one dead level, so that the water in many spots never flows off in the drains. The back and side streets are very dirty and without sidewalks. All the finest parts of the city are built of brick, stuccoed, and in this hot dusty locality, the stucco either crumbles off badly, or becomes very much discolored. Even the Royal Palace—one of the largest palaces in Europe, looks as soiled and begrimed as a Liverpool warehouse.

Nothing seems built completely. The Brandenburg Gate—the most imposing portal perhaps in the world—is constructed of brick, stuccoed in imitation of stone, and the only genuine thing on it, is the copper car of victory, crowning it.

Still refined taste has atoned for the want of scenery, or of building material. The architectural points of view seemed to me without an equal in any city of Europe, except Edinburgh. I shall never forget my impressions, when first walking down the broad street, "*Unter den Linden*," (Under the lindens)—a street perhaps twice as wide as Broadway, with a noble avenue of lindens in the centre. At one end, were the columns of the splendid Brandenburg Gate, like the portico of a Grecian temple, and at the other, as I stood on the bridge, was a view of as many noble buildings in various directions, as any modern city will show. The sturdy, compact-looking arsenal, the most original and consistent architectural conception in the city; the New Museum with its colonnades and brilliant frescoes; the little temple-like building relieving the foreground—a guard-house; the gloomy and massive palace behind the university, and seen through an interval of the houses, a square (the *Gens d'armes Platz*,) lined with imposing buildings and churches.

But there was about it all to me an interest greater even than the pleasure from its architecture. None but one who has felt, can understand an American traveller's first fresh feelings, in standing in scenes of old historic association. To me the whole was speaking of the Past. The old iron-hearted, indomitable king, whose campaigns I had followed when a boy, as if they were a tale of romance, seemed to me still to fill the scenes with his presence. The martial air over everything, the statues of general and soldier, the designs and sculpture, everywhere picturing war and struggle and victory, the buildings he had erected, and even the squadrons of men who marched incessantly by with the precision of working machines, all spoke to me of the stern old General and Martinet, who had himself by his unconquerable purpose built up a Capital and a Kingdom of soldiers. Everywhere, too, voices from Prussia's short, but glorious history. There right by me, the bare head whitened by a squall of November snow, as it might have been on many a battle field, the foot treading proudly over a dismounted cannon, and the sword waving triumphantly in the air, is a bronze statue of the fiery Blücher.

Across the street, in reflective posture, a marble figure of the man who beyond all others prepared Prussia, and organized her army for the grand struggle with the French in '14 and '15—Scharnhorst; behind him, as the trophies of the city, the cannon and mortars brought back from Paris, in 1816. And beyond, on the great gate, the car of victory recovered from Napoleon after the battle of Waterloo.

In the gathering darkness, as the thick ranks of soldiers hurried eagerly on over the bridge, towards the road for Southern Germany, or as some more enthusiastic shouted, "*Für König und Vaterland!*" (For King and Fatherland!) it almost seemed as if the Great Frederick might again appear in his three-cornered hat and careless uniform to lead the armies on to victory; or as if there were again an uprising of Prussia with her old war-cry, to oppose a combined Europe. But, alas! a most degenerate descendant sits on the throne of the "soldier-king;" and the contest, towards which they enthusiastically hasten, shall be but another of the valorous displays and cowardly retractions, which have marked the reign of FREDERICK WILLIAM.

The city, as I said before, shows everywhere the marks of a high culture and taste.

I have already visited an Institution, founded, I think, by the Government, whose sole object is to instruct gratuitously apprentices of the various trades in the fine arts, with reference to improvements in the patterns of manufactures, and in the designs of common utensils. The King has been very earnest in his endeavors to improve the taste of the people, and to beautify the city. The large galleries of painting and sculpture, and the fine collections of antique vases, coins and medals, are entirely open to all. He is putting up also a colossal bronze equestrian statue of Frederick the Great, by Rauch, in the Linden Avenue, and is now erecting besides one of the most tasteful and consistent structures which is to be found in Europe, designed as a building for the reception of the numerous collections of sculpture and works of antiquity, in Berlin. It is constructed throughout, as much as possible, in the classic style. The floors are, in most instances, of the most minutely tesselated marble, of all varieties of color. The walls, and cornices, and roof, are painted in the elaborate classic mode; every appropriate space filled with minute, exquisite colored figures, or with those strange devices from mythology, and history, and life, which one can still see in the houses of Pompeii. The columns are of every variety and color of marble, carefully chiseled, even to the finest leaf on the capitals. On some of the side walls there are bold, free, almost startling frescoes, by Kaulbach and Cornelius; and on others, genuine classic *alto-relievo* work, brought from Rome or Athens. The niche for each statue is painted appropriately to the character, with beautiful minute figures, and the wall-veils beneath the cornices are filled with mythological, grotesque combinations from the hands of German artists, as luxuriant, or wild, or sensuous in composition, as any which ever adorned the temples of Venus or of Bacchus.

The whole, like the ruined houses of Pompeii, or the remains of the palaces and baths of Rome, leaves an impression of the most wonderful combination of elaborate and solid work. It was the splendor and massiveness of an ancient temple, with the fineness of a modern miniature museum. I wandered a long time through the splendid halls and lofty porches, and could not but think, as I looked at it all, that there were some advantages from this centralizing of power in the Old World, which we must wait long for in the New.

But, as I go abroad among the people; as I see soldiers stationed at every corner and in every public place; as I find that a man cannot stir from his city and hardly from his house, without feeling this strong grasp of the central power; as I hear the desires of noble men expressed for something freer and better for their nation; and as I observe how confused and unsatisfied, and unhappy, the condition of these German monarchies is now, I feel how poor the exchange of this, with all its splendor and taste would be, for our free, unchecked society.

Soon after my arrival, an entertainment occurred quite characteristic of Berlin, and which is considered one of the great literary enjoyments of the season. It is the acting over of one of the old Greek plays, with all the appropriate accompaniments. In this case it was the tragedy of *Antigone.* Tieck, one of the first poets and literary men of the age, and Böckh, the great classical scholar from the University, were consulted as to the decorations and scenery. The choruses were translated by Donner, and the music composed for them was by Mendelssohn,—I suppose the greatest of modern composers. The more difficult parts of the scenery had been provided by the King himself, from whom, I believe, the whole idea originated.

At an early hour there was gathered in the theatre an immense audience of students and professors, and all the principal literary people of Berlin. The very first aspect of the scenery and stage, was strange. Beside the customary stage behind the curtain, there was another lower stage, in front, with entrances on each side for the actors. On each side of the curtain were beautiful fresco figures of the Comic and the Tragic muse. The curtain fell instead of rising, as in modern days; and the actors came in from the front, instead of the back—a much more difficult thing, by the way.—The principal characters alone enter from the opposite side to the audience. I believe there was some further arrangement also, which my classical knowledge hardly carries me through, such as the servants and one set of characters entering from the left, and another from the right. The scene was the front of a Grecian house—some beautiful columns,—an altar and small statue, with offerings upon it, and an opening occasionally into the peristyle beyond.

On the lower stage, was an altar with offerings of flowers upon it, around which were grouped the members of the *choroi*. These were old men, with long white hair, and holding staffs in their hands, in tunic and robe and sandals. There were two parties, each with different color and responding to one another in the chorus; the leaders sustaining the dialogue, where it was required in the play. Their "grouping" throughout—and their positions about the altar, which they were continually changing, were very striking. In the first scene, or "episode," Antigone is seen coming out of the house, with the graceful costume which the old wall-paintings give us of Grecian maidens, and with a classic urn on her head, which had quite probably been borne in that very way some two thousand years ago.

It is a very difficult play to act. The conceptions are, very many of them, so foreign to modern ideas; the allusions to old historical events and to Mythology are so very hard to render appropriately—and the expressions of Greek passion and pathos, sound so strangely in modern version, that it is not to be wondered at, if the acting had failed. Still, with all this, and with the fact that one accustomed to *read* dramas, is always disappointed, when they are *acted*, I found myself carried away by the whole representation. There is an idea, running through the whole play, of dark, inexorable *Fate* hanging over the unfortunate House, and urging them to mad crimes. And yet one can see, as perhaps the poet meant to show of all Fate, that after all, it is their own voluntary madness. These ideas were left almost painfully on my mind. Then the nobleness and rashness of *Antigone* as she resolves to defy *Creon's* and the State's command, and bury the corpse of her brother, Polynices. The inflexible will of Creon, as he dooms her to death, and denies the prayer of his favorite son—the betrothed of Antigone—for mercy, and his terrible grief, as he finds that with her, he has destroyed his son and his beloved wife, Eurydice. All this wild, fierce emotion, was wonderfully brought out—and in every part, came the glorious music of the *choroi*, as they sang alternately of the blindness of men in the hands of inexorable Fate; of the sweep and power of human passion; or of the unspeakable greatness of the All-powerful who sits above this—a passage worthy of Job. I have never heard music that was more thrilling, and there was in it all, a wild, strange tone, as consistent to that mysterious Fate hanging over this House. That tender passage too, where Antigone half excuses her own heroic devotion to her brother, which had impelled her to defy law, and almost to forget her love to her betrothed,

"Not for Hate, but Love, was I, by nature formed,"

was given with touching truthfulness. The death of Eurydice was beautifully shown, by throwing open the inner portals of the house, where were seen the funeral maidens gathered around a white form, with burning torches and flowers.

There was no division of the play into *acts*—only episodes. The whole throughout, in costume, decorations, scenery—even manners, in the most wonderful consistency to what we know of the Grecian modes; though probably the thing most inconsistent, was the music; which I suppose would have been far inferior in the original. Altogether, it was a very high intellectual enjoyment, and impressed old Grecian Drama on the mind, more than many a college lecture.

CHAPTER XIII.

LIFE IN BERLIN.

Nov. 1850.

I HAVE taken lodgings in a very pleasant street—the *Dorotheen Strasse*—near the Linden Avenue, and where several of the Americans and Germans, to whom I have letters, reside. My room is on the second story, with a pleasant exposure, and on the whole neatly furnished, though it has required a long-sustained argument to get rid of that enormous *feather-bed* coverlid. I pay four Thaler (about $2 80) the *month*, which is cheap enough; and the breakfast of coffee and rolls costs eight cents, and dinner at the cafès, from twelve and a half to thirty-seven cents, very neat and with several courses; so that living in Berlin does not seem likely to be specially expensive. My landlady must have been a beauty in her day, though she is very slatternly now. I scarcely ever saw more finely chiselled features. She comes in in the morning with my coffee, and wishes me *Guten Morgen!* in such a merry tone, and always gets my name wrong, sometimes making it Herr Bric, sometimes Brac, or Brahcy, or even Brass, and always apologizing in a compassionate way, as if the men were to be truly pitied who were forced to have such unchristian names.

I nearly always induce her to stop and chat, and being of rather a speculative turn, she is very fond of putting knotty theological points to me; which if I cannot solve, I avoid, by taking refuge in my bad German—a sufficient excuse to her for any amount of ignorance. She is the best-natured creature in the world, and of course never has anything done in time; never keeps any engagements, and lets everything run at loose ends. I have saved her conscience a great load by taking all our accounts and keeping them myself; paying her some weeks ahead, to keep her out of debt. She has a very pretty daughter, who keeps my room neatly, so that I am satisfied; though I must say, her utter unpunctuality is very provoking; and perhaps it is quite as much so, that I am entirely cut off from scolding! A man must be proficient in a language if he would scold well, and I cannot do it. Long words and book phrases will not serve, and I do not know Berlin slang, and could not conscientiously, even if I knew how, swear in German. Perhaps my looks and terrible English ejaculations and impatient German do as well, as she always at once beats a retreat with a half-comic, half-terrified look when I commence. Her own manners and those of the children are very pleasant; they never enter or leave the room without a bow and salutation to me. The husband, who is a tailor, has far more the bearing of a courtly gentleman, than most of our cultivated men, and always raises his hat when he meets me in the street.

I notice a similar peculiarity through all classes. In the *restaurante*, if a gentleman takes a place at the same table, it is always with a bow; if he reaches over for the paper you have finished, he uses some half apologetic expression, "*Ich bitte!*" The shopkeeper gives the morning salutation as you come in; and says "Empfehle mich!"* as you leave. No one enters an omnibus or a railway

* "I recommend myself," the almost universal formula in Berlin for

carriage without saluting the others. I have seen now many classes of the Germans, from the *Handwerksbursch* (apprentice) on his travels and the soldier in the camps, to the highest literary people, and I find through all, this "*humanity*" as the Latins used to call it; this open-hearted, pleasant, human way, as if men were really, without any poetry, "members of the same family." Men in the lower classes do kindnesses for you, and neither claim nor accept the "everlasting shilling," as in England. In a rail-car or public conveyance, people talk of their own private matters as if it was a thing of course that other persons would take an interest in them.

Something of my impressions may be due to *visiting*—one of the most unselfish forms of human life—still there is much, which cannot be accounted for in that way. The politeness too, seems genuine. It does not burden you; or make you feel that you are impolite, or appear as if it were worn for the occasion. It is a part of every-day, habitual life. Not a politeness, expressing itself in grimaces and bows; or fearing openness and downright words in others; but a quick, almost unconscious respect for others as *men*, which speaks constantly in German manners.

I have asked an English groom the way in the streets of London, and been told in answer "How the h—ll should I know?" An American workman would tell you very clearly—but in a fever of impatience at being stopped. A German stands—says to you with a half bow, "*Be good enough* to take the second street," etc., and touches his hat as he goes, which is, perhaps, a little too much of a virtue, and yet is a very pleasant thing.

I notice that there is one expression of deference, which neither the Germans nor the English often use, but which is almost univer-

parting, where *adieu* is not used. The old German expression, "Leben Sie wohl," (Farewell!) is seldom heard, except between intimates.

sal with Americans. I mean the word, *Sir!* *Mein Herr,* (Sir), is seldom heard in Germany, except from servants or inferiors, and is considered slavish between equals.

In general, the contrast in manners between our lower classes and the European, is very striking. It has often surprised me. The cultivated classes, in that respect, are very nearly the same, the world over. But why a poor man, or an uneducated man with us, should be so much less polished, than one in the same position in the old world, I have never been able to explain.

I used formerly to think it was a natural result of our new society, not softened as yet by the appliances and influences of an old civilization. But I have seen the manners and courtesy of the most complete gentleman in a Hungarian cattle-driver, whose whole civilization had not carried him above undressed sheep-skins and half-cooked meat. It is the more remarkable, as we are not naturally a grumbling, or whimsical, or domineering race, like the English; or a strict and pragmatic people, like the mass of the Scotch. We seem to have in our character all the elements of high courtesy, fearlessness, generosity, kindness—yet few of us are habitually courteous.

The causes begin early—manner, *expression* of any feeling is laughed at in childhood; later in life it is called a humbug; and afterwards in the gigantic, absorbing plans and pursuits of our American society, so small a thing as manners, or the promotion of others' happiness in these petty ways is altogether lost sight of and neglected.

As though feeling could grow where its expression is always pruned, and as though all our grand outward success were worth anything, if there be a basis in home-life of cold, unsocial, disagreeable intercourse.

The *type* also of religious character most reverenced, and very naturally so among us, has not included courtesy as one of its traits. We have forgotten the old patriarch, with his simple hospitality and native courtliness; and Paul, who could "become all things to all men," and have taken to ourselves as a model the severe, ascetic, form-hating Puritan. A character whose faults men have caught but too easily, but whose grand and massive virtues become more rare each day. There is a feeling too among our sturdy farmers and Western "boys," that any courtesy is unmanly. A feeling, boyish as it is, connected with our old English gruffness which we have inherited. If Kossuth has done nothing else in this country than show that a tact and politeness, like a woman's, is not inconsistent with the strength of an indomitable manhood, he has not been without his use to us.

There is something higher in Politeness than Christian moralists have recognised. In its best forms as a simple, out-going, all-pervading spirit, none but the truly religious man can show it. For it is the Sacrifice of self in the little habitual matters of life—always the best test of our principles—together with a Respect, unaffected for man, as our brother under the same grand destiny. In its lower and more common development in every-day life, we have very much to learn of the Europeans.

NOVEMBER 26.

Have just called on a family to whom I had letters, and who have already been very friendly to me. They are among the first literary people of Berlin, and are well known throughout Prussia. I found them living in the *third story* of one of these great houses. The door below was opened by a porter at my ring, and then on the third landing, their own door by their servant. They occupy only four or five rooms, and keep but one servant.

The sitting-room is more filled up, with various objects, than is usual in Germany. There are some exquisite ornaments, in plaster, scattered about, mostly casts from *antiques* in the classical Museum; a very much more tasteful mode of beautifying a room, for a man of limited means, than laying out all his money on one or two pieces of expensive and second-rate statuary. Few of us can afford to buy really good statuary, or fine paintings. Why cannot our American housekeepers learn that good engravings are a better ornament to a room, than poor paintings in gilt frames; that flowers set off a window better than tawdry curtains; and that casts of something truly graceful, or objects with a real meaning are worth all your second-hand marble nymphs, gaudy mirrors, or gilded cornices. They received me this evening, as they always do, cordially; not so much, I think, because I was a foreigner—for the Berliners see as much foreign society as native—but because I was a friend of their friends. I had found previously that they were *royalists;* and this evening we fell into a spirited discussion on our political creeds, which may have some interest to my American readers.

Men need, they urged in the course of the argument, a central, definite object for their reverence and obedience. In a Republic, there is no reverence for government; no *moral* tie to the centre; it is merely the bond of interest. There can be no loyalty to a President; he is, according to your own definitions, the "servant of the people;" and not always chosen because he will be the best servant. You tell me that your best Statesmen are seldom Presidents. All that is most poetic and noble is excluded from such a form. The only Government, resembling God's, is a Monarchy.

"We love our king," said they; and their voices quivered with emotion, as they spoke of the present chances of his being driven into exile. "Where he goes, we will go!"

I could hardly realise, as they talked, that I was conversing with persons of the present age; it seemed as if I were among the loyal cavaliers and ladies of chivalric times. Yet these were people of the highest cultivation, and accustomed to think on all subjects.

I have an unconquerable tendency to take in my own mind, the stand-point of the persons I am with, and on this occasion I was deeply impressed with the earnestness and the poetic tone of their views, so that, though I battled stoutly for Republicanism, I was a little blinded to the wrong of their opinions. I forgot for the time, that it is such theories among the cultivated and noble-hearted, which have helped to deliver over the forty millions of Germany to the blind caprice and heartless tyranny of twenty or thirty as weak and inefficient and unprincipled men, as have ever disgraced humanity.

I said in reply, that none of us in America considered our Government any the less "from God," or any the less an object of love and reverence, than they their Monarchy. We believed it to be the form especially springing from the wants and the nature of developed man, and thus directly from God. We believed God had thus far guarded it in its outward growth; and we loved it—would die for it, not as impersonated in any one imperfect ruler, but as expressed in the institutions it forms, and the fruits it everywhere bears amongst us. Even if we were sure of finding the "best possible man," to impersonate Government, and to rule us without check, we still would prefer our system. Our creed was that the highest development of humanity is insured by leaving the greatest possible liberty to individual development. And that under a few limitations, it would more and more be found true in our country, that the best government is that which governs least; until the good time comes on the earth when all outward government ceases, and the only checks on human intercourse are the Love and Principle of the individual man.

All which and a great deal more of a metaphysical and transcendental kind, I leave to the imagination of the reader, picturing an argument-loving American and a philosophical German sitting late at night over mugs of Bavarian beer, and some genuine German mystifying tobacco.

A warm shake of the hand when it was over, "*Schlafen Sie recht wohl und kommen Sie bald wieder!*" and I returned to my lodgings.

I take the liberty of quoting here from a letter which I received after I left Berlin, as farther showing the feelings of the Royalists, and the open-hearted German manner to a stranger. It is from Madame ——, who will pardon the freedom for the object intended.

BERLIN.

"I thank you very much, lieber Herr B., for the friendly sympathy which you have retained for us in the distance. Take with you our most cordial (*innigsten*) wishes into your Fatherland; and think whiles of the old custom of our dear Germany, that those who have once grasped hands, do not again forget. Do not let yourself be disturbed, if neither I nor my husband answer your letter as it deserves. We stand before great events. The Lord hath not yet torn aside the curtain. It will soon be shown whether elevation or ruin is our fate. One of either must happen; and as the heart of our dear, dear king is moved, so is the destiny of our Fatherland determined. Without the *Hohenzollern* there is for us no power and no respect on earth. "With God for king and fatherland!"

"A *Republic* is something great and noble. The history of the ancients teaches, indeed, that it has Tyranny as a companion, and ruin as its bequest. To me is a Republic like a beautiful woman full of glorious gifts, but *without* soul, like the lovely fable of Undine. * * * * * *

"You will not laugh at a woman's truth, if she tells you, that sometimes there is no pleasure like *subjection.*

"God grant his blessing on you! If you on the sea or on the soil of your fatherland have any desire to greet us, do it certainly, and my husband and myself will thank you!" And the husband adds in a postscript, "On the last day of your stay in Germany, receive our hearty greetings and wishes for your happy home-return. You will now be able to imagine how dear one can hold Germany, with all its wants and confusions. Think of us friendly the-other-side the ocean."

CHAPTER XIV.

A BERLIN DINNER-PARTY.

"Ich bitte, mein Herr! nehman Sie Platz! Der Herr Geheimrath erwartet Sie!" "Take a seat, sir, please! His honor, the Geheimrath, is expecting you!" said a respectable looking German servant, as he threw open the doors of a handsome parlor for me. *Der Herr Geheimrath*, or in every-day language, Mr. C. was a Berlin gentlemen in comfortable circumstances, who had formerly been in political life. I found him living, like most of the aristocratic people in the city, way up in the top of one of the great houses. I had entered through a large portal, the door of which was opened by a porter, in a story above, with a wire and pulley. Each story was occupied by a separate family, and I could see from the names above their bells, by persons of high rank. None of the stair-ways had any carpeting on them, but the material was rich-looking, apparently varnished oak in inlaid figures, and the banisters gilded. The walls in the hall were broken up by oval compartments, in which were pretty little colored designs of faces or figures, in the classic style, and were ornamented with arabesque borders—all having a rich and massive air, and entirely different from our own style of ornament.

Mr. C.'s drawing-rooms were truly German again. High, cheerful rooms, with painted ceilings, light curtains, many objects of Bohemian glass-ware, and vases of flowers scattered around; but no carpet on the polished parquette oak floor, and no heavy articles of furniture. On the whole, tasteful and airy, but somewhat bare com pared to English rooms.

Mr. C entered soon, and we fell into pleasant conversation. In the course of it, I said something about this mode of occupying each an *ètage* or story, and asked him, whether it was general? He replied, that there were not half-a-dozen families in the city who leased a whole house. The houses had been originally built of a large size by Frederick the Great to fill up the space, and since that all who built had followed the same style. It was much cheaper, too, for each family, "and we Germans you know," said he, "have not the objection of you English to living all in the same house together. It seems more *gemüthlich!*" *

I thought then and I have often thought since in our large American cities, as I have seen the immense burden of rents on young business men, how convenient and pleasant such an arrangement would be with us. For a man with family, a boarding-house is the last residence to be desired. And yet there is no other resort in our great cities, under these exorbitant rents. In this Berlin-mode, each family can be private, carry on its own house-keeping; and yet need not be at much more expense than in a respectable boarding-house.

The more I see of the middle classes in Berlin, the lawyers, professors, merchants, &c., the more I am surprised at the economy shown everywhere. Hamburgh seems luxurious by the side of it.

* I cannot translate this word, though "*cosy*" comes near it, in this place, except that *gemuthlich* expresses something higher—something of *feeling*.

No house with carpeting; and few with rich furniture even. A family seems seldom to have more than two servants. In some houses of wealthy merchants, I have seen the dining-room furnished with beds in curtained alcoves, so shortened are they for room. And in nearly all, some of the sitting-rooms are turned into bedrooms, as the first thing with a German is to have a place in which to chat with his friends, and after that where to lay his head. I see, too, that the Hamburg bountiful dinners are not in vogue here; and invitations are usually to supper—a substantial, plain meal. Yet there is the most constant and easy sociality everywhere; and it is apparent at once to the stranger, he is among people of the highest culture and refinement. Money seems to be spent readily on entertainments in music and art, and for social enjoyment; but not much on mere luxury or display. When a Berlin scholar, or man of business gives a party, he does it in a simple, unexpensive way, generous enough in its provision, but that not of a very costly kind. If he would ride out with his family, he quietly takes a *droschky* (hack). None but a few of the superannuated noblemen sport our New York equipages. Something of all this is due, without doubt, to the small means of the people; but more to their good sense. Towards the foreigner, there is less too of outward hospitality than in other German cities; but the want is more than made up by the lively, easy, intellectual intercourse into which he can be admitted; and the genuine interest taken in him, if he has anything worth being interested in.

But to return to my visit at Mr. C.'s. There was to be a dinner party, and the rest of the company were gradually coming in. The ladies were in full dress; the gentlemen had much the same appearance with any dinner company at home, except that the *moustaches* were more common.

After taking our ladies into the dining-room, conversation commenced at once.

"Sind Sie ganz *orientirt* in der Stadt?" (Are you thoroughly familiar with the city?) I find is the most general first question to me, the stranger. That use of the word *orientirt* was quite new to me, as it is seldom found in books till of late years. "Have you found your *eastings?* taken your bearings—known where you are—become familiar?" I suppose to be the meaning and derivation. It seems applied to almost everything.

The ladies in our chat were quite interested to know whether all the fine stories were true about the American gallantry to women. It was the paradise for women, they had heard. I told them of the universal attention shown them in public places; how a man would be thought "no gentleman" to let a lady stand on a steamboat or in a rail-road car, while he occupied a comfortable seat; and that a woman could travel through our country in safety, without an escort. They thought it must be "because there were fewer of the fair sex,"—a reason I indignantly repelled—whereupon they assured me kindly, they quite "understood why the Americans were such a free and happy people!"

It was very apparent in this dinner, as everywhere, how much better the Germans have the *art* of enjoyment than we. Of the particular courses I will not speak, as they were much handsomer than is customary in the middle classes, and would be no fair specimen of Berlin dinners. But the little haste through it all; the variety of small dishes intended rather to fill up the time and sharpen the appetite, than to gorge the stomach; and the general air of the company, as met rather for pleasant converse than for earnest gluttony, were all characteristic of this people, and very unlike American habits. Everybody of course just now is deeply interested in politics. The news has come of a skirmish between the outposts of the two great armies of Austrians and Prussians at Fulda, in Hesse Cassel; perhaps the first meeting of those opposite tides which shall desolate all Europe. The troops marching towards that little province are equal, they say, to the armies of Napoleon's time, in number. In fact, since 1815, Europe has not seen the gathering of such mighty masses of soldiers. The Austrian left wing, resting on Frankfort, numbers 80,000 men, mostly Bavarians and Würtembergers; as the king of Würtemberg hopes, it is said, to have his share of the plunder when it comes to the picking of Prussia—in the shape of the Prussian Rhine provinces. The centre now gathering in Saxony and Bohemia amount to 120,000 men, under the command of Radetzky himself. On the right, near the borders of Silesia, is a body of 70,000 Bohemians, who will penetrate the passes of the mountains, occupy that province, and act in co-operation with the centre. It is probable 150,000 Prussians will soon be concentrated there likewise.

The talk at table is that there are orders to the Prussian outposts to withdraw, from "strategical considerations." The only losses in the skirmish were two horses. They are describing too with great zest a picture in *Kladderadatsch*, (the German "Punch,"—a very weak mixture by the way,) wherein the Prussian soldiers are seen marching grimly away from a battle-field, on which are the corpses of two horses; at the same time all looking behind fiercely at the line of fat, easy Bavarians, and saying, "*Aus strategischen Rücksichten* (From strategical *back-looks*, i. e. considerations).

No one can believe that after this grand preparation, the king will now retreat; yet they notice that the tone of the *Deutsche Reform*, the ministerial organ, is becoming more submissive, and that there is a rumor, Holstein will be utterly given up to the troops of the Confederation. I can see the idea of yielding to those "beer-drinking Bavarians," galls them to the quick. There is a considerable variety of political characters in the company, one or two intimately connected with the king and attached to him; some of the old Constitutionalists who worked in '48 for a United Germany, and who are now becoming fast the most steady opponents of Government; and a few Free-Traders of somewhat democratic sentiment. Yet they all seem to have such a love for "poor Holstein," and they relate many a story of the oppressions going on there, which I know to be much exaggerated, though I do not care to tell them so.

It is plain, though little is said, that even the friends of the king are in doubt of him. "No one who does not know him," said one in a whisper to me, "should judge him. His misfortune is that he has too delicate moral perceptions. He dreads the responsibility of a WAR!" I had little doubt, in my own mind, that he dreaded much more rousing up the Democratic spirit in such a struggle—which, perhaps, afterwards neither he nor any ruler in Germany could put down.

I have never been in a literary circle before, where there were not some intellectual *dilettantists*, men who pride themselves on a philosophical indifference to subjects which are life and death to the masses. I do not know whether this comes from a want of heart or from cowardice, but I do know I would rather meet the coarsest boor with a meaning in him, than these literary *faineants*. There were none here, however; and with all the Berlin *persiflage*, I seldom heard any on such subjects. Men spoke of their country, and her future with an expression of pain, as of the disgrace of a friend.

At the close of the dinner, we all returned to the drawing-room for coffee, where the conversation became more general. There had been a great Panorama, in the city, of the Mississippi, and many questions were put to me about it. Nothing seemed to so arouse the imagination of the ladies as the idea of a "primeval forest," where the trees were not planted. They all lamented, however, that we "had no singing-birds in our woods!" I find this idea general in Europe. I told them that I had noticed no difference in that respect, though in England I had heard several songsters far surpassing any of ours, except the mocking-bird.

During the evening one of the gentlemen turned to me, and said in English, "Your country will soon have a different language from that which your fathers brought over!" I told him, I thought not. Taking all our classes, there was more pure English spoken than in England itself. Of course we should invent new words in new circumstances, but the old tongue would be always ours.

In reply, he reckoned up to my discomfiture the number of words added or changed in America; showed the change in English everywhere since Chaucer's time; alluded to the gradual variations which came over the classic languages, and thought English as likely to degenerate as Latin or Greek. It was a good instance of the German's learning and theorizing. The man knew far more of the technicalities of my language, than I did myself. I told him, however, that we had one great safeguard for the purity of the tongue for all classes, which the Romans did not have—our old *Saxon Bible.*

He allowed that, and said that it was equally the case in Germany. "There is no German like those plain, strong words in Luther's translation."

As we were upon the subject, I took the liberty of asking him whether some of the *purists* there, were not fearful of their own language? For of all disagreeable medleys, the modern conversational

German seemed to me the worst. "You have only to add an *iren* to a foreign word, and it becomes German; and near half your words seem of that kind, *amusiren*, *discursiren*, and a thousand others!"

He quite agreed with me. I told him, also, how few vigorous terse writers I found on political subjects among the modern authors; and that *Bülaň* seemed to me the only one who could at all compete with our essayists in style.

"It is too true, alas!" said he; "we Germans seem to have lost vigor of words as well as of character, of late years."

In colloquial language, nothing will so utterly surprise the stranger—yes, shock him—as the universal profanity among the ladies. In the best circles of Germany, I have heard more oaths in one evening, than I would in the same time from a ship's crew. "*Ach Gott! Mein Gott! mein Gott! Jesus Christus!*" rung over and over at the veriest trifles.

It was some time before I could accustom myself to it. Of course the words have no irreverent sound to them, and are used like the French "*Mon Dieu!*" still how so foolish a habit could have become so general among sensible people surprises one.

It is singular in the usual literary conversation, how little is said of modern German literature. Göthe and Schiller are "classics" now; and *Jean Paul*, is even quite *passè*, so that few of the young people know anything about him, except his inextricable sentences. This would not be so strange, for the great Teachers of a nation are seldom discussed in common talk; but among all the many romances read, there is scarcely one of the German. And an American is surprised to find himself discussing the naturalness of *Johanna* (Jane) *Eyre's* character, or the morality of Bulwer, or laughing over the remembered jokes of "*Bots*," (Boz) as they call him, just as he did at home. Cooper and Irving I find everywhere, and the children all know "Leatherstocking," and the Indian Chiefs perfectly, and have confident hopes of meeting him, if they should ever cross to the New World. In fact, the English and American novels are the mode at present in Germany, and there has scarcely appeared one of any worth for several years without being speedily translated into German. But the foreign work, which of all others has been read most eagerly by thinking men in Germany these late years, and which is exerting a most happy influence, is *Macaulay's History of England*. And if Macaulay never does any other good through it, than what is effected in this land, he will have accomplished a great work.

It is almost the first instance to the Germans, of history made dramatic; and in its exposition of the English Constitution, and its vivid account of the English Revolution, it is of incalculable benefit, and singularly appropriate to the present state of Germany. It is a new thing too, to the Germans, to see in union a genuine Christian belief and an ardent love of Liberty.

There is another writer too of England, the freest, truest, most earnest spirit of this century, whose influence seems to have been as great here as in his own country, or in America—Dr. Arnold. It is very grateful to those who have admired and loved Dr. Arnold in secret, to find that in distant lands and under foreign languages, that simple, truthful spirit, that warm heart, that free, practical, reverent mind are equally known and appreciated. Strange, how little is ever said of the man, and yet how wide and deep is his influence.

Though our American novels were spoken of warmly on this evening, and one or two of our scientific men, the tone was generally of pity at our devotion to "the practical," and our neglect of the intellectual. "But it must be;" said one of the learned gentlemen present, "it will be long before your people have leisure to give themselves to Art, or to any high intellectual cultivation in one direction. You must clear the forests first!"

I assured him we were not quite all "pioneers," and that he must remember the national mind had thus far been most applied, apart from directly practical subjects, to oratory and politics. In these, in specimens of eloquence and in a philosophical understanding of political questions, I thought our short records would bear a very favorable comparison with the best of classic times.

Besides, with us every man was far more generally furnished with information than in Germany. No German ever knew much out of his particular line of study or business. I told him, I thought in practical politics and useful information, he would find our "peasants" superior often to his learned men. Though under a severe temptation, which every American will sympathize in, I did not *gasconade*, and they all listened courteously. Indeed, the last thing a German can ever praise is "the poor Fatherland;" and he is quite too ready to believe anything good of other countries. "Yes—yes—*die Zukunft ist für Sie!*—The Future is for you!" said they gloomily.

"Society is worn out here. Perhaps Europe is to become like Asia. But you! everything is before you!" and as I wished them "good evening," the ladies assured me, if they ever were exiled from the old Fatherland, they would remember first our American gallantry to the weaker sex.

CHAPTER XV.

THE GERMAN PASTOR.

I WENT out on a Sunday lately to a pretty modern church in the *Thiergarten*, (the great park of Berlin,) where *Büchsel* preaches. The church is very fashionable, and almost the only one in the city which has a full congregation on the Sabbath. There were several handsome equipages of the nobility at the doors as I came up. I noticed that most of the pews within, had plates with the owners' names upon them, and that each family had its own key. The whole arrangement within—ornament, seats, &c. were modern, much like those in our best Episcopal churches. There were candles burning at the altar. Mr. Buchsel is a very simple, effective preacher, but exceedingly conservative, and devoted to the Government. His sermon was a beautiful, heart-felt discourse, on the "signs of the times." He deplored this "Brother war"—this strife of German with German; spoke feelingly of the dark days which had come to their beloved Fatherland; of the dangers threatening Prussia, and the death of the firm, true-hearted old soldier, Count Brandenburg, a member of his church, who might have done so much to avert these evils. These were judgments on the country for its atheism and irreligion; still it was every Prussian's duty to go forth in the strength of God into this war, on which their very existence as a nation depended, and He would be with them in their just cause. As I went out, I fell into conversation with a theological student, who was just going to be "licensed" as a preacher, but before he had passed his *examen*, was summoned to his regiment in the army! He was sorry, he said, yet he went forth feeling "it was a war for the Lord!"

I felt desirous to see how a Pastor lived and worked in Germany; and a few days after attending this service in Mr. B.'s church, I took the opportunity to visit one of the prominent clergymen, to whom I had letters.

Mr. K. lives somewhat out of the city, though still within the limits, and the walk to his house is a long one. We pass through a pleasant part of Berlin, which is comparatively new, and where this stucco on the houses, that looks so rusty and crumbly in other streets, appears quite handsomely. I suspect that in a dry climate and dusty situation the stucco never can be made to look well a long time. In Hamburg, with its moist atmosphere and sea-board position, houses with this plaster, no older than these in Berlin, made a far finer appearance. Our walk carries us through one of the large city gates, with a guard-house on each side. Officers are patrolling to and fro, prepared to search every hand-cart if necessary, or to pounce upon the luckless individual who has no passport. There, just beyond the gates, is the famous Royal iron foundry, where all those beautiful little iron ornaments which adorn the shop windows of Berlin are made.

A part of it, it will be noticed, is still under the builders' hands, the part which was burned down by the people in mere spite in 1848. Few such acts were committed in that Revolution; and about this gate was some very exasperating fighting. Beyond this, we pass along by the side of the railroad, built almost solely to connect the railway termini, so that in case of emergency cars could be sent from one to the other to convey troops from a distant part of the kingdom. These arrangements are now so complete in Berlin, that tens of thousands of soldiers could be transported in a few hours from the most extreme provinces to the Capital. Mr. K.'s house is a plain, one-story parsonage, with a pleasant little garden around it. The church, a modern-looking building, stands close by: I am shown at once into the "study," which has the somewhat unusual luxury in Berlin of a small carpet in the middle of the floor. The walls are lined with well-used books, showing from their titles that their owner has a strongly orthodox and Lutheran tendency. There is a very good selection too of English literature; and, as one almost invariable accompaniment of every German pastor's equipment, must not be forgotten the long *Meerschaum*-pipe and the bundle of choice Hamburger segars to offer to a friend.

Mr. K. is a man of talent and accomplishments, and could have easily held a position more honored in other professions, and certainly far more comfortable. But he evidently does not think of his circumstances; his heart is with his work. And a very considerable work it is.

The parish—the "*Gemeinde*"—over which he is placed, numbers, he tells me, 19,000. Of these, be it remembered, every child must be baptized, and, after it has reached the age of fourteen, "confirmed," or it will be entitled to no civil or legal rights. As a preparation for the confirmation, each child must receive instruction—*Unterrichten*—in religious subjects two hours a week for two years, from the pastor. It can be imagined what a task this imposes. One would suppose also, that the funerals in such an immense parish would take up a large portion of his time; but in answer to my inquiry he said, that though he had given notice that the offices of a clergyman were at the service even of the poorest, such was the indifference to religious ceremonies among them, that out of over 500 funerals during the year only about 80 were attended by a pastor. Large as this parish seems, compared to an American, it is quite small placed beside some of the parishes of Berlin. I am acquainted with one clergyman who has only one assistant, whose *Gemeinde* numbers 25,000, and there is another neighboring to it containing between 50,000 and 60,000 persons. Yet with all this, are their churches half empty, their weekly meetings scarcely attended, and all church enterprises almost lifeless.

I asked Mr. K. how he accounted for this extreme indifference among the lower classes in Germany to religion. He thought it the result, he said, of the old Rationalism, which had now somewhat left the educated classes and had begun to work among the lower, and was producing an utter want of faith in anything unseen. "There was one good aspect to it in Germany," he thought: "there was no mere resting in forms, such as one sees in England. *There were plenty of Sadducees in Protestant Germany, but very few Pharisees!*" The class where the purest religious feeling existed now, he conceived was the aristocratic. There was more being practically done now for humanity among the nobility than in any other grade of society; and he described how ladies of the highest rank, from the Queen downward, were engaged in these enterprises of the *Innere Mission*, and how they frequently left the most elevated stations to join the Protestant institution of *Diakoninnen* (Deaconesses) at Kaiserswerth, on the Rhine, and to give up their best years to labors of charity. There were not a few, even then, ladies of noble family, he said, working as common assistants and religious teachers in the famous Hospital for Females in Berlin, under the superintendence of the *Fraülein von H——*, herself a lady of rank. The middle—the most intellectual circles—he thought as yet more, if not unbelieving, at least indifferent.

His own efforts in his parish against this indifference of the lower classes, appear to have been constant and very comprehensive in their nature. He has mingled sociably with the people, and has won very considerably their confidence; and I observed afterwards, as we walked out, that all the little dirty children from every quarter run pleasantly up to him to get a shake of the hand.

He believes—in practice at least—in accompanying spiritual reforms with material. Accordingly he has built two houses, corresponding to the model lodging-houses in London, where healthy quarters are given to the poor at a low rent. Besides these, there are some other lodgings now being built, where he hopes he can furnish two rooms, comfortable and dry, for about *half a thaler* (36 cents) a week. In addition to this, a savings' society has been established in the *Gemeinde*, where the poor once a week deposit their money, and receive it in return at the end of the season in fuel or provisions, furnished to them at wholesale prices, by which the immense loss of buying at retail price is saved the laborer, and the temptation to spend, lessened.

Is it noticed how in all the best charities of Europe, that grand principle of *Socialism* is applied, of *combining*, in order to produce certain advantages to the laborer which shall not bear after them the bad effect of mere charities?

The above labors would seem to be quite enough for one man to perform. They are only a small part, however, of what Mr. K. has taken on himself. Twice a week he or some of his friends deliver lectures before a Mechanics' Society, which he has formed and provided with a library and newspapers. Once a month he holds a meeting for Foreign Missions; twice for Home Missions, together with divers religious meetings during the week, when he can get any one to attend. Then he has formed among them a "Society for the Sick," the members of which devote themselves to caring for the sick of the parish; a "Temperance Society," to work against the use of brandy, (*not* wine); a "Business Society," whose duty it is to provide work for the poor sewing women and weavers out of employ. In addition to these, by great exertion, a society has been formed to seek out the workmen who have fallen into difficulty, and to advance them money, without interest; and also another to take charge of infant schools, of which there are three in the parish. It must not be supposed, all these societies are managed in the effective way they are with us. There is little "voluntary" work among them. Mr. K.'s energy is probably the only thing which supports and keeps them alive. Still they accomplish something, and will undoubtedly do more and more. Besides all these duties mentioned above, there are two sermons to prepare every week for Sunday, and all the immense business of such a parish to attend to. To assist him is *one curate*, and from six to twelve voluntary co-workers, who take something of the place of our deacons. For such unceasing, anxious labor, as this must bring, Mr. K. receives, reckoning fees from baptism, confirmation, and marriage ceremonies as salary, about 800 thalers, that is, not quite 600 dollars, and his assistant perhaps 400 dollars. He smiled at the idea, when I asked if the pastor's salary was ever increased by presents from the congregation, and assured me very few ever took interest enough in the whole cause to do such things. These various facts he did not relate to me at all in any whining or melancholy way, but merely as facts which would be interesting to a stranger; and it was evident he himself was very little conscious of his self-denial, and very little troubled by his circumstances in any way.

I inquired in the course of the conversation, how his church was first built. A company of citizens in that quarter of the city, he said, came together and petitioned for a church. The King, in reply, made inquiries as to whether they could pay any part of the sum required? They could not, they said. Whether, if the church was built, they could in any way endow it? "They were utterly unable to do anything for it," was the answer. Learning that this was the fact, he built their church, endowed it, and thus became the *Patron* of that parish, with the power of choosing their pastor, and what may be called, the Presbytery. I asked my friend whether he felt no inconvenience from thus being under the patronage of the King. "*No, most certainly not,*" he said; "there could be no better." He was left entirely free; and the Presbytery, who aid him in managing the financial matters of the church, but in nothing else, were the very best possible men who could be found in the parish. It appears, they were selected with great care by his predecessor, and approved by the King. From what I hear, there seem to be three modes in Prussia in which a pastor is appointed:—by the King, as in this instance, where he builds the church, or where the *Gemeinde* are on the crown-lands; by some nobleman, who in like manner has founded the church, and has the privilege, like the English nobleman, of appointing his own clergyman to the living, though it should be mentioned here, with thankfulness, that no English custom exists of letting out the place to poor curates. The third method is, as in our own churches, the selection of the pastor by the congregation, which privilege is allowed them where they have built their own church.

The church of Mr. K. is comparatively a modern-looking building, and has the very unusual luxury among the Berlin churches of *being warmed.* In fact, I know nothing in Berlin which gives one a more vivid idea of the indifference of the population to religious observances than the cheerless, comfortless aspect of the churches. The opera houses and concert rooms of the city are all of the most cheerful, comfortable, modern style; but there are not more than two or three of all the churches where a man can sit through a morning-service without extreme discomfort, and even without considerable danger of an attack of rheumatism.

The situation and duties of Mr. K. would correspond very nearly to those of most German clergymen, except that as he has been some time in England, he has acquired a more practical, systematic mode of doing good than most of his brethren. It will be seen that the place is no sinecure.

My friend's opinions on the state of piety among the upper classes, expressed in this conversation, are to be taken with great allowance, as he was an enthusiastic royalist. Yet I am disposed to think, that in the main he was right. There is no doubt, that just now, "orthodoxy"—evangelical religion—in Prussia, is fashionable; that is, the King and the highest authorities favor the opinions and practices in that direction, and this would naturally have its influence. Indeed, all accounts represent the King as sincere in his outward piety, and as giving very substantial aid—though rather enthusiastically bestowed sometimes—to these benevolent movements. His manner, with respect to public worship, is exceedingly simple. I often notice him on Sunday, walking over from the palace to the *Domkirche* (the Cathedral) attended only by a single adjutant, and dressed like any other army officer, in great blue overcoat, buttoned to the chin, and with the usual spiked helmet. His whole bearing also, during the service, shows the same simplicity, and is very reverential indeed.

The practice of which my friend spoke, of requiring every child to receive so much instruction before being confirmed, is a great task upon the pastor, but it must be of very considerable benefit to the children. I notice that the children of my landlady, and in other places where I have been, the children of the lower classes seem to set a great value on the pastor's teachings, and read for them beforehand and talk about them afterwards—and I presume often they get almost their only real "instruction" from him. The clergymen themselves wonder how any land can ever do without a law, requiring religious instruction. And one of the first questions they ask an American, always is, "How can you be sure without a law, that your lower classes will not grow up utterly irreligious?"

It is not difficult, generally, to explain to them the immense advantage of our "voluntary system;" but they always take refuge at last, in the argument, that "it may be all very well adapted for a young country like America, but it will never do for such a society as this here!"

I have often asked them, whether there were not some who could not conscientiously make the "Confession of Faith," required by law in order to become a citizen. They say, and I suppose justly, that very few at the age of confirmation (fourteen years) ever have interest enough in the matter to be very scrupulous. However, I have one friend whose family took a more honest view of the subject, and brought themselves into very considerable legal difficulties, by refusing to make a "confession" which they could not believe. They escaped annoyance at length, by joining the "*Freien Gemeinden*," (German Catholics), though they could not accept all the doctrines of this sect. Its very simple creed, they could assent to, and thus received, what at present is a legal "confirmation."

There are cases of great tyranny under this law for enforcing Baptism and Confirmation. While upon the subject I should not omit to mention one which has attracted much attention recently, in Germany and England, and which is certainly one of the most remarkable instances of petty tyranny on any police record.

It appears on the 31st of March, last year, a child was born at Seehausen in Prussia, which the father wished to be baptized under the name of "*Jacobi Waldeck*," each name being that of a distinguished democrat. The officiating clergyman refused to baptize the child under such detested names. The father was determined it should be baptized as a Democrat, or nothing else, and accordingly was letting it grow up without the rite. Such a heathenish state of things was not to be permitted, and he was summoned before a court, and a guardian appointed to the child, who was empowered "to baptize it with or without the names desired" by the father, according as the Consistory (of clergymen) should determine. They decided that it should be baptized with the "usual names." The parents still refused to send the child, and the guardian was proceeding to administer a forced baptism, when the mother with her babe, suddenly disappeared, and could not be found.

A long search was made, and at length they were both discovered by the police in the neighboring village of Arendsee. They were immediately transported by the *gens d'armes* to Seehausen and put into prison. From there, at the command of the *Bürgermeister*, the child was taken by the soldiers, packed away in a basket, to the church, and with closed doors, the Bürgermeister and *gens d'armes* as witness, it was introduced into the great Christian family; and in a few minutes was carried back to its surprised parents a *thoroughly baptized Christian child!* This was not the end of the matter. The mother, says the legal reporter of the *Vossische Zeitung*, "has been summoned before the court, for resistance to an officer of the government, in the lawful performance of his duty, and has been sentenced to *two months' imprisonment*." From later accounts, it seems she has appealed to a higher court, but the sentence has been sustained!

Nothing has occurred for years, better fitted to throw light over the whole system of *law* in Prussia, and the feelings of certain classes as connected with it. Clergymen so horrified at democratic names, as to be willing to baptize at the point of the bayonet! And courts able to decide what *name* a child shall have, and sentencing a mother to the cell of the convict for objecting!

CHAPTER XVI.

PICTURES.

I AM disposed to think Art has reached a higher grade of cultivation in Germany now, than in any other country. Of the fine and elaborate school, we in America, have had very good specimens in the Düsseldorf paintings. But in the grand and bold works, one must go to Berlin or Munich, for the masters. I know nothing in modern painting, which can equal in genius and boldness, these frescoes and paintings of KAULBACH and CORNELIUS. They are the reaction of strong minds against modern frippery. Ornament, decoration, gaudiness—are nothing. The thought—the reality they demand and utter with uncompromising sternness. Beauty! for beauty is the highest expression—but if that is not possible, let the truth be bare and strong, is their principle. Not many words, not many lines, but a few bold and grand strokes!

An excellent specimen of their style, is Kaulbach's "Battle of the Huns," in Count Raczynski's Gallery in this city.

There has long been a tradition among various nations that those who perished in some great world-battle, in the very moment of fierce conflict, met again in fiercer fight after death. There is such a tradition in regard to a spirit-battle between Attila's army and the Romans. This picture takes its idea from that tradition. The scene is a battle-field, with corpses strown about, and beyond, the towers and battlements of Rome rising in the distance. The light is a pale, cold, unnatural light, like the light of early morning. From the battle-field the forms of the dead are rising. They are stupefied, half-unconscious at first; the warrior only faintly clasps the sword, and the spearman can hardly raise the lance; but as they comprehend the strange scene above, they seem to *burst* from the earth as if into a new existence. Imagination never pictured or scarcely dreamed of such a conception of *motion.* They do not fly, nor are they wafted, but they rise with a free, eager movement, as if their own spirit and passion pressed them up; as if they had powers of moving not possessed by man, or were creatures of a new element. Among the rising forms is a woman's, her face towards Heaven, and her hands clasped together above her head. The features are hardly visible, but the outline of form is the most free and graceful, I ever remember to have seen in painting. All have human features; but there are strange, fearful expressions on them, and there is something bloodless and unnatural about them all. Faces once seen, not easily to be forgotten; such as one sees in night-mare dreams.

Above is passing a strange, terrible scene. On one side, moving swiftly on through the air, is a host of wild forms—the army of the Huns. At their head, in half-oriental robes, supported by four slaves on a shield, stands Attila. He holds a scourge in his hand, and drives on before him a crowd of fugitives, who are grappling in fierce fight among themselves, or are fleeing before him, and on whose faces are the most terrible expressions which the mind ever dreamed of; looks of unearthly wrath, and fear, and malice, and revenge. On the other side are seen the warriors of the Romans, with noble and dignified faces, but saddened and almost fearful.

They do not move so swiftly; and they look and point at the cross which is borne in their centre. Before them, is their king leading them on as if to desperate battle; yet still with confidence apparently in the cross. Two timid, youthful forms, his sons, are clinging to his sides. Far in the heights of the air, other forms are struggling, seemingly in fierce conflict, but so mist-like and uncertain that one can hardly tell whether they are shapes only of the morning clouds, cr the spirits of the dead. Both armies appear to have risen from the field of battle, and others are continually rising to join passionately in the strife.

There is no coloring scarcely in the picture, except a faint yellow. But the outlines and expressions are bold beyond anything I have ever seen in painting. The forms seems as if they might melt away with the first morning light, yet they are animated with a passion which is almost superhuman. I do not believe throughout painting, such intense, absorbing rage and hate is pictured as in those faces, and always a passion which does not seem to belong to this life.

The first sensation before it is almost of shuddering. You remember the name which mankind gave in fear to this conqueror, "*The Scourge of God;*" his own conviction that he was sent by the Almighty; and the traditions even among the Christians of his connection with the Unseen. And as you gaze at the wild, dream-like picture, a feeling crosses over the mind, not easy to describe or account for. A glimpse for a moment as it were into what is not of earth.

I have always been much interested in galleries, in studying the different religious conceptions of painters. The large Musaem gallery of Berlin, though containing no great works of art, is excellent for this purpose, as it gives the best *historical* exhibition of painting in Europe, beginning from its Byzantine origin, down to the latest Dutch and Flemish masters.

In the very earliest of this collection, one finds little beauty of coloring or gracefulness of outline; but there is an intensity of fervor, an earnestness in their conceptions of the unseen, which puts at defiance all the more refined spiritualizing of later masters. You are very sure they meant what they painted. And when a drunkard in the future world is pictured as tied to two hideous devils, while liquid fire is pumped into his mouth by another devil, you are quite sure the artist's idea of punishment was an earnest one, to say the least. They are very *material*, all of them; and I have often thought in walking among these works of theirs, that it would make a man skeptical to think of them much. Still it is a terrible materialism, the materialism of a Dante, or of Job in his pictures of Deity. Every form or image which can convey a disagreeable or painful idea, is used to represent the sufferings of the wicked in the future world. Hideous toads are swallowing them—serpents with disgusting human faces are winding themselves around them—creatures for which there is no countertype, except in the creations of nightmare, are crawling over them. The revellers are having their orgies over again with lizards, and worms, and scorpions. The gluttons are crammed with loathsome substances. Others are sawed and turned on wheels, and crushed and roasted.

In their conceptions of future happiness they are not so striking. Perhaps it is less revolting to give material representations of pain than of pleasure. One is shocked, too, to see Deity itself pictured as a gray-headed old man. Their only heaven is an assemblage of immense numbers of simple-looking winged beings, with harps and violins and hand-organs; or rows of comfortable monks who are saved by angels from the abyss below. Still with all their stiffness and bareness of coloring, and material conceptions, there is such an evident fervor about those oldest masters of the Berlin Gallery, such a devotion, and such an *affection*, that they must ever be dear to the student of art.

When one gets down as far as Rubens, the representations are not so much of material torture as of *expressions* of pain, and of faces with demoniac malice. Beautiful female forms, with his wonderful flesh-coloring, are clasped and hurried away by demons, who look back with that terrible scowl of malignity which Rubens alone can fully give ; or faces are just seen through the darkness, writhed in contortions of pain.

In nothing have all the painters made so many attempts as in their picturing of the spiritual world, and in nothing have they shown themselves so inferior in the genius of expression to the great artists of language. Angels have again and again been attempted, from the beautiful, intellectual-looking youths of the Düsseldorf school, and the winged, Cupid-like children for which all the painters, religious and profane, have such a strange affection, up to the abnormal creatures of the earlier masters, composed only of round heads and large wings, but never scarcely in a single instance do they give one the idea of a *spiritual* being—of a higher existence under different laws. Perhaps the very appearance of *wings* immediately forces on us the idea of animals ; or perhaps their own highest ideal of angels was of pure, happy children. Raphael has ascended very high in his ideal when he merely paints children with an expression of intelligence and affection, unnatural to their years.

I am not surprised that the painters have thrown so much of their highest religious ideals, into the picturing of Christ as a *child*.

It was, perhaps, their unconscious thought, that God can easiest touch the sin-hardened heart, through the purity and simplicity of childhood.

Of Christ himself, no artist has ever had even a faintly adequate conception. It was some womanly monk's imagination, not the Bible, which has first traced the effeminate, sentimental features, that now cover the canvas through the schools of all ages. If those pages picture anything, it is a dignified Manhood; a character of strong and indomitable purpose; a nature filled indeed with boundless affections, but capable of the most sweeping indignation, and stern in inflexible Truthfulness. The Christ of the Bible is not the Christ of Art.

Still, with all the enjoyment which I have derived from European Art, I must say, I turn from it with a sense of disappointment. Not alone from the eternal disappointment of the soul with its ideal; but I had no thought that Painting, as an art of expressing human feelings, was so much below the power of expression in *Words.* Beside the great Painters in language, the most gifted Artists are poor. In all the range of painting, there are no lines of passion, such as Shakspeare draws. No such absorbing, hopeless sorrow; no such fierce, sweeping passion. There are no faces on the canvas which are half so noble, as those which look upon us from the pages of Schiller or of Scott.

There is so much, too, of superficiality, of want of earnestness about the best painting. *Repenting Magdalenas* are painted, and you forget all idea of the repentance in the beauty. Scenes of sorrow are drawn, and the eye is caught and absorbed in beautiful costume and graceful posture; and the great idea disappears. Then the greatest of artists have devoted their talents to such ignoble subjects; to conceptions which only could have arisen from a people altogether unmanned by luxury. It seems strange—one can hardly understand it—that a painter so gifted as *Correggio*, could employ his wonderful conceptions of beauty, and his power of soft, dreamy coloring, to consecrate subjects which would disgrace the foulest page of Grecian mythology, or of modern French literature. *Rubens*, too, of grosser and stronger nature, has given too often his life-like coloring and power of vivid expression to scenes which should have passed away with the sickly imagination which gave them birth. In truth, I have sometimes thought that these old Grecian conceptions, however much they have embodied themselves in the most beautiful forms of art, have done almost as much evil as good. It has needed centuries before Painting could break loose from them; and modern sculpture and the forms of monumental record, have not even yet reached any originality under them.

But it is not alone mythology, which is searched for its most debasing dreams. Everything in the Jewish History, which was the fruit of a wild age; every deed of lust and blood and unnatural crime which the Bible has recorded as a warning, is worked over and again, with delighted pencil, till the mind sickens of the Art, which could so revel in such scenes.

Not that painting should be a *hieroglyphic* art. Beauty will always have its own wonderful language—even if no other idea be expressed—a language, telling of the highest and most solemn thoughts. But Art can only reach its highest point; can only compete with its kindred, Poetry and Oratory, when the language from beauty of line and color and shading, all unite in expressing intensely and directly the one great Idea of the painter, and that idea is such as can thrill the noblest and purest feelings of the human heart.

CHAPTER XVII.

DRESDEN.

Nov. 1850-1.

I HAVE determined to vary my winter in Berlin, by an excursion to the other cities of North Germany. The weather is very bad now for travelling, as it rains almost every day. My objects, however, are so much in-doors, and so little with the usual "sights," it does not trouble me. I have taken lodgings at once here in Dresden, as being much the quietest and cheapest mode of living.

My principal object was to study Art for a few days in this quiet city, but I find everything in the greatest turmoil. My readers will remember that the little Kingdom of Saxony—not numbering so large a population as the State of New York—lies as a most tempting bait, right between the two great powers of Austria and Prussia, and it has been the jealousy alone of each toward the other, which has prevented its being swallowed up long ago. Well, at this present time, the King has taken it into his head to reverse the authority of the old Diet, and has allied himself with Austria, with whom are also his religious sympathies. His people, who are mostly Protestants, sympathize more with Prussia, but they have been obliged to yield, and the Saxon army has been *mobilized*, to give their assistance to the old Confederation. As Saxony lies in the direct line of the Austrians into Cassel, or of the Prussians towards

Vienna, there is naturally no little fear that their quiet, inoffensive territory may be the terrible battle-ground of foreign nations, as it has been so often before. Beside, the treasures collected by the old Saxon Kings and placed here in Dresden, would be altogether too great a temptation for the most virtuous government of Europe, provided there was once a war. Indeed, the jewels alone of the *Grüne Gewölbe* (Green Vaults), would pay the expenses of Prussia for years to come. Accordingly, everything of value among the works of art, which can be carried off, is being packed up and sent away to the old fortress, where they rested so securely during all the fighting and plundering of Napoleon's wars—the fortress of *Königstein*, on the Elbe, the only one in Europe which has never been taken—the old shelter of the Saxon Kings and Saxon treasures, and upon which, even the storm of war in 1812 and '13 made no impression. The whole kingdom is aroused, and as I came on from Berlin, I could see masses of troops all along near the borders, ready to beset the railroad, in case of an attack of the Prussians. Through the town, too, there is a continued marching of companies of "Jäger" or of cavalry, all attired for a rough campaign, on towards the Prussian boundaries. And beside these, horses and wagons, and heavy cannon, and an unceasing stream of straggling soldiers, over the old bridge so famous in Napoleon's great battle here, and all the accompaniments which an approaching war brings with it.

It will give an idea of the weight which these petty governments lay upon the people in Germany, to examine briefly the statistics of Saxony.

The whole population of this kingdom numbered last year, (1849) 1,894,431, or about half the population of the State of New York. The total expenses of government for the last three years, have amounted to about $5,720,000 *per annum*. Yet the whole civil and diplomatic expenses of the United States per annum, are only $7,339,000. The annual duties and taxes amount to over $3,611,000. The public debt is about $16,830,000. Before 1848, the Saxon army according to the laws of the German Confederation, numbered 13,000 men, together with 6,000 men in reserve.

In 1849, the new Federal allotments required two to every hundred of the population, so that the regular forces reached the number of 36,546, and 72 cannon. Out of the 1,894,000 inhabitants, more than 1,857,000 are Protestants, and yet they are saddled with a Roman Catholic Government. The old grandeur of Saxony has been very much reduced in this century: and the truly noble devotion of her king to Napoleon, during all his calamities, has cost her some of her finest territory, and occasioned in 1814 immense losses to her capital.

I have been surprised at the difference which mere political situation makes in the character of a people. It did not need a day's intercourse with my friends and acquaintances, to show that I was among an entirely different population, from what I had seen in Prussia. Saxony has been a small, unimportant country, having most to fear from contentions, and very little to expect in war, so that gradually the whole nation has acquired a peaceful, ease-loving, almost effeminate character. National pride it has not—only national fear; and the whole mind and strength of the country have turned to art and quiet intellectual pursuits. The proud, manly characters of the Prussians, one does not find here. Their scholars do not, as in Berlin, interest themselves in political matters. They "rather hide their heads in their books and specimens," that they may not hear the storms which are raging all around them. Every one you meet at such a time as this, is fearful or desponding, and one longs to inspire a little of the Anglo-Saxon *pluck* into them.

How constantly everywhere in Germany, do the evils of this miserablo system of little separate governments, come before my eye! It is as if every State in our Union were a distinct petty kingdom, with its own separate administration, its own expenses, its own tyranny too and hold over the people. All the burdens of a great government and none of its power! May God preserve *our* Union from ever splitting into the petty and factious and inefficient Principalities of the German Confederacy!

As I said before, everything was in confusion, and the most valuable articles of *vertu* packed up. By good luck, they had not begun on their picture gallery, and through the kindness of friends I gained admission and have been able to study its beautiful collection every day. The fine collection of plaster casts, and the tasteful, though rather meagre gallery of antique statues, was also untouched. I was kindly introduced also to the *ateliers* of the various painters, a cultivated, really original set of men. These artists are among the most celebrated in Europe, though they do not have the mutual assistance of a school, to press their pictures forward, as the Düsseldorf. Wherever I meet artists in Europe, I am most pleased to see that so many are men of earnestness and intellectuality—and with noble ideas of their profession. And among the continental artists, I have certainly not found, that a dissolute life and devotion to art, are at all necessary companions, according to the old prejudice.

Still I may be permitted to express the wish without impertinence, that among men of such generous purposes, for the sake of themselves and humanity, and for the sake of that noble Art, which they study, there might be a deeper religious character.

Art is not, in these days, fulfilling its highest destiny. And there are means of elevating humanity—not yet essayed—which belong alone to its field, and which the cause of Progress cannot do without.

HESSE-CASSEL.

December, 1850.

As the Conferences of Olmütz have just finished; and as the Conferences which are to determine the condition of Germany for the next year, are to be held in Dresden within a few days, it may be proper here to speak briefly of the matters in dispute.

It will be remembered, that during this last year, there have been two German *Unions*—the Austrian in the form of the old *Bund*, represented at Frankfort, and the Prussian, represented at Erfurt. The little principality of Hesse-Cassel at first joined the Prussian. But the Elector, being in want of money, and not being able to collect it in a constitutional manner, thought the old Confederacy, naturally, more suited to his purpose, and left the Prussian for the Austrian.

Twice he demanded supplies, not permitted by the budget, and the Chambers refused and were adjourned. The country was now put under martial law, though army and officials and people protested against such an arbitrary act. The Elector persevered, confident of his game, and appealed to Austria for aid.

The people, on the other hand, appealed to Prussia, and Prussian troops were marched in to protect this member of the separate Union (*Sonderbund.*)

The threats and bold bearing, and the sudden retreat of Prussia have already been incidentally mentioned. Her present position will best appear from the results of this conference between Schwarzenberg and Manteuffel, at Olmütz, (November 29, 1850).

These are thus reported:—1. That each government, together with its allies, shall appoint Commissioners to meet in Dresden, for the final settlement of all these difficulties. 2. That, in order to preserve order in Hesse-Cassel, the troops which the Elector may call in, shall have the right of passing over the Prussian military roads, and that, for the after preservation of law and order, one battalion of Prussians, and one of Austrians, shall be allowed to remain in the kingdom. Next, that Commissioners from each government shall proceed to Holstein and attempt to induce the government of the Duchies to reduce their army, and withdraw their forces behind the Eyder, and also endeavor to persuade the Danish government to send in no more troops into Holstein than shall be absolutely necessary for the establishment of order.

These are the principal points of the agreement. How do they compare with the former claims of Prussia? It will be remembered the Prussian government has always asserted that the old Union did not at all represent Germany, and, accordingly, had no right to interfere in the affairs of a member of the new Union and an ally of Prussia. This is altogether waived, and the legal existence of the *Bundestag* is acknowledged; or if not, it is quite clearly implied, in the authority conceded to her. Prussia had objected also to any invasion of Cassel, on the ground that she alone had the right of passage through the kingdom; and that any stationing of foreign troops there would be in effect the separating her Rhenish Provinces from the central. Here, however, such invasion is not only allowed, but the use of the "Military Roads" given to the foreign armies. She had claimed beside, that the cause of the Duchies was a just one. Her armies had fought for it, and her soldiers and means had supplied the insurgent troops. She had acknowledged their rightful independence, and had claimed Holstein as a part of the new German Union. This too is all quietly abandoned, and the deputies will *induce* the men, whom a year ago they honored as patriots struggling for their rights, to forsake their cause—"to withdraw their troops behind the Eyder!"—in other words, to hasten as fast as they can from a land where they are rebels and traitors! This is the result of Prussian diplomacy! Can we wonder at some slight discontent on the part of people, who have not learned this rapid diplomatic mode of changing *facts?*

In the mean time, how goes it with poor Cassel? The country is not a rich one, and, in the best of times, the people have a hard work to live. Now, not only has their court, with its profits, been dispersed, but, in the first place, an immense force of the Prussians has been quartered upon them. The Prussians have acted kindly; still of course, they consumed enormously the substance of the land. Now the Prussians retire, and close upon their heels, the Bavarians pour in over the land; more greedy, less friendly to the people. They encamp in their houses; they consume their carefully saved provisions, force the peasants to give up their horses for the cavalry, and are, in fact, bringing the country near upon a famine; so that in some parts, the price of provisions has arisen beyond all parallel. No sign of yielding, however, appears as yet in that quiet, but most steady population. The officers of the army, to the number of several hundreds, have thrown up their commissions and have left themselves and families without any means of support, rather than help to violate the Constitution which they have sworn to obey. Deputies of high character have gone on from Prussia, to induce the members of the Chambers to assent only in part to some of the unconstitutional demands of the Elector. But in vain. The people know their right; and, very quietly, but with a firmness infinitely nobler than any noisy courage, they stand by it. I have alluded to this resistance before. I never can think of it without a thrill of sympathy and admiration for that suffering and unyielding people. I do not believe History can give a parallel of a resistance to oppression so reasonable and so deeply founded. One wonders, as he looks at it, how the usual passions and excitement of men have been governed, that they could act so wisely and carefully. An open rebellion would have laid their country in a day, under an overpowering army of either Austrians or Bavarians, and the tyrannical, stupid old Elector would have been reinstated more firmly than ever. They have simply rested on their Constitution, and have tried the virtues of passive resistance. They are *suffering* merely for their rights. In my opinion, a better act for constitutional progress has not been done this century, than this quiet resistance of the Hessians. The spectacle of a whole people, calmly and rationally letting their land be trampled and wasted of almost its last morsel, by foreign armies, rather than yield an item of their Constitutional rights, has something in it, rather grand, and gives men the impression that there must be something here worth defending!

Of course the only result can be defeat—defeat by the overpowering brute-force of Austria—another act in that sad, sad drama, which began with Italy and Hungary; and which will end—where?

As I see more and more of these wrongs in Europe, I find myself praying with tears, "*How long, O Lord!* Is this heart-crushing Tyranny to be forever? Shall the day ever come when these oppressions, and this trampling on Freedom and Justice, and crushing of men's rights, cease? Shall these brave, free hearts, who have struggled and suffered so long for Germany, have no ray, no glimmer of hope?"

His ways are not to be judged from a year or a century. We will not doubt. Wrong and violence triumph now among men; yet not for ever, as He is good!

In the words of the mournful old chaunt of the Jews, "*Even in our day, O Lord! even in our day, build again Jerusalem!*"

CHAPTER XIX.

HALLE—STUDENT-LIFE.

Dec. 1850.

THERE are not many more disagreeable places in Germany than Halle in winter. The streets are narrow, and get little of the sunlight in them. The mud and water settles in the thoroughfares, and never runs off, and the luxury of dry, level sidewalks is altogether unknown—what are called "sidewalks" being jagged, macadamized paths, which are quite as muddy as the streets. The town, too, has an old, worn, dreary look, which might be interesting in another season, but is gloomy in this. Still, despite all this, for myself I am enjoying Halle quite as much as if it were a more beautiful place. It is a University town, and as is usual in such places, a cultivated, learned society has gathered in it. I could not form any very definite opinion of the tone of society in Halle, though, apparently the same fact holds here which does usually in exclusively literary towns:—that society becomes one-sided and less interesting, where there is not a mingling in it of men of various pursuits.

One of the *literati*, to whom I had letters, was Dr. Tholuck, and it happened the first night, as I called on him, I stumbled in on a little exercise which is quite peculiar to him. It seems he has always been very desirous of becoming intimately acquainted with the students, and for that purpose allows some to live in his family, and takes them with him on his travels, and is very familiar with them.

With the same object he has commenced during the last year or two, a kind of conversational meeting, where, however, he usually does most of the talking. There was such a meeting that night in one of his parlors, and as I came into the crowded room, he was giving an animated description of a journey he had taken the last summer in Würtemberg.

In personal appearance he has decidedly a scholarly air, with a fine forehead and keen eye, though in size he is somewhat small. He spoke with a clear, deep voice, much deeper than one would have expected from his reduced frame. He told, first of his travelling, then of the great meeting of the friends of the "*Inner Mission*" in Stuttgart (the *Kirchentag*, as they call the meeting), of the hospitality of the citizens, and the intense interest of all in the proceedings; then of their own discussions in the assembly, and the narrow escape they had from making it merely an arena of political contests, especially with reference to the Schleswig-Holstein question. Something of the objects and the great results, also, of the Inner Mission, were touched upon; and finally, he came to what was the more especial subject of his remarks—the former condition of the Universities. He spoke of Halle, of his connection with it, of the command which some five-and-twenty years ago came to him from the king, to take a professorship in that University which had so abandoned the faith of its fathers. He loved Berlin, he said; in Berlin was his home. His old friends, and many who sympathized deeply in his religious views, were there. He dreaded to leave it. In Halle, among a large and influential corps of learned men, there was only one pastor and a superannuated "*Candidat*," who could in any way stand by him. He was to go there, a young man, with unpopular opinions, to stem the general tide of Rationalism. He had many fears, but he at length resolved to attempt it. He then described in a most amusing manner, the condition of the University at the time of his coming—the universal rowdyism among the students; the highflown religious instruction, and transcendental tone even in prayer, so that the common people used to look on, almost stupefied. At first, he said, he only had four students who embraced the views he was supporting, and three of these were not especially remarkable for intellectual *acumen*, and the fourth rather prided himself on his deep religious struggles. Rationalism was all the vogue. To be an "*Orthodox*" was the mark either of a "*Dummkopf*" (dolt), or a "*Fanatiker*" (fanatic). In all that concerned Christian faith and practical religion the University was almost lifeless.

He did not relate the result of his labors. But it may not be unknown in America, that Tholuck's influence under a Higher, has been the means of almost *Christianizing* Halle. With a mind fresh and interesting—even if not always strictly logical—with a learning of wonderful extent and variety, and all the accomplishments of a "man of the world," it is not surprising he has gained a deep influence over the students and the University at Halle. The simple, humble, practical piety, too, which spoke out all through this speech, has worked its way among the minds here; and instead now of their being but one Professor with what are called "evangelical views," the whole Faculty, nearly, are of that school, and the exceptions are the Rationalists. Tholuck's orthodoxy, too, is not of that strict, narrow kind, which one finds now occasionally in Germany, as a re-action from Rationalism—the orthodoxy which dreads inquiry and forbids freedom. It is evident, his mind works freely on all religious questions. Some thoughts of his, of late, on a subject whose philosophical theory demands an investigation from earnest minds everywhere—"Inspiration"—have called forth no little opposition from certain orthodox quarters.

The close of his remarks consisted mostly of heartfelt advice on the difficulties peculiar to students—the conceit and self-confidence they are liable to, and the discouragement they will often feel in struggling with their defects, and the strange struggle which with them, as with all, rages between what they desire for the moment and what they desire really; what they "would," and what they "do." His tone was deep and full of feeling; and the earnestness of his manner and thought must have reached every heart.

I was considerably surprised in what I saw of Tholuck that evening. I had expected to find an elegant, somewhat mystical scholar, with no especial practical bias whatever. All his remarks, however, showed a keen knowledge of human nature, and even a somewhat *humorous* eye for its weaknesses. He had evidently been among men, and knew something of the art of managing them. As a speaker and preacher, too, he must be a man of no inconsiderable power. Perhaps fault might have been found with his speaking so often of himself; but, after all, when a man has accomplished so much as he has, it seems to me he ought to have the liberty of telling of it.

I found, while in Halle, that there were several Americans there, very intelligent, gentlemanly fellows. Through them I was made acquainted with the students. We met a circle of them first, at a "coffee party" in the afternoon. They were hand and glove with us in a few minutes; most social, easy men. A kind of romance and enthusiasm, too, about them, which is very refreshing. One of them told me, that no student ever saluted another with "*Guten Abend!*" (Good evening), but always "*Guten Morgen!*" (Good morning), as "with them it was always morning!"

We discussed politics; they were enthusiastic for freedom, but evidently had rather vague ideas of it. I told them, that "they, like all the Germans, did not have confidence enough in the people." They allowed it, and said they had no reason for it, thus far in European revolutions. We explained to them our system in America; and, after some discussion, they admitted its success, and very politely too, that we were "the most unprejudiced set of Americans they had met."

The walls of the room were covered with various spruce little figures of students, in outline or charcoal sketching. On inquiry, it appeared, these were the heroes of the respective "Corps" or Secret Societies in former years, and that their fame was thus transmitted to posterity. After a very sociable afternoon together, in which coffee enough was absorbed and cigars smoked to have shattered irretrievably the nervous constitution of any one but a German, we adjourned to a lecture, from which they promised us much entertainment. It was from ERDMANN, and one of the regular Historical Course—subject, "Student Life."

It was amusing to hear such a subject as this, carefully and laboriously analyzed, and the effect of it, as one element of German institutions, so closely traced. According to the lecturer the student was the "Aristocrat" of German life—in the class which possessed the most peculiar privileges and influence. Without going minutely into the lecture, I would say that the idea throughout was *not* that the student was a man of the world and with the responsibility and aims of other men, but that he was a member of a peculiar class—a class whose distinct existence was necessary to the welfare of the other classes of the country; and that, therefore, any sinking of the importance of this body, as occurs in a large city, or any uniting it with other classes, was very much to be deprecated.

I told our German friends, in returning home, that such a lecture could never apply to our country; that the students never have formed a distinct class with us, and we hoped they never would. We would prefer them to be like the other citizens of the State, and many of us found it one of the greatest evils of our sytem now, that College-men knew so little of the world.

They replied, and very justly, I think, that in Germany almost the only class which contains within it any free and independent principles, is the student-class. "We should have had no Resurrection of Germany in 1814," said they, "if it had not been for the universal movement among the students; and in '48, it was the students who headed the Revolution everywhere, and who stirred up the People!"

It is true, without doubt, that in Northern Europe, and even in Austria, the Universities, beyond all other Institutions of the State, are the repositories of free and noble ideas. The student is a sacred, inviolable personage, whose rights even the Austrian police dare not as yet invade; and we do not deny that any merging of these universities into other Institutions, or breaking down of the guards which they have thrown around themselves, is to be deeply deplored by the friends of Freedom. Still, I could not avoid thinking in this conversation, though I said nothing, that it was a bad sign for a country, when its boys are the leaders of its Revolutions. In America and Hungary, it was the prime of the manhood which headed the struggle. And that it did not speak very favorably for the boasted influence of these Institutions, that the Radical of the

University, so soon became a Conservative after leaving it; and that a government-office had with the majority such a tranquilizing and soothing influence over their enthusiastic ideas of Human Freedom.

In parting with my friends in the evening, I felt as if I had known them for years, and they assured me in the most handsome manner, that I was made for a student, and that I had "*die echte Deutsche Gutmüthigkeit!*" (the genuine German good nature!)

I notice in Halle, and in Leipsic also, more of the genuine student-costume than in Berlin, or in many other university towns. The high jack-boots, reaching up to the thigh, the jaunty little red or yellow caps, just set on the front part of the head, and the velveteen coats with curious devices, figure everywhere in the streets. Here, as everywhere, the students seem to differ very little in age from our own, though I understand the average age of entering at Halle is about nineteen, which perhaps is a little higher than in some of the New England colleges.

I like very much the bearing of the Professors and students toward one another, in these Universities. The manners are gentlemanly, but nothing more. There is no repelling distance on one side, or excessive deference on the other. They walk together and meet each other in society, and make excursions in company in summer; and the feeling between them is of friends, though of friends differing in years and experience.

It is rather amusing to see how the students in the lecture-room govern themselves, and indeed the Professor too sometimes. If a man comes in late, or makes any unusual noise, so that they cannot hear the lecturer, he is hissed in a manner which is decidedly unpleasant; and if the lecturer himself speaks so fast that they do not catch the idea, a sort of "*hush*" always passes around, and the unintelligible passage is repeated.

One evening while I was there I was invited to what is called a "*Verbindung*" among the students. My readers may know that all the students through the German universities, who are members of a "*Chor*," have what they call the "*Kneipen*," a social party, where they smoke and sing and drink beer in a way which would alarm a veteran toper. I was present in one at Heidelberg, and a more senseless, stupid, beer-swilling performance I have never seen in any tap-room of England.

It has been the desire of Dr. Tholuck and some others here, that something different might be formed, especially among the theological students, and that a society might be started in which any religious student could have social enjoyment, and at the same time sympathy in higher matters. Accordingly with this idea, the *Verbindung* was formed, and I suppose the majority of the members are theological students. As I came in, I found a company of some thirty or forty seated at a long table, each with his mug of beer and pipe before him, and all in the most animated conversation. I have hardly ever seen a more intelligent, genial-looking set of men, and the conversation was really very interesting, and often serious in tone. They evidently met, after hard study, for relaxation, and though there was great liveliness, there was no kind of excess. The evening was varied with some amusing mock-auctions, and various songs which were sung with the greatest spirit. One patriotic song, in which the valor of the Prussians was the theme, was sung again and again in a manner which showed something more than common interest in it. I observed that there were a few who took no part in it—probably students from South Germany who sympathized with the Austrians.

About eleven o'clock, I left the party, with very agreeable impressions of the *Verbindung* as compared with the *Kneipen*, and with the chorus of the valorous song, ringing long after through my dreams that night:

"*Die Preussen sind da! Die Preussen sind da!*"
"For the Prussians are there! The Prussians are there!"

CHAPTER XIX.

UNIVERSITIES— * * * * HANOVER.

I CANNOT leave Halle without expressing my sense of the contrast between the American and the German Universities.

Whatever our Colleges may have done, they have certainly in one respect proved a failure—they have never succeeded in producing any genuine intellectual enthusiasm whatever, among the mass of the students. I never yet met a set of College-men in America, who took any deep interest in their pursuits. The idea with most is, that College-life is a kind of wearisome sea voyage—the great object lying beyond—and that their first duty to the studies is to get rid of them. With some of the best minds, half of the most laborious efforts of the four years are spent in gulling tutors, and *rushing* through recitations on small capital. If the lesson is broken up, or the lecture put off, it is considered a victory. The teacher is the student's natural enemy in our Colleges. Those who do study, work so mechanically, for "honors," or under some equally unworthy motive, that it is hard to imagine any high intellectual interest in the pursuit. The thing is the more remarkable, as in all the intellectual pursuits of active life we find in America, the most absorbed enthusiasm and activity. But the moment we enter a College, even among men no younger than those without, it is all changed. The student's business is a *bore*—a task--a punishment—and the sooner it is over the better.

There are exceptions to these remarks; but I am sure that in their general truth, I shall have the agreement of the mass of College graduates throughout the country, whether they care to express it or not.

The appearance of things in a German University is utterly different, and one sees at once that the common idea of their pursuits, is quite another from that of our students at home. There is the deepest attention in the lectures. The students constantly discuss and talk over their studies. There is as much enthusiasm among them for an abstract theme, or a scientific subject they are investigating, as there is among the politicians or the business men without, in their pursuits. This studying is their business, their profession, and they know it; and the mass of them would no more think of *shirking* lectures, than a botanist would of getting rid of his flowers, or a lawyer of his briefs.

The feeling towards the teachers, too, is very different. With less outward deference than with us, there is a far deeper love and reverence—a feeling that these are great men among them, who are helping them on to higher stages of knowledge, and that any assistance from them is a kindness, and that their intercourse and instruction is a privilege to be received with gratitude.

I am aware that there are many exceptions to this, especially among the "corps members," and exceptions there naturally would be, where so many attend the University merely because it is required by their station in society; but among the great majority of those who enter the institution—as with us—for the sake of *education*, and who expect to gain their livelihood by their intellectual efforts, I am confident there is generally this high intellectual enthusiasm, an enthusiasm which seems to me almost utterly wanting in our colleges.

The causes of this difference will not be found in the greater youth of our students, as contrary to my expectation, there is very little difference in years. Nor will it altogether in the different nature of the studies pursued, as the last half of our course corresponds almost precisely with a part of the course in a German university. The great and prominent reason of this difference is in the fact that the German system is, from beginning to end, a *voluntary system.* No student is obliged to attend lectures. No account is taken of presence or absence. No strict supervision is maintained over him with respect to his studies. The whole matter is left to his own sense of responsibility, or his interest in the subjects taught. He is treated at once as *a man*—as a reasonable and responsible man. And the effect is, with a few exceptions, what we might expect—he acts like one. The idea is not in any way brought before his mind, that the studies are a task—a burden, placed on him by another. He can stay away or attend, as he chooses. The whole impression left is that study is a privilege, an intellectual pleasure.

This is not the idea in our colleges. And whether this be the right explanation or not of the difference, the fact is worth considering. And it is worth considering, also, that where the voluntary system is tried, as in our professional schools, the intellectual life, the enthusiasm for study, is far higher than what appears under the other system.

We know that against the evils mentioned here, many of the teachers of our colleges have struggled long and earnestly. That more than anything else, they have labored to infuse into college life a higher moral enthusiasm. If they have not succeeded, the fault, with many, has been in the system, not in themselves.

No one can doubt, of course, that even with these defects, our college system has done much for the thought of the country. But in my opinion, the great benefit of the course, the highest intellectual life, will be found to be not so much from the regular studies as from the *contact* of the students' minds with one another, from the general intercourse, from the "voluntary studies," and from those literary and debating societies which form the most original feature of our college course.

From Halle, I travelled by rail to Magdeburg, on my course to Hanover. I was interested to see the old city which had borne so many terrible sieges, and which is destined yet, if another European war takes place, to play an important part. It is probably the largest fortified town in Europe, and would require an army of more than 50,000 men to thoroughly invest it. Its importance consists in its artificial defences, and in its commanding the line of the Elbe. As I studied from the high Cathedral tower its long green lines of fortifications, and saw how marsh and river, and every contrivance of art defended it, I wondered more than ever at that utter prostration of the Prussian nation in 1806, which had delivered it almost without a stroke to Napoleon. There were heavy masses of soldiers in various parts of the defences, in preparation for the coming war, so that the war-like picture was complete.

From this city, a pleasant ride on the railroad carried me to Hanover, where I spent a few days most happily. I cannot refrain here from expressing my obligations to Prof. Oesterly, the court painter of Hanover, a most accomplished and truly religious artist, to whose courtesies I owe some very pleasant hours in the city. Everywhere that I went among the citizens, I heard accounts of their gruff, honest, indomitable old king.* He had come there (in 1837) from England, determined to govern absolutely, not so much because he objected to popular principles, as because he wanted his own way. The reputation which preceded him was notoriously bad. A brutal, imperious man; brave indeed, but under strong suspicions of having murdered his own valet; and disgraced by the worst immoralities—to such a degree, that he could not appear in the public streets of London, without being "groaned." His fame had not belied him, for he commenced a most unprovoked attack at once on the Constitution of '33, under the pretext of reverting to that of '19. The great fault of the former, in his eyes, being that one of its provisions declared the "incapacity of any heir to the throne who suffered under a physical or moral defect." His only son was blind. The country resisted his efforts, especially for the reason, that the last Constitution gave a control over the finances to the ministry. Many of the cities refused to send deputies to the Parliament, under the old Constitution. And several of the most prominent professors at Göttingen entered a public protest against this violation of the people's rights. Resistance only inflamed the imperious old man; and he swore, that he would leave them no Constitution at all. The Parliament was declared dissolved, and the professors were banished. The contest continued for some years between King and People, until the former had carried all his points, and his subjects had settled down into a discontented submission. Then, very characteristically, when not forced, he restored of his own accord many of their old privileges. The administration of justice was reformed; and though the old Englishman was arbitrary, it was found soon, he was always on the side of the poor man and of justice. He managed his own finances too, without a responsible

* Ernest Augustus, formerly Duke of Cumberland, son of George III.

ministry; but it soon appeared, they were much more honestly farmed than under the old system.

It is related of the King, that a poor countryman applied one day for an audience, and according to his rule that no one should be refused, was admitted. The man complained that the judge of his village neglected his duties—left the business with the clerk—and was amusing himself with hunting and sports, so that the poor could not get their rights.

Ernest heard him through—said nothing—but before the countryman could have fairly reached the city gates, was posting in a private carriage as fast as horses would carry him, to the village ot the unfortunate judge. The carriage stopped before the court, the King, in citizen's dress, rushed up the steps, demanded the judge, and found that he was engaged as described; called for the clerk, and substantiated everything through him; sat down and wrote off something hastily on a bit of paper and handed it to the clerk, and was rattling off again in his carriage. The clerk to his amazement, on opening the paper, found that it contained an order for the dismission of the judge, and his own appointment in his place, signed with the name of the *King of Hanover!*

Ernest had much of the worst English qualities. He was coarse and brutal; and it was said, he would curse and beat even the ladies in attendance, if they offended him. No one loved him, and the most stood in mortal fear of his anger. Still he had, too, something of the English punctuality and honesty. Before his reign, the court tradesmen and workmen were in the habit of executing orders with true German ease and leisure, whatever speed they had promised. With Ernest, if any man—carpenter or artist—did not have his task fully completed at the exact time promised, his work was rejected, or his services refused henceforth entirely. The people told me, that a great reform had been introduced everywhere in the Hanoverian business, through this exactness of the court. The King, too, always kept his word, and was inexorable to any one who did not. He has the glory of being almost the only sovereign in Europe who promised liberty to his subjects in 1848, without being compelled to it, and who kept his promise, after he had the power to break it.

In that year, the trial by jury, a fair liberty of the press, and a parliamentary system of two Houses, whose election was based on a property-qualification, was definitely settled in Hanover. Still, though liberal in its tone, the Government of Hanover has never corresponded in its fundamental principles with the wishes of the majority of the citizens.

It remains to be seen in a few years whether that liberty-loving people will remain as quietly under the blind, weak son, as they did under the strong, imperious old father.

It is probable, in these last years, the interest taken in the Federal question of Germany has removed public attention in Hanover, from their own difficulties. After the extinction of the Great National Assembly at Frankfort, the king of Hanover, as we have before related, formed an alliance (May 26, 1849) with the kings of Prussia and Saxony. The reservations, however, made by him in this alliance, gave him liberty to leave it, when it suited his convenience. And accordingly at the summoning of a new German Parliament at Erfurt, by Prussia, Hanover quietly broke her relations with the parties; and much to the vexation of Prussia, stood for a while separated both from the Austrian and Prussian ranks. This position, the confidence of the people in their king, and the weight of his character through Germany, have given Hanover much influence in the various crises, during this last year. To its honor, be it said, the Hanoverian Government firmly refused to have any share in the late tyrannical federal intervention in Hesse-Cassel.

The general prosperity of Hanover, the citizens say, has been much improved since the residence of their own king among them as the court draws many branches of labor to it, and the royal revenues are now spent within the country.

Hanover is the centre of another of those singular "Protection-Unions," which exist in Germany—the *Steñerverein.** Of this and the larger Prussian Union, the *Zollverein*, I may have more to say hereafter. It will be sufficient to observe here, that this Union founded in 1834, embraces nearly all of Hanover, the Duchy of Oldenburg, the Principality of Schaumburg-Lippe, a part of Brunswick, and certain small provinces of Prussia.

The basis of the Union is a lower rate of duties than that of its rival, the Prussian. Its commerce is principally through the ports of Bremen and Hamburg. Hanover has never been a manufacturing country; agriculture is the principal branch, and perhaps in consequence, she has always, thus far, inclined to low tariffs. One cause, without doubt, of the low state of the manufacturing interest, is in the burdensome laws with regard to apprentices in trades; requiring each one to travel three years in foreign countries; to be member of a corporation and to possess the right of citizenship, before he can set up business for himself.

The annual duties in Hanover, have amounted for several years to about $1,400,000. The commercial marine this year (1850) is estimated at 55,000 tons.

Hanover is not so populous as Ohio, numbering only 1,759,000 inhabitants, yet her expenses are more than $5,780,000 per annum, of which the king takes about $420,000; and the contingent which she must always stand ready to furnish to the Union is 36,000 men.

* See Appendix.

CHAPTER XX.

BERLIN AGAIN! WINTER AMUSEMENTS.

December, 1850.

I EXTRACT from a letter, as giving best my impressions on returning.

"DEAR T——: I only stopped for a short visit in Hamburg, and came back at once here to my old quarters.

"I did not go directly to my German acquaintances, but having *gekriegt* your letter and refreshed myself with it, I called on some Americans, whom I knew here. I was not at all prepared for the contrast. The truth is, I had been in Hamburg, as in a home; and the last night, my friends looked quite as blue as I did, at my leaving. Then to come right down among these men—all of them with a kind of supercilious indifference to everything—and a sort of *hardness* of manner which I begin almost to think, American—it was like jumping into a cold bath. It disappointed me, and I was glad to get to bed and forget it. This *humanity* of the Germans, becomes almost a necessity of life to one. To be able to meet men, as if you had an interest in them, and they in you—as if it wasn't poetry that you were "brothers," and it was no impertinence to talk freely of their affairs, or intrusion or impropriety to speak of your own—to have the abiding, underlying idea of your intercourse, all the while a kind of open-hearted, social *respect*. This is what I like so in them, and what I did not find in these fellows, and the want of which will *cool* me off so, when I get home."

One of our pleasantest out-door recreations now, is a skating-party on the *Wiesen*, or "Meadows," about a mile from the city, through the *Thiergarten*. We usually make up a party of ladies and gentlemen and walk out. The Meadows are some broad flats overflown by the water, making an admirable skating-ground; and the scene on them on a pleasant winter afternoon, is one of the most lively I ever saw.

The ice for a mile beyond is covered with a labyrinth of whirling, gayly-dressed groups; there a man cutting the most artistic and mysterious figures of the science; there two ladies skating off gracefully together; here a lady and gentleman hand in hand, or a whole line together, moving across, and again through them all, rushing on at a most alarming speed, the sled-chairs with ladies, pushed on by servants or friends—all moving and whirling and dashing around among one another, and yet no one injured or getting a fall. Then on the bank, other groups again—men renting skates, women with coffee-tables and cakes, boys with fresh flowers from the conservatories, and crowds of hacks and private carriages waiting to take the skaters, and scattered about through them all, that omnipresent and most inquisitive individual—the Berlin policeman—grand in helmet, blue coat and sword. Add to all this, to complete the scene, a clear winter's air; the rich light of the sun, far sunk in the south, falling over the groups, and just tinging with rose-color the white columns of smoke; and for a back-ground, the delicate tracery and dark masses of the old trees against the cold gray eastern sky.

There must be nearly a thousand people out, some days, from all classes, young and old, ladies and gentlemen, and the ladies in their prettiest dresses, much as if for a fashionable promenade.

I have never seen a more graceful exercise for women, and the most here were well accomplished in the science. It has only been tried among the ladies of Berlin for a few years, since one of the Princesses set the fashion, though now it is quite the mode. The most surprising thing to an American was the number of elderly men joining in the sport—men of station—the Professor and students together, or the worn-out business man coming out to have one of the free sports of his youth over again.

I know of nothing, in the habits of foreign nations, which struck me at first, as so entirely new, as this love for out-door sports. In England, I did not pass through a village, without finding the green cricket-ground; and, be it remembered, not with *boys* at play on it, but men—men often of rank and character. Later in the season, were the boat-races, where the whole population gathered; gentlemen of the highest rank presiding, and the nobleman and student tugging at the oar, as eagerly as the mechanic or waterman.

In September, we were making our foot trip through the Highlands of Scotland, and we scarcely found an inn so remote, which was not crowded with gentlemen, shooting, riding, or *pedestrianizing* through the mountains, and with the zest and eagerness of boys let out of school.

On the Continent, with the exception of Hungary, there is not uch a passion for exciting field-sports; but the same love for the open air. In Paris, a pleasant day will fill the *Champs Elysèes* with cheerful parties, sipping their coffee under the shade; or watching the thousand exhibitions going on in open assemblies. And in the Provinces, every man who can have a spot six feet by ten in the free air, uses it to sip his wine, or take his "potage" therein.

In Germany, the country-houses seem to be made to live out of doors, and people everywhere take their meals, or receive their friends in balconies and arbors. Every city has its gardens and promenades, which are constantly full. There are open air games too, where old and young take part; and in summer, the studying classes, or all who can get leisure, are off on pedestrian tours through the Harz, or Switzerland, or nearer home.

There is throughout Europe, a rich animal love of open air movement, of plays and athletic sports, of which we Americans as a people, know little. A Frenchman's nerves quicken in the sunlight, even as the organization of plants; and a German would be very old and decrepid, when he should no longer enjoy a real tumbling frolic with his children. The Englishman, cold as he is in other directions, would lose his identity when his blood did not flow fresher at a bout of cricket, or a good match with the oar. We on the other hand are utterly indifferent to these things. We might pull at a boat-race, but it would be as men, not as boys; because we were determined the Yankee nation should never be beaten, not because we enjoyed it. We do not care for children's sports. We have no time for them. There is a tremendous, earnest WORK to be done, and we cannot spare effort for play. It is unmanly to roll a ball in America. Our amusements are labors. An American travels with an intensity and restlessness, which would of itself exhaust a German; and our city enjoyments are the most wearying and absurd possible.

We like being together well enough, but our gregarious tendencies are nearly always for some earnest object. We can crowd for a lecture or political meeting, but as to gathering in a coffee-garden or in a park, it would be childish (or vulgar).

I have noticed here this contrast to the Germans, because a most important subject is bound with it—a subject which must more and more demand earnest attention from our scientific men—I mean, *our National health.*

We are an unhealthy race. No one can doubt it, who sees the old races of Europe. Our faces are thin, complexions sallow; dyspepsia and consumption are universal in a land, which in all physical comforts, presents the greatest advantages for the preservation of health. Life may be as long in the average, but it is much less enjoyed. An American is as capable of strong muscular effort, and is as enduring as a European; but he does not get half the *pleasure* from his vigor. Indigestion and nervous diseases sour the life of half our people. The evil increases too; and the probability is, the health of the Nation is degenerating. These facts are notorious in Europe, and our sharp, worn American faces are known everywhere. There is much disease and bodily weakness among the poorer classes of the Old World; but in classes, enjoying equal comforts, it will be found that the Americans are confessedly inferior in robust health. The dyspepsia, which so curses our whole population, is comparatively unknown among the older nations.

In accounting for this, too much weight, in my opinion, is laid to the effects of climate. I could not see in North Germany in the autumn and winter, or in Hungary in the summer, that the differences in climate were very appreciable. There were the same sudden changes, the same extremes of heat and cold, and an atmosphere quite as remarkable for dryness as our own. The great and sufficient cause will be found to be, in this very difference in respect to out-door exercise and amusement.

We work too hard, and play too little.

Our nervous and digestive systems cannot sustain such an intense action of brain, as the American life demands, without frequent pleasant muscular exercise. The people need out-door manly sports, and healthy amusements. Those wearing, formal city enjoyments, with late hours and unhealthy fare, and those most useless trips to crowded watering-places, must be dropped for something German-like—something cheering, healthful, boyish—or we shall be a nation of dyspeptics.

Other causes for our sickliness, can be found in our general habits—our diet—our excessive greed for money—the little heed we give to quiet family enjoyments. And if in these respects, I shall be able to show how much vitally important to our future we have to learn from the Germans, I shall have written to good purpose.

As a practical conclusion, I would say to every man, who would deserve well of his country, play! play more—patronize, encourage play!

Why should bowling-alleys and cricket-clubs be given up to "fast men?" Why should rowing-matches and yacht-races, fencing bouts and boxing lessons, fishing and shooting, be any more the privilege of "the world," than the church? Why should not respectable, moral, religious people go into any, or all of these as they fancy, and invigorate their bodies and cheer the mind? Do not let us grow old and dyspeptic, because we are growing more religious.

Let there be something of healthful boyhood in us always! No sports, but what are pure, humane and moral in tone; but where there are such, let no notion of asceticism, or false dignity restrain us! Of course each one will have his favorite amusement; whatever it be, let him remember it is nearly as important for his health of mind as his regular work. For my own part, as a "brother of the angle," I most recommend the "gentle art."

Those cheery mountain-walks, the clear dashing brooks, the air, the light, the easy occupation, which always absorbs just enough to let the full, almost unconscious enjoyment of scenery pour into the heart. It makes one a boy again to remember!

DECEMBER, 1850.

The concerts still continue, and are a great treat to us Americans. Every Friday afternoon, we have in the coffee-gardens out of the city, instrumental concerts, where Beethoven's symphonies are given with a skill, which no band in America could equal. The entrance fee is *six or eight cents*, and each visitor is expected to order a cup of coffee, or mug of beer. There are ladies in the centre of the building usually, but how they bear that condensed atmosphere of tobacco-smoke is a mystery to me. Where I sit on the side, I could hardly see the orchestra for the thick clouds; and though somewhat hardened to "the weed" myself, I had once or twice to cut a symphony in the midst; all enjoyment being out of the question, amid such a burning of bad tobacco.

As a specimen of these concerts, I give a programme for an evening lately, in Liebig's saloon.

OVERTURES.

Iphigenia, by Gluck.

Midsummer Night's Dream—Mendelssohn

Don Juan—Mozart.

Coriolan—Beethoven.

SYMPHONIES.

G Major—Haydn.

The Andante from C Major—Mozart.

C Minor (5th)—Beethoven.

Of the other concerts, the most celebrated are given by the *Sing-Academie.* This is an association founded by Fasch in 1789. They only hold some three or four concerts during the year, and usually sing Oratorios and Masses. This season they have given Haydn's "Creation" and a Mass by Cherubini, together with Handel's "Messiah" and "Sampson," and Mendelssohn's "St. Paul." The admission fee is seventy-five cents and fifty cents; when they sing in the Garrison Church, only twenty-five cents. There are beside two or three similar societies, but less important, which perform oratorios. The best orchestral music is from the Royal Orchestral Society, which gives a series of nine concerts. I copy as a specimen of their evening, a late programme. On this occasion only three symphonies:

1 Symphony C Minor—Haydn.

2. Symphony A Major—Mendelssohn.

3. Symphony F Major, (8th)—Beethoven.

More commonly there are two Symphonies and two Overtures, as on January 16.

1. Symphony C Minor—Gade.

2. Overture to Fingal's Cave—Mendelssohn.

3. Overture, Coriolan—Beethoven.
4. Symphony Pastorale—Beethoven.

The price of admission to these concerts is the same as at the other—seventy-five and fifty cents. They rank so high, that seats are taken by families year by year. The orchestra numbers from one hundred and sixty to one hundred and seventy members, of whom one half must be all the time occupied. The services required are performances in the theatre and opera, and private concerts for the King. Every member must pass a severe examination before he is admitted; and with thousands of players, the great object of their ambition is to become a member of the Royal Orchestra. The salaries are small, but are increased, so as to support the members when they are superannuated.

The usual price for the chance concerts, corresponding to those we have at home, is seventy-five cents. For Jenny Lind's, it was one dollar fifty, and seventy-five cents.

There are also Quartette and Quintette Soirèes, given by the first artists in Berlin; similar to Eisfeldt's in New York and those of the Mendelssohn in Boston.

The rehearsal of the royal bands before the guard-house, is in itself a fine entertainment. From fifty to one hundred instruments are in play, and you hear music such as you can only hear at home in our best concerts.

Of Church music, not much can be said. I have often listened with intense delight to the choir of men and boys in the Cathedral. Artists tell me, that there is no choir equal to it in the world—not even that of the Sistine Chapel. They sing the Psalms and Chants from Mendelssohn, Neithardt, and all the best composers. I heard, too, once, *Mozart's Requiem*, from a grand choir of operatic singers in the Catholic Church.

DECEMBER, 1850.

A very pleasant "birth-day party" came off last night at Pastor ——, one of the purest *Pietisten*, as they call the Evangelical orthodox. I went at about eight o'clock, and found quite a large company already assembled; and *tea and rum* being passed round. Pastor —— received me in his usual cordial way, and I found a number of my acquaintances present. If I might be allowed to especially mention any, whom one meets in the Berlin circles, and whose names are already widely spread in other lands, I would not omit the genial and eloquent Krummacher, a man so favorably known in America; Nitsch, the most scientific and profound of the Berlin preachers, and the successor, I believe, of Schleiermacher, Snetlage, the court-preacher, at whose house such pleasant companies of English meet; Lepsius, whom I had not the pleasure of knowing personally, famous for his researches in Egypt; and Curtius, the youthful Professor of Grecian Art in the University, a man who, I do not hesitate to say, will win the gratitude of Prussia, when the results of his free and earnest course of instruction with the young prince—the future king—shall appear.

There were several rooms open this evening. In one there was music; in another were people playing chess, or looking over prints; and in another, the elder part of the company engaged in conversation. All was easy and social, and very little of forced enjoyment appeared. At half-past nine or ten began the most social part of the evening around the supper table, with the sparkling wit and lively conversation for which the Berliners are so famous. I was struck that evening, as I have often been in these supper-parties, by

9

the superiority of the Europeans over us Americans in the *art of conversation.* We are better orators, but I suspect seldom so good *conversationists.* Is it that as a nation we are too earnest for "small talk?"

Another peculiarity in most of German society which would at once attract an American's attention, is the much less prominent place *woman* takes. It is very seldom, you hear a lady taking any great share in table conversation. There are very few subjects on which her opinion or her feelings seem to be listened to with much attention. It is quite evident she has a very different position from what is given her in American life. And I may add, I think without presumption, that it is seldom in completeness of education, she can claim the same position with the ladies of our educated classes at home. There is something too, perhaps, in the exceeding strictness of the rules of society here with regard to the intercourse of ladies and gentlemen, which may have checked that lively, intellectual converse, which, after all, forms often one of the best means of education.

But to come back to our supper-table. The Berliners are not at all gross eaters, but they hold firmly, at least in practice, to the good old German idea—of good eating being the aid of kindly social feelings. Through all the old world much more of the best social life is over the table than with us in the new. Our first course here was fish, the Berlin pike, a fish resembling our pike, but coarser and softer. The salmon from the Elbe too, or the carp from the Spree, are much eaten in this way at supper. This was followed by roast meat, with preserves or pickled fruit. Mutton is the common meat for this, sometimes venison or turkey. Then came the pudding or the confectionery. We had, as an imitation of the English, a genuine "plum-pudding," greatly to the glee of the children. According to the popular idea it can only have the true English flavor by heating it in burning alcohol; so that there was a long line of blazing plates down the table, and a great deal of sport for the children, even if no better pudding. The last course, according to the universal custom, was black bread and cheese.

Through every course light wines were passed around, either Bordeaux or the sour Rhenish.

Towards the close, one of the Pastor's friends rose, rapped on the table for silence, and bade the company fill up for a birth-day "health." Every glass was filled, and the speaker commenced. He mentioned the long and close friendship which had existed between him and their revered host; described with a comical touch their early difficulties in the ministry; spoke in a tone which called the tears to many an eye of the dear hearts who had been with them in the Morning, and were gone now as they drew towards the Evening, of the struggles his friend had had with the infidelity and indifference of the nation, and the abundant success which had been granted him. "God too had dealt mercifully with his family," he said, and *she* was with him still who had so sustained him in his starting. He was before a company of friends, and he could not avoid speaking with thankfulness of the light which she had thrown around the pathway of them all—that abounding cheerfulness, that patience, that entire forgetfulness of selfish pleasure! He would propose "the health and long life of their two esteemed friends, the Pastor and his wife!"

It was drank with many a *Hoch!* After this followed several speeches, all full of that genial home-tone; and about half-past eleven, we broke up. The evening had been a delightful one; and there was much to interest me as I recalled the conversation.

Political subjects do not form a great topic just at present for

Berlin table-talk. Every man of whatever party is so thoroughly dissatisfied with the present state of political affairs, and so hopeless of the future, that it seems as if any mention of the subject was carefully avoided, and they all took refuge in their wit and their literature to escape the thoughts of it.

As I see the quick joke pass around and hear especially those keen stories which the Berliners so delight to tell, against the heavy, "material" English, it often seems to me like the wit of the Greeks as their degradation was coming on, against the sturdy Romans; the wit of an intellectual race which is losing its power to act.

I have spoken before of the unbelief or indifference on religious matters which meets one everywhere in German life. There was little of it apparent in such a company as met at my friends; still, in general, it is a trait of Berlin society.

The city seems still somewhat to deserve its old name, "*The Voltairian Berlin*;" though one must confess there is nothing of the *maliciousness* of Voltaire in its unbelief. And yet from this, there is much less danger to one mingling with the Germans than would be supposed. If I might be allowed to speak of my own experience, I would say, and with deep gratitude, that my faith has only been strengthened by my experience of the want of faith among the Germans. I feel this the more gratefully, for after all, when the best and noblest spirits around one, doubt, it is seldom that even the strongest belief can remain altogether unshaken. So far as I can judge, too, the faith is not in this case from that home-sick love which every man under almost any religion, feels for the teachings of his childhood in a strange land. But I cannot help seeing that the Germans are not at all happy under the change, that there is a dissatisfaction, a sense of want in their present condition, which speaks most painfully of the injury they have done their own natures. And besides, the more I see of them and of men generally, the more I am convinced that even in the *practical* emergencies of life, no height of moral principle, no nobleness of character, can in any way take the place of the religious Principle; that there is a certain "ground-trait," a certain *reliableness* even in every-day difficulties in the religious character, which no mere moral culture can ever give, and which is, to my mind, one of the best proofs of its origin.

It will make my impressions of German Social Life more fresh to others, to give an extract from a private letter written about this time.

"My Dear J.—* * * I want to tell you about my friends. I have spoken often of Mr. T——. He is a retired merchant, living in a very pleasant house; a warm-hearted, social, sensible man. * * * Fräulein F., his daughter, who keeps house for him, has a kind of suffering, pressed-down look, which wears off as she becomes interested in the conversation, and which is owing, probably, to a great sorrow a few years ago—the death of her betrothed. She is full of kindness, with the shape of head and marked features, which indicate strong feelings. She is simple, heartfelt, and self-sacrificing, and her kind manners give one the impression, at first, she is very amiable and nothing else; but after a while, you see under this, that there's a strong understanding and a very vigorous character. Her mind is not the *most* highly cultivated, but in all this family there is such a taste for Art, that it in some degree has made up for this, and she has an excellent practical sense. Her impulses are kind and noble—and she will *grow*. * * * I will not describe her sister. She might have been a genius in other training—as it is, she is the simplest—sometimes most deep-seeing, unpracticalest, *phantasirendste Fräulein* (*most phantasizing* young lady) I know—yet again not highly cultivated, except by her own dreams. There is one son at home—a merchant—been in Southern India some years—rather witty and boylike. Like all the family he *draws* well. The other children are married, and all live close by in the same block. One is an artist; a deep-feeling, under-thinking, somewhat sceptical man, with decided genius. * * * I visit here every day—sometimes to Morgencaffee (morning coffee)—generally to Frühstuck (breakfast) at eleven; chat with the ladies; go down with the father and visit his friends; dine with them, when I am not engaged out; then after dinner walk with the ladies, and in evening call on others, or meet them again at half-past eight o'clock to supper. The meals are the most pleasant and social affairs I ever saw.

"I am inclined to believe, dear J——, and don't laugh!—that the true view of human life, would bring in *eating* as an important element. Not eating as a mere means of animal pleasure, but—first as the embrace and the kiss are at once the expressions and the aid of affection—so eating as an expression of joy and an aid of sociality. We might wish to have sociality and the higher intercourse freed entirely from the bodily influence, and purely spiritual. But they never are; and for some wise reason, there is no lofty emotion which is entirely separate from bodily states.

"I am disposed—not like Jane Eyre and perhaps Emerson—to believe that the true course, is to *sanctify eating*. Not to look down upon it—but to make it a means of the higher influences. This seems to me the idea of the Bible. As was natural in an early age, eating in the Old Testament was always the expression of happiness and sociality. In the New, is it not remarkable, how much

Christ is spoken of *at meals?* His noblest thoughts, his freest out-pourings of real feeling are at the table, where good cheer has been. His best speeches and teachings are often at dinner. The peculiar rites—yes, the only rite—which he transmits, is the changing of the convivial meal into a remembrance of Him. His appearance after the crucifixion is at the breakfast table. And His last appearance on earth, is at a dinner in the open air. Is not this the idea of the *Grace?*

"As Charles Lamb said, 'He could not see why he should thank God more for a dinner, than for a new pair of boots!' I have felt this so, that I have asked God 'to bless us in this, even the smallest action of our lives!'

"But is not the real idea, that the meal is one of the best aids of sociality and best expressions of happiness; and that in that time of friendly, pleasant intercourse, we especially want the aid of God and His company, in making it all noble and good?

"Is not every meal a Lord's supper—and should not every Lord's supper be a social meal?

"Is not this the healthy, natural idea of eating—of a man, who had not been a glutton and was now *reacting*—with good appetite and social affections? I fear this sounds irreverent in some parts, but it should not. Of course, you will say it is 'dangerous,' and that if Appetite and Duty were in the same path, men would go with a rush. I do not mean to say, you know, that I hold precisely this—but something like it—at any rate, you can think of it. Don't think that my lips are smacking now with the remembrance of my German dinners! If I could have a tip-top Senator Meyer German dinner, with eighteen courses and wines, all *by myself*, I should not prefer it to my *bouillon* and *gänseklein* (soup and roast goose) for seven and a half cents—but give me a company or family-dinner, where thought and kind feeling and language are waked up by the good cheer, if it be only tea, and bread and butter, and I confess I do like it far better."

CHAPTER XXI.

THE GERMAN CATHOLICS.

December, 1850.

Among my friends here, are a family, to whom I have become especially attached, who are followers of Ronge (pronounced, *Rong-gay*), or "German Catholics," as they are called. I have been attracted to them by their genial humanity, and their free, democratic principles; and through them have become acquainted with several of their persuasion.

I accompanied them last Sunday, to hear their preacher, Mr. Braũner, who was formerly a Catholic priest. A small, meagre man, who spoke with a fire and enthusiasm, you would not expect from his appearance.

His sermon was on "Love," showing the progress of love for the individual, to the wider and more unselfish love for mankind; touching sadly on the evils now, which are cursing Germany, but full of confident hope that a better Future was dawning on humanity, when Love should govern the relations of rulers to subjects, and state to state, as well as those of man to man. The heaven-appealing oppressions in Hesse were denounced in a tone, which I have heard yet from no pulpit in Prussia; and the supineness and time-serving disposition of the Protestant clergy met with a stern rebuke.

"Let us have courage," was the conclusion. "Time will change it all! We are going hence, soon to be absorbed into the world-spirit (*Welt-geist*); our feeble and selfish love to be merged into His eternal and ineffable Love; and the times and events all tend thither!"

The whole—church and preacher—struck me as in consistency with this Ronge movement—the union of the old and the new, of the venerable Past with the reforming Present—chanting of liturgies, with a popular, transcendental sermon; antique panel-pictures in carved oak, set into modern brick walls; and dear old stiff paintings of martyrs with gilt images of saints, lighted by nineteenth century chandeliers; and to crown it all, a man who had been a Catholic priest, declaiming over one of the carved pulpits of the middle ages, on unlimited democracy, and denouncing tyranny as boldly as an American stump orator. It is to be hoped, the analogy goes no farther, for the church had all the inconveniences, with none of the associations, of the old buildings; it was very damp without being antique.

In walking home with my friends, I told one of them—Madame ——, a very *spirituelle* and benevolent lady—how much I had liked the sermon in the main; that it seemed to me freer and bolder than any I had heard; but that some allusions towards the close, were hardly plain to me. "Do you all believe," said I, "that your souls are absorbed into God, or are you only speaking figuratively?"

"We do," said she, "and the most of our sect, though it is not an article of our creed."

"But, that our souls have no individual existence at all after death?" I inquired.

"They live in God," she answered, "in so far as they are pure and good. The evil in them perishes. God and they will be one!"

"And do none of you expect to meet those you love, again?" said I. "Have you no hope of living on and working for others' happiness? Is your *Ich* (I) to disappear altogether and forever? Can you bear to think that this half-life is all?"

"We can bear to think what God has appointed us," she answered. "We believe that our friends and ourselves will be happier, or rather better, by complete union with HIM! We do not ask for a reunion with them, but for something higher—a reunion with God!"

"But can you preach this to men when they are in suffering and sorrow? Can you tell them that there is no remedy for this—no other life, where there is peace and rest again? Are they to die with no hope beyond? Is this most incomplete, mysterious existence to be all? How are you ever to place motives in the Future, before the sinful, if there is no Hereafter?"

"That is it!" said she. "Precisely for that reason, we believe God takes away a future life, except as it is in Himself. You Protestants have frightened men into goodness, or bought them with promises. We want a holiness which does not care for a Future, which rests in God alone. We do not believe in the goodness that fears Hell, or looks forward to Heaven. Our idea of holiness is that Love which embraces all, without thought of anything but the happiness of those who need happiness. Not selfishness, not looking to reward or praise, but the Love of Truth because it is truth, even if there were no God; the purpose to sacrifice happiness, pleasure, everything for those who are suffering and helpless and guilty."

"We believe, Herr B., that just as Protestantism with its spiritual life has supplanted Romanism, so this belief of ours will gradually cover the world. It may need time, but it is sure; it has God's Spirit with it!"

I will not detail the conversation farther. I was impressed with the beauty and purity of their ideas, and their enthusiasm for them, though it could not but be sad to me, believing that these theories without their beautiful accompaniments would gradually work among the masses here, and produce, as they have done so often before, universal skepticism and irreligion. I inquired after we reached the house, whether all their preachers were equally bold on political subjects. "Yes," said they; "we want men who are not afraid to speak of rulers as well as ruled, and our ranks are crowded with those from the Protestant churches, who cannot believe that system true; they say that no pure faith could support clergymen, so conservative and truckling to authorities, (*Obrigkeiten*) as these in Prussia."

I must here, though not denying the errors of this sect of German Catholics, express my hearty admiration for the tone of their preachers on public matters. Theirs are the only pulpits where a man dares gets up and speak a word of sympathy for the immense masses of crushed and oppressed men in Germany; the only place where one hears of the rights of the subject, as well as of the "respect for authorities," and where the idea is sometimes broached, that one of the results of Christian Love is to be FREEDOM for man.

I asked my friends, whether they had experienced no annoyance from belonging to such a heretical sect. "We have," they said, "the Government is bitterly opposed to us. We are not even legally recognized yet; and our children may lose the right of citizenship possibly, from not being confirmed by an orthodox pastor."

I saw much afterwards of these persons, and of various members of the sect, and, I must confess, that in practical benevolence, in a genial humanity, and in all the evidences of a sincere love of God, they seem to me quite equal to any of the more orthodox denominations.

The German Catholics are to occupy no unimportant place in the political development of Germany, and a brief account here of their progress and principles may be of interest.

Probably few of my readers will forget the thrill of surprise and hopeful feeling which passed through the American people when, a few years ago, the news of a bold movement in the heart of the Romanist Church of Germany, and of the formation of the new sect of the "German Catholics," came over to us. Not many, probably, know the singularly different direction the whole movement has taken since that time.

It will be remembered that after the Congress of 1815, the general position of Roman Catholicism in Germany became, from the re-action of the French Revolution, as well as the measures of the Congress and various other causes, much strengthened. Footholds were soon gained even in the Protestant States, and rights were publicly granted to the Pope and his ministers in Hanover, Bavaria and Prussia, such as before they had not even ventured to claim. Encouraged by this success, further attempts were made, and the marriage of Protestants with Catholics was attacked with a vigor and lordly authority which might have belonged to the proudest days of the Roman Church. These last efforts struck at the very heart of society, and threatened to disturb the peace of thousands of families through all Germany. In Silesia and East Prussia, especially, the excitement over them was intense, and even the government of Prussia entered into a controversy on the matter. At length, as a climax to these efforts, a grand blow was struck in the provinces of Rhenish Prussia. There, on the great highway of nations, in these matter-of-fact, unbelieving days, a leading Archbishop of the Church of Rome had the presumption, and not only the presumption, but the success, to collect more than half a million of men from all parts of Germany, at immense expense and suffering, to worship an *old coat*, which he affirmed to be the coat of Jesus, and to induce them to give their trouble and money as an offering to it! One can hardly understand it; and if it were not for the most convincing records, we should say at once it was one of the fictions of the enemies of the Church of Rome. Yet such was the fact, and a fact dating only seven years back! This was the last, however, of these attempts to bring back the middle ages. Amid the lull of astonishment and indignant feeling through all Germany, at such a daring assault on human Reason on so grand a scale, there came forth from an obscure priest in Upper Silesia, a letter—a letter whose thrilling effects through the German nations we cannot understand, without appreciating the preparation of the people for it, caused by these various movements of the Romanist Church—the *Laurahütte Letter* of Ronge. "For a long time," it begins, "like a fable, like a tale, has it rung in our ears, that the Bishop Arnold of Triers, has exhibited for worship and religious reverence, a piece of clothing called the coat of Christ. Ye have heard it, Christians of the nineteenth century! Ye know it, German men! Ye know it, teachers of the people and teachers of religion! It is no fable and tale—it is reality and truth!" Then, after a vivid exposure of the idolatry, as well as the injury to the poor people, in expenses which they could little afford, from the exhibition, he says: "Bishop Arnold of Triers, I turn myself then to you, and in virtue of my office and calling as priest, as a teacher of the German people, and in the name of Christianity and the German nation, I call upon you to put an end to this unchristian exhibition of the holy coat, to withdraw the article from public notice, and to make the scandal no greater than it is! For do you not know—as Bishop you should know—that the Founder of the Christian religion left to his disciples and followers, not his coat but his Spirit? His coat, Bishop of Arnold of Triers, belongs to his *executioners!*" Without following the letter through farther, we would only say, it is a most impassioned, spirited appeal against the imposture, and shows a mind burning with intense hatred of oppression in all forms.

It met at once with a response through thousands of hearts. Within twenty days one congregation had separated itself from the Catholic Church, at Schneidemühl, and their priest was to be heard celebrating the mass in the German language. In a little longer time, Ronge himself was summoned to assist in the formation of a large and influential church in Breslau, composed altogether of those who had been Catholics, and based on the freest Protestant principles; while the idea spread itself with more and more power that a new and glorious Church was to be formed, freed from the defects of the Romanist Church, and yet so independent of the Protestant as to attract those from the Romanist body, who would otherwise find many prejudices in their way. Such was the first influence of the "Laurahütte Letter."

To Ronge himself this does not appear to have been any sudden movement. According to his own account, and what other evidence I can get access to, he had been now for four years deeply agitated with indignation at these mummeries of the Church which he had once so filially trusted, and with doubts of the whole soundness of its system. In 1839, with hopes of a quiet, useful calling, as religious teacher, he had entered a seminary for the education of priests. He was not there long, without finding his confidence in the general spirit of the church shaken; and from that time till he entered on his office as priest in Grottkau, in 1841, he appears to have become more and more conscious of the unmanning, debasing influence of the principles in vogue among his brother priests.

In entering on the sacred office, he tells us he was determined that for his part he should be, in the true sense of the word, *a Teacher of the people*, and that without fear or hypocrisy, he would speak, what he thought the truth. Under such a determination, he naturally soon brought himself into trouble. And during the next three years, at various times he found himself accused of all kinds of heresies—of wearing his robes too short and his hair too long, of teaching German history in the children's schools, of deviating too much from the catechism in his instructions, of talking too much of faith and too little of works, and divers other misdeeds of the kind, until at length a letter of his, addressed to the Cathedral-Chapter at Breslau, exposing various corruptions and superstitions in their midst, caused his suspension from his office. During this suspension, while at *Laurahütte*, he wrote his celebrated "Letter."

In regard to the subsequent career of Ronge not much can be said. He appears to have assisted for a while in the formation of the new churches among the German Catholics, and to have given his impassioned, spirited style of writing, heartily to the aid of the new movement. Men hailed him for a time as a second Luther. But gradually, whether from the fact that in cultivation and general learning he did not correspond to the place he was taking; or because so long in a cloistered life, he had lost his practical power over men, his influence became less and less. Then occurred some events in his private life, in respect to which there are very different opinions. In fact in regard to these as well as the general character of the man, it is very difficult to get any definite information.

The orthodox and conservative parties detest him, the Catholics hate him, and the *Freien-Gemeinden* seem equally strong on the other side. The fact, at least, is certain that he married another man's wife, though it is claimed she had been first legally divorced. Soon after this, a violent letter appeared from him against the King of Prussia, and in order to escape trial and the imprisonment which was threatened, he fled to England, where he is probably living at the present time.

Whatever the man may have become afterward, every appearance shows him to have been honest and sincere in his first movement against the Roman Church. It was no easy thing for a quiet recluse to leave his calm pursuits, his companions, his means of support, and, without any knowledge of the results, to step out boldly in the world and strike such a blow as that against the corruptions of the Old Church. It was a bold, manly stroke, and for that let us give him honor.

But to our account again of the *Freien-Gemeinden*, or German Catholics. The first important church, as I have said before, was formed at Breslau, and under the freest Protestant and Congregational principles. The supremacy of the Pope, forced celibacy, "confession," were rejected, together with the practices of praying to saints and worshiping relics. The Scripture was to be opened to all, the church services to be performed in the German language, and entire freedom of conscience and belief to be secured to each man. Every *Gemeinde* or "congregation" was to be entirely independent, and to have the power of choosing its own pastor; and if synods met, they were to be endowed with no power other than advisatory.

This was followed by the founding of numerous other churches through Germany on a similar basis, and in 1845 the first Synod of the new sect assembled in Leipsic. The principles declared by this Synod were similar to those stated above, except that after great discussion, a new form of creed was established, very much the same with the Apostles' Creed, with the exception that nothing is said of "Christ being the Son of God," or of his "dying for our sins."* And now began to appear the great direction of the sect. It was not so much in maintaining of the doctrine of faith as opposed to works, nor in the opposition to the Roman Church, that the movement found its life. It was a struggle for *perfectly untrammeled belief.* All the freest, most ultra thinkers through Germany

* We give an abstract of some of the principles of the Creed, set forth by this assembly at Leipsic.

(11) "The foundation of the Christian Faith shall be singly and alone the *Holy Scriptures*, whose interpretation and exposition is given entirely to the Reason, penetrated and moved by the Christian Idea."

For Creed they give among the articles, (12) "I believe on God the Father, who created by his omnipotent Word, the world, and who governs it in wisdom, justice and love. I believe on Jesus Christ, our Holy One. I believe on the Holy Spirit; a holy, universal Christian Church; the forgiveness of sins, and life everlasting. Amen."

(9) "We allow full freedom of conscience, free investigation and interpretation of the Holy Scriptures, limited by no external authority; we abhor all force, hypocrisy and all lies, and we find in the difference of the interpretation of our articles of Faith, no ground for separation or condemnation."

(10) "We recognize only two Sacraments—Baptism and the Lord's Supper."

Marriage in the 13th is declared a civil contract, and (14) "We believe and confess, that it is the first duty of the Christian to exercise his Faith in works of Christian Love."

joined it—all those most filled with enthusiasm and not always most judicious in their efforts for the progress of freedom and liberal ideas among men. Its basis soon appeared not so much a religious one as simply the *desire for freedom.** The wildest forms of religious belief started up in the sect. The personality of God was denied and the existence of a future life. Men were mere emanations of the great *Weltgeist*, (World-spirit,) to return and be absorbed in Him at death. The divine authority of the Scriptures was only a dogma of Jewish tradition, and any other character to Christ than that of a pure and benevolent philosopher could never be maintained; and there arose a wing of the party, represented by Wislicenus, who could not rank otherwise than as infidels and atheists. The sect naturally attracted the attention of government, and it was supposed most truly to be a nursery of democratic ideas and dangerous political sentiments. In Vienna, where the *Gemeinden* had numbered some 10,000, the whole society, in the reaction of '49, was utterly suppressed. In Prussia they have had many difficulties, but have succeeded in keeping their foothold. By the Constitution of this year, all religious societies are allowed their legal place in the State; but it remains a question whether this is a religious society or a corporation—an important question for the Gemeinde; for if the pastor is not a legal pastor, no child baptized by him can have

* *Wagner* in his Report to the Assembly of German Catholics at Halberstadt 1849, thus defines their principles of Union.

(1) "A Protest against the Old Church, with all its tendencies, traditions and doctrines, with its power and its claims, and (2) the unlimited struggling after knowledge and perfection in the spiritual ground, and after the unconditional independence of each congregation."

Uhlich defines their principle, as "The freedom of the human mind." *Herrendorfer*, as an assertion that "all knowledge comes from the Thought of man; a Divine Revelation, there is not."

a citizen's rights—can hold property, or peddle goods, or shoot an enemy of Prussia, legally! As I said before, their practical benevolence and their popular sympathies, I heartily respect. There are many individuals too among them whose views are not very dissimilar from our own. But, as a whole, one can find little religious character in the sect. The wildest, vaguest dreams of German philosophy appear to constitute their religious belief, and to be the object of their faith. In practical sympathies they are eminently Christian. It is not, however, as a religious party that the existence of the German Catholics is important under any aspect. In that character the sect will soon die out. But it is as a party cherishing the freest principles, as a combination where sympathies may be nursed and plans formed, affecting the political future of Germany, that it is worthy of attentive consideration;—and it is as such, that I shall watch with deep interest its future operations

CHAPTER XXII.

POLITICS.

DECEMBER, 1850.

I HAVE just been conversing with Mr. ——, one of the leaders of the opposition party, and a gentleman very favorably known in the political circles of Berlin. He has resided some time in America, and his acquaintance with our system of government, and with the Constitutional forms in England, give him a great advantage in the debates of the "Chambers." I observe that he is frequently called upon in doubtful points of order or legislation. He tells me that he has great hope through all these present difficulties. He thinks the nation are desirous of supporting a Constitutional Government, and that they only at present need experience. The great drawback, he and every patriot find in their present system, is in the number of office-holders, through each branch of the Legislature. He has no fear, however, that this will not be remedied, and believes in a few years that this Monarchy will take the position of a thorough Constitutional Monarchy.

Still there is quite enough in the present condition of Prussia, to make any reflecting man serious about its future. A stormy session of the "Chambers" has just been ended by the king's summarily adjourning them till the middle of January. It was a short session, but it was long enough to show what the temper of the country is, towards the ministry; or, in other words, towards the policy of the king. Bolder words have not been spoken in any representative Assembly of Europe, than were by certain members of these Prussian *Kammer*. They have denounced this whiffling, vacillating policy, which is endangering the honor and the position of Prussia, as an independent monarchy. They have exposed the folly of a government which began with such mighty preparations, and contented itself with such mean results. They remind the ministry, that in the beginning their claims upon Austria were many, and such as might rouse the whole nation to support them; that they then demanded that no troops of the *Bundestag* should settle the internal affairs of Hesse—a country in which, as belonging to the later German Union, Prussia and her allies alone had the right to interfere; that any such attempt must be at once desisted from, as being an insult to Prussia and a separation of the two parts of her monarchy by a foreign force; that a new Union should be formed, where something beside Austria and Absolutism should have a voice; that Schleswig-Holstein should be left to maintain her own "good right," or that the dispute should be so settled that the Duchies could form a part of the great German Union. These were positions which the Prussian people could stand by. They were claims, to urge which, 200,000 men had left their business and their homes, at the call of government, with an alacrity unknown in the history of military recruiting.

But now, after all this brave opening, what was the close? A whole people had been aroused to arms; the most magnificent preparations known in modern warfare had been made; and what, according to the confession of the ministry themselves, had they gained, or supposed they had gained? Simply and principally the *right for Prussia to occupy the military roads through Hesse*—a right which had never been decidedly questioned, and which was not even mentioned in the early period of the dispute; and secondly, the opportunity of holding some "Conferences," between the various powers of Germany. At this period of the session of the Chambers, the results of the agreement entered into at Olmütz, between the Austrian and Prussian Governments, were not known; except as they could be gathered from the speeches of the ministers; but those two claims mentioned above, were supposed to be all which the Prussian diplomatists had succeeded in establishing. The issue shows that hardly even those were maintained.

The most spirited speech of the session was made by *Herr Von Vincke*—a speech which in skillful management of arguments, and in ready, lively oratory, has very few superiors in parliamentary orations. It was the great "Constitution" speech, and told with wonderful success. A more complete, thorough *exposé* of this changing policy of the ministry could not have been made. *Manteuffel*, the Minister, tried to reply, but it was manifest he had a bad cause to plead, and that the sympathies of the Assembly were decidedly with the "Left"—the opposition—and he had finally to acknowledge he would much rather be where "*Spitz-Kugeln*" (pointed bullets) than where "*Spitz-Reden*" (pointed words) were flying. In Von Vincke's speech, and in all the others, the King's name is hardly mentioned; or, if he is spoken of, it is done in the most respectful manner. Still the tendency of it all, was evidently to weaken, in the most dangerous manner, the royal authority. The king was known to be at the bottom of all these inconsistencies and changes; and every sarcasm and every bold attack was really a blow at him. When one of the orators closed a vivid statement of this fickle, dishonoring policy, with the words "*Away with the ministry!*" it must have been felt by very many, that these strong words were equally true against the head of the ministry, and that, if the servants disgraced Prussia, the master was at least equally guilty.

Without doubt, the great motive of this attack on the ministry is *not* a desire for any constitutional improvements. The mass of the delegates have very little conception what a genuine constitutional government is, and just now their ideas are quite in another direction. It is the Prussian pride that is injured by this assumption of an authority in Cassel, which Prussia had claimed alone. That the Bavarian—the stupid, heavy-headed, beer-loving Bavarian—should be giving the law to one of Prussia's allies, in utter contempt of her threats! This is what galls so the national pride. That the great antagonist of Prussia—the rival in power, and the representative of a different religion and different politics—should be usurping a right which Prussia had claimed and had not been able to maintain! It is this, much more than the questions of freedom involved in the contest, which has aroused so thoroughly the popular mind. Still, all the best and noblest spirits, undoubtedly always under the success of Prussia, see the success of the great principles of freedom which she represents in Germany. They regard any concession as a concession to that immense absolute Power at the East, whose influence now is so visibly seen in the affairs of Germany. And the humbling of their country is the humbling of the last defence of constitutional liberty in this part of Europe. As one of the Delegates said, in the late session, "the Prussian pride rested on an unstained, an honorable history; but what would become of national honor, if an ally in the time of its trouble, in an attempt so reasonable and so constitutional to restore its rights, were left to be crushed by a foreign power?" And, whatever may be true of the great body of the members, I have certainly been struck by the tone prevailing through the speeches of the leaders of the Opposition—a tone of recognition, all the while, that the great idea of this struggle is, that it is a constitutional struggle. The great men, who, throughout Prussia, through the press and in the chambers have been dealing such heavy blows against the ministry, undoubtedly believe, that they strike in the cause of constitutional freedom The multitude, however, want *War*—war against their overbearing enemies, and they are indignant that the Ministry have so disappointed them.

In the mean time, everything seems to go on gloomily enough for the Constitutional party. Right under the very eyes of the Representative Assembly, with the law fresh on their statute books for the liberty of the press, one of the most prominent editors of Berlin is banished from the city, without an hour's notice, or the form of a trial. Nothing has happened for a long time, that shows better how few Constitutional rights they have in Prussia. This man was not an agitator, did not belong to a party, where even a reproach of lawlessness could be fastened. His paper—the "*Constitutionelle Zeitung*"—is one of the ablest and most respectable journals issued in Germany. It appears, after attacking for a long time, in the most able manner, the policy of the ministry, he at length wrote an article against the king; hinting particularly, that the king was playing into the hands of Russia,—and either in that article or one soon after, comparing his course to that of one of the Stuarts, and warning him of a similar end to his family. This was not done as plainly as I have put it here; still it was very bold, and there was something undoubtedly in the last comparison, which was peculiarly offensive. No one can have studied the character of the present King of Prussia, without being struck by its great resemblance in many points, to that of James II of England, and in others, to traits which that ill-fated family ever displayed. The same lofty ideas of kingly prerogative ; the same remarkable cultivation as an individual, with James II, and the same inefficiency as king. All the fickleness, all the double-dealing, and all the tyranny which ever characterized the worst of that house; and which, with him, as with them probably, is not so much the result of a bad heart, as of a weak head.

It was this, most probably, which gave the peculiar point to Dr. Heym's attack. The king had the opportunity to summon him, according to the fine-sounding "*Press Law*," to a trial for libel. Or, according to that late provision which the ministry made themselves, and which the Chambers have hardly thought of assailing, he might have confiscated the paper, and the sum deposited by the editors. But, with a littleness which has rarely been known in kings, he personally at once has ordered the man from his home into a disgraceful banishment. *Frederick the Great*, used to command the numerous libels put up in the streets against him to be pasted *lower down*, so that every body could read them! The contrast in his descendant is striking!

All the free Journals in Germany now are put under strict censorship. The ministry are making constant use of the ordinance before alluded to. The mode in which this Ordinance was passed, will illustrate the present condition of this most Constitutional Monarchy.

In June, 1850, an attempt at assassination was made upon the King, by a discharged soldier. The act met with universal indignation from the nation. The king, however, either really supposing it revealed the wicked passions fermenting among the people, or using this as a good pretext, enacted through the ministry a temporary law for the Press, (June 5, 1850). The whole proceeding was utterly opposed to the Constitution. This instrument contained a provision in regard to the Press, and can only be changed by a vote of the Chambers. The law, too, thus summarily passed by the king, was of a most oppressive nature. According to this, every journal issued more than three times in the week, must deposit with the public authorities, a sum varying from 1,000 to 5,000 Thalers, which sum is forfeited whenever, *in the view of the judge*, the journal has endangered the public security. A more secure, quiet repressal of the liberty of the press cannot be imagined. In addition to this, the law enacts that transit by the public mails shall be forbidden to such papers, as the police may deem expedient.

As was well said by one of the members in the Session just closed, "the ministry might with equal right, without trial or sentence, forbid the transit by public coaches of such members of the opposition, as the police might deem expedient!"

In fact, the Government is everywhere drawing the reins tighter; and when in addition to this, it is mentioned, that in Prussia, the only body through which the Constitutional Party could have an influence, is suddenly adjourned, quite probably to meet for a longer adjournment, and that the absolute parties in Austria and Prussia are, without doubt, now combining to carry out their own objects, we may well say, that it looks gloomy for the cause of liberty in Germany.

The discontent at the result of the "*Olmütz Conferences*" I find very great, and report says, the Prince of Prussia—brother of the king and next heir to the throne—a brave soldier, arbitrary enough, but true as steel to his word and to Prussia's honor, is quite as much dissatisfied with it as the people. I was conversing recently with an army-officer, who told me that when the news of those stipulations reached Berlin, and there was such a danger of a revolution, he "*could not* have fired on the people," and that multitudes in the ranks felt in the same way.

I have felt sometimes, in these old States, a momentary regret in comparing the *rawness* of our American society, our superficial cultivation, with their elegant and finished culture. But the moment I have turned to the political relations—to the complicated difficulties and long-standing abuses—to the capricious tyranny of rulers, and the astounding ignorance of subjects in these European governments, I have felt satisfied. Learning and Refinement *can* spring up even in the wilderness; but whether Freedom will ever grow where Slavery has so long been, seems a more doubtful question.

CHAPTER XXIII.

CHRISTMAS.

My landlady has been rushing in now and then of late in the mornings in an excited way. "Ach! Herr Bric—*pardon!* Herr Braez! are you not getting ready for the Weihnachts-Fest?" or, "will you have no *Fest* on the Weihnacht—you must join in ours! But I know, you Americans work too hard for such things!"

I assure her, we do play sometimes, and ask her how she means to celebrate it. She has put up a nice large Christmas tree in the kitchen, she says, and the children are cutting out gilt spangles and fastening on candles, and then they are all to go next day to the Arabian Circus. I see, too, that the husband is bringing home an armful of presents, though the poor man is hopelessly in debt, and must creep in and out in the stealthiest way, to escape the needy-looking men, who are always lying in wait for him, with "accounts."

There is a shoemaker's family, too, I have often noticed, in the back basement, a very bright industrious set, but so poor. My landlady says the man only earns twelve groschen (30 cents,) a day, and she always gives them what there is left of her own dinners, but "the children look very hungry some days—*die armen!* (the poor things !)" I see, however, as I walk by, through the low window, a green Christmas tree, and the children are tying on the bits of candle. One gay evening in the dull year, at least. I find the whole city alive with preparations. Children hurrying about in the highest state of excitement; handsome carriages rattling from one shop to another; gigantic dolls staring you in the face everywhere, and gorgeous trees of wood and gilt paper, flaunting at every window.

The square by the *Schloss*, (Castle,) is green with Christmas trees; and behind it are long rows of booths, each one filled with all imaginable articles, and each booth with its price. "Here, everything for 2½ groschen, (six cents)!" "Here for six groschen!" &c. The *pfeffer-kuchen*—the immemorial cake for Christmas—are selling off by the loads; and the walls are all covered with advertisements of books, songs, exhibitions, concerts, dioramas, circuses, for Christmas.

I am surprised at the hold the festival has on the whole population. There are not a dozen families so poor, as not to have their tree and pfeffer-kuchen on the Weihnachts-eve.

Even the preachers have alluded to it now for some weeks. Their analogies would be childish to us, but are evidently all real to the people. I went last Sunday to hear *Büchsel*, the preacher, of whom I have before spoken. Almost his whole subject was the Christmas Festival.

He reminded the people how much reason there was for being happy; that for a time now, they should put away their cares, and think of the great Gift of which this "*Fest*" was the memorial. As those were the unhappy children who have no home and no presents on this joyful evening, so were the men pitiable, who had not received the Greatest of presents from above. And, as the child who is unhappy or discontented, while receiving on these Christmas days so many marks of love from his father, is most ungrateful, so are they, if they are gloomy now, while celebrating this festival in memory of *their* Father's love.

At an early hour in the evening, I was at the house of a friend, who had hospitably invited in an English gentleman and myself, to share in the Christmas festivities.

We were at once shown into the dining-room, where the whole family were gathered, the children in an excited state of suspense; only one or two of the older people being allowed to make mysterious visits into the parlors, where the presents were being arranged. Of course, none of the children would, for worlds, have broken in before the appointed signal of the bell; but they were continually making little incursions to the key-hole; and the grave old father was kept in a constant frolic, in driving back these attacks.

The excitement was raised to fever-heat when a large Christmas-box came suddenly in from a married daughter at a distance, packed full of unknown treasures. These were all carried into the parlors; and after a little longer waiting, the bell rung, the doors were thrown open, and we all rushed in a promiscuous throng into the bright rooms. In the centre stood the large Christmas tree, all blazing with lights, and gilt, and tinsel; the presents hung upon it. We stopped to admire it, and especially the pretty little oratorio made of pasteboard, with wax candles, where were the mother's presents; next to hers came the father's, and then the sons' and the daughters', and so on.

Great were the huntings at once, each for his own. The mother had a surprise for the father, and the father for the mother, and the children for both, and even the little youngest, who was altogether overwhelmed by the outcries at first, became quite consoled when she found the stores of enormous dolls and unnameable animals, which were her part. The strangers were not forgotten, and we each found a pleasant memorial, with a spicy little epigram attached. As a traveler, I received with some books, a box of Berlin *sand* as a specimen of the place, and with a delicate allusion, that I would have it occasionally " thrown in my eyes," in some of my investigations.

The verses on each set of presents, as they were read off, were received with shouts of laughter ; and when the father, a clergyman, found a nice cigar case, with a bit of witty-poetry, there was a general clapping. After this, there were games and various quiet amusements, until at length in the middle of the evening, the mother said, " We will have our Christmas hymn, now ! " So she sat down to the piano, and all the little ones were made quiet, and the whole family sung one of those sweetest of old German hymns, speaking of HIS patient goodness—of their own unworthiness, and the gratitude which they all for ever will owe to Him.

I was rather surprised at the half-solemnity of the evening—the almost subdued happiness, and I asked them, whether they would ever *dance* on such an evening? " Oh no ! " they said, " scarcely any family would."

I left in the middle of the merrymaking, as I had been invited to another friend's, whose family I much wished to see.

The night was cold and blustering, so that the contrast was very pleasant as I stepped again into a warm, cheerful room, with tree and candles and presents, and met the hearty greeting. There is something about this German Festival, which one would seldom see in our home enjoyments. People do not seem to be enjoying them selves, because it is a "duty to be cheerful;" and because a family-gathering is a very beautiful and desirable thing. They are cheerful, because they cannot help it, and because they all love one another.

The expression of *trustfulness* through the children of these families; the open and unconscious affection shown by them all, was very beautiful to see. They were all so happy, because they had been making one another happy.

As I recall our hollow home-life in many parts of America—the selfishness and coldness in families—the little hold HOME has on any one, and the tendency of children to get rid of it as early as possible, I am conscious how much after all we have to learn from these easy Germans.

There is a compensation, to be sure, in all these matters—our faults connect themselves with our strength—and a boy is an independent, self-reliant man with us, when he is in leading-strings in Germany. But there is growing up in our cities, a hankering after exciting pleasures, an aversion to the simple and pure enjoyments of home among the young, which forbodes badly for our family-life.

Materialism—the passion for money-making, and excitement, is eating up the heart of our people. We are not a happy people; our families are not happy. Men look haggard and anxious and weary. We want something more genial and social and unselfish amongst us. A piety which prompts to petty self-sacrifices, and takes a pleasure in them, as well as in great. Any family-festivals of this kind; anything which will make home pleasanter, which will bind children together, and make them conscious of a distinct family-life, is most strongly needed. Good people are to recognize that there is a religion in Christmas feasts, as well as in prayer-meetings; that a father who has made his home gloomy, has done quite as great a wrong to his children, perhaps, as he who made it irreligious. We want these German habits—these birth-day and Christmas festivals—this genial family-life, without the German weaknesses, if possible.

In my friend's family here, there were the same genial enjoyments, as in the other—perhaps even more subdued. I found myself again remembered kindly, with Christmas-tokens, so that I quite forgot the old family circle over the waters, which used to have its cheery gathering this evening—now wide scattered and broken.

At the close, my friend read some touching, beautiful letters from Luther to his boy, which fastened the children's attention quite as much as they did mine.

After this, came the merry Christmas Eve supper, with the ancient Berlin dish for the occasion, *carps stewed in beer*, followed by the Christmas-cake, *pfefferkuchen*, which to the unitiated may be described as a mild form of ginger-bread, sweetened with honey.

Then at a late hour, hearty shakes of the hand, "*Viel Glück!*" and many good wishes for the future, and my first Christmas Eve in the German Fatherland was over.

CHAPTER XXIV.

THE GERMAN UNION.

THUS far in my travels through Germany, the question has constantly arisen to my mind, " *What is this German Union*, about which I hear so many and such ardent thoughts ?" What has it been in former times? Was there ever a " United Germany," and is it probable that there ever will be?

I must confess to a very vague and indefinite knowledge previously, as to the answers for all these queries; and not improbably, I shall have many companions, even among historical scholars, in my difficulty. We all know, either from German literature, or from European Journals, of this intense and almost poetic desire through the German race for "Unity;" we know also, that there is a Confederated whole, called Germany; but what the nature of this Confederacy is; on what pact it rests; what basis this desire of Union has had in past history, or what probabilities there are of its realization in the present time, or what are the causes of the strangely high-wrought German feeling on the matter, probably but few even among intelligent men can explain.

In investigating this subject, I must forewarn the reader of some very dry chapters. Still, the facts to be given are indispensable to a correct understanding of Germany, and the movements even now at work within it.

The Germanic Empire of history—the basis of the present Confederacy—dissolved through the influence of Napoleon in 1806, may date its origin from the year 962, when Otho the Great, King of Germany, gained, by the conquest of Italy, the title of Emperor. The kingdom thus elevated into an Empire, was made up of five different nations, each governed by its own prince, and all united under one elected monarch. Its limits, especially on the east, were by no means those of modern Germany; still, in the main, they were determined by German Nationality, and the provinces and kingdoms lying beyond the territory of the original tribes, though belonging to the empire, were not represented in the Diet of the German States. The development of the empire, from this time, gradually into the Confederacy, which ensued, is very curious, and altogether different from the political changes in any other country of Europe.

In France, and through all the feudal kingdoms, the different provinces or duchies were bestowed by the King on his favorite vassals as temporary governments, finally reverting to the Crown as fiefs, the result being, that each kingdom became at length a compact whole and the king absolute ruler. In Germany, on the other hand, there was a principle of law from the first, that the Emperor should unite no fief to his own property, nor hold one which he had possessed before his election or accession. The effect of this regulation and of other causes was, that gradually each of the Dukes or Electors became independent of the Crown; and the German Empire, in place of being one State under the command of a single head, resolved itself into a Confederation of States, yielding a nominal obedience to their elected ruler and diet, but each, in fact, independent and self-governing. This result was not obtained without difficulty. From the crowning of Otho to the peace of Westphalia, the history of the German Empire presents nothing but a scene of unintermitting discord and quarreling. The Emperor oppressing the Electors, and the Electors encroaching on the imperial right; the princes carrying on war against one another, and against the cities; the cities forming unions against the princes; and the knights combining against them all. In the eleventh century, Henry III succeeds for a short time in exercising almost absolute power; but his posterity is soon dispossessed; and in the thirteenth century, says Hallam, "The place was now become a mockery of greatness. For more than two centuries, nowithstanding the temporary influence of Frederick Barbarossa and his son, the imperial authority had been in a state of gradual decay. From the time of Frederick II, it had bordered on absolute insignificance; and the more prudent princes were slow to canvass for a dignity so little accompanied by respect."

In 1220 and 1232 the territorial independence of the princes was first legally acknowledged by the Emperor, by two decrees, in which he engages "Neither to levy the customary imperial dues, nor to permit the jurisdiction of the palatine judges within the limits of a State of the Empire."*

During all this period, up to the peace of Westphalia in 1648, Germany, though nominally an Empire, was scarcely, on one occasion, able to exert any combined power on the rest of Europe.

There was no national army of any account; no metropolis; no representative of the government, except an impoverished Emperor;

* Hallam.

no union between the separate provinces; no court to decide upon their differences, or permanent Congress to give them all a combined influence. Germany was neither a powerful Confederacy of States, nor an absolute monarchy. Its strength was spent in internal dissensions. Besides the existing wide divisions into dutchies and archbishoprics—each almost an independent state—the Empire, as if to make more absurd the claim to a German Union, was split up at different times into various internal Unions, each a rival to the other. There was the Hanseatic Union in the fourteenth century, or Union of the free cities; the Electoral Union; the Rhenish Alliance; the Union of the Knights; some of the leagues being expressly formed to oppose the action of the Imperial Government.

As the last source of complete separation of the different parts, was the spread of the Protestant Reformation; and, before the close of the seventeenth century, the distinction between the Protestant and Catholic States of Germany, grew to be as great as that between the different nations of Europe.

The old Constitution of the German Empire, though giving, as we see, no efficiency for foreign action, was somewhat more useful for internal administration; and, even if the Diet could not unite the whole confederacy for an effort against strangers, we must allow that it could at least sometimes protect a weaker member of its own body against a strong. However, it needed five centuries, before even a Federal Court could be formed to settle the national differences, or an Executive established to carry out the decisions.

The first great exposition of the German Constitution is in the Treaty of Westphalia, 1648; and on this as a basis, have rested the internal relations of the Empire, up to the time of its dissolution. Through the whole treaty, the different provinces of Germany are recognized not as members of an undivided kingdom, but as separate states. Each of the princes is established "in his entire right of sovereignty over his own territory, in the power of making war, concluding peace, and forming alliances," whether with the other princes or with foreign states; the only stipulation being that "such alliance shall not be to the injury of the Empire." The central power is stripped of almost all prerogatives of control over the individual states; and the different parts are settled in their relations to each other, much as if they were hostile countries.

So little is there of the constitution of a confederacy in this document, and so much of a treaty regulating the rights of conflicting states, that the principles settled here, have formed the basis of the European code of international law, since.

There is no appearance, certainly, thus far, of "German Union" in the constitution of Germany. Nor did this treaty tend to promote it. The weak, it is true, were better protected by its stipulations, against the strong; but the forces of the Empire were just as useless for any foreign object as before. Various causes also tended now to sink still more the dignity of the Central Power.

By various means, and through the strangest reverses, always rising strongest after defeat, gaining alike from marriage and alliance and even reverse, by robbery, and by purchase, by accident and by scheming, the House of Austria was building itself up an Empire, which would surpass even the ancient empire of the Czars, and under whose brilliancy the name of the German Empire would quite be lost.

The King of Austria was, indeed, the Emperor of Germany, but all the forces which he could lead in his imperial capacity, were not a third as numerous as the standing army of his own kingdom; and those could only be collected under the greatest difficulty and opposition. The great power of Central Europe became Austria and not Germany.

A century later, also, another state suddenly rose in Germany, by a series of successes even more wonderful, and by acts of fraud and injustice, even more base—Prussia. It is not my purpose here to trace the growth of this petty Dukedom into one of the first European kingdoms. It is sufficient here to observe, that the successful position of Prussia in the eighteenth century as the Protestant rival of Austria, destroyed the last semblance of unity to the German Empire. Germany was lost out of view, as a separate state, and Austria and Prussia appear henceforth on the field of European politics. The German States were still nominally provinces of an empire, but were, in fact, independent powers, holding a loose confederacy for the maintenance of internal peace, and clustering around the two great Kingdoms, who were for the future to dispute the power and the territory of Central Europe. The last blow to the falling empire was struck in 1806, when fifteen of the German States separated themselves from the Imperial Alliance, and formed the *Confederation of the Rhine*, under the protectorship of Napoleon. Thus was the old Empire of Charlemagne, after a nominal existence of more than a thousand years, in fact, dissolved; and, in the same year, Francis II completed the legal act of dissolution, by relinquishing the crown of the Empire, and declaring himself simply, henceforth, Emperor of Austria.

The Confederation of the Rhine, supported alone by the power of Napoleon, fell with his falling fortunes; and in 1814–15, the German States, with their European allies, met at Vienna, to reconstruct Germany, and to give it a constitution, which should in some degree remedy the evils of the past, and answer the enthusiastic wishes of the People.

To the Constitution here given, after many changes and some almost magnificent experiments, has Germany again returned; and he who would understand the present position of the German States, will perhaps find it worth his labor to accompany us in a brief survey of the provisions of that Instrument, and of the changes wrought upon it, in the few succeeding years.

The first gathering of the Deputies to the Congress of Vienna in November of 1814, was amid the almost boundless hope and enthusiasm of the whole German race. A mighty effort had just been made to cast off foreign oppression. The people had risen to the aid of their princes, with an exalted heroism and a self-sacrifice, such as has not been seen in the popular movements of modern days. Something of the solemnity, and of the inspiration of those stupendous events, which had delivered Germany from the power of Napoleon, still rested on the nation and its rulers. The first proclamations of the sovereigns have almost a religious tone. And in the preceding year, at *Kalisch*, they had called upon the German people to "struggle with them, with heart and mind, with good and blood, with body and life for the return of Freedom and Independence to Germany, and for the restoration of a worthy kingdom in suitable form, as may please the peoples and kings of Germany, and such as, in its traits and outlines, may spring from the original spirit of the German race; so that Germany, renewed in youth, vigorous and united, may take a position among the peoples of Europe."

"For this object," too, said Prince Metternich to this Congress, "have the people seized arms; and all the States who have joined themselves to the great alliance, have declared themselves at their entrance, for the same end."

Already previously, (May, 1814) also in Paris, the allied sovereigns had declared, that "the States of Germany shall be independent, and united by a Federal tie."

Everything seemed to promise that Germany would at length be established, as her patriots had so long and ardently desired—as a vigorous Federal State, governed by a Parliament, at once representing people and princes, able to act with power in foreign relations, yet made up of independent States, each possessing its own popular constitution. Unity of Germany and provincial constitutions, were the objects, everywhere, before the hopes of the people—to which many added a Federal Court, empowered to decide upon differences between the States. How these expectations were realized will be hereafter seen.

CHAPTER XXV.

THE GERMAN CONFEDERACY.

THE first year of the Vienna Congress passed away with scarcely one tangible result. The old spirit of Austrian diplomacy seemed to have settled down on the members; and amid the universal stretch of excitement among the people, incredible time and breath were wasted in the most superficial matters of ceremony; and wordy plans succeeded plan, until there seemed no end to the discussions. The sudden return of Napoleon from Elba, at length aroused the Deputies to the times in which they were living; and with a marvellous despatch, the document was prepared which was to be the ground-work of the Constitution of Germany. The essential articles, concerning the internal government of Germany, were as follows:—

(Art. 2.) The object of the German Confederacy is the maintenance of the internal and external security of Germany, togther with the independence and inviolability of the confederated States.

(Art. 3.) All the members of the Confederacy have, as such, equal and uniform rights.

(Art. 4, 5, 7 and 9.) The general interests of the body shall be discussed and arranged at a Diet, in which each member shall have a vote, (either a single vote or a share in a collected vote). This Diet is appointed to sit at Frankfort-on-the-Maine. It is perpetual, and the period of its adjournment must not extend beyond four months, at the most. Austria is to hold its presidency.

(Art. 10.) The first business of the Diet, after its opening, will be the settlement of the fundamental laws of the Confederacy, and its organic relations, in connection with its internal, external, and military relations.

(Art. 11.) All the members of the Confederacy promise to unite together against any and every attack, and when a war takes place, they pledge themselves not to enter upon any secret compact, nor conclude any partial armistice or peace with the enemy. Meantime, they reserve to themselves the right of forming alliances of every kind, but they bind themselves down not to conclude any such alliance, which may injuriously affect the welfare and security of the country, or be opposed to the interests of any one individual member. At the same time, the members shall not be allowed under any pretext whatever, to carry on a war against each other, but shall lay all matters of dispute before the Diet, which shall either mediate or adjudge, and to the decisions of which the parties must submit.

Article 13.—*In all the States of the Confederation, there shall be a government by Constitutional Chambers (landständische Verfassung.)*

Articles 18 and 19.—The subjects of the German princes shall have the right to pass from one state into another and to accept of either civil or military offices therein, if no military engagement already binds them to their native place. The Diet shall occupy itself with the formation of laws for the liberty of the press, and against piracy, as well as for the commercial and trading intercourse, between the states of the Confederation.

Besides these provisions, there were stipulations with regard to the religious rights of the various sects; and others regulating the military contingent for each member of the Confederacy. The army was to consist of 300,000 men, to which Austria contributes 94,000; Prussia, 79,000; Bavaria, 35,000; Würtemberg, 13,600; Hanover, 13,000; Saxony, 12,000; Baden, 10,000; and the other members in proportion. The commander-in-chief for the whole army, is appointed by the Diet, to whom he renders the oath of duty and service, and from whom he receives orders and authority.

Such was the gift of the Congress of Vienna to the German people, in return for their heroic efforts and sufferings.

Even the ambassadors* of some of the monarchical powers of Germany had expressed the desire before the meeting of the Assembly, that the future constitution should contain at least provisions for a Federal Court to decide between subjects and the rulers; that provincial representative constitutions should be guaranteed by the Confederacy, and a popular representation have a share in the Diet. None of these were given. There is no approach made to the Unity of the People. No Federal Court is established; no executive department; no representation abroad; no common code of law. Neither people, nor provincial legislatures have any share in the government of Germany. And so little weight had the 11th article, even at the time, enjoining that "no member of the Confederacy should conclude a partial armistice or peace with the enemy," that at the second Peace of Paris, Austria and Prussia alone of the Confederacy, were parties in the treaty, which was to settle the affairs of Germany. In truth, it was not a unity of Germany which was gained, but a unity of her princes.

Neither do popular rights fare better. Liberty of the press, publicity of trials, and trial by jury—so long demanded—are nowhere bestowed. Popular representation in the legislatures, is not secured; and the provincial constitutions are not protected. The only answer to the universal cry of the nation for a constitution, is answered by the enigmatical words of Art. 13. "*Landstandische Verfassung*," skillfully contrived to mean a constitutional government, based either on popular representation, or on assemblies ap-

* Von Stein, Humboldt, and others. (Stein's Leben. Entwurf der Deutschen Verfassung. Die Gegenwart, 1848. 12th Heft. Wirth's Geschichte der Deutschen Staaten, vol 1)

pointed by the Government. Pure monarchical rule is the principle recognized throughout. Constitutional Government is the exception.

The result, in fact, of this long hoped-for Congress, was not to make Germany more united, or more free, but to throw more power into the hands of Austria and Prussia; and to strengthen the rule of the princes over the people.

It will be seen, as we go on, that the progress of events from 1815 to our day, has only confirmed these tendencies; that more and more the German Confederacy has been changing into a Confederacy of princes, and the Diet of the League, yielding itself up into the hands of Austria as an instrument of absolute power, until the sudden and terrific outburst of popular passion in 1848, has scattered the whole structure to the winds. That the new Government raised by the people has proved as unsatisfactory as the old, and that this year, (1851) has witnessed a return to the princely Confederacy of '15, more unconditional and more absolute than ever before, and to a prostration and oppression of the people more hopeless and more complete than in the worst days of the Past.

The acts of the Vienna Congress, naturally aroused a universal discontent among the free spirits of Germany; which showed itself during the next four years, in very manifest forms. The students and young men especially, felt the disappointment, and vented their feelings, sometimes a little extravagantly. The governments professed to be alarmed. And at length, when in the increase of the excitement, KOTZEBUE was murdered by a crazed young man, a student and a member also of some of the secret clubs, they sounded the alarm of a universal conspiracy for murder and revolution among the German youth. A more unfortunate act for German liberty never occurred, than this maniac-blow of the over-wrought student. It gave to the princes the pretext, so much desired and so influential upon the whole conservative party of Germany, for passing stricter measures. The Conferences at *Karlsbad* were the result, and in Sept. 1819, a new set of ordinances still more thoroughly enslaving the nation.

These were directed especially to limiting the freedom of the press and to strengthening the central power of the Diet. A commission was appointed to watch over the execution of the decrees of the National Assembly. Another to investigate all revolutionary movements, with powers to arrest any suspicious or dangerous individuals, and to control any local authorities. Officers, too, are chosen to watch over the universities, and report the names of those professors whose instructions are opposed to the spirit of these Conferences. A professor displaced on this ground can enter no other university in any State of the Confederacy.

No writing, it is also provided, under twenty pages, can be printed without the consent of the State authorities; and any State, where such writings are issued, dangerous to the public welfare, will be held responsible to the Diet.

The Diet, too, shall have the right, at pleasure, of suppressing any such printed writings in any State of the Confederacy.

It will be seen that these decrees throw a very great power over the individual States into the hands of the princes, and almost completely muzzle the popular press. The despotism was completed by the "Closing acts of the Vienna Congress" the next year—(June 1820). Among these, we only quote the following:

(Art. 57.) As the German Confederacy, with the exception of the free cities, is composed of *sovereign princes*, so must in consequence of this fundamental idea, the collected power of the State remain united in the ruler of the State; and the sovereign, by the Constitution, can be bound to co-operate with the Chambers, *only in the practice of definite rights.*

(Art. 58.) The sovereign princes united in the Confederacy, shall be hindered or limited in their federal obligations, by no provincial Constitution.

Article sixty-one forbids interference by the Confederacy in the contests between rulers and the chambers, unless through the resistance of the subjects to the authorities, the internal tranquillity be disturbed; or unless the government, after the use of all lawful and constitutional means, appeals to the assistance of the Confederacy.

Thus was Metternich's policy triumphant. The ruling power is declared to be vested alone in the princes. The provincial legislatures are not only under the control of these princes, but also under that of the Diet. The great constitutional right—that of raising the revenue—is taken from the Chambers. The powers bestowed on the separate rulers, are so vaguely worded, that they would admit of almost indefinite extension. And the unity of Germany is at length secured, by giving nearly absolute power to the organ of its princes.

From this time (1820) till 1848, the Diet of the German Confederacy has kept on a regular and consistent course of oppression. The people have cried for "Unity" of government, and the Diet have given them "Unity" of police. Nothing has been done for Germany. No German fleet appointed; no representation abroad; no common law; no united postage, or united revenue system, or common weight, or measure, or coinage. But wherever free thought could be stifled; where the press could be curbed, or the university watched; where associations could be restrained, or the efforts of an oppressed population to regain its rights be crushed, there has been unity of action enough on the part of the Diet. Every year it has sunk in the respect of the people. In 1824, it is found passing laws which utterly destroy the independence and the lowest rights of the provincial chambers.

In the year succeeding, there is no object of a revolutionary character so insignificant, in which the National Assembly of Germany cannot interfere. It legislates upon political clubs, on popular festivals, on radical newspapers; it passes acts against red cockades and democratic hats; and at length, it is seen in 1834 enacting four solemn decrees on the travels of German apprentices! It had become, amid the contempt of the people, the great police-office of Germany.

The news of the Revolution of '30 in France, spread deep excitement through Germany. The people became more urgent in their demands; and insurrections took place through various provinces. No good result, however, ensued. The government saw that any popular representation in the National Assembly, would limit the power of the rulers. And each feared to take measures for any greater unity of administration, lest in the new Constitution some of the rival governments should gain the ascendancy. If there were to be a united Germany, Austria dreaded that Prussia would become the executive head; and Prussia feared to take a second place to Austria; and the smaller governments apprehended their being entirely swallowed up by the two combined.

So again did Germany—the "patient, much-suffering" Germany with its forty millions of inhabitants, resign itself to be robbed of its rights, because thirty princes—mere men, and very common place men—could not arrange their petty and interminable rivalries and jealousies.

As I study the records of this time of darkness; as I observe the inquisition-like watchfulness of the police, the open and unrebuked acts of oppression, the subserviency and poltroonery of leading statesmen; as I see in the correspondence of men of the period, the indignation and discontent, working terribly through the middle classes of the people; and at the same time, the step of the oppressors bolder and steadier than before, I am recalled to the present aspect of Germany.

The Diet of '51 differs not a hair's breadth from that of '31, unless in being, if possible, more absolute and more unprincipled. There is the same discontented, unhappy, oppressed Germany.

To the wise man of that day, there were warnings in the movements around him, of that terrible convulsion which in a few years was to shatter almost every throne in Germany. Are there not signs now to the watchful observer, darker and even more threatening?

To follow through the acts of petty oppression, or wide injustice which characterize the history of the German *Bundestag*, or Diet, till 1848, is happily beyond my present object. In February, 1848 a member of the Second Chamber of Baden, rose and offered the motion, that a petition be addressed to the Duke for the formation of a popular Chamber, in the Diet. The motion met with universal applause through Germany; and amid the increasing murmurs of revolution from every side, was discussed with the utmost freedom. The talk soon became openly of a new "German popular Confederacy." The governments were alarmed; the Diet put forth proclamations; but in the midst, the news came thundering through Germany of another French Revolution, and a *French Republic!* All saw at once that the days of the old *règime* were numbered.

Six months before, words disrespectful to the Diet were high treason. Now a Prussian minister dared to say, that the "Constitution of the Confederacy was so much worthless paper," that "he would know nothing of the Confederacy, as a Confederacy of sovereign Princes." And another, (*Bodelschwingh*) that "the Constitution of the German League was something more than a piece of paper, on which were written the articles of Confederation, a mere treaty—that it was a powerful, mighty Being—a brotherhood of forty millions of Germans!"

The Diet made every struggle for existence. It issued liberal proclamations; it voted the old German colors, which it had once so stringently denounced; it proposed to the Governments to send deputies to Frankfort, to revise the old Constitution. But it was too late. The people could not believe, that anything good could come out of the *Bundestag*. And on the 31st of March, 1848, a Revolutionary Assembly had met at Frankfort, composed of about five hundred deputies from all parts of Germany, to deliberate on the election and formation of a grand new NATIONAL PARLIAMENT.

With this almost self-elected body, (the Fore-Parliament) and with its successor, the National Parliament, the old Diet strove hard to agree. But it found continually, that its young rivals were encroaching on it; that the law-giving power was first taken away, and then, by the formation of a "provisional central power," its executive office was reduced to nothing; and that all parties, princes and people, had lost respect and confidence for it.

At length, on the 12th of July, 1848, it terminated its existence, by the President of the Diet formally transferring its rights and authorities to the Administrator of the new Federal Germany, ARCH DUKE JOHN.

Whether, says a spirited writer in the "*Gegenwart*" of '49, the

German League was also dissolved by this dissolution of the Diet, is still a question. One thing is certain, The League which the sovereign German princes and free cities had made, and whose organ and representative was the German Diet, is on the 12th of July, buried for eternal times. Over its tomb, has the League of the NATION been erected ; a new covenant with a new meaning is made, to which also the new form will not be wanting. May soon to our descendants, the disgrace of the old League, be only an incredible fact!

Alas! the writer himself has probably lived to see the "Old League returned "tenfold worse than before."

CHAPTER XXVI.

THE LAST ATTEMPTS FOR GERMAN UNION.

Of the German National Parliament in 1848–9, I do not propose here particularly to speak. It is an interesting historical fact, but in no way closely connected with the present condition of Germany. The attempt was a splendid experiment—thus to build up, on popular representation, a consolidated empire, of thirty independent sovereign states. The intense hopes and almost passionate expectations of the lovers of freedom through the whole German Fatherland, followed the effort. The Germany, which the Professors at Frankfort would frame in one session, was such as the Past had never seen. It was neither the old Empire, with its rival and conflicting States; nor the modern Confederacy, with its union of despotic princes. It was a free, popular, compact Germany. The forty millions of the German race were at length to stand, as one people in Europe. A new state, more powerful than the Germany of Charlemagne, of Frederick II, or of Charles V, was at once to be erected. Prussia was to disappear as Prussia; Austria to be only a second-rate power; Saxony, Bavaria, Hanover, to be only provinces in this mighty kingdom. A common law, a common coinage, a common force was to rule from the Baltic to the Adriatic—and an executive to be chosen with powers such as the old German Emperor never dared to claim. All this grand Empire was to be governed by a constitutional Parliament, based on free, popular representation—a magnificent project, and formed under the influence of the noblest purposes. Still, we are forced to confess it was one for which Germany has never yet shown herself prepared. Innumerable difficulties incumbered the Frankfort legislators on every side. They knew nothing themselves of practical politics. Each one had his own political theory, elaborated long in the study or the lecture-room; and now, on this grand theatre, it must be displayed and realized. Endless, hair-splitting discussions occupied the golden time, when they might have firmly settled their authority over the whole nation. Questions pressed upon them, also, which might have puzzled much older legislators—the relations of the Central Power with the different States, and the obligations of the States to this new, undefined general government. The democracy besieged them on the one hand, with their demands for a universal license, and the governments, on the other, asserted the independence of the separate kingdoms. They could content neither party; and asserted rights over each, which the other would not aid them in maintaining. In excluding the non-Germanic provinces, they offended Austria; and in their democratic discussions, alarmed Prussia. Even the offer of the crown of the new German Empire could not win over the Prussian king. And when, at length, they called in the soldiers of the princes, to save them from the violence of the people, it was felt that their day of power was over. The first formal intimation of the helplessness of the Parliament was given in May, 1849, to its envoy, by the Prussian Minister, who coldly "declined any foreign interference in their interior affairs," and recommended to the Central Power, to "confine its attention to matters nearer home."

Nothing daunted, that body (May 10th) made a bold declaration that a recent act of Prussia—her interference in the Dresden insurrection—was a violation of the public peace; whereupon (May 14, 1849) the Prussian Government proclaimed the authority of the Parliament at an end, and that it "was no longer the representative of the German Nation."

With this terminated, so far as its influence over Germany was concerned, the existence of the German National Parliament.

Despite this sad failure of the popular attempt to form a United Germany, the efforts were still continued on the side of the princes.

The king of Prussia now made overtures for a German Union; and on the 26th of May, (1849), struck a league with the kings of Saxony and Hanover, known as the "League of the three Kings." In this Union, twenty-eight States were gathered. It was not claimed to be a universal union, but according to one of the articles of the Treaty of Vienna, was formed as a separate league (*Sonderbund*) within the German League.

As an offset to this, Austria (September 30) instituted a Federal Commission or Executive Council, to take the place of the executive administered by Archduke John; thus forming another German Federal Government.

The "League of the three Kings" did not enjoy a long existence. The kings of Saxony and Hanover soon found that its great object was to make Prussia the leading state of Germany; and as they no longer had need of Prussian soldiers to restrain their turbulent peoples, they abruptly retired, with the declaration, that "the measures of Prussia for forming a Federal State were hardly opportune, when the whole of South Germany was wanting."

"German Union" was in fact now nearly given up, and the struggle was to be between Prussian Union and Austrian Union. To complete the division, the smaller kingdoms, Bavaria, Würtemburg and Saxony, in their fear of the two great rivals, formed (February 27, 1850) another Union. Thus did the opening of 1850 show to the world, as the result of the enthusiastic struggles of 1848, for a united Germany, no less than *three* separate Unions, rivals and enemies, within the limits of the German Confederacy.

The king of Prussia did not yet, however, entirely abandon his efforts for a confederacy. Whether with his ideal enthusiasm he had really formed a scheme for a United Fatherland, which, with characteristic fickleness, he as easily threw aside; or whether he merely intended the whole movement as a *blind* to his disappointed people, is not to my mind, from the result, clear. On March 20th, he summoned a Congress at Erfurt, seriously to consider the formation of a Federal Germany. The plan laid before this body, for the Constitution of the German Empire, was perhaps too democratic and too favorable to unity, to please even the court itself.

Within a month, the Congress was dissolved, to be replaced by a "Congress of Princes," who were to meet the 10th of May, at Gotha, to consult for similar objects. On that same day, however, Austria had taken a much more important step, which has determined the condition of Germany up to the present time. With a bold forgetfulness of thirty-five years of popular discontent and fearful suffering and out-bursting rebellion, under the old German *Bund*; with an insulting defiance to all Prussia's efforts and those of the nation for a new confederacy, she calmly summoned the plenipotentiaries of the German Governments to Frankfort, on the 10th of May, to hold the full session (*Plenum**) of the old Diet.

In other words, she returned formally, to the Vienna Treaties of 1815, as the basis of the German Constitution. Of her success in this apparently difficult and presumptuous undertaking, I shall not here speak minutely. It is enough to say, that by bold bearing and shrewd diplomacy, she ousted Prussia from every new position, degraded her in the eyes of her own friends, and succeeded in carrying every point of her daring policy.

Germany, so long agitated, torn and wounded in her struggles for National Freedom, and Unity, now lies calmly under the old arbitrary regulations of 1815; governed by the detested *Bŭnd* ot confederated petty tyrants, with the House of Hapsburg at the head, enjoying an unchecked dominion, such as her proudest emperors have not held.

That the Past gives but little hope of a union for Germany must be painfully evident, even from this brief abstract of her history. There never has been a United Germany. The old Germanic Roman Empire was only an ill-adjusted League of independent states for the sake of internal peace. The modern confederacy has been only a Confederacy of princes, banded to oppress the people. Kings, who from motives of ambition or of romance, have labored

* The *Plenum* was the legislative body of the Diet, with sixty-nine voices, of which each state had at least one, and some four. The smaller Executive Council had only seventeen voices, of which eleven States had each one, and all the others only six. The discussions in regard to the number of votes to each state, formed, afterwards, the most important part of the proceedings at the "Dresden Conferences," in 1851.

to rebuild a grand German Empire, have equally failed with Parliaments and representatives elected to construct a popular state. Every experiment has had its trial, whether coming from the prince, the professor, or the popular statesman—and each has come to nought.

Neither do present appearances promise better. There are now in Germany, taking the statistics for 1849,* *thirty-eight* separate, independent states, containing 46 millions of inhabitants. Of these the two largest, (Austria and Prussia,) have nearly 28 millions, or more than half the whole number. Of the others, the three kingdoms, (Hanover, Würtemberg, and Saxony,) have not any one, a population as great as London; and the seventeen smallest states, or more than half of the whole, have not together, more inhabitants than Paris.

The population of the different states ranges from 6,500 (Princedom of Liechtenstein,) to 15,648,000 (Prussia.)

Each one of these petty states, princedoms, duchies, and kingdoms, has its own distinct government; its own code of laws; its own past history; and especially, its own ineradicable jealousy of its nearest neighbors. The only bond to this multitude of states, is a common language and a common blood. It is manifest from the very statement of their population, that the two largest powers completely hold the others in check; and that no attempt at Union can succeed, in which both these do not join.

When it is remembered that these two States are the representatives of different religions, and of different political schools; that behind them lies a long history of bitter hatred and warfare; that each has its national pride and local interests, must we not fear

* Die Gegenwart, No. 25, 1849.

many a year will pass yet, before a German Union is framed by the union of Prussia and Austria.

It is true, our own American Confederacy of heterogeneous races, and religions, and interests, might give us hope for Germany. But with us, there is not this past history of intense jealousy and unceasing dissension; there is not the local boundary, which at once separates religions and interests. The Frenchman of New Orleans, the Catholic-German of Ohio, and the planter of the Carolinas, look back to the same history, and work often side by side with the Anglo-Saxon and the Puritan. But for the Prussian to forget he is a Prussian, or for the Austrian to sink his memory of a proud history, for the Saxon, the Bavarian and the Hanoverian to bury their time-embittered jealousies; for one and all, Monarchist and Republican, the Jesuit of Vienna, and the Rationalist of Berlin, the passionate Southerner and the cool North-German, to unite and form a new compact Federal State, seems as yet like a dream only of the lovers of Freedom.

Yet it shall not be always so. It is manifest through the whole history, that it is the PEOPLE who have always most longed for union. They have seen that liberty from these thirty tyrants, could only be secured by their own harmony. A united, popular Germany would throw off as encumbrances, this horde of petty oppressors.

When, at length, there is a Germany with a *common people* educated for Liberty, when revolution is a struggle not for license but for rights, then will there be the first approach to Unity. A free Germany must be a united Germany. Sectional jealousies will disappear in the great victory of popular rights. Prussia may still be Prussia, as distinct from Austria, as with us Massachusetts is from Louisiana; but, with a people disciplined for freedom and with no princely houses to foment the jealousies, what is there to hinder them at length from combining for great public objects under one common Constitution.

If the nations of Europe ever learn the lesson of self-government from these many defeats, we believe that Germany may at length, realize the old dread of her patriots—A German Union.

CHAPTER XXVII.

A PRUSSIAN OFFICER—AND THE ARMY.

JANUARY, 1851.

I HAVE been holding a very interesting conversation to-day with a Prussian gentleman, a retired officer, Colonel ——, well known to the Americans here. He is of the old school, having served under Blücher; and was wounded, I think, at Waterloo, and afterwards pensioned. He has all the Prussian pride, and that military corps-feeling which the government has so cherished. A devoted Royalist, though just now it seems to pain him, as we speak of the king; and we are quite cautious about alluding to these late events. He thinks this recent disgrace in Cassel before the Austrians is all from "the evil counsellors of His Majesty." "New men are in," he says, "who do not care for the honor of Prussia!" According to his account, and the general opinion, the tone of the army has been wonderfully raised within a few years. No flogging, or brutal punishment is allowed now. A man previously sentenced for a criminal offence is never admitted into the ranks. There are "courts of honor," too, among the officers, which can punish, and severely, any infringement of the "code." Their decisions in weighty matters are submitted to the king. Every means is used to give this high, gentlemanly tone to the army. The officers (of the line) must all be men of education, and pass an examination at every new step in rank. Every private can reach the highest place, if he only show merit enough. Colonel ——'s account is entirely substantiated by what I observe everywhere in Berlin. The city is crowded with soldiery, but the manners of officers to privates are the most exact possible. A failure in courtesy on either side is considered an offence. An under-officer was recently put under arrest for neglecting to touch his hat to a superior; and there is a story told of a Lieutenant B., who lately met a private in the street, and in return for his salute, stopped and chucked him under the chin, in an insulting way. The soldier, though bitterly offended, remained true to his military *etiquette*, touched his hat again with the words, "I report myself insulted!" and at once entered a complaint. The Lieutenant was publicly disgraced.

I find soldiers generally in society here; and there is a very considerable sprinkling of epaulettes in the lecture-rooms at the University. The three years course at the Military Academy demands a certain amount of time to be spent in the University. Besides this school, there are Artillery and Engineering Schools in the city, Riding Schools and a Medical College for the Army. Everything shows that the greatest possible pains are taken to make the soldiers' profession, an educated profession.

I asked Colonel ——, whether the soldiers ever took part in political life at all? "No," he said. "An army, in the nature of the case, must obey; and we do not permit the soldiers to take oath on the Constitution. We all obey the king alone. Besides, according to the Constitution last year, there can be no assemblies or elections in the army, and we hope there never will be. May God long preserve our gallant host from these poisonous democratic movements!"

Did not he fear combinations among them?

No; for the officers are usually so distinct from the privates, and from such different districts, that they would not easily unite. Besides there is a great deal of *esprit du corps* in the militia, (Landwehr) as the battalions are raised each from its own district, and represent that part of the country. As for the regular line, they will never combine, with God's aid, except as in 1814 to defend their country. "No, monsieur; it is not Democracy which our brave army has to fear; it is these misguided men who are now at the helm of government. If our soldiers lose the sense of Prussian honor—*alles ist verloren*—all is gone!"

My friend, the Colonel's, views were equally *exaltirt*, as the Germans say, or enthusiastic on everything pertaining to the army. He even defended that ugly, blue frock-coat, a garment made apparently neither for peace nor war—too ill-fitting for a citizen, and too plain for a soldier. The spiked leather helmets, he assured me, were also the most convenient head-pieces, and were often bullet-proof. The miniè, or *Zundnadel* rifle, so much in use in the Prussian army, he says will strike its mark a half-mile without difficulty, and is a very great improvement. Other military men, I find, do not speak so well of it. It is cumbersome; and takes much time in the cleaning and loading, and is very liable to get out of repair, they say.

Whenever I converse with a Prussian soldier, or study the military system which has formed him, I am struck with the skill with which a nation of soldiers is thus educated, and put at the disposal of one man. An organization so compact, so easily managed, and, at the same time, so calculated to uphold the sovereign, has, perhaps, never been witnessed in history. The army of nearly 800,000 fighting men is not a set of war-machines, like the Austrian troops, or of blind, ignorant devotees, like the Russian. It is a proud, chivalrous, high-spirited body. It is entirely separated from the State; while its internal organization is essentially popular. No political sympathies are allowed. Its thoughts and feelings are all turned within itself. Merit, talent and bravery can win the highest rank; and the soldier is taught early, that the honor of his corps and his King are especially entrusted to him. He owes no allegiance to the State. The king is his Commander-in-chief, and alone has the power of promoting him.

It will furnish a clearer idea of the power thus put into the hands of the King of Prussia, to give a brief description of this famous military system.

Every young man in Prussia, on reaching the age of twenty, is liable to be drafted into the ranks of the standing army. No substitute is allowed; and except in princes of the blood, no exceptions are made—not even for the nobility or the clergymen. If he is drafted into the infantry of the line, he serves two years; if, into that of the guard, three years. If, however, he be a volunteer, and can show a certificate of previous examination, proving a certain moderate degree of scientific education, his time of service is shortened to *one year*, at his own expense. A part, too, of the regular service is often shortened for the others, by their being placed in the "Reserve," as the regiments are not filled out in time of peace. Whenever the army is to be prepared for war, or *mobilised*, the Reserve step into their respective regiments again. Though all the men through Prussia twenty years old are liable thus to be drawn into the ranks, not more than half are drawn annually. In 1846, it is reckoned that there were 160,000 men in Prussia of that age; of these 77,779 were called out, and only 39,790 sent to the regiments—

the rest being kept as Reserve. The regular army numbers 138,810; with the Reserve 225,550.

Besides this, there are two divisions of militia (Landwehr); and another body of reserve (Landsturm). To the first division belong all the men of the kingdom from twenty-five to thirty-three years of age, or those who have served five years in the line. The time of service in this is seven years. This body is designed mostly for defence, and numbers (in 1850) 174,616. It can be used, however, for external war, in aid of the regular troops. The second division takes all those who have served seven years in the first and who are between thirty-three and thirty-nine years. This is employed for fortresses and for internal defence alone. It numbers 175,196.

The last reserve (Landsturm) is never called out except in case of an invasion by the enemy within the country, or in any great danger, at the command alone of the King. To it, belong all who have served in the other divisions, who are yet under fifty years of age, and all who have not served, from seventeen to twenty years of age.

The standing army, with the two divisions, would reach the number of 574,362; and on a war footing would not be far from 600,000 men. Adding the last reserve of militia, and the Prussian host would amount to nearly 800,000 fighting men.

This immense host, too, be it remembered, is not a multitude of raw soldiers, such as we usually call militia; but nearly all men, drilled for many years in military exercises, commanded by carefully educated officers, and animated by a common military pride. A more tremendous weapon has scarce ever been in the hands of a modern State. It should be borne in mind, too, that since it was used with such fearful effect upon Napoleon, it has hardly been wielded in these modern wars. In 1806, the army had become thoroughly vitiated by luxury, and altogether turned from the popular and spirited direction given to it by the Great Frederick. It needed the fearful and disgraceful punishment, which Napoleon inflicted, to bring it back to a suitable spirit. Under those days of sore trial and crushing disgrace, it learned a lesson which it will never forget; and with the skillful organization of SCHARNHORST, it resumed its old character. It was popularized; ranks were thrown open; new honors held forth; and the ancient *esprit du corps* evoked. Every nerve, too, of the lamed and exhausted kingdom was strained to fill it. And with success. Of all the attacks which beat back the iron columns of Napoleon in the disastrous campaign, that ended in the battle of Paris, none were so unrelenting and so irresistible as those of Blücher and his fiery Prussian corps.

In these late years, the army has been only occasionally employed; and then for no cause which could especially arouse its spirit. To shoot down democrats in Baden, or extinguish revolutions in Dresden, would hardly satisfy the old Prussian pride. The war in Holstein against the Danes was of a more popular nature. And in this the Prussians swept everything before them. This winter has witnessed the first grand preparations for war in Prussia, since the campaigns against Napoleon. The whole nation rose, as they did in 1814. Had this king possessed the genius or the spirit of his great ancestor, he might have led a conquering army from one end of Germany to the other. At the head of the whole liberal party of Germany, with a nation of soldiers confident of victory, nothing could have withstood him. Twice has Frederick William thrown away those grand opportunities which fortune seldom offers men even once. The first time, the imperial crown of Germany was within his reach. The second, a whole people stood in arms at his summons, burning for vengeance. By his timidity in the first, he has alienated the whole liberal interest of Germany; by his fickleness in the second, he has lost his greatest support, the devotion of the Prussian army.

Who shall say, that in these strange weaknesses of its rulers, Providence is not bringing on a better day for Prussia?

This great army organization, is an immense expense and loss to Prussia. In 1848 there were in the kingdom 1,794,051 men between the ages of twenty and thirty-two. Of these, more than *one quarter* were withdrawn from all the pursuits which tend to increase the wealth or the happiness of the people, from all care of their families, and all steady labor, to spend their time in military drilling. Everywhere in the country, one sees, that the fields are tilled by women, while the men are leading idle and mechanical lives in the barracks of the cities.

All active thought is extinguished, except in professional matters; practice in political affairs is lost, as the soldier, "*Nach der Natur der Sache*," in the nature of the case, as my friend the colonel said, cannot be a citizen. The whole system over the modern Prussian tends only to make him a loyal feudal servant of his lord the King, and of the great "Prussian Royal Army."

Besides the loss, in the absence of so many able-bodied men from all useful pursuits, Prussia pays in time of peace for her army, $19,150,000 per annum—or nearly *three times* the sum paid for the same object by the United States, with a population ten millions greater, and a territory a hundred times as large, to defend. Still, the Prussian finances have always been managed with extraordinary economy. The whole pay of a private is only from 2½ to 3 groschen (6 to 7½ cents) a day. In 1847, the clothing for every private soldier only averaged $7.50 for the year; and it is estimated that each soldier only costs the state $135 per annum for food, lodging and all expenses.

Of the whole expenses of the Prussian Government, the army take somewhat more than forty per cent.

CHAPTER XXVIII.

A PROFESSOR'S EVENING PARTY.

February, 1851.

I WAS invited last evening to a small party at Prof. ——'s. I went about eight o'clock, as the invitation was to tea, and found the company just assembling. The same plainness here, again, in the furnishing of the rooms, which I observe everywhere. No carpets, furniture light but pleasing, and pretty shows of flowers throughout. The writing-desk in the corner, is arched with a trellis-work of vines; and the deep alcoves of the windows show through the curtains, flowers and tropical fruit, arranged so as almost to give the effect of a bower. There is to be, contrary to the custom, only a little dancing at this party, and the most of the time shall be for conversation. An especial god-send too, such a company is to the Berlin young people; for generally the laws of society for the intercourse of young gentlemen and ladies, are the strictest possible. Every gentleman is assumed—before anything is known to the contrary—to be of lax principles. He cannot walk out with a lady; he cannot accompany her to a meeting, a concert, or a theatre; he must not see her at her own house, except in company with her mother, or guardian. She never goes into company, without an older relative; and for her to invite any young gentleman to her house, would be the greatest breach of etiquette. The proper place for intercourse between the sexes, is considered to be the ball-room; and the few words passed there, are usually the basis, and often the main part of their knowledge of one another, before the parties become more nearly connected. Of course, there are exceptions to this—families where all the free, social intercourse of American life is carried on—but, in general, this treating of the two sexes, as if they were morally dangerous to one another, is kept up through Germany. A stranger never suffers from such rules. He is charitably supposed to be utterly ignorant of them, and can break over as many as he chooses I certainly transgressed them *ad libitum.*

Beside many pleasant young people in the company this evening, there were a considerable number of scientific men. In all society, I think the pleasantest set, is usually the scientific. The study of the natural sciences seems to give a freshness and geniality to the mind, which no other pursuit does. Of those who meet at different times in the scientific circles of Berlin, there occur to me with pleasure, the genial Mitscherlich, professor of chemistry, the Roses, Humboldt, who appears even yet in social circles, with all the liveliness of youth; the brothers Schlagentweit, who, though mere boys, have won a European reputation from their researches in physical geography in the Alps; Professors Dove and Magnus, and many an other.

It is pleasant to an American to find certain of our scientific men spoken of and respected among these, as authorities; Dana in Mineralogy, and Gray in Botany, seem as well known among the learned in Prussia, as in New England. Silliman, too, is everywhere gratefully recognized as the founder almost of natural science in our western continent.

I found myself in the course of the evening, how, I forget, in easy conversation with a young lady, over Goethe's "*Wahlverwand-*

chaften," or "Instinct Affinities," as it might be translated,—a novel the most dangerous possible to a weak mind. The story, it will be remembered, represents two married people unsuited to one another, but who each find the objects of their sympathies in another couple living with them. The struggles and the sorrows in the temptation, and the final triumph of instinct over all obligation and duty are most painfully pictured. I had no thought of any one ever defending it, as other than an exquisitely drawn picture of passion. But the lady, who though young is well known in Berlin for her genius and her noble heart, did not hesitate to say, that it contained its truth. Partly to draw out her meaning, I ridiculed the whole idea, in the strongest language.

It was altogether striking to see the noble and free way, in which she roused herself to maintain the idea of the author. It was a delicate matter to handle; but in full, free tones, she told me we could not appreciate the great heart of a Goethe. He believed—and she believed that there was an affinity of one heart to another, which was above all law. God himself had created it! There are instincts which no one can govern. And even if the tie is not broken legally, there is a relationship of heart!

"But he would do away with the obligation of marriage; he would make a communism in wives!"

"No;—he would make us more creatures of instinct, so that our marriages and everything may be more natural. Now are we not all artificial! We fear to think, or act, or feel, as our hearts prompt us. People who are so cold and dry, may talk of *laws*, but the men of heart do not own such laws. Goethe believed that men are mere *shells* now, and that every one feared to be himself."

"But do you not believe," said I more seriously, as I saw how much in earnest she was, "that the greatest thing man can ever do, is to govern Passion for the sake of Duty?"

"No, a greater is to be able to let all passions free. If we were harmonious, there would be no duty and no work—all would be pleasure."

"What, still on your electic theory," said a friend coming up; "our practical American friend will hardly understand your loose philosophy—I must explain!"—The explanation the reader himself can make.

I give this, though the rich tones and language which fastened it for many a day on my mind, are mostly forgotten, as a specimen of that philosophy, which has crept among many of the noblest minds of Europe; a philosophy which, in one aspect, I can heartily recognize, but which, in another, would make Passion and Selfishness the guides of the soul.

In another respect, it is a specimen of what I so much like in European society, the free, unassailable manner, in which a refined lady will speak of such subjects. That universal prudery, which so hampers a man in America and makes him ignore half the facts of life, for fear of treading on some unknown delicate sensibility, is never seen in European circles. It is boldly assumed, what every one knows to be the fact, that both sexes are equally aware of a great variety of things, and where the allusion is natural, no one troubles himself about it.

There were in our company, this evening, two who were invited as betrothed, and I was very much struck with their manners towards one another. I think in an Anglo-Saxon company, the fact would have been dropped out of view as much as possible, and certainly the slightest expression of their feelings would have been intensely dreaded by the parties.

But here there was the whole evening, an unconscious beautiful expression of affection and confidence, which really, I think, gladdened the whole company.

You never thought of watching them for it, but you never thought of anything else with them. Love seemed to speak out as naturally from their tones and glance and manner, as friendly feeling did with us. Nothing else would have seemed in place. It was above criticism,—above surprise even—though if any other of the young bachelors were like myself, they retired with a sufficiently vivid appreciation of the woes of bachelordom.

I often have observed this *naturalness* of expression among the Germans. It is more apparent in the families, of course. There are not in all my memories, pictures so warm and glowing, as of some of those families in North Germany; families where the look and language of Affection were not blurred by that everlasting formalism and coldness and selfishness which hangs over our households; where love was without dissimulation, neither worn for duty, nor worn for effect; where mutual kindness and self-sacrifice and affection had so long been, that the very air and aspect seemed to welcome and sun the stranger.

This habit of expression in love affairs, appears to be carried rather too far, sometimes. In Hamburg, it seemed to me that every one knew when any lady was engaged; and a broken engagement, or even a disappointment in love was as fair a topic for conversation before strangers, and as generally known as a marriage. The parties must evidently talk of such matters, in a way altogether averse to our English feeling.

In our entertainment on this occasion, I am happy to say, there was no card-playing. Generally this is the universal amusement of thé Berlin circles, especially in the mercantile and in the aristocratic classes.

I sincerely hope this amusement will never become as general in American, as it is now in European society. Why any company of intelligent and social people could ever have adopted it, seems strange to me. It is a complete stoppage on the pleasantest enjoyment, after all, of life to the man of sense—conversation. Besides, we Americans should never be able to play for counters or dimes. We should be a nation of gamblers, inevitably.

In one of our rooms this evening, the dance went on, most spirit edly. Here, as everywhere in Germany, the dance is an entirely different affair, from what it is with us at home. There is a life and spirit in it, which contrasts most pleasantly with the solemn and measured ceremonials in our parlors in America. For the first time, I gained the true idea of the dance—a musical, joyous, childlike expression of good spirits.

"What! you dance not?" said a young lady to me, whom I knew well, in English, as I stood watching the merry groups.

"No, I never dance!"

"Perhaps you are from the *Pietisten*, who think it wrong to dance?"

"Oh no, I like to see it very much!"

"Are your country people so strict as the English in dancing and Sabbath-keeping?"

I told her, I thought they were in the last, but that a great many good people approved of dancing. Still we did not have *that* dance among us.

"*So!*"* said she. "That is one of our prettiest dances—a

* This *So!* is the *Indeed!* of the Germans, which they always transfer to English, when they speak it.

Hungarian dance. See, the gentleman *pfeift*—what call you it? whistles!"

A Hungarian was at the piano, and he commenced a running accompaniment by whistling the air, which had a very enlivening effect.

"They say your people never play; they work always!" said she again.

"Yes; it is too true," I answered; "we make our play, work."

"But we poor Germans have nothing else than play to do," said she with a half-sigh. "How should I like to see America! The Nature must be grand there. But then you Americans are so *praktisch*, (practical)."

I said, I did not think we all were; and asked her, if she had read the volume of Poems, (Homes' Poems) which I had lent her.

"Oh yes!" said she, "I am so much obliged! There is no other poetry like it. It is utterly characteristic—so fresh and original—and how simple! remember you that of the old man?"

"And the mossy marbles rest
On the lips he once has pressed
In their bloom!"

"But then so practical! No German young gentleman would so write to his bride, as that one who speaks of his dollars and shillings; and his presents, which he shall not again have!"

I could not restrain a good laugh. The poem was that one of Homes'—

"Of my cooings and my billings
I do not now complain;
But the dollars and the shillings
They will never come again!"

I was obliged to explain to her, that to us Americans, that was the very joke.

"*Ach Gott!* I see. You are a strange people!" and she took my arm into another room.

"Is it true," she asked, as we sat down together, "that your ladies in America sit still in the houses, and read, and cause the husbands and the servants to work everything?"

"Oh, no!" I answered; and then tried to explain to her the position of woman in American society.

"So! It is very different here. You see that lady across the room, very stout, with ear-rings, and light hair, that is the Frau Professor and Geheimrath S——, but she goes down every morning and cooks in the kitchen till eleven hour. I myself divide my house-holding with my sister; and since six months, I have kept the accounts, and I go to the markets, and look the cooking every-day over, and brush the rooms and clarify the dishes. The next six months will my sister take; and oh! will I not be glad!"

I assured her, she would have an easier time in America in many circles. Yes, she was sure she would. She liked America, even much better than England. She had been in England, and it did not please her.

I asked, why? "Well, I was so afraid all the time. People are so much more strict as we. I did not dare to do anything. In Germany, we can act in the public places as we choose—and no person considers us—then we are not so stiff and cool to the strangers. I always so feared to be laughed in England. Then the English so have the *spleen!*"

I did not agree with her about the English; and asked her, what she meant by the spleen?

"Why, do you not know? The low spirit which in their bad

weather comes on—the oddities, such as you Americans have not, nor we Germans—the *spleen!* *Par exemple*, see you the Herr Engländer by the table, the tall, fresh young man. We all know him. He is very honorable and good, and is much *gebildet*—I mean, educated. A true friend also, but so odd—so, as we in German say, unexplainable. He shuts himself in his room up for many days sometimes—then he becomes very social; then again he studies all the night and sleeps the day through. In the bad weather, he is so gloomy, that we pity him; but if we say, he is at once displeased. His Frau Wirth says, that he much money to the children gives; but that he drinks tea infinitely, and has fourteen pairs of boots for winter! This is the *spleen!* You understand, Herr B.?"

I expressed myself entirely satisfied.

I inquired soon in regard to the fashions in the room, whether they were German, most of them?

"*Ach*, no!" she replied; "it is not thought so *noble* to dress in German fashions. We borrow the French. I sometimes think we have nothing original, unless our musique. No one reads a German novel now; and in the South, they often teach the children never German, only French and English—" "Will the Herr Americaner be good enough to take the lady out to supper," said the hostess, interrupting us.

"Very lucky!" whispered my companion, as we walked into the supper room, "for otherwise, we should have sat at the lower end among the children and stupids."

The soup was passed around, while I helped my lady to tea flavored with vanilla, with a few drops of rum.

"Do you know," said I, "you would utterly shock any of our tea drinkers by such a mixture as that?"

"I know it is not English," she answered. "You will find it

through all Germany. We think the tea will not awaken us at night, if we sprinkle in rum."

"Is it so," said she again, after a little while, "that you in America have those heavy English breakfasts with *meat?* How can you? It is so gross!"

I defended the habit as well as I could; at the same time, making an insidious attack on some of the standard German dishes, especially the *Sauerkraut.* She held up her hands in a comic astonishment, "*Mein Gott!* Not to like *Sauerkraut?* Where *have* you educated?"

The conversation of the table now began to turn towards me. A gentleman near, asked me in regard to my plans of travelling in Hungary in the summer. I explained them. He said, he would strongly dissuade me. Hungary was a very uninteresting country—half barbarous. There was nothing there to see. No works of art—no theatres—no good hotels or roads. The country had scarce ever been heard of till this late red republican outbreak. "It was a wild, lawless insurrection, and the land has not yet recovered from it."

As the Hungarian was gone, I took up the defence of poor Hungary. "I was not sure of the facts," I said, "but I had a different impression of the struggle." I commenced in German, and then, waxing warm, left it for English. I described the commencement of that heroic struggle—pictured the old Constitution—told my opponent, that he and his countrymen were not prepared to appreciate a Constitutional struggle—and in my ardor, from the deep stillness at the table, began to fear I had offended the political prejudices of some; when I was interrupted, as I stopped for breath, by "Vortrefflich!" (excellent!) "the vowels have even a clearer sound than ours, and the consonants are smoother. A strong language but not so clear, not so many small words in speaking, as German!" And I found, that my English, much more than my ideas, had been listened to, so I turned again to German; and it is a curious fact, that the speaking a foreign language varies as much, at different times, and depends as much on moods, as any *extempore* speaking. When under a strong flow of excitement, I could always speak good German.

I spoke now in words which my opponent could not help attending to, of the wrongs of that unhappy land, of its noble and rational struggles for freedom, of the crushing attacks of Russia, and of the Austrian tyranny, of whose abuses we heard each day in the papers.

I could not avoid, as I was upon it, and as I knew my audience well, speaking sadly also of the oppression over the dear old German Fatherland. I alluded to their strict police laws; to the open acts of injustice from the authorities everywhere, and mentioned that well known measure of injustice by which, lately, liberal editors had been imprisoned and banished. I said that the times seemed dark in the Old World—and that we in the New looked with pity over to all this, and longed to right it again. I had spoken with very considerable feeling and the company had listened intently; but here I was interrupted by a gentleman whom I knew to be somewhat more acquainted with America, than the others. The words I can only imperfectly give, but the rebuke will never leave me.

"Sir," said he, very earnestly, "we admit that the times look dark here in Europe, and that there is much wrong here, but we do not admit the right of your country to rebuke it. There is a system *now* with you, worse than anything which we know, of tyranny—your *Slavery*. It is a disgrace and a blot on your free government and on a Christian state. We have nothing in Russia or Hungary which is so degrading, and we have nothing which so crushes the mind. And more than this, we hear now of a law, just passed by your National Assembly, which would disgrace the cruel code of the Czar. We hear of free men and women, hunted like dogs over your mountains, and sent back, without trial, to a bondage, worse than our serfs have ever known. We here in Europe have many excuses in ancient evils and deep-laid prejudices, but *you* the young, free people, in this age, to be passing again, afresh, such measures of unmitigated wrong and oppression! We have not been able to understand it."

I must say that the blood tingled to my cheeks with shame as he spoke.

I could say nothing in defence. I told him party-movements had carried this act through, which I could not understand. But, as to the existence of Slavery, he, like all foreigners, labored under a great mistake. That I, that my countrymen at the North, had nothing whatever to do with it. We detested it. We condemned it. But we, in the free States, could not reach it; we were not responsible for it. And even if we were, it was a momentous and very difficult question, how it was to be done away. Sudden and complete emancipation would often be only a curse to the slave. I then tried to unfold our Constitutional system, the peculiar independence of our several States.

They understood easily, and admitted there were many more difficulties, than they had supposed. Perhaps, unfortunately, there is nothing that a German understands quicker, than the evils of a Confederacy, where the members have their independent rights.

The company at length rose from the table. "You have well your Fatherland defended," said my companion, as she took my arm into the other room, "but perhaps you will think once more, before you speak so hard into German tyrannei, again! And it is posseeble, you may even sometime find good in the *Sauerkraut!* Now let us shake hands, I like so your English custom, and you have not yet learnt the hand to kiss! *Gute Nacht!*"

CHAPTER XXIX.

BERLIN FETES—NEWS.

Feb. 11, 1851.

WITHIN the last month the city has been enlivened by several brilliant *fêtes.* First, in January, came the festival commemorating the origin of Prussia, as a kingdom—the 150th anniversary, and therefore especially celebrated. Now, there is a grand levee, which makes the rusty old palace gay again, in honor of the king's taking up his residence in the city, for since 1848, he has not deemed his *liebe Berlin* quite safe enough for a residence, and has held his court in Charlottenburg, about five miles distant.

It is the first levee which has been held in the Palace since the Revolution of '48; and report says, it is the first time the queen has entered the building, since that terrible day when the fate of *Marie Antoinette* hung over her; and when the shouts of the populace called her out on the balcony, to look at the ghastly corpses, as they were carried into the Palace-court, of those who had died fighting against the throne. A friend of mine, who was in front of the Palace the day after this, says it was a humiliating sight to witness the forced complaisance of the king with the crowd, shaking hands with the *Blouses* and the ragamuffins of Berlin; and his servants emptying the palace cellars to supply them with wines and delicacies. Of course, all this is forgotten now. Such an occasion is almost the only one in the year which calls out the country gentry, and we have a display of liveries, the most unique. Many of these worthy gentlemen have only means to appear once at court, and the old carriages and dresses are carefully preserved for this opportunity.

There are all imaginable colors of livery, and powdered and ruffled coachmen in the style of Louis XIV's time, with the ponderous vehicle and outriders, side by side with the graceful carriage and simple footmen of the modern court-beau. They are pouring on in a continuous line to the castle gates, while the mounted police are keeping the way clear amid the crowd. The people are having great enjoyment in cracking jokes at this display of the thread-bare nobility.

The *Fest* in January, though not more showily arranged, was to me much more interesting. It is difficult to realize that this powerful kingdom has only been in existence 150 years; and that its brilliant history dates almost within the memory of the living.

The name too, of Prussia, is taken from one of the rudest and poorest provinces in Europe.

In 1417, Frederick, of the family of *Hohen Zollern* of the Burgrave of Nuremburg, *bought* from the German Emperor, the province, which now constitutes the centre of Prussia—*Brandenburg*. To his descendants in 1618, was conveyed by marriage the "Duchy of Prussia," a fief of Poland, and a desolate province which had been won and held by an Order of Teutonic Knights. The title of Elector of Brandenburg, was merged into that of Duke of Prussia; but it was not till after the splendid victories of Frederick William the Great, and the spoils gained in the Peace of Westphalia, that Prussia was fully recognized as an independent state. It was at length raised to the rank of a kingdom on the 18th January

1701, by Frederick II crowning himself as King of Prussia. It needed, however, sixty years before the Republic of Poland would deign to acknowledge its old fief, as a kingdom.

From the peace of Westphalia, the history of Prussia has been a course of continued and skillful acquistion. Marriage, negotiation, war and peace, defeat and victory, have all alike added to its territory. What it has not openly plundered, it has gained by cunning bargain or by fortunate accident. The Saxon provinces, the Pommeranian, the Rhenish, the Westphalian, have all been won in these modes, and the history of the acquisition of Prussian Poland is still fresh. Like many of the German States, Prussia is a disjointed country; and were one to judge only from present appearances, it would be natural to predict that another half-century anniversary would not be celebrated by the Prussian kingdom. The inhabitants of the Rhenish provinces, with their warm southern blood, their popular sympathies, their French customs and laws, are as diverse as possible from the loyal and aristocratic population of Brandenburg, or the sturdy and often chivalric farmers of Prussia, bred up only to the old German ideas. And again, the proud Polish gentry of Posen, the mechanics of Silesia, and the easy intellectual Saxons, form other as irreconcileable elements in the Prussian State. Free institutions would, we are persuaded, unite even these opposing populations. But with the present system of a centralized monarchy, we believe that parts of Prussia—especially the provinces on the Rhine—will become more and more alienated, and that any well-sustained attempt on the side of France to regain them, would, in a few years, meet there with a welcome reception.

SILESIA.

Accounts come each day, in the papers, of the sad condition of one province of the kingdom, Silesia—the *Ireland* of Prussia. No description of Prussia or of recent Prussian administration, would be complete, without some mention of the mournful history of this district.

It will be noticed on the map, that there is one point of Prussia protruding down between Poland and Austrian Silesia, to the south-east of Breslau; this forms the province of Upper Silesia.

The province, it appears, is a barren country, inhabited mostly by weavers or small farmers, professing the Catholic faith, and kept by their priests in a state of great superstition and ignorance. In 1847, their potato crop, on which they almost entirely depended, failed; and their other harvests, which had been gradually growing worse, this year were poorer than ever. They lived much during the autumn on roots and poor vegetables, and meal mingled with chalk or stone. The winter set in with an unexampled severity—and the year 1848 opened on a scene of suffering and destitution in Upper Silesia, such as the word has seldom witnessed. Men wandered haggard and starving in the streets, grasping food where they could find it. Corpses lay unburied on the way-sides. Houses were filled with the dead, and no one knew of it. And the officers of the government, who forced open the doors, not unfrequently found the famishing wife in the arms of the husband who had been dead perhaps for days. We will not go further into the details. All that is disgusting, heart-sickening in human misery, was experienced by thousands and tens of thousands in this Prussian province. The Catholic clergy labored incessantly among the sufferers, and the

"Sisters of Charity" were known, not seldom, to have slept in the snow, while going about to help the starving. But all aid was of no avail. As the spring came on, to the horrors of famine, were added the raging of a fearful pestilence, caused by the unburied dead, and the foul nourishment on which the inhabitants had lived. The priest was swept away with the sick whom he would relieve. And even the immense establishments for feeding the people, erected by the Catholic clergy, were of little use. The whole population were so weakened and hopeless, that the highest wages could not induce them to labor, and they could hardly make the necessary exertion to receive the food which was offered them. The Government, for a long time, paid no attention to the complaints from the province; and it was only, till in some districts one-fifth, and in others, nearly a half of the population, had perished, that it deigned to contribute its aid.

The causes of these terrible calamities are to be sought, as in the so strangely similar Irish sufferings, in many sources. Disproportionate taxation, division of the land into great estates, *absenteeism* of the owners, a bad government and corrupted religion, and finally, all these working on the character of the people, till they themselves became so lazy and inefficient, that no good government could save them. These, with sudden events in the natural world, may account for that terrible famine and pestilence in Upper Silesia. As I said, the Romanist clergy have been working nobly there. No sect in Prussia was found to show such self-sacrifice, such heroism, amid these scenes of pestilence and death, as these Catholics showed.

Herr Wichern, whom I mentioned in Hamburg as leading the operations of the "*Innere Mission*," has carried his indefatigable efforts even to this distant province. And strict Protestant though he be, the Catholic clergy have joined with him, and in the common society of the "Mission," they are working together for this wretched province; their especial design now is, to establish orphan asylums, as there are said to be some *ten thousand orphans* in that country. The bishop has even consented to send some of his young clergy to Wichern's *Rauhehaus* in Hamburg, for the purpose of learning his system in the management of such institutions.

The news comes to us now, (February, 1851,) of a protest of France against Austria entering the German Confederacy with all her provinces. A very natural step—as any such successful movement on the part of Austria, secures the whole German confederated army in her favor—and completely frees her from all present apprehension for Hungary or Italy or any of her disaffected states—inasmuch as a revolt in them would be a revolt against the Union of forty millions of Germans. France has no wish to see Austria thus strengthened.

A much more interesting piece of news to me is the appearance of Webster's letter to Hülsemann, in full, in the *Constitutionelle Zeitung* (Constitutional Gazette) of Berlin. It is attracting great attention, and will be read in every coffee-house of North Germany.

There is no greater infliction upon a newspaper-loving American, than the German press. No one understands, apparently, how to publish or how to edit a newspaper in Germany. The dailies in the largest cities are not one-third the size of our common country papers. There is seldom any good foreign correspondence, or foreign news, little important telegraphing, few connections with distant quarters, and no great talent in editorials. The advertising is carried on in a separate sheet often, from the reading sheet, and the great object of advertising lost. What news these journals contain, is so badly arranged and given out, that I have frequently gained a more distinct idea from articles in the London Times or Daily News, of events transpiring here, than I have from daily reading of half a dozen local papers. Except in the large cities, families seldom take newspapers; they are read in coffee-houses or club-rooms. The best journal, in my opinion, of Germany, is the Cologne Gazette (*Kölnische Zeitung*)—a bold, spirited, free-spoken journal, which has been prosecuted twice this winter by the Prussian Government. It represents the liberal constitutional feeling of South Germany. The correspondence from abroad, and the arrangement of news, seems to me much superior to that of the other German journals. In Berlin, the organ of the Ministry now is the "German Reform" (*Deutsche Reform*)—a journal of fair ability, and of course, strongly conservative. The *National Zeitung* is the democratic paper—sometimes permitted to speak a bold word; the *Constitutionelle Zeitung* is the leading constitutional paper of Prussia. This has occasionally articles of much spirit, but is usually too heavy. It takes the middle ground now between the Democratic and Governmental party, and has been strongly for war. There is also a German *Punch* in Berlin (Kladderadatsch), whose principal characteristic, is its unbounded impudence.

In Hamburg, the *Nachrichten* has a good circulation, though by no means remarkable for genius. In Southern and Austrian Germany the *Allgemeine Zeitung* (Universal Gazette) of Augsburg, has long had the greatest influence. This has been a very able journal, and for statistical and scientific articles, scarcely surpassed in Europe. Now, however, it is conducted in deadly fear of the Austrian or German police, and has lost much of its life.

The best paper of Vienna is not the most liberal—the *Lloyd's*. The editors write under the eyes of that accursed detective police, and of course, can say little to any purpose. They have been permitted to speak in financial matters, and there they have uttered new and bold truths.

American papers are seldom seen in Germany. The *Times*, of England, and that most non-committal and prudential journal, the *Galignani* of Paris, are everywhere. What American will ever forget their really home-like look in the German *cafés?* How often wearied by the strange streets outside, or by the foreign gossip within, have I settled myself down over their columns, as if for a chat with a countryman, just from home!

The influence of the *Times* throughout Europe, is wonderful, and one of its strong, practical, carefully-prepared "leaders" makes almost as strong a sensation in Germany as it does in London. The *Times* represents the great *common sense* of England more than any other paper; and it is these practical articles of it, penetrating into the bombast and idealizing which cover these German affairs, that give it such an influence—or at least make it so feared by the leaders of the parties.

CHAPTER XXX.

A VISIT TO THE CHAMBERS.

"WHAT do you say to making a call upon our Prussian Chambers?" said a friend to me one morning, as we were chatting in my room over the morning coffee. "An acquaintance of mine, one of the members, has offered me a ticket, and we can get it as we go along."

I assured him, I should like nothing better; and we at once sallied out, to be in time for a good seat.

My companion was a young merchant of some property, and an ardent, almost violent Democrat. We usually had a great deal of discussion together—agreeing very well in the main principles, but differing on detail; I finding him somewhat ultra and unpractical, and he me a little tainted with the "*verdammte Reaction*," as they call the conservative tendencies.

"There are some of those accursed soldiers again!" said he, as we came upon a company drilling in the fine avenue "under the Lindens;" "and the old 'Haùdegen' (Slasher) at the head, I believe. Think of him for our next King!"

It was the Prince of Prussia, the King's brother, a heavy-looking, stout soldier, who was cantering up and down the line with a few staff-officers.

"Tell me," said I; "these soldiers are quartered on you, are they not, whether you will or no?"

"Yes," he replied, "there were two of them put upon me last month; and I only got rid of them by paying their *Kosten* elsewhere. I hope as a citizen of Prussia, I should always be willing to support our brave army, if they were fighting for the people or the country. But now I know, they are nothing but tools of the King!"

"I hear," said I, as we passed the position of the staff, "very favorable accounts of the Prince's son. Those who know him well, tell me he is far superior to his old father. A very honest and good-hearted young man, with high purposes to benefit the nation, they say. He may make you a good King!"

"No; it is impossible," said he, "the whole kith and kin are utterly unreliable. You cannot trust them; and the best thing for Germany would be to take off the heads of the whole brood!"

I laughed at his excitement; and asked whether he would not, at least, acknowledge that the present king and his nephew, (the heir presumptive) were religious men; and were trying to spread abroad religious influence.

"No;" he answered, "it is not so. You mustn't get your views from those *Pietisten*. All the religion they care about, is to have a State Church. See what the old King did—trying to make us religious and belong to his church with the bayonet. And then take this reign. That old hypocritical tyrant, Eichhorn, (one of the State ministers) tried for years to choke all thought-freedom—and would not even appoint a school-teacher, unless he was an orthodox! The King has broken every promise he ever made to our people. It was not till four years ago, that we had the first shadow of a Constitution, though his father promised it, in 1815;

and now our "*allergnädiste*," (most all gracious) breaks it every-day. His piety is to pay preachers to delude the people!"

"What!" said I, "do you think all the preachers hypocrites too?"

"Oh no; not that. But they are paid by the King, and are naturally influenced by him; and they preach to please him. Who ever heard a word from them against tyranny, or for the oppressed, or for the victims all through Germany to these execrable princes? When did they ever speak for poor Cassel, or Holstein? They talk often enough of the '*Obrigkeiten*,' (the authorities) and the godless Socialism—and these impious attacks on religion and government; but who ever heard a free word from them? I don't believe in such religion! *I would rather have Infidelity!* We must sweep away kings and preachers, before we can be free!"

I told him, I agreed with him as to the public teachings of these men, though I liked them personally, and thought them very self-denying and good men. "It all comes," said I, "from your State Church. You must have a free voluntary church; and then you won't confuse religion, and the abuses of government together!"

"But look!" said I again, as we passed the bridge of the canal, "there's a specimen of your German practicality—just like what you are doing in Constitutions—six men doing the work of one, and all hindering one another!" The six men were engaged with poles and ropes, in pulling open the gates of the lock, a work which one Yankee would easily do with a lever.

He laughed, and admitted it; and we turned soon into the alley of the post-office, as it was hardly time for going to the Chambers. "You send passengers as well as letters by post?" said I, as we entered the court-yard, full of coaches, just ready for starting.

"Certainly. Everything—mail-coaches, rail-roads, telegraphs, are government property here."

As we walked down the narrow street from the Post-office towards the large bridge, my companion showed me with ardor the different points, where the people had forced the soldiers back in the Revolution of '48, till they retreated across the bridge to the castle.

"You see that corner house there!" said he. "Our people did almost the only violent thing, which was done in those days, on that building. There was a wretch of an officer lived there, who sheltered some of the soldiers as they hurried down the street, and let them fire on the crowd from the windows. When we reached there, the fellows were on his story in a moment—the doors broken through—and out came through the windows the fine mirrors, the pictures, the chairs, every possible article; and a great heap was made for a bonfire below. They were beginning at one room, when the servant-maid rushed in, and said it was hers; and not one article was touched! I had gone off at a little distance at the time, but I remember now of seeing one poor fellow tumbled into the heap; and then beaten and flogged by the crowd, with everything tney could lay their hands on. It seems, he was one of their own number, who was caught *thieving!*"

We now made our way to the "Chambers," and after presenting our tickets, took a good seat, near the diplomatic benches, in the gallery. The House would not meet for some half-hour yet, and we had time enough to look about. The appearance of the building outside and in, was not at all remarkable. The hall, where we were, was of oblong shape, with various galleries, a curtained box for the royal family, a slight desk and stage for the speaker, and seats for three or four hundred members. There was no very rich furniture, yet all neat and cheerful, and well-kept, and altogether, a much more comfortable hall of legislation, than the English Hall for the Commons, which I visited last year.

"There's *Vincke!* Do you see him?" said my companion, "the stout man in a snuff-colored frock-coat, with a rather important air, here in front! He's the leader of the opposition now, was one of the old Constitutionalists. You saw his speech the other day, the best we have had this session— tremendous cuts on Manteuffel!"

"And there comes *der Teufel selbst*, (the devil himself!)" It was the Prime Minister, *Manteuffel*, who entered by a side door, followed by a page, bearing his port-folio. He took his seat on a little raised platform, behind a long desk—the ministerial benches—and quietly received the members who came up to pay their respects. A little and insignificant man he is, except in the outline of his head, which shows decided intellectual power. His face has an expression of much shrewdness. This man guides now the destinies of Prussia, and probably will for years to come. He has ousted the military Radowitz, has adopted the pacific and cringing policy—and avoiding war, he has managed, even while yielding to Austria, to strengthen the material interests of Prussia. Whether all the tergiversations of his administration are to be laid to him, is doubtful. He has a difficult master—and it must need great skill to adapt his policy to the ever-changing tendencies of Frederick William.

Among the crowd, I was pointed out Beckerath, Camphausen, Count Schwerin, Prof. Tellkampf, and many other eminent members of the Liberal party.

PROF. TELLKAMPF is well known in America. He has distinguished himself this winter, in all constitutional discussions and debates on points of order, by his minute knowledge. His acquaintance with the American and English Constitutions is very exact, and stands him in good stead.

The house was at length called to order, and the members took their seats; those on the right being occupied by the friends of the ministry and those on the left, by the opposition. The members do not wear their hats like the members of the English Parliament; and in general have not so independent and careless an aspect, but seem more like a company of gentlemanly well-fed office-holders, as in fact, most of them are.

The discussion opened on the late *Press-ordinance*, enacted, as I have before explained, by the ministry in an illegal manner, while the Chambers were not in session, and completely cutting off in its workings, liberty of the press.

The discussion was rather spirited, though in general, the speaking was awkward and uneasy. Von Vincke made a short speech which was listened to with marked attention. He has all the ease and force of our best orators, and must be a very effective speaker, I should think, when thoroughly aroused.

The Ministerial party defended the Ordinance as a temporary measure, and made the usual objections to the license of the press. The Opposition attacked it, especially on the ground of its arbitrary character, and defended free speech, and urged the old promises and the guarantees of the Constitution for Freedom of the Press.

There was nothing new to an American in the discussion, except the fact that any members of a Constitutional Parliament could be found, to defend a measure, so obviously unjust and arbitrary.

This is the second Chamber, or Lower House. It dates its peculiar formation to the constitution given last year (Jan. 31, 1850). The members number 350. They are chosen by electoral colleges, made up of electors from certain fixed districts, or certain cities, numbering at least 10,000 inhabitants. The qualifications for a member are that he should be thirty years of age, in full possession of civil rights, and a resident of Prussia three years. For a voter, the conditions are a residence of one year in his parish, property to the amount of one hundred Thalers, (about $75,) or a payment of the parish taxes, and at least two Thalers of direct taxes; and furthermore that he should be of a sane mind, and twenty-five years of age. Apparently a very liberal basis of suffrage.

The First Chamber is composed of the princes of the blood, and of certain members of ancient princely families; of members nominated by royal order, whose number shall never exceed one-tenth of those chosen by the people; and of the regular representatives from the nation. Of these last, sixty are chosen by two hundred large landed proprietors in each province; thirty-eight by the common councils of the large cities, and six by the professors of each of the six universities.

After some time, spent in listening to the closing speeches on the debate, which grew more and more dull, my friend and myself left the hall, and I accompanied him to his house, for a lunch after the long fast. "The worst of it all is," said he, as we walked along, "there is such a quantity of office-holders among them. The Constitution reads well enough, but it says nothing about three-quarters of the members being in the pay of the Government. We can carry no liberal bill through, of course.

"Then we have no good hold on the king, by the purse-strings, as you have in England. To be sure, the Chambers have a nominal control of the budget—but *die dümmen!*—(the stupids!)—they don't know what it's worth, nor how to keep it. Oh die Deutsche Gutmüthigkeit! the German good nature, it is infinite!"

I spoke of my pleasure in Vincke's bearing and words. "Yes," said he, "he and the old Gotha party (the Constitutionalists) are trying all they can to undo what they did in '48 and '49. But we Democrats do not care for them. They defeated us then and brought back the Reaction, by their accursed theories. If there is another Revolution, we shall soon sweep them from the board! The only hope for Germany now is in unlimited Democracy. These half-men are not the men for the times!"

I expressed my disagreement; that these men seemed to me rational liberalists, who thought the people unfit for a Republic, and would give them what they could bear. They wanted a free constitutional government like the English. I told him I did not like to see parties separated, as they were now in Prussia. "The Democrat and the Constitutionalist ought to unite, to gain the best form of government possible under the circumstances."

"What! you a Republican, advocating these courses! You have learned this from your conservative friends here. Did you know that that Constitutional party ruined Germany, when they had everything in their own hands? They can't save us. It is too late. We have tried gentle measures long enough. No—to the devil with them all! A Republic for us!—Universal suffrage!—Free speech!—No State Church, and a chance for social reform again! This is the Democratic doctrine! You think me, perhaps, too much excited and unreasonable. But you have not been here! You have not seen all Germany buy its liberties with blood, and then entrust them to these scholars. You have not seen us wait and hope and pray, always believing that these great, learned men would work us out something, and then, at last, to find, that they were only engaged over their own selfish theories and hobbies! To forget this great crushed people in their damned professorial quibblings!—But here we are—come in, and we'll take a bite!"

We went in, and were soon over a very good cold joint, an excellent German *Wurst*, some unnameable pickles, and a flask of wine. After a busy engagement with the eatables for a few minutes, to stay our appetite, I went on to tell him, that we, in America, did not believe in that kind of Democracy. We believed in bestowing on a people what they were fit for, and in *educating* them always for the highest freedom. That our liberty was not the product of a moment, or a year—it was the fruit of generations of political habit and training. "You do not know our system," said I, "though the best explication of it ever made was by a foreigner, De Tocqueville—

"Ach yes—I have read him. But take a glass of wine before you begin your argument. It is the Cap-wine;* a very peculiar wine; I think you never saw it; sweet as Tokay."

"No, thank you, not this morning. As I said, or meant to say; this is a most thorough system of political training with us. Every village and district and state, is a distinct political school; the one represented often in the other, and each fitting for the other, so that the boy, and then the man, gets a constant training, through life, in practical politics. Our municipal constitution, as you call—"

"I see," said he, "it is precisely what Stein meant to found here in 1808, and a whole-souled man he was, even if no Democrat! But you are neglecting the joint; allow me!"

"Well," said I, "our principle is this;" and I entered on a long explanation of the American Constitution, showing its wonderful influence in political education. I then told him, that for one I should hope more from seeing that or a similar municipal constitution

* Wine from the Cape of Good Hope, occasionally drank as a cordial in North Germany; a sweet, pulpy wine.

planted in Prussia, than from the most successful revolution. "Not but that a revolution would be preferable to your present oppressions —but the only lasting liberty, I am persuaded, must spring from such institutions."

"I think you are right; but, *mein lieber*, we have tried all that. We had an excellent municipal constitution promised us, and then made out last year. But, Ich bitte—beg your pardon—light a cigar—they are the best Hamburger, though of course not equal to your American. When you get back to your rooms, just look in those documents you are poring over, and you will find that a Constitution very like the one you have sketched, was published last year. And now, where is it? The '*all-graciousest* king' reigns by the grace of God, and he never will suffer a piece of paper to come between him and his beloved subjects. He keeps it in his pocket. (He referred in these words, to an expression used by the king, in one of his speeches to the Chambers.) No, mein Herr Republicaner, there is no use! You would be a Democrat, if you were here. There is nothing to do with this *Gesindel* (rabble) but to get rid of it! Our German *Volk* will bear long, but not always. You can have no idea of the petty oppressions over the lower classes. All associations forbidden; even an evening party was broken up lately, because the dancers were Democrats and the *Gasthaus* was a liberal house. The only free sects we had, the German Catholics—your friends, the T.'s, belonged to them, you know—are declared illegal. And now we cannot own a house or peddle cigars, without being confirmed in that —— State Church. Pardon me—but it is *enough* to make a man excited!"

I asked him, after some farther discussion, in regard to the first Chamber, and the nobles, whether they were of much account. "No," he said, "they were not. No one cared for them, or respected them especially. They have not wealth or talent enough to give them influence. They make up fine liveries and carriages for the king on the *Fest* days, but the people scarcely know any one by name. The king has a pet-theory that he must be surrounded with a chivalric corps of peers. He has tried a great deal to build up a House of Lords, as in England, but without success, Gott sei Dank!" (God be thanked!)

"So," said he at length, as I rose, "you must go . . . Well; leben Sie recht wohl! and may your Fatherland never come to be like our poor Germany—the Reaction or the Revolution to choose between. Adieu."

The constitutional history of Prussia only dates four years back. The father of the present king had promised in the universal enthusiasm of Prussia in 1815, to bestow a constitution on the kingdom. The gift was delayed from year to year, by various pretexts, and at length the old king died. At the accession of the present king, in 1840, all parties confidently awaited the long-promised instrument. It was still withheld; and it was only till the increasing discontent of the people almost made it necessary, that it was finally given (in 1847.) The constitution then bestowed was framed after the feudal and chivalric principles, so favored by the king, and did not at all suit the present condition of Prussia. The Parliament was made up of the eight Provincial Assemblies, and the representatives of classes, and did not represent the people. The king evidently had no plan of founding a constitutional monarchy, but rather of establishing a feudal rule, which should rest on the loyalty, as well as the mutual antagonism of various ranks in the state.

This Constitution soon gave place to another in 1848, and then again, after further changes, to the Charter of 1850. Over this, there were long discussions between the King and Parliament. He was urgent to carry out his favorite plan of a hereditary peerage, and to make perpetual the feudal fiefs held nominally in the kingdom.

The Chambers were equally opposed to both of these aristocratic measures.

The king, at length, yielded on the fiefs; and compromised the question of the peerage, by consenting to postpone the nomination of the Lords, till August, 1852. By this Constitution, the present Chambers were granted; and the law, establishing the responsibility of the ministers.

The King in bestowing it, still made a reservation for his much loved theories of regal right.

In the course of a characteristic and eloquent speech to the Chambers, he said, "in Prussia, the King alone must govern. And I govern, not because it is my pleasure, God knows! but because it is God's ordinance. Therefore, also, I WILL GOVERN!"

The Constitution was well received; the only exception being the disposition of the Poles in Posen towards it. They demanded a distinct provincial organization to their province, incorporated since 1848, in Prussia; and not obtaining it, their deputies retired from the Chambers. The most important portion of the Constitution was, probably, that relating to the municipal regulations; published in two distinct laws, March 11, 1850; but never yet carried out into practice.

These are worth considering briefly, as constituting the best possible political reform, if they ever are realized.

The laws relating to the reform of city governments date as far back as 1808—those establishing legislatures in the Provinces, to 1823 The difficulty thus far with all these measures, had been, that they rested too much on the feudal basis, and threw the power into the hands of the country gentry. According to the new law, the government, in the first place, of the parishes (*Gemeinde*) is left with the people. Every native-born Prussian, aged 25 years, and possessing property to the amount of $75, or paying the parish taxes together with $1.50 of direct taxes, is a voter. The administration of the parish is committed to the common council, (*Gemeinde-rath*) elected by the people. This, in parishes of from 1,500 to 2,500 inhabitants, numbers twelve members ; in towns of from 90,000 to 120,000, sixty members. Beyond 120,000, the allotment is six for every 50,000. The qualification for this body is determined by property—half the members being landed proprietors. The session lasts six years, and is always public. The Council chooses the board of aldermen, (*Gemeinde-obrigkeit*) who administer the executive authority, and whose number vary according to the population. The parish has the power of changing its own internal government, by a particular statute, subject to the approval of the council of the canton, (*Kreise*). In the smaller parishes, more power is given to the lords of the manor.

Previous to these laws, as I have before said, the influence was entirely in the hands of the nobility—this was especially the case in the provincial Legislatures. By the new laws, the deputies to these bodies are chosen by the assemblies of the cantons, (*Kreisen*). Every person is qualified to be a member, who has owned property within his district for three years, or who is engaged in a profession, and aged thirty years. Every canton sends a deputy, if the population be below 60,000; if above, two ; and one for every 50,000 beyond. The Session is six years, and is public. These "State Legislatures" are at the head of the internal administration of Prussia. The royal power is represented with them by a Lord Lieutenant, (*Ober-praesident*) who is obliged to present every year, a report on the administrative condition of the province.

These Legislatures, in some provinces, have given the King already much trouble, and very probably will much more. The fiery, liberty-loving deputies in the Rhine Assembly, the independent Poles in the Assembly of Posen, and the sturdy farmers and landowners in the Province of Prussia, who are not forgetful that they form the kernel of the kingdom—have all spoken bold words these last few years against the encroachments of regal power. The Legislature of Brandenburg feels too much the influence of the court, and along with that of Pommerania, has distinguished itself by its cringing and servile attitude. The Saxon Assembly has been somewhat bolder; but the Silesian and the Westphalian again have shown the "reactionary" tendency.

Under this State government, (of the *Provinz*) come the governments of the districts, (*Bezirk*) and of the cantons, (*Kreise*). That of the districts appears to have only a minor importance. The cantons hold the principal administration, after the States or Provinces; and are in many respects, almost independent of the central power. Their administrative bodies are elected by representatives chosen by the parishes, (*Gemeinden*); and the qualifications for membership, are a house or other property within the canton, and the payment of the class-tax, (about $6); if the property lies beyond the canton, the candidate must possess an estate worth 5,000 Thalers, or have an income of 500 Thalers. In addition, he must be thirty years of age.

The especial office of these Canton assemblies is the division of taxes. They meet, also, for six years, and renew themselves every two years by a third. As they are elected by representatives from the parishes, their basis is equally popular, with that of the parishes.

The crown is represented in these bodies, by a provincial councillor, (*Landrath*) who must be heard whenever he demands it.

It will be seen from this brief sketch, that this new municipal Constitution is of a very popular nature, and though possibly a little cumbersome, is eminently adapted to train the people. It would give them, what all their schools and universities and learned men do not—*political education.*

In the various councils of parish and canton and district, in the large and stormy Assemblies of the Province, in the thousand little offices, executive and financial, which the Constitution creates, each man would gain a familiarity with political principles. The great defect, which appears now in all the German political enterprises, a want of skill in the *details* of politics—would in a few years, be very much removed by such a system. The Prussian peasant would get the idea thoroughly infused into him—of a self-administered government. He would come more and more to trust in the ballot-box, and not in the bayonet, for political reforms, and in time, we might hope that, like the Englishman or American, he would be a supporter and advocate of Self-Government, almost from instinct. In respect to such a system, I should say, what I said to my friend, that "I would hope more from its adoption for Freedom, than from all the Revolutions of a century."

CHAPTER XXXI.

A SUNDAY IN GERMANY.

My landlady came in this morning with my coffee, unusually neatly dressed, "Herr B., you must hurry! you will not be ready for the Domkirche (Cathedral)!"

"Why, what is there, this morning?"

"Did you not know? This is Lent, and we have not been to the theatre the whole week, and I have cooked puddings every day, and now there will be some beautiful music for the king, at 8 o'clock! Are you not Christians in America?"

"I thought you said you never went to church!"

"I do not usually; but now one must go for the sake of the little ones, and then you know, no one stays away in Lent!"

"Do you like Prediger Nitsch, as well as you used to?" said I, after a little further conversation.

"Yes, I do like him, but I find it hard to understand him. He seems to me the only honest one. Perhaps it isn't so, in America, Herr B., but you know here, the preachers do not believe what they say, and we all know, they do not care for us common people."

I told her I found many of them very good men indeed, and

doing much for the poor; "but what makes you think they do not believe what they say?"

"How can they? You will pardon me, for perhaps you believe so, but how can they believe that miracles ever happened. Why should we not have them now? And then who supposes God would have created us poor sinners just to be miserable always, after we die? I do not often speak of these things, mein Herr, especially before the children, but I do not believe in the God of the *Pietisten.* I have done very many foolish things, and I was a gay pretty young girl once, though you would'nt think it now; but if I should die now, I should have no fear. Perhaps that will be all of me—the dear God knows best; one thing I am sure of, He will treat me kinder than I would treat my dear little ones. I always remember what Schleiermacher said once in a funeral of a child, here, 'There is hope of a tree, that if it be cut down, it will sprout again, but man dieth, and where is he? Yet one thing we are certain of, the little one and we, are in the hands of the All-Merciful, and whether we shall exist or not, it shall be well with us!' I think so also, Herr B!"

This speech of Schleiermacher, I have often heard from others beside my landlady, so that there is probably some foundation for it; still it must have been uttered very early, as his later writings show an unwavering faith in Immortality. Our conversation I will not follow further; it was soon interrupted by the summons to the church. It was a bright, peaceful winter-like morning, as I stepped out, the fresh snow over everything, and the spires and towers of Berlin, standing up cold and distinct against the clear sky. Cheerful parties were returning from the morning concerts held in the coffee-houses out of the city, all hastening towards the Cathedral. These Sunday concerts, I understand, are to be forbidden in future, by the government, which is determined to have Sunday more strictly observed.

The walls, as usual, are all covered with placards of the grand entertainments for this evening; though, it being Lent, the King's theatre will be closed. There is much excitement, apparently, about one play which is to come off to-night—*Julius Cæsar*—as only last week an opera not nearly so democratic in its sentiments, was forbidden, and the crowd expect the police will interfere in this.

No one seemed to have any private seat in the Cathedral, and I took a good one in front. It was very cold and damp in the building. The soldiers crowded in so thickly, that very many stood up, but there was no disorder. At length the king entered the gallery dressed in his usual blue overcoat, with only one officer in attendance. The service at once began with a chant, and then a young man in a gown, apparently a *Candidat* or theological student, stepped forward on a low platform, and read the service, while the responses were made by the choir. He read appropriately, yet with deep feeling of the great wants and sorrows of the human soul, of its infinite needs, its essential weakness, its dependence, and its love for the Highest One, and the music answeredin tones of more than earthly sorrow, or of repentance, or joy, or hope. It was a sublime service, as given in that crowded Cathedral, with the best trained choir, perhaps, of Europe. I never hear a good liturgical service in any church, without being conscious of how bare is the simple form to which I have been accustomed at home. From a man of real life and feeling, prayers of the heart are beyond all forms and liturgies. But how seldom is he to be found! How much of our present church prayer, is the most utter and monotonous form and repetition, without the advantage of its being a repetition selected by the best taste, and hallowed by the associations of many centuries. Would that some new service might be framed, where the prayers of the moment, of the heart's feeling, might be mingled with prayers, culled from the Bible and from the best aspirations of the holy men of the past.

Our preacher was one of the regular chaplains, and appeared to view in a high box or pulpit, in another part of the building. He opened with a short introduction, then read his text, and then preached from memory. The sermon was a quaint one, upon the subject of *Sampson's life*, the object being to draw an analogy between the history of Prussia and the experiences of Sampson! The contamination of the people by French influence under Frederick the Great; the merging of their own morals and taste into the French, and the subsequent degeneration, and disgrace under the French rule, was found pictured in the sinful intercourse of Sampson with the heathen. "He took a wife from the Philistines." His principles were injured and his strength weakened by this union, and he fell utterly into their hands. Still, through it all, he retained his faith in God, and this, at length, wrought out his salvation. So with their dear Fatherland. Through all those years of weakness and dishonor, she still held, in some degree, to the Faith, and when finally, she was delivered, it was because Infidelity and French sensuality were repented of, and the people believed in God again. Sampson, still later, fell into the hands of the Philistines, and again, through his intercourse with the Philistine harlot. So with Prussia. She will not keep herself from the Delilah of French infidelity, and socialism, and falsely-called Freedom. Again, like Sampson, she has fallen in these late days of the Revolution, into the hands of the Philistines, and "who shall say, whether she shall escape, like the Jewish leader, only by her own ruin? "Meine geliebten!—beloved! these are dark days for Prussia! A godless, heathenish spirit is abroad. Men are seeking to uproot all Law and Religion! They cry Liberty, but they are really seeking license, indulgence. The people do not believe on a God, they do not respect their lawful rulers. They revile the church. See the excesses of the Revolution, and see here, what they have resulted in. Look at these outbreaks in Hesse-Cassel and in other parts of Germany. Blood and disorder, and irreligion, are the fruits. These are what the Socialists, the Revolutionists, and all who are stirring up the ignorant crowd, seek. No, to have true liberty, we must return to the Faith of our Fathers, we must learn to honor our rulers, we must attend to the instructions of the clergy. In every way, we must be separate from this French Delilah—the Socialism and Unbelief—then only will strength return unto our poor Fatherland!"

The sermon was listened to with profound attention, and was really eloquent in many passages. It was followed by a hymn and short prayer, and the congregation broke up.

As I was walking home, I was joined by a young gentleman, an acquaintance, who is at the head of a manufacturing business of some extent; not a man of University education, but of quick intelligence. We spoke of the sermon, and its quaint analogies, and at length he said, "I do not know how you feel, Mr. B., but such sermons sicken me of the Bible!"

I told him I detested them.

"There was not one generous or noble word," said he, again, "in the speech for these millions of poor, oppressed men in Germany. He spoke as if the whole of these immense wrongs rested on the ignorant and degraded people. He did not even mention the promises which have been broken over and over by these princes; nor the deception and injustice practised so long by our rulers. Who has made the people degraded? Who keeps them so? One would think from him that the masses had no rights."

"And that allusion to Cassel," said I, "seemed to me base, and ungenerous and false."

"I am glad you think so. But these things are what we hear all the while. There has not been a wrong or an act of tyranny these last ten years, which these men have not supported from the Bible. And, for my part, I have come to abhor much of the Bible. If it upholds a system like this, I shall not wish to know more of it."

I told him I was sorry he felt so about the Bible. To me, its spirit seemed to be the very spirit of liberty, and for myself, the highest aspirations I had ever had of human freedom, I believed prompted by it. My most ideal dreams, I said, of what humanity might at length attain to—the highest possible perfection to which society could progress—were always only the realizing of the simple words of Jesus. This has always been to me, said I, the proof of the divine origin of Christianity, much more than miracles or historic evidence.

He acknowledged this was true of the New Testament, but the Old, which these preachers used so much, "How did that answer my conceptions of progress?"

I told him that I looked on it, in the main, as a history of the first development of the race, where complete growth was not to be expected. "Yet, even there," said I, "I find ideas and pictures of human progress, far beyond that age or any age since. That grand Future of Justice and Love for mankind, which Isaiah paints, is beyond even our highest theories. Yes, and nothing to me so completely foreshows what the purest of your patriots in Europe might feel. Kossuth, for instance—"

"Kossuth is no Democrat!"

"Well, any who hate oppression and long for liberty. Nothing, I say, so sounds like what they ought to speak, as the words of these Jewish prophets—that passionate love for their country, through all the dark days of oppression—that hope irrepressible of liberty for their native land, and thus for the world, and the belief never to be shaken in the God of justice, and in a happy Future for humanity. Is not all this fully equal to the spirit of our nineteenth century? Isn't it a great way beyond your cowardly German faith in progress?"

He confessed it had never struck him quite in that light. "But," said he, "I cannot escape my early prejudices. I do not desire to disbelieve. I sincerely long for some support to faith, but, as I have little time to study, my impressions of the Bible are mostly taken from the teachings of these men. And now I cannot separate them from their arguments for tyranny and injustice. I know it is not reasonable; possibly it would not have been so, if I had been brought up in America; but now the Bible seems to me an instrument of priestcraft. My first emotion towards it, as I see these tremendous wrongs among my poor people, is almost of indignation. And I find many of my workmen have the same feeling, or if they have not consciously, it affects them, and they prefer beer-drinking to hearing such things. I always argue against them, when they say anything, yet I must confess to thoughts of the same kind."

I told him I was very sorry that he should have been forced to such a view of the Bible, but that he must leave these (to him) "blind guides," and study for himself. I thought our American Liberty was planted on the Bible, and if he would only look, he would see that the spirit of Christ everywhere is the spirit of liberty.

Such are the views I hear throughout Germany, from the honest-minded and the earnest; the seekers for truth and lovers of freedom. I respect the Protestant clergy of Germany; they are, in general, self-denying, laborious men, who have certainly not entered on their profession with any motives of selfish advancement or ease. But I cannot avoid seeing that they are losing their hold on the heart of the people. Their connection with the State, their associations, their education, unite them to the upper, not to the lower classes. They do not sympathize with the people. They are not "with the age," and the age will leave them.

When the next Revolution comes in Germany, as come it will, woe to the Protestant clergy! The storm which is gathering against royal power, and the privileged class, and the accumulated abuses of ages, will burst fearfully on them also. It will be found that they have built on the sand.

Clergymen in America! This is a fact worth considering by you. Your influence over the American people has been great; greater, perhaps, than the moral influence of the clergy has ever been in any land. It has been gained by the deep-seated conviction among all, of your sincerity, of your unwavering love of Liberty, of your hearty sympathy with human progress. It is remembered, that your body led the Puritans, that you aroused the people, and even led them in the struggle of the Revolution; that you have stood first ever since in the promoting of social reform, and the defence of genuine Freedom! For this, you have the full confidence and affection of the nation.

But if the time ever comes, in which your Order is found siding with the powerful against the weak; if from motives of paltry fear, or of caution, or of selfish interest, you are seen upholding wrong, however legalized and sanctioned; if the voice which has so often rung for Freedom, is heard on the side of oppression; if the holy influence of your office, the sanctions of the Word which you teach, are turned to support the strong in high places, and to press down the helpless—then is your influence over the American heart gone! Nor is that all. If Religion and the Bible are made to excuse or defend Tyranny—"away with the Bible!" will be the cry. And we shall have an Infidelity wide-spread, worse even than the German—because all the best impulses of the age will gather around it.

Let us be warned in time.

In the afternoon of this Sabbath, I attended a meeting of the Baptists, in a distant part of the city—quite as simply conducted as the services of our least formal sects; and with an air of unassumed sincerity and spirituality. After this, I took that pleasantest of all walks, the Sunday evening walk in the park, adjoining the city—the *Thiergarten*. Many parties were out enjoying the bracing winter air; but on the whole, not especially gay or noisy. There seems much less dissipation on Sunday, in Protestant than in Catholic Germany. In the evening, I was invited to a friend's, Pastor L——, a man much beloved in Berlin for his simple Christian character, and well known for his talents. There was some pleasant singing of hymns by the family—those earnest old German hymns—in the early part of the evening; and about eight o'clock, we sat down to supper. Dried goose flesh, *Wurst*, tongue with bread and butter made the principal part, followed as a close by a large pudding with a cup of tea to each. We were a long while eating, and still longer talking. At length, the things were cleared away; a huge punch-bowl was brought in, the pipe filled for the Pastor, and a cigar offered me, and the cups being passed around, the long conversation of the evening began.

I spoke in the course of it, of the hymns they had been singing; how very expressive and heart-felt they seemed to me. Yes, they said, the old hymns were a treasure to their people, only next to the Bible. "They have become so identified with various parts of our lives, that we cannot do without them. This hymn for instance has been sung at thousands of death-beds.

"'Mein Jesus ist mein Leben, und Sterben mein Gewinn; ihm hab Ich mich ergeben, in Friede fahr ich hin.'

"Have you Americans hymns, that you love so much? We Germans, perhaps, feel music more than you."

I told him, I thought that our people had a great love for music, though of course they were not so cultured in it, as the Germans. And I believed the most intellectual part of us, felt the music in church-service quite as much as the ignorant, "for it is the language of the heart, and the head is not offended by it, as in many of our religious forms."

"To which of your sects do you belong, Mr. B.?" said Madame

"To the *Independenten*," I answered, and then attempted to explain the position of our Congregational churches—"*selbst-ständige Gemeinden*," as I called them.

"Are they Lutheran or Reformed?" was the next inquiry. Their creed was more from Calvin, I said, though we did not make the same division as in Germany.

"Is not the splitting up into so many sects a great evil with you, in America?" they asked. "It does not seem right that the Church of Christ should be so divided!"

I replied, that if these sects were rivals, or were continually quarrelling, or if they felt each that the other was out of the church, it would be so. But as it is now, they only represent a few of the infinite differences of the human mind. "You here in Germany, in the United Church, are in fact just as much divided; that is, if you are honest. You yourself, Herr Pastor, have told me of the very great difference of opinion in the German Church, in regard to the doctrine of eternal punishment, and I think, if you ask each thinking man, you will find quite as great a variety here of theological views, as are shown by our sects."

They allowed it would probably be so.

"What surprises us most here in Germany, about America," said the pastor, "is that you sustain so religious a state and such a steady *self-government*—for we have taken that word into German—when you are getting from Europe all our wildest elements. You have our proletairiat, our escaped convicts, our reddest Republicans, our Socialists and Jesuits. I myself hardly believe the American Republic can last, with such a continual pouring in of these classes."

I told him the fiery Revolutionists cooled down there very fast, having as much as they could do, to earn their "*bŭtter-brod*," and besides, finding nothing which needs revolutionizing. "And as for the immigration of your proletairiat, your paupers and your rogues, it is an awful evil; but for my part, I am glad that there is one land where the man who has gone wrong before, can start afresh. We do not want the refuse of your prisons on our shores, but we do offer hope to the outcast again, and if his influence is bad, with God's aid we will meet it."

"*Gut!*—good!"—said they all; "a health to your Fatherland!"

"Thank you! I think," I added, "you are under some mistake in regard to our Socialists. I find every one here looks on them as the worst people."

"What! You do not think that there is anything good in Socialism?"

"Certainly I do. Socialism as Communism, the voice of common sense everywhere condemns. And it is very plain, that Europe has passed its sentence on the Socialists, as a party. Perhaps those in Europe may be worse men than ours in America. But I think with us, the movement will have its good effects. Our Socialists especially advocate the raising up of brute labor, by uniting it with Capital and making it responsible. And you will find in many of our manufactories the workmen holding shares of the stock. They encourage Association, too, especially for those who cannot protect themselves. Then, for my part, I think it good, particularly in our crowded cities, that they preach up so continually the advantage to *every man* of owning land, and through its great advocates in the *New York Tribune*—have you seen this journal?"

"No; the only American papers we ever see here are the New York Herald, and the Staats Zeitung."

"Well, through the articles of that paper, though very few agree with its theory, much attention has been drawn to the laboring classes. We begin to feel more the claims and rights of the poor. You understand? We are not Socialists; but many of us think there are truths in this Socialist movement."

"But do you not at least fear the Catholics?" said the pastor. "We are in much alarm here in Prussia. Some report—though I do not credit it—that His Majesty himself is influenced by the Jesuits. And we hear that they are making great advances in the Rhenish provinces. Will not the enemy soon be in like a flood everywhere, even in your free land? I fear it, mein Freund."

I answered that many good people feared it with us. I did not. Jesuitism was behind the age; "and if it ever influences America, it must be very different from what it has been."

"Ach!—you don't know it as we do, Herr B——. It changes everywhere."

"But, *Vater!*" said one of the children, "you must not forget to let der Herr B. tell us about the Indian chief, he promised. To think that he has really seen the *Indianer*—only they are very often not at all as Cooper makes them, and he says that they wear old hats and long coats, like other people. Do tell us, Herr B.!"—and accordingly I am drawn into a long description of a poor tribe I once saw and its chief. "Oh! how hard it must be for them to leave the old hunting-grounds!" they all say at the close; and the *Frau Mutter* half brushes away a tear, as she thinks of the sad lot of the exiles, and the pastor says solemnly, "God will hold your Fatherland accountable!"

"But tell us more, Herr B.," the children say, as they cluster around me, "about the great steamboats you told us of once, which have so many thousand people in, and the cars with sofas and fire-places, and the buffaloes and all that. We want to hear again!" So I spin another long story, when, at length, it is time for the children to go to bed. We all leave the table for the other room, and family prayer is held; a short, heart-felt exercise, breathing with love and charity and child-like dependence on the Giver of all their mercies. The children embrace "the father" and me, and are taken up stairs. I say a few words of parting, kiss the hand of the Frau Mutter, and am conducted to the outside door by the pastor, where he kisses me on both cheeks, "Gott sei mit Ihnen!" (God be with you!)—*Gute Nacht!*—and I return home. The Sunday has been a happy one to think of, though after all, there are no church services like those in one's native tongue.

The sermons, as usual, have disappointed me. Since I have been in Europe, I have listened faithfully to the preaching in the countries of the highest culture, and I am satisfied that in that mode of influencing men, the European nations are not at all equal to us. It is not only in a *facility* of speaking—which is much more generally possessed by our people than by any other unless the Hungarian—that I find this inferiority, but in the genial sympathy with humanity, and in the thorough intellectual cultivation of oratory, by which alone a great part of the community can be reached. In Scotland, where the preachers have a greater influence than in any other country of Europe, the sermons are models of consistent and thorough logic; and I know nothing more interesting than the sight of a Scottish audience, settling itself down with such an air of comfortable enjoyment, to the hearing of a lengthy discussion on some of the driest, *knottiest* points of a technical theology. Still, with all this, and though the Scottish oratory is often of a very effective kind, and the Scottish clergymen of the Free Church, since that grand, noble act of "Separation," take a position which no other clergymen in Europe can take, it will be found that their preaching has very little hold of great masses in the community. The sympathies of the preachers are not with the immense classes of the poor and degraded. The Scottish religious thought is trammeled by systems. The ministers denounce from the pulpit, and they lay down their dogmas; but, as they themselves confess, there are large classes, both of earnest, inquiring minds, and of degraded, sunken characters, whom they never at all influence.

In England, oratory is by no means so generally cultivated as with us; and sermonizing in the Church has become often a mere form, while in the Dissenters, it is not generally supported by the highest culture, or most thorough labor. At least, that was my impression in England. The French pulpit oratory is often very touching and beautiful; full of an affectionate earnestness—sometimes not sufficiently chaste; but usually showing much pathos and poetry; a style, which under a free-church system, might be developed into a very effective means of influence.

In Germany, there are two distinct styles of preaching, so far as I have observed—a very abstract and obscure style, and a superficial and "popular," the latter much predominating. Whether this is owing to the fact that the preachers must address so many very ignorant people, or to some deficiency in "*the practical*" in the German character, I do not know; but certain it is that the German preaching, at least in Prussia and Saxony, is usually inferior in intellectual power, and very little adapted to make any lasting impression on any one. The sermon is a well-meaning religious exhortation, not well delivered—for the Germans are seldom good speakers—but pathetic to the weaker part of the audience, and sometimes flowery. For deep and earnest thought, which penetrates men's minds and rests there; for the eloquent expression of the preacher's own life and experience, one must not go to the usual German preaching; and, quite naturally, there is very little interest among the majority of the community in preaching.

The best pulpit orators I heard, were Dr. Tholuck, Wichern of Hamburg, and one or two of the Berlin pastors. I would not take it on myself to say where exactly the preachers are at fault; for very many things are to be considered, in an old country, with almost hopelessly ignorant classes like this. But such, in general, is my impression of German preaching.

CHAPTER XXXII.

THE UNION OF THE GERMAN CHURCHES.

THE traveller in Germany will find himself with surprise, on entering certain Protestant churches, under a form of worship which seems to him scarcely to differ from the Catholic. The clergyman is going through with similar manifold genuflections and movements to and fro, before the altar, or is singing passages of the worship with his back to the audience; candles are burning before the crucifix at mid-day; there are old pictures over him and images of saints on the walls, and everything reminds him of the church whose power has always been in her striking and sensual ceremony.

Again, he will enter other churches and join in a worship plain and simple as the simplest to which he has been accustomed in any land. A prayer, a hymn sung by the congregation, the sermon, and the closing blessing—and then perhaps will flash upon him the history and the opposing tendencies of those two minds who have left their ineffaceable impress on every nation of Christendom—LUTHER and CALVIN,—and he will see that he has been standing before the embodiment of their thoughts and feelings, in the forms of the "Reformed" and the "Lutheran" churches. If he should carry his researches still farther, he will find, especially in North Germany, churches where both the modes of worship he has seen before seem combined—where the "wafer" is not used at communion, but the candles still burn at the altar; where the clergyman sings the service, but the service itself is "Reformed;" where the creed speaks of Calvin and the ceremonies of Luther; and then, on inquiry, he will learn for the first time, with surprise at his ignorance—if he be in my own situation—that these forms are the results of a most important religious Movement, which has been going on for more than a century in North Germany, and which has called out more bitter feelings and at the same time more ardent hopes, than any other religious movement of the age—a movement whose thorough success would have changed the whole aspect of the German Protestant Church: I mean the attempt for the *Union of the Reformed and Lutheran Churches.*

I wish in this chapter to enter into an examination of these efforts for a Union, both because of their very important influence on the present state of the German Church, and because of the very little knowledge there is generally on the whole subject.

In doing this, it is not necessary that I should speak at any length of the differences of these two churches, or of the minds which founded them.

Luther, we all know, clung to the Past, loved a strong mingling of "the material" in his worship, and could not avoid a tone of mysticism in his creed; Calvin and his school were men more of the new times—men of clear intellect, of abstraction, of progress.

They do not seem to me either of them to have been so much opposed to one another, as rather to have represented different sides of the human mind. We are all Calvinists or Lutherans, almost by nature, and sometimes we become one or the other, as our years or our circumstances change. For my part, I must say my sympathies are always with the Lutheran and my practice with the Cal vinist. I should like to believe with such men as LUTHER, and COLERIDGE, and BUSHNELL, that there was a mystic, mysterious influence in the partaking of the Lord's Supper, deeper and more sacred than that from a mere "memorial;" or with Melancthon, that an unseen power acted in Baptism, which made it something more than a "symbol." I could hope that their belief would prove the true one;—but it will not stand the cold touch of Reason; it does not fit the "compasses of Logic"—and I must doubt. Yet those are the minds which are much the most interesting, with whom one can have the deepest sympathies, whom one can most love, but with whom, alas! one cannot *think*.

To understand this subject of the "Union," it will be necessary to go into historical detail somewhat, and the research will necessarily be dry. Yet this detail is indispensable to understanding the present condition of religious parties in Germany, and it opens an important movement, in regard to which there is very little known in America, among those who ought to be much better informed.

The dissensions between the Lutheran and Reformed churches in Germany, had been now almost for centuries one of the crying evils of the Protestant Church. Theological bitterness and controversy had well nigh exhausted itself over the points of difference. Churches had been severed which should have acted together in the same great cause; and the contest had reached such a height among the common children of the Reformation, that not only the preachers of one side would not interchange with those of the other in performing church services, but that even Lutheran families would not associate or intermarry with Reformed. It was not till the eighteenth century, that any great effort was made to heal these dissensions. Princes had occasionally issued proclamations, but it was always found that "Orders from Cabinets" had very little influence over the *odium theologicum.* At length, in 1730, the Centennial Festival of the Reformation, or rather of the formation of the Augsburg Confession, took place, and it was anxiously desired that all parties should join amicably in it. Accordingly the preachers from both churches publicly recommended the two parties, "in speaking and writing, to preserve theological prudence and suitable moderation and calmness, and to avoid all abusive expressions or invectives against those related in the Faith!"

At this Festival, several distinguished men ventured to speak out in favor of a union of the two parties. The son of Bishop Jablonski boldly asserted that "the difference of opinion did not concern the ground of Faith." More impressively still, a certain Dr. Töllner, in his Miscellaneous Theses, declares that "the easiest and most attainable means of union, was a common *Declaration,* that the difference of opinion is no essential ground of separation between the two churches, and that they should unite in the great ideas of the Reformation." All these efforts by prominent men, and the general friendly influence of such a festival, had a good effect in preparing the minds of the people for a nearer union hereafter of the opposing sects. At the close of the century many other voices were raised with the same object; and among them that of Kösler, of Epping, in a somewhat remarkable appeal: "We have a great, an immortal work before us, which in earlier and later times the most celebrated philosophers, princes and kings, have attempted in vain—the *unity of Lutherans and Reformed,* or rather the melting together of both these Protestant religious parties into one. Calvin and Luther shall embrace before the altar of Religion, break their shepherds' staves, and deliver over the sceptre to the Genius of Protestant Freedom alone! The names 'Reformed' and 'Lutheran' shall die away (*verhallen*) forever, and only the name of 'Protestant' be given and taken," &c., &c.

In 1800, an address of Simon Van Alpen appears to have pro duced much effect, wherein he says: "Of no giving up of this or that doctrine, no yielding of this or that sect, is the talk; and as little would we introduce a community of goods, or melt together the means of the different parties. No; we will only think upon this, how good and beautiful it is to be in union. We will only work for toleration, for sociality, for harmony of spirit, but never *force* Faith—Unity!"

At this time, as the result of all these efforts and perhaps of greater enlightenment, there began to prevail a much more friendly spirit between the two churches. The preachers interchanged in church services and even in celebrating the Communion, and the families of one party were known not unfrequently to intermarry with those of the other. There seemed hardly an objection in some places to a formal union, except in the difficulty of arranging the property of the various denominations. In these years, too, Herder uttered his voice for the uniting of the sects, though warning that "only two things can unite opposing religious parties—*Time and Truth!*"

Here, in the beginning of this century, came the sweep of war over Germany, and began the long years in which the power and the laws of a foreign conqueror were fastened upon Germany. The immediate effect of Napoleon's "Confederation of the Rhine," by its prostrating all religious sects to the same level and bringing them all under the same laws, was undoubtedly to unite and soften their differences of doctrine. But the greatest influence arose from the nature of those wonderful events during the first years of the nineteenth century. The common sufferings of Germany, the long years of disgrace, the sudden, inspirited, almost religious uprising against the French, the well nigh miraculous deliverance, all conspired to deepen the religious feelings throughout the land. Even in the complicated diplomatic negociations of 1815, and in the later Conferences, there is a religious tone manifest, which is very singular indeed, and which, if we consider the astounding deceptions of the princes at the time, we might regard as mere hypocrisy. But the inconsistencies of human nature are manifold, and we are justified perhaps in believing that, even here, there was a basis of truly religious feeling. With this general state of feeling through Germany, as the Centennial Festival of the Reformation in 1817 drew near, the desires increased among all parties for a nearer union of the churches. A day of truer freedom and unity seemed dawning for Germany,—why should not the common disciples of the Reformation, pitted against one another so long in fierce contest, at length join hands over their common principles? What better expression of gratitude to God for His dealings with Germany, than this harmony of His servants?

These feelings, strong and deep, were wonderfully increased that year by an "Appeal," made by the king of Prussia with reference to the Union, to the various "Consistories" of the monarchy. This "Appeal" is the basis of all the subsequent proceedings in Prussia. We will extract briefly from it:*

"Already have my enlightened predecessors—now resting in God—Prince John Sigismund, Prince George William, the Great Prince, King Frederick II, and King Frederick William II, made

* I copy these extracts from an old newspaper of the year 1817, containing the Appeal in full. And I would say here, that the details given in this chapter are taken from a great variety of histories and newspapers, or gathered from conversation with those well-informed on the subject—as indeed no comprehensive account of the whole movement exists, so far as I know.

the attempt with pious earnestness, as the history of their lives and governments prove, to unite into one Evangelical Christian Church the two separate Protestant Churches, the Reformed and the Lutheran. * * * * *

"Such a true religious unity of both churches, as yet only separated by outward differences, is suitable to the great objects of Christianity; it answers the first views of the Reformers; it lies in the spirit of Protestantism; it is healthy to household piety; it will become the source of many useful improvements, often only hindered by the difference of confessions, both in churches and schools.

* * * * * *

"But much as I must desire that the Reformed and Lutheran churches in my kingdom should share with me this my well-tested conviction, yet equally far am I, in my regard for their rights and freedom, from wishing to force them or to determine their choice in any degree in this matter. This union can only have a true value, if neither indifference nor persuasion have a share therein, if it comes from the freedom of individual conviction, and is not a unity of outward form alone, but a unity of heart." * *

We will not follow it through farther. Suffice it to say, it contains the most admirable principles of church unity, is written in a lovely tone of toleration and of true Christian feeling, and forms, in connection with succeeding events, one of the most beautiful instances in history of the utter contrast between the public professions of princes and their actions. However, at the time it made a great impression, and the long-wished for Union seemed to many at length close at hand.

Schleiermacher took up the subject with great earnestness, and with him, as presiding officer, a synod of Berlin preachers from both churches met to adopt suitable measures. The king had already made known his intention of celebrating this Festival of the Reformation, by uniting the two court churches of the different sects into one "Evangelical Christian" Church, and partaking with them in common of the Lord's Supper. In agreement with the above, this Synod decided that in the parishes the names "Reformed" and "Lutheran" should no more be applied to the different churches, but the name "Evangelical Christian," and that they would all unite at once in the communion—the only change in this last being, that bread should be used instead of the wafer, and that simply the words of Christ should be said, "Take, eat, this is my body," &c. Still, it was added, that both in this union and in this change of ceremony no change of doctrine or uniting of confessions was implied, and that no one who joined them should be considered as having left his own church. At the same time notice was given that the *Candidats* in Theology who presented themselves for examination before the Consistory of this church, could be of either Confession.

The "Union" was now an organized thing. There was a "United Evangelical Christian Church" in Prussia. Thus far, matters had gone on well. Before the assembling of the synod, the uniting seemed almost a natural process; but with the proceedings of this body began many objections to arise. It was noticed, with distrust, that very many of those most prominent in the efforts for the union, were men of no especial earnestness of Christian character. The harmony in many quarters seemed very much like the harmony of indifference. It was urged too, with much force, that the union was a merely apparent union—a melting together of ceremonies which never would have differed from each other, unless they had represented different opinions. Time, it was claimed, would have done much more for true union. The Berlin synod had been in too much haste to pluck the fruit. Despite these querulous voices, the king was determined to carry the matter through, and accordingly, in 1821, issued a public "Church-Service" (*Agende*), which he ordered to be adopted in the "Court Church" and cathedral of Berlin, and which he recommended to the other parishes of Prussia. The service here recommended is the one, with some slight modifications, at present used by all the united churches in the kingdom, and it may not be superfluous to examine it briefly.

It will be remembered that the Reformed churches of Germany early simplified their form of worship as much as possible, while Luther, in the churches under his influence, preserved many of the traits of the old Romish ceremony. Still more than the Lutheran worship, did the form in the Church of England approach the Roman Catholic form, while the creed of that church leaned to that of the Reformed. Accordingly in this new Prussian Church-Service the model taken is the service of the Church of England, with the design of satisfying both parties in the German Church. The great points of difference between this and the old Lutheran form, are in the words spoken at the Lord's Supper, and in the change of certain expressions in the Litany. Various passages, too, which appeared to smack too much of the "old orthodoxy," in this new form are modernized. At the breaking of bread, under the Lutheran service, it is said, "*This is* the true body of Christ Jesus, which shall strengthen us," &c. In the United-Service, "Our Lord and Holy One Jesus Christ *speaks*, 'This is my body,'" &c. In the Old, in the prayer, "As we now purpose to celebrate the Supper of our Lord, wherein *he has given us his flesh for food, and his blood for a drink*," &c. But in the New, merely "As we now intend to hold a *memorial-meal*, which has been established by Him for the strengthening of our faith," &c.

The Lutheran exorcism at baptism, "Depart, thou unclean spirit, and give place to the Holy Spirit!" becomes "Let the spirit of impurity give place to the Holy Spirit!"

The forswearing of the devil under the old form by the baptized, in three separate questions and answers, is simplified into "Dost thou deny the Wicked (*Bösens*, which may mean either a person or a thing) in all its (or *his*) works and being?"

Our limits will not allow us to go more particularly into an examination of this service. Suffice it to say all the old expressions with reference to inherited depravity are softened, all allusions to the existence of Satan as a being are carefully rooted out, together with the Lutheran belief of the *bodily presence* in the bread and wine at the Supper. The whole has besides a much more *modern* look than the Lutheran services, and is filled with more expressions of homage and obedience to the king, "the highest bishop," than are the former.

The official publication of this church-service, and the prospect of its soon being forced upon the nation, at once aroused all the old slumbering spirits of controversy. From far and near, from Lutherans* and Reformed, from the Unionists themselves, came the attacks on this new mode of worship.

* Among the very strong opposers of this service, at this time, was Steffens, and as he was a man of feeling and vigorous thought, it may give an idea of what modern *Lutheranism* is, under its best forms, to quote some of his thoughts on the "Communion Supper."

"Through the communion the whole mystery of Redemption sinks in its rich fullness into the feeling personality. * * * * What Christ believes, what impregnates his whole life, what overpowers death—this becomes by the sanctifying presence of the Redeemer (in the Communion Supper) Certainty, Enjoyment, Nourishment. Only he who knows the being of Love (and *he* only knows it who has *lived* it) can comprehend this inner Inspiration. All that we think and will, every lurking idea of the spirit

The Lutherans disliked it because it omitted their peculiar doctrine with regard to the Communion, and because of its modern half-rationalistic tone. The Reformed could not endure the Romish customs it enjoined—of singing at the altar, and burning candles before the crucifix, and the half Catholic arrangement of the liturgy. The indifferent objected to the King's assuming to himself the ecclesiastical power, and among the Unionists, one who had been most prominent in the first movement—Schleiermacher—came out with characteristic boldness, and denied that this *jus liturgicum* was included among the royal rights; in other words denied that the king had the right to prescribe in what way his people should worship. All the opposition, however, could not delay the progress of the "*Agende.*" In four years, it was adopted by nearly 6000 churches in Prussia; the government requiring a direct yes or no, as to its reception, from every preacher. And in 1826, directly against all the beautiful principles of toleration put forth by the king in the beginning, it was forced upon every parish under governmental influence. In 1830 it became the legalized mode of worship in the National Church.

One would have supposed that this would have at length settled the subject of the "Union." Bnt it was very far from doing so. The great question now arose what peculiarly the Union was? Was it merely a union of ceremonies? If so, what was it worth, and how could ceremonies be changed without in some degree im-

everything which we gaze at and enjoy, as great and noble—body and soul, pressing themselves through to a higher spiritual union, step to meet the present Holy One. All which he was and will be to the world: all which he taught and suffered, forms itself anew in us. His words are HIMSELF—are Spirit and Life."

"I am no theologian, * * * but the Communion Supper seems to me the highest, the most important, most mysterious of all religious acts.'

plying a change of the opinions which they represented? Was it a union of creeds? But this idea, it was well known, was strongly deprecated by some of the most strenuous supporters of the measure. Besides, if it was such a uniting of opinions, what was now the common basis? Was it the Augsburg Confession, which was the only one on which they could appear to be in harmony? But here, there was the insurmountable objection that the Lutherans held to a different form of the Confession (*invariata confessio*) from that recognized by the Reformed (*variata.*) Beside all this, the difficulty arose as to the point whether the United Church was the National Church or not. The supporters of the movement claimed nationality for it, as vehemently as the opposers denied. So that now there was not only fierce dispute on the question *what* the Union was, but *where* it was. To these endless quarrelings over the long hoped for "harmony," was added the intense opposition of the "old Lutherans," who would have nothing to do with the Union, who abhorred it as our Puritanic ancestors would have abhorred being "united" into the Church of England. In Silesia and Breslau, this opposition rose to a determined resistance. And here the king, forgetting the beautiful sounding principles which he had uttered in the beginning of the movement, proceeded to *drive* the opposing sects into a union; "united" clergymen were installed over unwilling congregations by companies of infantry, and those who would not "harmonize" were sent to prison, or driven to foreign lands, to acquire a more fraternal disposition.

So vanishes the beautiful dream of Christian Unity! The king, however, still continued his efforts, and in 1834 issued the "Cabinet Order," on which the present dispositions of the Prussian Church rest. According to this document the Union is a matter of free resolve; the reception of the new Church-Service does not include the Union in itself: and furthermore, churches that wish the pastors about to be placed over them pledged on the "Augsburg Confession," are allowed this privilege.

But we will quote a passage—

"The Union purposes and intends no giving up of the previous Confessions of Faith, nor is through it the authority, which the confessional writings of both churches have thus far had, in any way abrogated. By the connection with it, will only the spirit of moderation and mildness be expressed, a spirit which would not let the difference of single points of doctrine in the other Confession, be held as a ground for denying it outward churchly society."

The last movement of any importance with reference to this matter, is the assembling of the "General Synod" in Berlin in 1846. Nothing, however, of the existing relations of the churches was changed by this body. Their efforts appear to have been directed to an ingenious and benevolent plan for jointing together a Union by the aid of a double-meaning Confession. For instance, in the "Ordination-formulary" proposed by them, in the expression "God the Father and the Son," &c., the *comma* is introduced after "Father," with the design of leaving the liberty to those who wished of applying the name "God" to the Father alone. And in respect to Christ, the word "*Self-privation*" (*Selbstentäusserung*) is used, and the words, "of the glory which he had with the Father," are expressly left out. Throughout this form for Ordination, Scripture terms are as much as possible alone employed, so that the preacher who pledges himself to them may apply his own interpretation. The object of the Synod seems to have been, by means of such an elastic Confession, to bring all the clergymen under one union, and then to have allowed each church to propose its own particular form of faith, (if it so desired) to the candidate for Ordination. The plan fell through, however, and the present Prussian Union rests on the legal basis of the "Cabinet Order" of 1834.

An apology, perhaps, is due to the reader for carrying him through such a mass of dry detail. But it is only by these historical facts that the present condition of the Prussian Church can be understood; the parties into which it is divided, and the hopes and feelings which have gathered long and which still exist in connection with these parties. It is believed, too, that the facts here presented are exceedingly difficult to obtain in any clear and compact form, even in Prussia itself.

It will be seen, that the result, after all, of these many governmental efforts to unite the opposing sects is a failure. There is no more real unity than there was in the old days of bitter controversy. What harmony there is, either began before government put in its aid, or is the result of the present wide-spread indifference to the whole subject of religion and its ceremonies. Lutheran and Reformed, indeed, worship often now under the same forms, but either holding different beliefs of certain dogmas, or with no earnest belief whatever. Probably the next generation, brought up in this "Unity," will be entirely indifferent to the theological controversies of their fathers. But whether this harmony, connected as it is with that *deadness* of religious life always the effect of governmental interference, is of any value, is a question.

Another great result is the important ecclesiastical power allowed the king by the Union. With his right as "Patron," of appointing the clergymen to a great number of the churches of Prussia, with the power he has assumed, of imposing a Liturgy on the people, and with his privilege of either nominating or approving the members of the "Upper Consistory," the great ruling Synod of the kingdom, he has certainly a very extensive and dangerous influence over the Church of the nation. Indeed it is the opinion of very many that the only object of Frederick Third's many efforts in this matter, was to strengthen the power of the crown. This is possible. But the general history shows the King of Prussia during at least the years of Napoleon's rule, to have been a weak man much rather than a bad man. And accounts which I have heard in private, of his remorse in later years at the forcible measures he had employed to fasten the Union on the people, lead me to think his motives might not have been bad. However that may be, the results are the same, and they at least show us that the great problem of the "Union of Sects" is not at all solved in the Prussian Union.

CHAPTER XXXIV.

A DAY WITH A BURGER.

I HAVE been invited to spend the day with my friend T., just out of the city. It is beautiful Spring weather, and I find it very delightful to be strolling out in gardens again, in this mild air. There are young ladies in the company, the daughters of my friend, and a university student of theology from Halle, a young lawyer just about to pass his *examen*, and a sociable clever fellow of middle age, who may be a physician or a scientific man of property. They call him Doctor, and I am told he is a strong Free Trader. Some other young ladies have come in almost with me—true specimens of German beauties, with oval faces, flaxen hair in ringlets, pure speaking complexions, and eyes of clear, deep blue, of which you can hardly say whether they are more expressive of reflection or feeling. There seems a good prospect of a very sociable day.

"I suppose you did not know, Herr B.," said one of the young ladies, as I came in, "that we are having a holiday for the mother's silver wedding?" I told her I did not, and unfortunately, did not even know what the silver wedding was. "So! I suppose you have no such things in your practical Fatherland. *Bien;* in Germany when a couple have been married twenty-five years, they celebrate the silver wedding, and the friends make them presents, and if they are good *fromme Leŭte*—pious people, they go to church and have a ceremony, and it's all a grand holiday. We Berliners leave out the church part, but we always have a merry time. Of course, you know no more, what the *golden wedding* is."

"Alas! no."

"That is for the couple who have been married fifty years, and it is the custom in many parts, for them then to be married over again in church!"

I professed myself very glad to have part in such a pleasant thing, and we turned to join with the rest of the company.

The ladies at once sat down with their baskets of worsted and silks, and we of the male part, strolled out in the gardens. I asked soon in regard to the betrothal in North Germany—whether that was also much celebrated. They said, it was not; there was usually a formal announcement—nothing more. "You will find," said the Doctor, "that these pretty customs of which you hear so much as German, are not much observed in North Germany. They are more Southern. We here are more cosmopolitan. I have been a great deal in England, and I notice very little difference in outward matters, between our country and that. We are more social, and we like a good home-chat and frolic; but as for superstitions and interesting customs, we have few of them."

I told him, that there was one thing in which I found a great difference between the two countries, and for which I liked the Germans—that was, the very few distinctions of rank here. "I have never heard," said I, "a German talking about any other class or set, as if he especially troubled himself with it; and for all that is said, I should never know that an order of nobility existed here."

"You are right, to a degree," he replied. "We Germans usually enjoy what we have, without asking whether others enjoy more or less, and we know little about the English, and as I understand your American—jealousy of those above us. Perhaps it is, because no one ever expects in Germany to be anything more than his father is."

"But," interrupted the young lawyer, "the Herr Americaner has not known all our ladies yet. If you only could see the stout lady of our *chef*, how indignant she is if a single title is left out. 'The Madame Councillor of the Court, and Professor and County Magistrate, &c. &c.' I have only to string all these together, and add a *von* in the end, and I can put her into a heavenly humor!"

"Yes, our *Advocat* has hit it," said the other, "there is a very foolish fondness for these titles among certain people, but in general our nobles are of no account. They are neither rich nor talented, and of course, blood alone goes a very little way."

I questioned the *Advocat* as to his profession, in the course of the conversation, whether he studied a regular course, and whether he could go at once into practice?

"No;" said he, "and that is the worst of it. I cannot practice or afford to marry for ten years after passing my examinations. The drudgery is tremendous. Our code involves such an immense amount of study on the sources of the present law, on the collateral law, on so many branches of law, I must pass three very severe public examinations, and then I receive a small salary from government, and can either be a pleader, or solicitor, as I choose. The work is enormous. It seems to me, I was a fool for ever beginning it!"

I asked how the jury courts worked.

"Miserably," said he; "it is an absurdity to suppose that twelve of our common Germans would either be honest or knowing enough ever to sit in judgment on any important case. Why should it not be left to a court of judges, educated for that very purpose?"

"But your judges are appointed by Government;" said I. "Are they qualified to decide on a case between the Government and the people?"

"Yes; quite as much so as the other party. Professional character alone would generally impel them to decide honestly. The fact is, Herr B., we have before our juries, just such pleadings as you may remember in that famous case of *Peekveek* (Pickwick). Our jurymen are a mere *Gesindel*, (rabble) and would be completely blindfolded by these Sergeant Bootsfoots, (*Buzfuz*)—how do you call it?"

I laughed at finding this classic of legal actions in the German; and the conversation turned, as it always will when that enclycopedia of fun is mentioned, into a delighted and hearty recalling of scene after scene of Pickwick.

"But, where are the young ladies?" said the Doctor, as we entered the house again, through one of the large windows on the balcony. "Why you know, Doctor," said one of those who had come in with me, "that we all have come rather early; and Fräulein S. must oversee the kitchen awhile, and L. is engaged up stairs. You find all this," turning to me, "*echt Deutsch*, genuinely German, I dare say! We hear ladies never trouble themselves about such things in America." I assured her it was quite a mistake; it depended entirely on the lady's position and circumstances. "Well, you at least see a difference in the place a lady occupies in the two countries!" they continued, "confess that your American lady is very much flattered."

In the large cities, I allowed it was so often; "but in the country and in our small towns you will find our ladies as sensibly treated as you could desire; and many of them are good housekeepers." Still I told them, I had beforehand expected one difference, and I had found it everywhere the fact. They inquired what it was, and why I had expected it?

"I have always observed," said I, "in your literature, in the correspondence of your cultivated people, that the women very seldom are allowed to hold as high a position, as with us. Now take that life and correspondence of Richter, a man who had the most exalted theories of woman's capabilities; and whose wife was an uncommonly accomplished person—he always writes to her and treats her, as if she were his housekeeper or head servant. You see the same thing pictured in his 'Flower and Thorn pieces'—you have read that?"

"Oh, no; no one reads Richter now."

"Well," said I, "I think I see the same thing in the feelings of the men generally. They are afraid of having women superior to them; and you never find, at a large table or in a company, that a woman's words are listened to as respectfully, as in America!"

"*Schön!* good!" said the ladies, clapping their hands; "we always said the same thing. What do you say to that, Herr Doctor?"

"Oh," said the Doctor, laughing; the Americans like the women to be *blaŭenstrümpfe*—blue stockings! We want a woman, a woman. What's the use of Greek and metaphysics to her? She must know how to sweep and cook, and take care of the children—that will do for her!"

"As for Richter," said the Advocat, "he's no authority; we all know he drank brandy and water too hard the last few years, to write to any one decently."

"Yes; it was *traŭrig*—melancholy!" said the *Candidat*, who had been listening in silence thus far.

"No, Doctor," said I, "we want no blue stockings; but we do

want a woman to be something more than a housekeeper. We believe that woman's education is only just in its commencement now. We cannot see a reason, why a person of the finest capacities, and destined in life to exert the greatest influence which one human being can ever exert over another—a mother's—should be cut off in her intellectual training, just where we begin. We think that a woman should in every respect be equal to a man, in which her nature is capable of being equal. We want a companion, a friend in a woman—not a servant."

"*Vortrefflich!* excellent!" said the ladies.

"But," said the Doctor, "see how it would be! We should have a whole race of 'emancipated women;' each knowing a little Greek, or Hebrew, or Philosophy; and then thinking that she knew everything. Look at these pedant-women now—pah! there's Madame T——, who always turns everything into its relation to the Kantean system, and who lets your coffee get cold, while she is lecturing! I would rather have a Bavarian apple-woman for a wife!"

"And very pretty women they are too, I can tell you," said the Advocat, "especially the Munich, in the little gilt caps."

"Besides," he continued, "a woman cannot in all respects equal a man, intellectually; and she cannot have time, at least in our poor country, to study metaphysics and the cook-book at once. She must not neglect the household!"

"But," said one of the young ladies, "it is all the fault of you men. If you would do with fewer puddings, we should have more time. Every one of us could learn all that is necessary in housekeeping in one-tenth of the time we spend at it. It is your luxuries, which make us so busy."

"You must let me explain myself," said I. "Remember, we

Americans do not want learned women, but educated women. What we desire is not books and languages and metaphysics, and all that, but the result of these—the power of thinking and appreciating. I believe generally among the most highly educated people, there is the least said about the *means*. We do not care what books a man has read, or how many languages he knows; but we ask, can he think for himself? Has he thoughts and judgments which are worth hearing? So with a woman. I conceive that a woman will cook a turkey better, for being educated."

"No, no;" said my opponent, "she will put salt into the *Pfannekuchen*, (pan-cakes) instead of sugar, like our learned Fräulein C., when she was so absorbed in the study of the early Greek tragedy. Besides, what's the use? She never has been equal with man; and she never can be."

"If learning were common among women, there would not be these difficulties," I replied. "No woman is conceited now because she knows French. We do not expect, that she will be equal to man in all respects, but we think she has some finer and superior capacities. As for her neglecting her natural duties at home, I suppose her instincts would always restrain her. One of our writers says, that probably no woman would ever desert an infant for a quadratic equation!"

"Will you close the discussion in a friendly way," said one of our hostesses, coming in, "by first trying a little of our German housekeeping? Lunch is ready!" and we all walked out informally to the dining-room, where we found a table set with flowers and some pretty fruit from the conservatories, *Wurst*, tongue, bread and butter, and beer. My friend also came in, and the talk went round with animation. "There's nothing I do so envy you Germans," said I to a young lady next me, "as your *bread!*"

"Why! do not you have good bread in America?"

"Very seldom. I suppose it is owing to our yeast not being much obtained from breweries. Our bread is always too heavy or too light."

"That *is* a misfortune! But you must go to Vienna, if you would eat good bread! and such puddings! The *Strudel!* Have you those much in America, Herr B.?"

"Oh yes. We eat all that kind of dishes, much more than you here. The universal breakfast over the whole land, of rich and poor almost, are these *Pfannekuchen* of buckwheat or Turkish corn, eaten with molasses, or syrup. I suppose you never tasted any *syrup?*"

"No, not that refined syrup, though we have heard in the books very much about it. But what a droll breakfast! You must eat *sweets* a great deal more than we."

Our attention here was called, by a growing discussion between the Doctor and our host upon *Free Trade.*

"Mein lieber Freund," said the Doctor, "you will find Austria is ruining herself by her close protective system. She has been obliged, it is true, to raise every kreutzer possible on account of her debt, but those heavy duties are crushing very much of her resources. See the change in the export of wool alone, both from Hungary and the other provinces. She may have built up one or two manufactures, though I doubt that, but her general agricultural interest is exceedingly damaged. Depend upon it, you cannot interfere with the natural laws of trade, without injury. I believe that with these enormous prices of foreign articles in Austria, these few inflated manufactures, and the depressed condition of the agriculture, there will soon be a tremendous crash."

Our host argued in return, that very many of the difficulties in the Austrian Empire, resulted from the wasteful expenditure on armies, &c., and that at least, the condition of the linen and silk manufactures, and the coarse cottons, spoke favorably for the high tariffs.

"No," said the Free Trader, "it does not. They have gained to the loss of the other interests of the Empire. And it will be equally so here, if we unite with the Austrians on a high protective system. Prussia has now in our Customs' Union, tariff enough. It is a pity that all Germany has not a common system of tariff, but when we do have one, it should be based on the lowest protection or on Free Trade. I do hope we shall carry this out eventually."

"But," said the other, "our silk and iron manufactures demand more protection. They say, they can do nothing against the French and English."

"Well, if they cannot, let them sink. Why should we pay more for an article, merely because it is made here. Of course, Prussia *must* always be more or less dependent on others. It is strange, people do not understand this here. Everywhere else in the world, the tendency is to a liberal system. Belgium has just renounced her old protective theories. Holland has had low tariffs for some years. Sardinia offers free trade to all, who will return it to her. England grows rich on it, and America tends more and more to it every year—though your Secretary Corwin," turning to me, "has some most maedieval ideas on the subject. Then the only parts of Germany, which ever have been really prosperous, in a mercantile respect, have always been free traders. Bremen, Hamburg, Frankfort —the Hanse-towns."

"Still they are only commercial cities," the other replied.

"Not at all. Hamburg has now most flourishing manufactures. There is one of the largest factories in Europe there—the *Meyers*, built up under free-trade—a factory, which imports its wood, &c., from America, and sends back the same in canes and whips *to America!*"

"A poor business for the United States," said the other.

"*Gar nicht!*—not at all! or they would have found it out. Ingenuity is paid for better, somewhere else."

I inquired, here, what the policy of Prussia would probably be in this matter.

"We cannot tell," said the Free Trader; "the Government has no fixed policy, and the people in general know nothing about the subject. If we decline this high Protective Union offered by Austria, it will be more because we hate Austria, than because we like Free Trade. There are some manifestly absurd provisions in the present Tariff—especially in determining the duties by *weight*—which we shall induce Government to change. We are arousing the thinking men everywhere, and holding meetings continually—by the way, there is one next Monday evening in the *Englischen Gasthaus;* will you attend?—and we hope gradually to bring our policy away from the protective system."

We now returned again to the drawing-room, and sat chatting or reading, or amusing ourselves, as each one pleased, the rest of the morning. The young ladies were surprisingly industrious; the daughters of our host running out every few minutes to see to the household arrangements, and the others keeping up an incessant sewing or embroidery-work.

I speculated in myself then and have often since, as to the difference between German ladies of this class and ours at home. There is a great contrast, though precisely where, it is somewhat difficult to say. Nearly all those in this company spoke several different languages yet there was singularly little interest in books or literature among them. At first, too, you would have said that they were very free and independent in thought, and you would have given them credit for earnest investigations, which had brought out such free results; but, after a little while, you would find that Freedom of thought was their *Orthodoxy*, and that their independent thoughts were merely the echo of what they had been taught. You would see, that the attaining these results, had not required at all the mental or moral power which the same would with us. Yet, with them all, there was a very happy natural intelligence and quickness; on the whole, however, much less culture and power of original thought or reasoning, than with ladies in the same rank of life at home. Where they were superior, was in a certain *individuality*, a certain simplicity, and natural following-out of their own bent and tendencies; and, also, in a spontaneous easy expression of themselves.

Our ladies at home, especially in New England, strike one as too much cut in the same pattern, as under a similar mould—not *intellectually*, but in their habits, tendencies, sentiments. It is seldom you meet any one with us, either man or woman, who comes before you as a spontaneous, natural person—one who really feels and expresses feeling, as she has it, and not as she thinks it "proper" to have it, or as she is taught she should have it.

A New Englander, like an Englishman, is for ever thinking, "What will others say?" or he is dreading "humbug;" or an iron system of duty and obligation has been around him so long, that it has crushed in his easy, spontaneous impulses.

In each of these German women there was a greater *distinctness* of nature; a play of passion and feeling, which might be ill-governed sometimes, but which was very beautiful because it was *hers*, and was the effect of no instruction or public opinion. The Continental people seem to me, in general, to show more of that most pleasing and exquisite variety of nature, which God has bestowed on all His works, and which no Creed and no System has the right to mar.

It is possible the "expression" here was much improved by the full and sweet tones of these ladies. I know not why it is, but our Yankee schools or Yankee air, has given rise to the most disagreeable intonation, which any where disfigures the voices of a cultivated people. An American (from the Northern States) is known almost any where in Europe, from his nasal twang and whine.

Want of refinement and education will produce in every country, bad modulations and tones of voice, which even in different languages, do not essentially differ from one another. But in America, people the most refined show this nasal defect of tone. It is comparatively rare, in New England, to meet a lady without some tinge of it, and the preachers manifest it almost universally. I have no doubt that if any one physical cause could explain the superior natural oratory in our Southern States, during our whole history, it would be their superiority in voice. It is remarkable how seldom the Americans themselves are conscious of this defect.

Throughout Europe—especially, however, in Ireland and Hungary—this richness of tone struck my ear.

Strange! the power of the human voice, when strung with genuine passion, or when bursting up, as it were, directly from the deep places of the heart! I have listened to tones in those old Irish homesteads, and I have heard voices by that death-bed of a Nation—in Hungary—voices of home-affection, of sorrow, of love for native land which many waters should not quench, of indignation at long-suffered injustice, which thrill constantly anew with an undiminished power over my memory, and to whose tones, the chords of my soul cannot cease to vibrate, while they move to any feeling.

In our rather desultory conversation, I was answering their questions about America, and philosophizing in traveller style upon the differences of our two nations, when I said something about the shape of head of the Germans, and the breadth of the front part as greater than in the American, corresponding to their greater ideality and hopefulness.

"What! you do not believe in that, Herr B.?" said one.

"Certainly I do," I replied.

"But is it possible," said the Candidat from Halle, "that Phrenology is generally believed in America?"

No; I told him; it was not. It had been so much employed as a humbug, that most sensible people quite doubted it.

"What is that? *Hoombooc!* Herr B.," said one of the ladies. "Explain!" I translated it as well as I could, for the German language is not capable of conveying that compendious term in one word.

"We here believe," said the theologian, "that Phrenology is a materialistic system; and inconsistent with the idea of the free agency, which the Holy Scriptures teach. Besides, to use your own word, Germany has found the humbug so much in Phrenology, that the educated (*gebildete*) do not have any confidence in it."

In reply, I unfolded my own ideas of the science, and I must do the Germans the justice to say, that they have the most courteous and candid way possible of listening to new theories. If you should present an argument which denied your opponent's identity, or which proved that the moon was made of green cheese, a German would always listen with attention, as if there was a possibility of there being some basis of truth, somewhere in it. I told them, that we did not believe that the brain determined the mind, but that certain traits or rather tendencies of the soul were connected with certain shapes of the head, just as they were with certain shapes of the features. And that the value of the science to me, was not in the manipulation, or in the determination of character from the head, but in its *analysis of human nature.* It was the only *practical* mental philosophy which I knew. It was the only one which analyzed and put together *tendencies* (Eigenschaften) of character, and showed the results which they form in the every-day developments of human nature. It did not so much make a strict metaphysical division of the mental faculties, as it took up and explained the separate tendencies, which lie as it were at the basis of each soul, and which shape human nature, as it *practically* is, in the various relations of life. The old systems favored abstract thought on the human mind, and the searching of one's deepest consciousness. This concerned itself more with the observation of human nature, as it appears around us. I thought its value as a practical philosophy could not be better shown, than by the universal use of its terms, now through both England and America.

As to its Craniology, its division of organs on the head, I considered it defective; yet in its main principles, I had never known it fail with any head.

They all listened very courteously, though I suppose with perfect scepticism; and it was proposed I should make a trial on some of their heads.

I may say here, that of all means of entertainment, in a set of ale-house tipplers, among a ship's crew, or in a fashionable drawing-room, before gentle or simple, I have never found anything half so *taking*, as a phrenological examination. To the traveller, Phrenology is worth a host of accomplishments.

Though a no very good "manipulator," I made some good hits here; and we kept up the laugh for some time, until the old servant put his head in the door, and bawled, "The dinner is on the table."

The dinner in Berlin is usually at one o'clock, except when company is invited, when it is delayed to three or four o'clock, after the business hours are over. Our dining-room here was a high, bare room, with walls and ceilings painted in pretty patterns, a tall white porcelain stove in one corner, and a sofa, together with a few plain articles, by way of furniture. There was no carpet on the floor, and the room had in general a naked aspect. It was used mostly as a dancing-room.

The table was very prettily set out; the desert-fruit and flowers being in the centre, and a handsome show of Dresden china and of graceful dishes, surrounding them. No grace was said; and one of the young ladies commenced at once by helping the soup, which was passed by the servant.

"How find you the German cookery?" said the lady next to me, in English. I told her, I liked it very much—much better than travellers generally do—especially the soups.

"The travellers judge so from our guest-houses—*inns*, I mean; where much fat is employed. But have you not the soups?"

"We had them," I said, "but nearly always cooked so as to be indigestible."

"That is very unfortunate, for we regard them the healthiest victual."

After the soup came the boiled beef, cut up in small pieces, and handed by the servant to each one. This is eaten without vegetables. This was succeeded by small bits of a roast chicken passed again to each, and eaten with pickles and preserves. The Bordeaux red wine was now passed, our host pouring first a few drops in his own glass, and then helping his right hand guest. When he pours the last glass, it is the custom for him to empty the last drops also into his own glass. This wine is not stronger than claret, which it very much resembles. No lady in the company took wine. I observed, that both gentlemen and ladies used finger and teeth on the chicken, in primitive fashion—a common habit of ordinary life in Germany. Our middle course, was a pudding and sauce, after which came the great dish of roast beef, the only meat carved by the host at the table, eaten with various vegetables.

"Is this quite different from your home dinners?" said the lady at my side again.

"Oh, yes;" I replied, and described our American meals.

"*So!* pudding last! how droll! But which think you most healthy?"

I thought the German diet, especially as her countrymen did not eat so much pies and pastry, as we Americans; and despite the long meals, were not so hearty eaters.

"*Ach!* Here comes the dish of dishes!—the—*pardon!* how call you it?"

"*Salad!*" and each one set to work, preparing his mixture, as for the especial dish of the day. Through the courses, all ate very slowly, and conversation continued in the liveliest manner.

"Now, confess! Herr B.; is not this infinitely more *comfortahble*, than the rich English dinners?"

"That is a genuine English word, you know," said I, "and the English think they have comfort in perfection."

"*Ach!* no;" she replied," I have been at those dinners in England. They are horrible! So stiff. I could not dare to say, once! We Germans do not find *comfort* in sofas, and carpets, and the wine; our comfort is in friends and conversation, and in the *feeling*. You know our word. I find it better—*gemüthlich*."

Our last course was black unbolted rye bread and butter, with a little fruit and confectionery, and after some farther chatting, the whole company went to the drawing-room, for the coffee, and the gentlemen to smoke.

"How much more pleasant is this," said my companion as we went out, "as your English way to leave the gentlemen to drink and talk without ladies—as if you were ashamed."

"I think so too;" I replied, "we seldom do that in America. But how *can* you housekeepers bear this smoking in your parlors? I should think you would be obliged to smoke yourself, for defence."

"No? Why should we oppose it? Is it not better for them to be in habit to smoke with us, than without us? Beside it never trouble me. I like it now. But do not think we smoke. No respectable lady smokes."

"I see Fraülein N. is making the coffee," said I, "Do you never leave it to servants?"

"Oh no," she replied, "it would never be so good. We always make it fresh on the table, for it must not long *kochen*—what is the word—boil. It only drops very slowly through a—a—crossing of—"

"Sieve," I suggested.

"Ja! a sieve and paper very thin. But have you good coffee in America?"

"No; not often. I have very seldom drank good coffee, at least in a hotel. We do not know how to make it."

"Here is your coffee. You must put no cream in it, but sugar much. Will you light your cigar?"

"*Danke Ihnen.*"

"Have you not as yet learned, Herr B., that *thank you*, in German, always means, nein—*no?*"

I told her I ought to have learned, for I had lost many a dish at public tables, by saying *Danke!* to the servants when they offered it.

After our coffee, came various games and merrimakings till evening. Other friends called with presents and mementoes to the *Frau Mutter;* good wishes were said and pleasant speeches made, and at length, after a hearty supper at 10 o'clock, on broiled sturgeon and Bavarian beer, the company broke up, with abundance of *Adieus* and *Empfehle michs*, and *Good byes* for me.

On reaching my lodgings, I found I had left my key inside—a rather blank prospect, as it would be too late probably to find a room in a hotel. In the midst of my cogitations, I heard a cry far up-street of "*Wächter!*" and I remembered there was a useful member of the community, who patrolled the streets at night, with keys of the houses, to be furnished for a few *groschen*, to any luckless individual, who was locked out like myself.

So I commenced in a stentorian voice, "*Wächter, Wä-ä-chter!*"

"What the *devil* are you yelling in that way for?" said a voice close by, and I found one of the night-police in helmet and sword just behind me, looking in anything but a Christian humor.

I answered shortly that "I wanted to get in!"

"Well, you need not make such a —— of a noise, if you do!"

"Every one does it, I hear the cry every night," said I, as the Wächter came up and turned the lock, "and you might learn a more civil way of addressing a stranger!" I added, at the same time, discreetly getting inside the door.

CHAPTER XXXIV.

THE UNIVERSITY—RATIONALISM.

An account of Berlin society as it appears to an American, would be altogether incomplete without speaking of the many American students who are attending the University, and who have met in such pleasant circles this winter at the houses of Mr. Barnard, our Ambassador, and of Mr. Fay. They are in general very intelligent, gentlemanly fellows, and far better representatives of our country than one usually meets in the travelling public of Europe. A large proportion are from our Southern States.

The choice of studies among the working part of these young men here and in other universities of Germany is remarkable, and seems almost to show a new tendency in our studying classes. One for instance is engaged in investigating the whole family of languages related to the Anglo-Saxon, with a view of explaining the early English literature; another is at work on the Sanscrit and kindred tongues, with a special reference to philology; others on the study of music as a science; others on the higher branches of chemistry; and one with an enthusiasm most worthy of success has travelled through many difficulties to Berlin to gather the documents for a *Life of Beethoven*, and intends even to walk to Vienna to collect the last materials for his work.

The day has probably passed by in our country, in which such studies as these can be objected to as "unpractical." It is beginning to be seen that human life is made up of a great many parts, and helped on by a great many different pursuits, and that Sanscrit has its place among them as well as shoe-making. For one I am rejoiced at the work these men are doing. The reproach against our nation in an intellectual respect has been its superficiality—and without doubt, often deserved. Such workers as these, for they are hearty, faithful students, will do much with the immense advantages offered by German libraries to remove this reproach, and to give a more thorough direction to the Mind of our country. Nor is there danger to be feared for our students, from the influence of foreign institutions in Germany. If anything would make a man republican or disposed to give the very highest value to the "practical," it would be an experience of the infinite confusions and inefficiency which appear now in German affairs, and of the political oppression which curses the people.

Whatever may be said of the older students, there is a most decided objection to the practice, now beginning to be common in our country, of sending *boys* to these foreign Universities. Not to mention the want of sympathy it almost invariably causes with our own institutions in the student's mind; and the weakening influence it has on his power to use his own language—a loss not to be replaced by a knowledge of all the foreign languages in existence;—it is beside a most terrible experiment. No one has any idea of the dangers which surround a young man in these foreign Universities. Even in the worst of our Colleges there is some glimmering of the good old religious influences of our fathers; there is the restraint of acquaintances and the fear of future loss of reputation. Here, of all these good influences, there is scarcely one which can still work.

Some of our good parents appear to have a great confidence in Berlin, as the centre of Protestantism, and in its orthodox influences. But it is a most sad mistake. In my view there is but one city more dangerous to a young man, on the Continent—Paris. And Berlin is only better than Paris in that vice here is more gross, and therefore more offensive.

In regard to Berlin, as a place of study, it is difficult to advise. The choice of a University depends so much on the personal plans of each student. There is no doubt that the Berlin University is not by any means equal to what it was a few years since. The loss of such men as NEANDER, and JACOBI, and LACHMANN in one year has made no slight difference. Still, now, in all branches there is quite enough of talent to satisfy even the most fastidious student. Where such men as RANKE, and RITTER, and BÖCKH, and BOPP, and HENGSTENBERG teach, there can be no very great deficiency The usual course among the foreign students is to try different Universities, avoiding Berlin in the summer, as it is an exceedingly hot, unpleasant city at that season. The expense of living in Berlin is small compared with that of our own cities, yet it is nearly double the expense of the smaller University towns. A student could live here very comfortably I think, on $300 a year, including the cost of clothing and every necessary article except books.

As a place for learning German, Berlin is not at all to be recommended. There are so many Americans and Englishmen whom one would not, if he could, avoid; so many Germans who speak excellent English; and it is so difficult to board in any private family, where practice in the language could be gained, that almost every foreigner residing here, finds his progress in German very slow. Still as a place where German life in its most interesting aspect can be observed, where German politics and religious movements can be best studied, where Music in its highest forms can be enjoyed, where the most intellectual and accomplished society of the Continent has gathered itself, Berlin is of all others, the city to be chosen by a foreigner for a residence.

I cannot bid good-bye to Berlin without speaking of a gentleman there to whom every American who has been of late years in that city must feel sincerely grateful,—*Mr. Theodore S. Fay*, at present the Secretary of the Embassy. A man in whom fifteen years of diplomatic life have not worn away manly simplicity and truth of character; one in whom we can see that the purest Christian traits are not inconsistent with the refinement and accomplishments of a man of the world. A genuine whole-hearted republican too, well representing our country. He is the last to wish to be spoken of in this public way; yet I cannot refrain from giving utterance to what I know is the sentiment of most Americans who have resided in Berlin with regard to him.

Before leaving North Germany, it is right that I should give my general impressions of a very important subject; and yet it is a difficult matter, on which to speak. I refer to the *Religious Character* of the German people. Religious Principle is not at all to be tested, as many are accustomed to test it. Its manifestations must be as various, as are the forms of human nature. No local and external measure can fit its infinite developments. Especially is this true of the *intellectual* expression of religion. Believing that the worst heart *may be* joined with the purest creed, and that a simple, loving Faith may be connected to the most wild and crude opinions; conscious that in our practice and instincts, we often reject what we professedly believe, I would never test a religious character by its usual language of expression, or by its avowed system of belief.

I had thought it possible, that even under the wild theories, the unsparing criticism, the apparent Skepticism of the Germans, I might find in practical life, the humble, fervent, loving heart, worshipping almost unconsciously to itself, the Infinite Being. But I am compelled to say, in my experience thus far with *the mass of the people*, I am disappointed. Religion does not enter as a great element into society in Germany. It is not a principle any one considers, in estimating the influences at work on the people. Few appeal to it, or speak of it as one of the great facts in human life. Very little seems to be sacrificed for its great objects. There are seldom enterprises under it for the poor, and the helpless, and the unhappy. Not much is given or suffered, through its impulse. There is seldom *expressed* worship. In fact, I do not believe there is a heathen land where less outward ceremony of worship is seen. The churches are half empty, and one beholds the painful sight of a church *attended only by women and children*, as if Religion was a thing belonging only to the weaker part of the race. It is not that the men one meets are bitterly hostile to religious truth, or abusive towards it; but there is a sort of *deadness* to the whole subject among them, an indifference, or a kind of smiling, quiet incredulity, which comes over one chillingly and sadly.—Of course there are numerous exceptions to this. Men with whom we can have the delightful consciousness that in distant lands, under foreign languages and a different culture, there is a certain bond of sympathy and principles and common hopes uniting us; about which little can be said in words, but which forms one of the most pleasing evidences of a common Christian Faith. And I believe, that in many of the families, the beautiful home-virtues—the Affection, and Self-sacrifice, and cheerful forbearance and geniality, are the appropriate expressions of their Love to Christ; perhaps even higher than our bolder and more heroic expressions. In what I have said, I speak only of the mass of the people.

There are favorite aspects, however, to the effects of this Rationalism. It seems to me it has done away with intellectual narrowness very much from the theological circles. No one dares to step out on the arena now in Germany, with a crude, bigoted, ill-equipped opinion. He knows if it cannot stand the attacks of the sharpest criticism and the most vigorous philosophy, it must go down—no matter if all the authority of ages is at hand to back it. The consequence is, the theological mind of Germany is very well furnished, and possesses a certain candid mode of looking at subjects, a certain readiness to acknowledge Truth wherever it is, which has not been a general virtue in the theological class. I meet a great many who belong to the strictest of the orthodox, the most extreme "*Pietisten*," and who hold the Evangelical views with all the strength and depth of feeling any one could desire, yet I have nearly always found them men of real liberality, ready to admit that their own particular view did not embrace all of the truth, and disposed to see what there was of truth in opposite views. Certainly in no country of the world could a Theological History be written like that which has appeared here within a few years from Hagenbach—a work so clear and strong in its own religious purpose, yet recognizing so candidly even in the vagaries of a Schiller, or the Romanism of a Schlegel, all that there is good and noble in them.

The man whose spirit, as we believe, most works now in Germany, modifying the influences of Rationalism, and reaching those who are world-wide from him in their theories or their philosophy, is Schleiermacher. His philosophy is passing by, his merciless criticism has lost its power, his daring speculations are scattered to the wind; but that simple, fervent spirit, that candid, truth-loving mind, that *life* so thoroughly imbued and inspired with the one great TRUTH, which, as we believe, has been the life and the inspiration of the best spirits through all ages—the truth of "GOD MANIFEST IN THE FLESH," of God, made near to man through human sympathies and a human life—this all works, and will not soon cease to work through the German people

CHAPTER XXXV.

SOUTH-GERMANY AGAIN.

"Es ist ein harter Schluss
Weil ich aus Berlin muss!
So schlag 'ich Berlin aus dem Sinn
Und wende mich. Gott weiss! wohin;
Ich will mein Glück probiren,
Marschiren."

So humming the student-song, I bade good-bye to Berlin. My friends had parted from me, as only German friends will; and I felt almost like leaving home for strangers again. It is the hardest part of traveling, that you just build up a satisfactory friendship, when it is all demolished, and you go on to new experiences. And it is hardest of all in Germany, where confidence and kindness are so freely shown the stranger.

I have found DRESDEN in its full spring beauty—so green, sunny, quiet, trustful—a beautiful city now. The parks and gardens and squares full of pleasant groups, the women sitting sewing, and the children playing in the sunlight, or listening to the bands of music. Oh! when will an American city learn so to provide for its free population, health, beauty, broad fields and cheerful landscapes, as these German princes have done for their subjects?

Among the other sights I have come upon, is a *children's garden.* A merry company of children, in bright dresses, are dancing on the hard ground round a pole, hung with flowers, under the instruction of a spruce dancing-master. Others swinging, rolling the hoop, or running through the paths ; others at some pretty calisthenic exercises under the trees. There are a few candy and cake tables on the outskirts. Only two or three nurses have the charge of them, though there must be nearly fifty children there. It appears, the mothers club together, hire the nurses and the garden, in order to save the expense of separate nurses, and at the same time to secure healthful open air sports for the children—an idea, perhaps, worth something for our large cities.

APRIL.

I have just dined with Rev. Dr. ——, one of the most popular and distinguished preachers in Germany. He laments, as usual, the want of any earnest Christian life among the people, and especially among the young men. You never meet a young man with any high, noble aims, unless it is *professional* to have them—the result, he says, of German Rationalism. He thinks we are getting, in America, a very bad importation of Rationalistic German Theology. He asked me what I thought of the present political condition of Germany. I told him candidly, and expressed how faint my hopes were for the future.

" It has seemed to me possible," said I, " that the German race has played out its part in the world's history—that it has irretrievably degenerated, lost its vigor, manliness, energy. We know such instances constantly occur in history. Look at the old Spaniards, and the Dutch and Italian Republics, and compare the same peoples and cities now. Perhaps it is so with Germany. Perhaps, until this race is united with some more vigorous, it will continue to become more and more weak and inefficient. I must confess, I am astonished on every side, at the practical weakness of your people. Even those, who know their rights, have no spirit in asserting them!"

"A bad outlook, certainly, for us!" said he. "You may be right. Such things have been. Alas, for poor Germany! Bad government, and especially this universal irreligion, have brought this about! But, mein lieber Herr, have you no fears for your own country—look at your *Sclaverei!* (Slavery.) I must say that if that does ruin your country, we in the old world, shall lose faith in Humanity! It seems to me, sometimes, yours is the last *experiment* in self-government—that grand English word!—who would ever trust it, if you fail?"

In reply, I detailed at length our difficulties in that matter, and my hopes, ultimately, of a change.

He hoped also; "but it is a strange fact," said he, "and one that much shakes my hopes, that during all ages Republics have rested on a *basis of slaves!* I have thought that it might be almost necessary to the system—one class made intelligent and free, by being freed from menial labor through the service of another."

I was able easily to show him, that our Republic differed essentially in this from the Classic States; that Slavery with us was rather a fungus, an evil from without, than a foundation.

I suppose it is said over in public speeches at home, no less than fifty-two times in the year at least, that the United States is the great example to the tyrannical Governments of Europe, and the hope and comfort to the oppressed, &c., &c. And possibly some of us have heard it so much, that we begin to doubt whether it is so true after all. But if one will only mingle with the various classes of Europe, the low as well as the high; if he will really get hold somewhat of the thought and feeling of men, he will not only never doubt the truth of such expressions, but he will feel that he never began even faintly to realize them. The existence of our Republic is a stubborn, unconquerable FACT, which speaks more to the minds of the masses here, than volumes of argument. The supporters of the arbitrary forms of Government may prove most conclusively that our Constitution is defective, that Republics are not consistent with the highest development of man. They may bring forth beautifully the theories of monarchy, and show the divinity of its origin, and almost demonstrate its *necessity* to mankind—but there, ever in the background of their theories, looms up over in the West, the great prosperous FREE STATE of the age—the undeniable happy existence of a self-governed people. No argument can get around it. There it is! People have become so well informed on these matters, that here in Germany for instance, no discussion is ever carried on in the Parliaments, or through pamphlets, on any great change of Government, without at once the example of the United States being adduced. I am struck with that, as I attempt to penetrate the immense mass of pamphlets and "Debates," which any one must work through who would understand German politics. The first thing to be overthrown by the Legitimist writer or orator, and the first to be presented by the Democratic, is nearly always the practice in our Republic, and the success of such and such a provision under our Government. And the orators in the German "*Kammer*," will not unfrequently discuss an article in our Constitution with as much spirit, if not with the same objects, as the members of our House of Representatives at home.

But I am bound to say, there is another side to this picture. America is known widely—her glory and her prosperity; yet there is one stain on her escutcheon which is blazoned still more widely—*Slavery*. I sometimes think the German papers take a real pleasure in giving details about this evil of ours. Some foreign journals, the Russian, for instance, contain more about our slavery difficulties, than any one subject connected with our country. The first objection you meet in an anti-democratic pamphlet against the "Model Republic," is the system of oppression within it. I have often wondered to myself, how a Southern gentleman could ever travel through Europe with any comfort. There is scarcely a drawing-room on the Continent, where, if the subject of the United States is brought up, one will not hear one voice of indignation against the system of slavery. Through all the best circles, among the noblest and best men, in every land, and especially in Great Britain—men whom the traveller would most like to associate with—the universal feeling is, if not of indignation, of something still more annoying—of pity for the supporters of such an institution! How often have I, within the first fifteen minutes of acquaintance, been asked about that great evil in our society; and it is such a comfort to be able to explain that I have no part or parcel therein, that my government has none, that the responsibility rests not with us, and that there is many a man among us, who gladly would lay down fortune and life to aid in doing it away, if there were any possibility of success. No one can imagine the public opinion of civilized Europe, till he is here, on this matter. Indeed, I must be allowed to say, the tone of the whole civilized world, is far higher and nobler on this question, than even that of our free States

Probably, much that my friend the clergyman said, of the want of religious earnestness among the young men is true. It corresponds with my own observations in North Germany. Still, let the German *spontaneity* and a clear sense and sound Christian principle go together, and there spring up the most beautiful combinations of character I have ever seen—natures such as are seldom found under our English civilization. I have just been making a visit to Madame ——, to me a marked example of this. I extract from a letter—

"On reaching the town where she lived, I at once left my card and letters, rambled about, delivered other letters—and called again in the evening; my introductions were from her mother and sisters whom I knew well in ————; and I had a letter, also, to her husband, a young scientific man of note; so that we had many common topics. We fell at once into the midst of things—a conversation easy but under the surface, and leaving something to be remembered when it was over. I spent tha evening there, and was invited to a supper-party the next—dined there the day after, and then went to a famous Castle with them, and staid till a late hour the last evening.

"I have never known a woman with so happy a balancing of qualities, and yet so little extraordinary.

"Imagine an oval face, a fine, soft complexion, fine auburn hair, nose slightly *retroussé*, yet not too small, good forehead, with the head rising nobly over it; 'Benevolence,' full, as a phrenologist would describe it; Ideality, large; the emotive faculties full, and the passionate, moderate; Comparison and the logical, large; and hazel eyes, full of feeling and thought, working continually in a quick, eager way; a mouth, just half on the edge of running over into a laugh, and a tall, full woman's form.

"She has a true woman's wit—that sort of playful, fine warding off, and quick catching of others' expression, but without the least sharpness to it—always under the control of the kindest feelings. But her glory and beauty, and that which speaks so in ever-changing language in her face, is that overflowing life, and interest in others, her *geniality*, the highest trait, or result of many traits in any human character; yet in her, accompanied with an exceedingly sharp, instinctive, keen knowledge of human nature. One gets the idea of no soft amiability in her, no blind benevolence; and at the same time, not as in our New England geniality, of a kindness, the result of a sense of duty. It is natural, keen, overflowing, genial—not exactly affectionate, or passionate, or principled—a happy combination of all.

"Then add a mind, very highly cultivated—independent, worked out opinions—strong moral sentiments—much ideality, coloring all her language and thought, but even more reason to limit them—a *vitality*, as of ardent, healthy youth, but always very tasteful and beautiful, and a great musical talent—and have we not a happy product? I have not exaggerated a single trait, except as one must necessarily in writing, abbreviate.

"Her husband is utterly unlike her. Calm, solid, deep in his learning—no ideality—and as yet from his easy disposition, led by her greater life, though in the end, his solidity may outbalance her activity. Manly, in that he had just as lief others should see, she led him.

"She talked of his foibles and of educating him, and of their educating one other, laughingly told me of a way he had of being stupid at precisely a certain hour in the evening, and wanting to go to bed, and how she had broken him of his habit!—described to us how he would keep up his *puns* after they were married, which was insufferable—before, an attention, now a bore!

"Is not all this truly German, with a two days' acquaintance!

"Her husband is aliberal Constitutionalist; but she is a Republican, as fully as I am myself. She is almost the first German woman, I have seen, who has the deep indignation of a generous heart at these crushing wrongs in her Fatherland. Her religion is very simple and fervent, yet utterly and entirely separated from all *necessary* bonds to form and externality, a mingling of Freedom and Faith, such as I have seldom met. She and her husband are deeply interested in efforts for the poor; in Sabbath Schools, and charitable movements here—the first instance of the kind I have encountered among the learned laity. Her very strong love for home, and for every detail about it, was truly German.

"We talked infinitely in those three days, and I know her better than I do many years' acquaintances. She speaks English beautifully, though we generally spoke German.

"The charm of her is, that happy mingling of animal, cheerful, genial traits, with real earnestness of character. She is one, who wins her servants and the lowest as well as her equals, to herself,—not because she tries, nor because she does it to please her own vanity, or for effect, or for duty, but because her nature flows out thus kindly towards all. Then with this, working continually, is a clear-sighted intellect and deep religious sense.

"The memory is a light over my path. I remember not so much a noble, or an intellectual, or a witty spirit, as a genial, clear-headed, refined, religious *woman*, who met me a stranger, as a friend. I shall never see her, and may never hear of her again. But I am grateful that God has created a few such happy combinations of qualities, and that I have known the embodiment!" * * *

CHAPTER XXXVI.

PRAGUE.

I NEVER remember to have taken a more interesting railroad ride than on the route between Dresden and Prague. The road, for the great part of the way, winds up the valley of the Elbe, through the "Saxon Switzerland." The first few miles are in the open country on the banks of the Elbe, with the green hills, covered with the vine, rising on the other side. But gradually the river is forced in between the mountains, and the track is obliged to accompany it, and we found ourselves puffing along right under immense jagged precipices, then cutting through in a dark tunnel a rocky promontory then rushing across, on solid bridges, some bend of the stream, with the wildest of scenery around us. It was like a railway through the Alps. If any one of my readers has travelled up the Naugatuck road in Connecticut, or followed the lower valley of the Wye, in England, he will have, on a smaller scale, a very good idea of the Dresden and Prague Railroad. This road has only been opened a week, and I could see all along the route, signs of the grand celebration they have just had at its first opening—great festoons of evergreens and flowers over the station houses, and varieties of decorations everywhere. By its completion, the traveller can leave Berlin at 7 o'clock in the morning, reach Dresden at 12, stop an hour and a half, and be in Prague by 9 o'clock in the evening, and, spending the night in Prague, can reach Vienna the next evening, so that the two capitals are, in fact, within thirty hours distance of one another. Many hopes are felt for the great Bohemian city from this line, and it is thought her manufactures will now pour themselves more freely into the Northern *Zollverein.*

The road seemed well-built, and must necessarily have been very expensive. This makes no difference, however, in the prices, as the Austrian railroads are all government property, and the fares fixed without reference to the cost of building. On this and most of their roads I have known, the price for the second class passengers—which perhaps represents the average—is 11 kreutzers per German mile, which is about 2½ cents the English mile. The seats in the Austrian cars in the second and third classes, are arranged like ours. The first class has *coupès*, or little separate compartments, each with two or three seats.

One of the most striking objects on the route was the immense fortress of *Königsstein*, perched on what seems an utterly inaccessible precipice. It boasts, you know, of being the only inexpugnable fortress of Europe, and has formed the refuge, many a time, of the Saxon kings and their treasures. In modern warfare, such a strong-hold is of no great importance, and would hardly repay the trouble of taking.

As we passed the Austrian borders, I felt the excitement which every traveller feels at entering a land he has heard of so often, and where such new forms of life will open to him, and I looked eagerly out of the windows to see if there was anything in the appearance of the country, to remind one of the old bigoted Empire. The first objects peculiar were the multitude of saints' images and crucifixes along the road. At every turn of the track, and on every high point of the banks, these memorials met the eye. The white-coated officers, too, appeared in the villages, and the Bohemian language could be heard oftener at the stations. The Austrian paper began to show itself, and I had my first sight of a little expedient which surprised me much at the time, though I have found it common enough since. I bought a trifle of a woman standing by the cars, and handed her a *bank bill* of six kreutzers, (about four cents). The article cost three kreutzers, and she tore off half, and gave me the other half! I saw a man afterwards tear a ten kreutzer into *four pieces*, and pass them in the same way. No one passed or received silver.

The talk of the people also around me sounded more "Austrian." They were discussing that question of questions for their country, the currency—and what the *Gulden* were worth, and the chances of bankruptcy, &c. I ought to mention here for the benefit of travellers, that my Prussian gold and paper brought me a premium of about *thirty-three per cent!*

I was very glad from the conversation going on around, to get some idea of this perplexing Austrian currency—this "*Guldenschein*" and "*Guldenmunz*," and these complicated kreutzers and groschens. A man has to keep a sharp look out, or he will be continually paying *Münz* for *Schein*, or in other words, two and a half times as much as he should. The innkeepers have a way of presenting their bills in "Schein money," and the unlucky traveller will be paying over in an extravagant manner, until he remembers that he settles in *Münz*. That is, if the bill is ten Gulden *Schein*, it means four Gulden common money—a very considerable difference in a long bill.

Another very characteristic thing in the cars, was the conversation of two men near me over the new Tobacco Law and the "cursed monopoly." "A man could not even smoke his pipe now, without being taxed by the Government!"

It was a beautiful sunny spring afternoon as we rushed over the railroad bridge at Prague, and the first sight of that crowd of towers and Moorish domes and turrets, as they rose one above the other on the hill side, crowned by what seemed a mosque on the summit; or stretched away on the other bank of the river among the multitude of houses, was very striking. I had at length reached the antique Bohemian capital—once the Paris of an old civilization, and now filled with monuments which make it, perhaps, the most interesting city of Europe. An interest which is increased by the strange movements of which it has been the centre during these last few years.

Thinking over such matters, and quite ready to be interested in anything, I walked out after engaging a room in a hotel, to see the old city. Not having any guide with me—and not wanting any—I wandered around quite at random in the narrow old streets. In fact, among all the pleasures of travelling, I know hardly a greater, than the first independent wandering through the streets of one of the old historic cities. You do not feel *obliged* to learn anything. You are not bored with guide books, or guides. You are deciphering yourself all the while, the thousand strange inscriptions written all around you; written in various architectures, in the style of the monuments, in the age of the buildings, and even in the faces and bearing of the inhabitants. I have found by experience, that the Past never comes before one's mind as in these first few moments, and I lay more value on these first impressions, than all the guide book information afterwards. The next time you see the hoary monument and crumbling walls with Murray in hand, or with monotonous "Commissionaire" at your elbow, exploring their history—

their glory has all departed, and you see nothing but very sooty stones or common-place statues; and are quite likely, in the midst of the most entrancing historic associations, to be speculating on the chances of the next election at home, or wondering whether it is not time for "lunch."

THE OLD BRIDGE AT PRAGUE.

I had not rambled long before I came on—what is perhaps the most interesting object in this interesting city—the old Bridge over the Moldau. You know the Moldau separates Prague into two parts, the old city and the "*Kleine Seite*," (Little Side). These two quarters are connected by two bridges, one beautiful modern chain-bridge, and this solid, ancient structure.

This is lined at the distance of every four feet, with statues and images. They are rough affairs, and peculiarly battered in the various bombardments which Prague has undergone, and especially in the Revolutionary contests of 1848. Still they are very characteristic, and speak forcibly of the long history and of the superstition of the nation. The turbaned Turk, and his companions the demons appear frequently, and are really terribly dealt with by the artists, while the saints always figure in great glory. There is one of the monuments which, though coarse, shows a good deal of power. You see a dark hole in one of the stone buttresses, with a fierce-looking Turk on one side, and a ravenous dog, just springing forward, on the other; within the hole are three saints, whose faces just appear, and really more dolorous, forlorn-looking visages one seldom sees. They are praying. Above, forming the statue for the bridge, is a group of Christ and some of his apostles, breaking the chains of prisoners, and apparently about to descend to the three saints in the dungeon. The great statue of the bridge is *Nepomuck's*, who seems almost the patron Saint of Prague. This is of bronze, with five stars about the head to represent those which appeared on the water when he was drowned. He seems, from all accounts, to have been a very good man in the middle ages, and to have been thrown into the river from the bridge, because he opposed one of their Kings in some way. There is a difference of tradition about him. But there seems little doubt he met his death in a manly rebuke of the King's vices.

I stopped some time near his statue, to get the whole aspect of the scene. It was a curious mingling of the new and old. There was the venerable bridge, with its battered and quaint images—the same old bridge that Wallenstein's forces had tramped over, and where many a hard fought fight between bürgers on one side, and the garrison on the hill, on the other, had swayed to and fro. Now, handsome modern carriages with liveries, and new hacks, such as one sees in London or New York, of the prettiest styles, were hurrying over. Yet, right alongside of them—the *oldest* sight to me in all Prague—were sane, keen-looking men of this nineteenth century, walking, and taking off their hats reverently to this image of Nepomuck! I watched for some time, what kind of men especially did this—and though, of course, the lower class were most particular in the matter, yet men of all ranks and classes seemed to do the same. It was my first experience of a genuine Catholic people—and I went away wondering.

The evening drew on, in these rambles, and I hastened to a friend's house, where I had left my letter of introduction and a card, during the day. I had been long expected, and it did not need many minutes, with the truly German sociability, for us all to be on the best of terms. A number of their friends came in, in the course of the evening,—mostly Professors in the University,—and the conversation soon fell on the Bohemian school system. These gentlemen were German professors, invited by the Austrian government to this University, and what is more singular still—Protestants. Their remarks on the general cultivation and school arrangements in Bohemia were anything but complimentary. They describe the teachers as wretchedly paid, till within a year, in all the common schools, and the *Gymnasia*, or schools preparatory to the University, as in a miserable condition.

The Austrian Government, they tell me, has been making, this last year, immense efforts at reform—and the first change in the Universities has just commenced. These are now all put on the same basis as the German Universities—that is, the studies are thrown open to the students, and they are allowed to choose their own field to work upon, and are free from all restraint, except the examinations necessary for entering most of the professions.

Another change, too, which has exceedingly gratified the Bohemians, is the putting the Bohemian language on an equality with the German, in all public schools and universities. So that there are a good number of lectures now delivered in this university, in the Cheski tongue. The students, according to the account of these gentlemen, are very poorly prepared for a university course, and the labor of a professor is much less pleasant than in a German University. These divisions of Nationality have even affected society, and this divides itself into the German and Sclavonic, which is unfortunate, especially as the Germans are so few in number. The Bohemian part, according to all accounts, is much inferior to the other, in cultivation.

It was related, by one of the party, as a sign of the feeling prevailing through many in the town, that a friend of his, a man of considerable influence in the Slavonic party, had recently had a seal made, with the figure of a *Cossack* above, and below the words "*Immer nach dem Westen!*" "*Ever towards the West!*"

These impulses for a *Slavonic* Nationality, of which Prague was the centre in 1848, and by which it is still agitated, are to me, one of the most singular developments in history. I do not understand them.

They were first carried out into action in 1848, and produced most momentous effects. The old kingdom of Hungary was shaken by them into disjointed fragments. Bohemia itself, was split off from Austria. Their influence reached Poland and the provinces of Russia, and even the principalities of the Danube, wherever a tribe of the old Slavonic stock yet lived.

If these Slavonic tribes had been of one language and religion, all this, though remarkable, would have been less strange. But with many of these tribes, it would have needed the scent of an ethnologist to determine that they belonged to one "nationality." Their religions were different, and their languages—though all of the same family—now so unlike, that in the great Slavonic Congress in Prague, in 1848, the different members could not even understand one another, and a foreign tongue was the organ of the much hoped-for "Union."

Their interests and their past history were widely separate. Yet was the movement very deep and far reaching. It affected some of the first minds of the Slavonic race; and the Slavonic literature here in Prague and elsewhere, has shown in these last few years such a progress, as it has not since the time of its bloom in the twelfth and thirteenth centuries. To our ideas, the movement seems fantastic and useless—hardly more singular and unpractical, if the whole

Celtic race (the Highlanders in Scotland, the Irish, the Oriental tribes from which they sprang, all who anywhere belong to that stem), should unite and agitate to form a great "Celtic nationality!" I consider it as one of those visions for which these people in Middle Europe have so often lost realities. They have fought for "nationalities," and have forgotten Freedom.

CHAPTER XXXVI.

WALK TO THE LAURENZIBERG.

I MUST confess it—more interesting to me than the old Bridge; more than Huss's pulpit, or Nepomuck's Statue, or Wallenstein's Horse, or the Hradschin Palace, was a certain clear-sighted, genial woman, and an accomplished, intelligent man, here in Prague, true children of this nineteenth century. I met them a stranger, and left them such friends, as I scarcely have in Europe. It is difficult, except with people of peculiar culture, to meet on all points under a foreign language. There is always something coming up at an unexpected moment, which strikes one aback—which is not to be accounted for on our ideas—which is *foreign*, and you see no possible way of explaining it. But it was not so with any of us here. My friends were from North Germany, highly cultured, with the best German candor and freedom of thought—but with a certain earnestness of character, which is not so common in Germany, just now. People of the world, yet with that real German simplicity and friendliness of manner. They both knew America well, and seemed to take almost as deep an interest in its future, as I myself. Though in an Austrian state, and though loyal subjects, they felt and worked for the great poorer classes of men, recognizing it as a duty before the enjoyment in learning, and before even the regular round of religious duties, to help th se great masses who are so helpless. I think my friend is almost the first German *Gelehrter*, (scholar,) I have met, who is at all devoting his talents to popular education. I was glad to tell him, how well his name was known among American scholars, and that his few efforts in science had reached so far.

To-day we have been taking a long walk to the Laurenziberg, a high hill, which overlooks the city. It is a glorious spring afternoon; the trees are in the first freshness of foliage; the green fields in the valley glisten pleasantly in the sunlight, and the fragrance and softness in the air make one's heart glad. Every one is out enjoying the fine weather, and there are unusual numbers here to-day; for it is a religious holiday, and the people are making pilgrimages to the chapel on the hill. There is the Slovack with his broad-brimmed hat and soiled sheep-skin mantle thrown gracefully over one shoulder, ready to sell his little wares to whoever will buy. There the ruddy Bohemian peasant woman, with kerchief about her head, and bright-colored dress, reading piously her prayers. Right by her clatters along the Austrian soldier, with sabre, white coat and dainty little cap. And once I observed a tall Hungarian hussar, in his short blue cloak, sauntering moodily by, thinking perhaps of his far away Magyar fatherland and its crushed people.

As we climb the hill, we pass groups kneeling before the little shrines on the road-side, and even occasionally kissing devoutly the glass before the images.

We speak, as we pass in our walk by old historic scenes, of the new land over the waters. And amid these relics of an old feudal government, I am describing that which is ever new to the Germans, and of which I never weary of speaking to them—the success of this grand modern experiment in Self-government.

We climbed for a long time, following the throng of pilgrims toward the chapel on the hill, until at length on the summit, the wide, grand view of the valley of the Moldau opened before us. These panoramic views are never the finest to me, yet this gave a very distinct idea of Prague. The rich golden sunlight was pouring over the scene, but did not obscure at all the forest of towers and spires and domes and Moorish-like turrets, which characterize the city. In the midst of the valley wound the Moldau, dividing the town into two parts. On the banks toward the hill where we were standing (the *Klein-seite*), the houses rise one above the other on the hill side, till the summit is crowned by the immense structure of the *Hradschin*, the old palace of the Bohemian kings. The whole of that part has just the appearance of one of the old feudal towns, with the castle on the summit, from which the baron can rush down in his forays upon the peaceful citizens. Indeed such has been almost its character; and that solid bridge which connects this side with the "old town," has been the scene of many a fierce fight in olden time.

Below this, forming a very pretty object in the view from where we stand, is the new chain bridge over the river.

On the other end of the "Old Bridge," rise the massive buildings of the university, where, once, more than 30,000 students were gathered. Even yet it is one of the most numerously attended universities in Europe. Beyond this, to a great distance on that side of the river, stretches out the "Old City," varied with innumerable towers and fantastic spires, which, mostly built in the Byzantine style, give a peculiarly oriental air to the whole place. On the outer limits can be seen those immense hospitals for the sick and the insane, for which Prague is now celebrated. The population of the city is only 120,000, yet the buildings are so numerous and grand, that it makes a very imposing appearance. It is stated that even with this comparatively small number of inhabitants, the city is some twelve miles in circumference.

We stayed long, enjoying the different views, and only as evening drew on, turned away for our walk home. I went back a moment, to take a last good-bye of the old city, which seemed even more rich and fantastic in the evening light,—then followed my friends down the hill, quite sure that its like I should never see again.

As we went down, we stopped to look at some of the little chapels on the roadside—they were nearly all filled with pictures—some of no inconsiderable power—representing the sufferings of Christ. The people kneeling before them, seemed earnest and engaged. We stopped in one place to rest on some stones, near a dark entrance, where persons were going in and coming out continually. We hardly dared go in ourselves, until at length, the lady of our party ascertained that strangers were allowed to enter, and that a fragment of the holy Sepulchre of Christ was exhibited there! Accordingly we all crept through the passage into one apartment, and out of that into a small gloomy cave, lighted with one lamp, and hung with black. On one side of it was lying a full-length, wooden figure of the naked dead Christ, with his bleeding wounds, and above, the cross on a fragment of stone, which I suppose must have been the relic in question. In front was a plate for the offerings. The whole was very well arranged and had an exceedingly oppressive effect on one, and I must confess we were glad to deposit our kreutzers, and get out again. One may judge, how well contrived it was for affecting the common people.

In all these ceremonials, we agreed it was *possible* for a truly

Christian spirit to be engaged. Whether that was the fact with these people, or not, was quite another question.

We returned in the evening to my friend's house, or rather suite of rooms, which by the way are much handsomer than would be those of a gentleman of his station in Berlin; and then over a good supper, continued a pleasant conversation till a late hour.

APRIL

To-day my friends and myself have climbed the Cathedral tower, which, with the hill, gives an elevation of some 500 feet over the surface of the Moldau. On the summit, we found a droll, sociable fellow, the warden, who had lived up there for many years, and who told us of his "high-born son"—born 250 feet above the ground, and 500 and odd above the river! His description of the old buildings we could see, was very well given indeed.

To one of them, there was a melancholy interest for us, in that it was the place where the revolutionists of '48--mostly young students—are confined. It had been a nunnery, but is now a State prison. They are allowed, he said, to walk around in the court, we see there—"most of them, poor fellows, are sentenced for many years."

Another building which equally spoke of late events, was a new, strong fort, just out of the city, built on a hill side, where the only possible range of the cannon was *over the city*. The Government are evidently securing themselves against any repetition of the scenes of '48.

In the afternoon, in company with a Bohemian gentleman, I visited a great variety of interesting objects. Perhaps nothing of all these was more striking, than the old, tangled, gloomy burying-ground of the Jews—an immense field, right in the heart of the city, filled to every square foot of ground with plain slabs of stone, and overgrown with very ancient twisted trees and vines. It forms, throughout, one of the wildest, strangest scenes imaginable.

We asked our Jew guide about the little pebbles on some of the tombs. These were laid, he said, by those who came to the tombs to pray, and it was his private opinion that the spirits came back into the graves when a good man prayed.

It is a curious fact that the Jews here are almost entirely on the German side, against the Slavonians. They are quite numerous, numbering some 8,000, out of a population of 120,000.

My companion was a genuine Slavonian, and seemed to hope much from the recent measures of the Austrian Government with regard to his countrymen. The equal position now of the two languages in Bohemia, and the complete abolishment of serfdom through the whole Empire, would do much, he thought, for them.

The plan adopted in Bohemia in this freeing the peasants, is that the State should pay one-third of the loss, the peasant himself another third, and the master take upon himself the remaining third. Such a measure causes an immense loss to the landholders, and occasions a very complicated mass of business for the Austrian Government to settle, as not unfrequently the rents for years from the peasants' labor have been mortgaged. It was the opinion of this gentleman, though a Catholic, and, so far as I could judge, a Conservative, that the attachment of the whole Slavonic race was very weak, indeed, towards the House of Hapsburg.

MONASTERIES.

Later in the day we visited some of the old monastic establishments where my companion had been educated, which are still cloisters and hospitals. It was strange to be wandering around through the long corridors, and under the rows of old pictures, and to be meeting real, living monks. I must say, however, there was nothing in the arrangements which smacked of the comfort-loving tendencies of which the brethren have been accused. Everything was plain and simple,—even the "Refectory," though a grand, arched hall, had a table just set, which would have hardly contented a common laboring man with us.

The chapel was the only exception to this plainness. Here the treasures of ages seem to have been expended in gilding and carving, and monuments, and every variety of rich painting.

One establishment which I visited,—that of the "*Merciful Brethren*"—had an admirable hospital arranged within, with all the most modern practical conveniences, and some hundred or more patients. These are admitted and taken care of by the "Brethren" without charge; and what I was especially glad to hear, no preference was given to any particular religious faith. The Heretic or the Infidel, is equally admitted with the Catholic. The means for this are gained by the personal solicitations of the Brethren, from house to house. Verily there is many a good side to the old Romish Faith.

CHAPTER XXXVII.

A BOHEMIAN LADY.

PRAGUE, APRIL, 1851.

AMONG my acquaintances here, is a very intelligent Catholic family—Bohemians—who have treated me with much kindness. They have taken me out in their carriage, among the antiquities of this famous city ; and have sent their own family tutor with me, to show me over the various places of historic interest. I came in to-day, after a ride, and took "afternoon coffee" with them. The house has a most dingy, unpromising exterior, and the outside door at the head of the great stair-way, opens into a kitchen, through which we pass to the parlor. Yet the parlor is richly furnished beyond almost any I have seen in North Germany—massive oak chairs, deep sofas, carpets, heavy curtains, and rich Bohemian glass in abundance. The lady is evidently a woman of the world—has been in England and France—speaks French and German, as if they were native languages to her; and is beside a person of real thought and intelligence. Her husband is a merchant, much interested in the new rail-road operations in Austria. He wants extremely a rail-road chart of America, and I have promised to get him one, if possible.

While waiting for our coffee, I asked for a glass of water, and the Bohemian servant brought in a pewter vessel, looking very much like what we should use in our quarter of the world for a *watering-pot.* I thought it was odd; especially as the hostess seemed so much like a lady of the world; still in such a queer house and queer city I was ready for anything, and did not feel at all sure but that this might be the regular drinking cup of the inhabitants; so I took it, and was bringing it to my lips very gradually, when the lady caught a glimpse of me. "*Mein Gott!* You are not drinking out of that!" and the servant was ordered sharply, this time in Bohemian which she understood, to bring a glass; and then such a laugh, as we all had—especially the children and myself! The coffee was at length brought in, and a small cup of it with a glass of ice-water, and a sweet cake was passed to each one. In our conversation, I made an allusion to the grand religious ceremonies, then going on in Prague, and told her, I had seen that morning in the Cathedral near the Castle, for the first time in my life, the *Confession.* It had left a deep impression on me—the kneeling, humble penitents, pouring out so the history of the heart into the ear of *man.* It seemed a tremendous instrument of power. I asked her, what she had observed of its practical influence?

"Oh! Confession," said she, "like a great many of our ordinances, and of the ordinances of other churches, was good in its origin, but has now been much abused. So far as I have observed, among my servants and the common people, the influence is very good. It is very desirable for such persons, you know, and for most persons, when they are confessing their sins, to have a distinct idea of them. Merely saying, 'I am a sinner,' is not enough; the man must see clearly where he sins, and then he can more truly repent; we think confession to the priest meets this difficulty."

"Have you ever known direct effects of it?" said I.

"Oh, yes, often," she answered. "I have had again and again things restored to me by the priest, which had been stolen either by my servants, or others. And many and many a family strife here has been healed by our confessors. Of course, everything told them in the confessional, is sacred; still they can use it often for good. I must allow that very often it is abused. Very many of the common people put it off till such a time as this, and then there is such a crowd, that the priest has no time to give good advice; and the penitents themselves hurry it over in such an indecorous manner!

"And there are such absurd confessions! I wonder how the good fathers can bear it! There is Madame L——, they say, is always mourning with tears, in the box, that she has made bad butter, and keeps the dinner waiting—"

"*Peccatum mortale*, in my opinion," murmured her husband.

"Then the Frau Z——, who laments so often that her house is not washed every fortnight! Still on the whole, I find the influence good."

"But do you feel no reluctance at unfolding all your faults and foibles in this way to another?" I asked.

"*Gewiss nicht!* certainly not! How can I; and how can any Christian woman who really wants her faults corrected, and confesses for that purpose?"

"*Ich bitte*—pardon!" said a young lady, a friend, who had just come in, "I cannot agree with Madame —— in that! I find confession a great bore! I shall never tell my secrets to any one!"

I said something then about the dangerous influence on the mind of the priest from hearing, for a few years, such a history of the human heart.

"I do not see that," she said, "on a pure-minded man. I allow that very great care should be used in appointing a confessor; and for my part, I always prefer a private confessor, who understands my own character and peculiar difficulties."

I did not ask her, whether she thought this confession could really obtain *absolution* from the priest, for the whole manner in which she defended it, evidently supposed the contrary.

"I have been on your interesting old bridge to-day," said I, "and I see the people taking off their hats to the statue of *Nepomuck.* Do you all do that?"

"Ach! no. Nepomŭck was a very good preacher and priest in his day, and died for the truth, and is very much reverenced here; still no educated Catholic would take off his hat to his statue—we only bow to the image of Christ, which is at this end of the bridge."

In my visit to the Cathedral, I had bought at the door a little copy of a prayer to Nepomŭck, and now showed it to her. She looked it over.

"This praying to saints, you know, is not commanded by the church," she said. "Of course, there is but *one* real "Intercessor." Yet I find it very natural. Sometimes I believe it fully, and then again I cannot—I do not know. The whole subject of the next world is very mysterious. Who can tell, but that those we love, and the good of all ages, still have an influence on us here? I love to believe it," she said, looking up for a moment, her eye kindling with feeling. "How glad should I be to think *some* were still by me!" She stopped, and her husband took the opportunity to make his escape.

"There are a great many ordinances and ceremonials of the Church," she continued, "which I do not feel at all necessary for myself. I have no need of public worship. I am conscious of worshipping the Infinite better among His works. These fast days are useless to me, and generally disturb my health, and so with confession often; but I observe these, because wise and good men of the past have recommended them, and because I shall influence ignorant people—my servants for instance. They always connect real heart religion with such forms, and if they neglect the one, they will be very apt to become weakened in the other."

"I am glad you think so about fast-days!" said her friend, "they give me such head-aches!"

"In my opinion," she continued again, "the greatest defect of the Catholic Church, as compared with your Protestant, is the *celibacy* of the clergymen.

"This ordinance, like the others, I think was very good in the beginning. In the earlier ages and the times of persecution, marriage interfered with the duty of the priest; but now, in my view, this forced celibacy is the great cause of the ignorance of our native priests. No man of any cultivation and refined feelings, will place himself where he alone of society is cut off from the most tender enjoyments and the best discipline. Besides it makes our priests form such dishonorable connections, and which from this very rule, become often sinful to them.

"Nothing pleases me more in Protestant countries, than to see the confidence with which clergymen are received into the families.

"No respectable family in Prague will admit a priest to regular intimacy. Besides, I do not see how a priest can ever advise, or console, or sympathize with a family, who has never had himself the cares and responsibility of a family."

"Are the foreign priests as illiterate as the native?" I asked.

"No, not at all," she replied. "The Jesuits are men of very high cultivation."

"Ach, yes—what an excellent teacher was my dear Father C—; out so skilful! I should have been one of the sisterhood certainly, if he had staid!" said her friend.

"It is not probable," said the other, "that the Jesuits will ever return. They have left so bad a reputation here."

We conversed in this way some time, and I found her in all her thoughts with the same beautiful ideality and religious feeling. At the close I told her how glad I was, to get the views of an educated Catholic on these matters.

"I must have quite wearied you," she answered. "I have talked very frankly about my faith, and I will tell you frankly, what I find so objectionable in your Protestant mode of worship. It is too bare and cold for me. There is no appeal in it to the feelings and the imagination. Human nature is made up of many parts, and I believe imagination has its claim, as well as the reason. Your forms may be different in America, but those I have seen in the Reformed Church here, never affect me in the least. And in England, at least in some churches—people seemed to me to come together to hear an essay, and not to worship the dear God! Perhaps I am saying too much. You will understand me. I *must* follow the instincts of my nature, and they are never satisfied with your forms!"

It was not the time to argue the matter; so I only said, that we did not exclude feeling from our services, but "preferred to excite it by other means, through the reason, by oratory and persuasion. And we too employed poetry and music."

I was deeply interested in the conversation, and have given this lady's expressions, as much as possible, word for word.

As I left, I thought of the beautiful words of Lavater, which have often come over me since, in Roman Catholic countries.

Der kennt noch nicht dich, JESUS CHRISTUS!
Wer deinen Schatten nur entehrt,
Mir sei, was dich nur, Jesus Christus!
Zu ehren *meint*, verehrenswerth.

Wenn's Täuschung wur, nur Fäbel ware,
Es fable nur zu deiner Ehre;
Es mag mich drücken und betrüben
Um deinetwillen, will ich's lieben,
Erinnert's nur an dich, tragt's nur
Von dir, die allerkleinste Spur!

CHAPTER XXXVIII.

VIENNA.

A FIFTEEN hours' ride by rail carried me from Prague to Vienna. I know nothing more enlivening than travelling in this fresh spring season. It makes one grateful to see the world so beautiful. Then this incessant meeting with so many varieties of minds; and finding friendships and affinities with people of such different culture and habit! It is very pleasant. Prejudices wear off fast. One meets so many, who unwaveringly swear to that as black which their neighbors call white; one finds such firm prejudices on the most opposite matters, that it seems hardly worth while forming very fixed opinions on small matters. I find, too, I come more and more to the conviction, that men belong to just the same family, have just the same weaknesses, foibles, and virtues, whether they speak German or English, wear moustaches, or are close-shaven, sport beaver or turban. The thought, too, settles on me, half unconsciously but very deeply, from seeing so much of oppression and degradation—of the great Want and unhappiness of mankind. I find myself, also, strangely and unpleasantly losing my sense of the importance of the *individual man.* Men are used in masses, like cartridges for war; or they give themselves in flocks to their rulers for such ignoble purposes; they are so fixed in circumstances, and so apparently beyond good influences, that I lose confidence in individual Reform, and have more in the great Causes, which shall change the whole structure of society. Not, perhaps, a logical effect, but a natural.

Every new station, showed, as we went on, the presence of a very different people from the North German; the swarthy, dark-haired boys, the number of beggars, the chapels and crosses by the way, and the animated talk and gesture of people were all characteristic of a more southern race.

In the afternoon, at an angle of the road, we came suddenly in view of a line of massive blue mountains in the distance. Why did my pulse throb quick at the sight?—They were the hills, where a nation had made its last gallant, unflinching struggle for life. The first glimpse of a land, which had always seemed too heroic and dream-like to me, that I should ever see it.

The Carpathians! HUNGARY!

The neighborhood of Vienna was indicated, as a large city is usually, by the different style of men, whom we saw. People more unobservant of strangers, more quick, keen, social, unformal; and at the same time, more polite. A very pleasant population must the Viennese be, if these are good specimens.

Our passports at the last station were strictly demanded; but the baggage was passed easily. In fact, I am surprised everywhere at the politeness of the Austrian police. My quarters were soon taken up; and to-day, I have been on the *Prater*—the Hyde Park of Vienna; and the best place for viewing the outside of the city.

A grand spectacle it is—almost the most brilliant I have seen in Europe. Otho, the King of Greece, is here, and the young Emperor gives an entertainment to his guest, by calling out all the finest equipages into the Prater drive. The people, too, have turned out in multitudes, and every walk and road under these grand old oaks and lindens is filled with a most picturesque crowd. Here, on this alley on my right, sweeps down a dashing cavalcade of riders, with those fine-limbed, deep-chested horses, such as one seldom sees anywhere, except in England. At their head is a young officer, with the white military coat and a diminutive little green cap. His features could never be mistaken by any one who had seen the portraits of the late emperor, as those of the House of Hapsburg. A brother of the Emperor, as you may learn from the crowd. In the great alley on the other side, comes a fine open carriage with gentlemen in red caps; Turkish officers, as you hear, who are in Vienna studying engineering. Then some riders in the gay and graceful short cloaks and plumed shakoes of the Hungarian noblemen—the few at the court who are yet allowed, as if in mockery, to wear the much-loved costume. After them a modest carriage with a kindly-looking man within, and a boy at his side. The crowd all salute him with great heartiness. It is the father of the Emperor, who declined the crown, it will be remembered, at the abdication of his brother in 1848, in favor of Francis. The boy at his side is his youngest son.

Following, and quite putting to shame his simple equipage, appears the most splendid carriage of the day, with four handsome horses, and gilt trappings, and out-riders and footmen. Within is a little man with a red cap and singular costume, who keeps almost continually nodding to the people. He looks like a court-fool. This is the Sovereign of the old Classic Land—the *Bavarian King* of Greece. Not far behind is a simple, neat carriage, looking something like one of our large buggies, but with two perfectly trained, powerful horses. There are two footmen in white liveries behind, and in front sits a young man driving. He is dressed in the usual costume of an Aus trian officer, white coat and small green cap. His face has a thin and worn look, and gives you an impression of a person of no great strength of character. He chats easily with a friend at his side, and occasionally with a gentleman who rides near by. He holds the reins well, and seems an accomplished "whip,"—and that is all you would ever notice in him. Yet that man is, perhaps, the most important personage of these times; the absolute monarch of the Austrian Empire—the Conqueror of Hungary and of Italy—the Leader of Germany and the great and almost only "Defender of the Roman Catholic Faith." On his will, depend perhaps the liberties of Germany, the continuance of Hungary as a nation, and the safety, if not the existence, of Protestantism in the empire. Do you notice the gentleman who reins up near him, so easily and steadily;—a fiery horse; a man of sharp features and keen eye, with full whiskers, looking much like one of our New York "*fast men?*" This is *Count Grünne*, the chief favorite, the initiator of the young Emperor into the mysteries of dissipation, and the great authority on all matters of the chase or the table. He has acquired, it is said, a boundless influence over the young man's mind; and through him, the whole thoughts and attention of the Emperor are given up to horses, and dogs, and soldiers' uniforms, and all manner of trifles. Alas for thee, Hungary, and Italy, and Bohemia, when such are thy rulers!

I know no so grand expression of wealth and rank, as fine horses and carriages. They give an idea of *power*, which scarcely anything else can express. The Austrian nobility is one of the wealthiest in Europe; and of late years, they have devoted much attention to the breeding of horses. The display to-day in horses is much superior to any I have seen, except in London. Their best blooded animals are crosses of the Arabian with the English hunter.

After this royal party, came an indiscriminate crowd of all imaginable liveries and costumes, whirling rapidly by. There is Metternich's carriage—next him a little fisherman's box with a rough, fast trotting nag; then Esterhazy's, then a nobleman's, then a hack, then a buggy, and pressing close after them, amid the laugh of the crowd, a large-wheeled, long-thilled sulky, like one of our New York Third Avenue *turn outs*. Uhlan lancers and Austrian dragoons; *Grenzers* from the "Borders," and *Jägers* from Bohemia, Hungarian Huzzars, and Viennese police mingle pel-mell in the hurrying line. The alleys are equally lively. There the neatly-dressed gentleman from the city, then the tall Tyrolese with green hat and feather, the Turk in turban and robes, the Greek with his graceful red cap, the Slovack with sheepskin and broad-brimmed hat, and the peasant women with bright handkerchiefs about their heads; all merry and happy, for the pleasure-loving Viennese are in their element in such a scene as this. I follow the crowd almost at random. There is an exhibition of the "Gigantic English horse;" just beyond in a tent, "The unrivalled panorama of the Mississippi;" and wedging my way out of that crowd, I find a large company seated at tables under the trees, eating ices or drinking coffee, while an excellent band is playing in the balcony of the restaurante in front. After a quiet enjoyment, sipping an ice and watching the party-colored crowd, I turn off more to the left towards the "Sausage park," as it is called. Here they are, the *Volk*—the populace—of Vienna in their element! Dances, jugglery, circuses, gymnastic performances, swings, sail-boats full of children sailing in imaginary ponds around revolving poles, beer tables, sausage tents, fruits, meats, puddings—everything in the open air, and all mingled together in endless confusion. Every one full of the enjoyment, and very unconscious of everything else.

In Berlin, in such an entertainment as this, there would have been a moustachoed, helmeted policeman at every beer-table. Here, except on a "drive," to regulate the procession, I have scarcely seen one. As is well known, the Austrian paternal government likes nothing better than to see its good-natured subjects altogether, absorbed in show and pleasure. Theatres, and wine, and women will drive all impertinent political questionings out of their heads. Yet probably here, there was not a tent or booth, or small assembly, which had not its "secret police" officer, or its "government agent." In Austrian diplomacy, tyranny must never be shown, where it can be avoided.

Sunday, April.

I have just seen another and more serious side of Vienna-life which has impressed me very much. I know not why it is, but there is something to me in the early beauty of Spring, more thoughtful and solemnizing, than any other aspect of nature. And I have often wondered, whether our spring Revivals in the American churches, or the long and serious time of religious penitence and worship in the Episcopal and Roman Churches, might not connect themselves somewhat with this feeling. However that may be, there is an appropriateness which neither Cant on the one side, nor Superstition on the other, can destroy, in the reviving of religious feeling with this beautiful revival of nature. I had felt this through my whole journey, and it was with no slight readiness for religious impressions that I entered this bright Sabbath morning the old Cathedral of St. Stephen. The building is capable of holding some three or four thousand people without any inconvenience, and this morning it was full throughout. A scene, most solemn and impressive. I had never appreciated before the power of the Catholic worship. Of course in our country one sees nothing of it, and in France—at least in Paris—the people are so indifferent, and the whole service is so dramatic, that it produces no great effect. On the Rhine, too, there are such crowds of spectators in the churches that a general air of earnestness is wanting. Here, however, despite the immense crowd, there was the stillness and solemnity of our own most affecting religious services. Scarcely any one was looking around to watch any one else; very many were kneeling on the stone pavement in silent prayer, others reading from the prayer-book, or bowing before the altar to partake of the communion wafer. Everything added to the impressiveness. The massive and antique architecture, the soft-glowing light, the shadowy arches, the ornament, rich, yet in harmony with the old and time-worn building, and everywhere tending less to dazzle than to impress.

If there is anything in proportion, in grandeur, in harmony of outline, in beauty of form, and of coloring, of itself adapted to call out or to aid religious feelings, then was the old Cathedral of St. Stephen wonderfully framed for religious worship. The pictures too! One evidently gets no appropriate idea of religious paintings as they are placed in galleries. They were never made to be set in rows in bright, bare rooms, with sharp-eyed *connoisseurs* clustered around them, any more than the beautiful thoughts and passages of Shakspeare to be gathered in one book. They must be taken with their natural accompaniments. Here, in a shadowy niche, with just light enough to see the upturned look of pain, and while the rites of worship are still going on around, a "Head of Christ" is peculiarly affecting; but when one hundred and fifty of them are in one hall, with all kinds of Satyrs and doubtful Nymphs distributed among them, the effect is gone. These stiff old pictures of martyrs and saints too, which look so out of place in a modern gallery, seem entirely appropriate and natural in these venerable churches. I could not but feel the effect of them in this Cathedral. There were pictures of Christ in his sufferings, rough, but powerfully drawn, which in the solemn stillness I could most vividly realize, and could hardly gaze at without tears. The martyrs, portrayed in their torments or their triumphs, seemed for the first time like the ideal of the artist; noble and pure men, who had died for the truth.

To these sources of impression was added the full and rich swell of music, which softened by the distance of the choir, reached one's feelings with an indescribable, touching effect. Surely one of the objects of Church music is to soften the feelings and prepare the mind for religious thoughts; and in this respect, one must allow that no form of worship is superior to the Roman Catholic. The full force of it, I felt that morning. And, as I knelt in prayer with the crowd, I could not but believe that in all the superstition around me, there were many who worshipped the Invisible Being as purely and spiritually as I. I felt glad to think that all which this mummery originally pictured, was equally reverenced by me. This mild and suffering face which meets one on every column, this bowed and stricken form, are representations of Him whom Protestant and Catholic can equally adore. This cross carved on every beam and in every niche, which the crowd mechanically imitate with their gestures, is the emblem to us, too, of the Greatest of all events. These men, pictured in all forms of pain and torment, are those whom we equally with them, can reverence as the noble martyrs for Truth.

I was glad that the idea at the ground of this worship was no false one, and that in its origin, and sometimes now, in its practice, there was something true and good.

I went out conscious that it had not been the worse for me, being in the Catholic Cathedral, and half ashamed, as I met a procession with a crucifix, that I did not take off my hat too, with the crowd.

These were the first impressions from the Catholic worship; but I am bound to say, what hardly need be said, that there is an entirely different side to the picture. Nothing is more calculated to destroy any good impressions with regard to the Romanists of Austria, than a sight of the priests themselves. I am in the habit of judging much from the form of the face and shape of the head, of a man's character, and I must say, more unpromising physiognomies and "organs" I have seldom seen, than on these men. There was a *sneaking*, under-handed expression to them which could not belong to men whose manhood had been properly developed. Their heads were, some of them, base, and animal, and sensual; or so deficient in the intellectual and so developed in certain moral propensities, as to indicate most distorted natures; or, as was the case with most, with a full intellectual shape, but with an expression of astuteness, cunning, suppleness, very disagreeable to look upon. I did not see one genuine, manly, intelligent face. Then, to observe the slavish adoration of the crowd to them, to watch their own mummeries, to become more and more convinced of the ignorance and stupidity of the masses, whose education mostly depends on them,—all this, step by step, has given me such an impression of the curse which they are to the whole nation, that I have felt ready to vow myself forever more, to the most Puritanic simplicity, rather than to bring upon mankind again this accursed hierarchy.

CHAPTER XXXIX.

LIFE IN VIENNA.

I FIND the mode of life and manners among various classes here, quite different from that in North Germany. Nobody seems to live at home much. A friend invites you to meet him at a *café* or *restaurante*, instead of his house. You find your acquaintances in gardens, and promenades, and concerts, and wine-saloons, and seldom anywhere else. People come before you as more lively, gay, passionate, than in the North, but with less intellectuality. The subjects for conversation are more from music and dress, and incidents in every-day life. Books are not much read or spoken of; and important or serious matters seem generally avoided. Yet are the Viennese a very social, kind-hearted, cheerful people, with much real force and deep feeling I am convinced, if they were in circumstances to awaken it.

The ladies dress much more richly, than in North Germany, though in the morning you will often see a lady of rank riding round to the shops in an old merino and a common velvet bonnet, which would almost shame one of our belles. With the fashionable classes, the day begins at noon. After a light breakfast, comes the drive in the Prater, and amusement till the dinner hour, from 4 to 6. The time for receiving calls is from dinner till 7½ o'clock, the hour for opera. After this, at 9½ and 10 o'clock, the parties and balls begin, and last often till 8 or 9 in the morning. Though rules for intercourse are very strict, all accounts represent the aristocracy of Vienna, as the most dissolute in Europe. *Liaisons* seem strangely public; and married ladies drive out with their lovers. Prince Schwarzenberg is living openly now with the wife an officer, who is said to be quite proud of the *honor!*

APRIL, 1851.

I went last evening to call on a mechanic, to whom a friend in Hamburg had given me a letter. He is living in one of the suburbs, in the third floor of a large house. He received me most heartily as an *American.* A dark-browed, dark-haired man, who looks just the one for a leader in a desperate enterprise. I met him cordially, but let him lead the conversation. He did not wait long.

"I wish I was in America! I would go there, but there may great events happen here, in a few years, and I want to be on hand. Ach! you are happy there! Here *they* have conquered. Nothing but tyranny and priestcraft for us!"

"You saw the Revolution, I suppose!"

"Ach, yes! I see you are to be trusted, from this letter, and I will tell you. I fought through every street with these accursed soldiers! We did not yield an inch without blood. Come to the window! You see that long line of blotches along those handsome house-fronts there?"

"Yes."

"Those are from grape-shot. We lined those fine houses with picked shooters, and the soldiers could not get on a step—and so the battery kept up a tremendous fire right through that broad street. They could not dislodge us, until they got some men around in the gardens, in the rear of those houses. *Mein Gott!* what a time was that! I had a company in that—you see it—that tall stuccoed building. There was no escape in the rear—and, in front, the grape swept like a tempest. So I went up to the attic, and a part of us kept up a continued fire, while the rest broke through the wall into the next house—and so we went on from house to house, sometimes climbing over the roof. I went last—and lost but one, poor fellow, who was picked off, just as we were scrambling over a roof."

"Have you any hopes of trying it again," said I.

"Certainly. This war shall never end, till tyrants or people are gone. I know how the working-men feel. Give them another chance, and they will fight till the last man. *We cannot bear this long!* Taxes, spying—every damned annoyance of tyranny. We get little work—we have no kind of freedom—and then we are paying all the while for these immense armies. You have no idea of the brutal oppression here. Every day *women* are publicly scourged—you must have seen the *Notizen* on the walls—and if I should go out with a white hat or a long beard, I would be in the guard-house in an hour!"

So he went on, in tones earnest and passionate, telling of the wrongs and sufferings of the laboring classes—the dark eye kindling at the thought of fighting the good fight over again with the hireling soldiery. A determined, dangerous man for the Austrian authorities, when the next struggle comes.

To-day, I have delivered some letters to a genuine Vienna gentleman, living in the centre of the old city, where, strangely, are the most aristocratic houses. Very polite, profuse in his offers of service; evidently could make nothing of me. A traveller, not interested in theatres—not going to the Casino-ball—lives in *lodgings* and *en route* for Hungary! An anomaly to the Viennese. He accompanies me to the door and bows me out with the sweetest "*Unter thänigster Diener!*" (Most humble servant!)—and I receive a note of invitation in the evening, directed to Herr *von* B——.

I find a great deal of genuine activity in the government, in matters of education. The Ministry have kindly furnished me with documents, and every convenience for studying the system. COUNT THUN, himself, has been truly friendly. A condensed sketch of these improvements has already been given to the public.* The main points are the introduction of the *voluntary system* in the Universities; and the connecting the various popular schools by gradations with one another. I am convinced that there is a spirit of real reform abroad; and that the Professors and the Ministry of Instruction are laboring to raise the standard of education. The great drawback, which either originates with Count Thun's rigid Romanist views, or from the obstinacy of the priests, is that many of the people's schools must still be left in the hands of the clergy. The influence of the Catholic priesthood is one of the great causes which check all progress in Austria.

I find the Protestants have a very precarious foothold here. They

* "Hungary in 1851," p. 3. A full description of the improvements in the Austrian School System, put forth by the Austrian Government, has been deposited by the author in the Yale College Library, New Haven, Ct., for public examination.

are barely permitted to exist, and are in constant fear of having their meetings broken up, as those of the *Freien Gemeinden* or "German Catholics" have been. I attended the Protestant service last Sunday, in a room like one of our large "conference rooms." A very simple, fervent exercise, and much more satisfactory than those which I have listened to, generally, in North-Germany.

APRIL.

My friend ———, a scientific gentleman and known as a man of liberal sentiments, asked me to dine with him to-day, and meet a small number of his friends. The hour was to be four o'clock. I rung at the time—the door was opened by a smart-looking man-servant in livery, who conducted me to the drawing-room, where Mr. ——— met me with the usual oft-repeated "most humble servant," and warm shakes of the hand—and then led me to *die gnädige Frau*" ("the gracious lady"), as they call the mistress of the house. There were several rooms opening into one another, very handsomely furnished—much more richly than the houses in North Germany. The floor was oak in mosaic and waxed. No books on the tables, but many Chinese articles, and vases and mirrors. The walls delicately painted in frescoe and arabesque—a so much more beautiful style than our papering. This room was filled with little ottomans and sofas, like our own parlors. The ladies were in full dress, and looking very pretty, though in general the cast of face was a little different from the common German type—more harsh and passionate—half-brunette. The manners of all were very cordial and easy.

"*Himmlisch!* Heavenly! heavenly!" I heard soon from a group in one corner, and on going there, found them looking at some beautiful little specimens of Bohemian glass-ware.

"Have you anything half so pretty in America, Herr B.?" said one to me; "look at this *Ampel!*"

It was a beautiful little hanging glass vase for flower-vines, the prettiest ornament in the German houses, swinging amid the curtains of the window, or on the balcony. I expressed my admiration for it, and the conversation then turned on the ornaments in American and German houses. "*Ach!* you will not see," said one, "such pretty furniture in our houses now as once—it costs so much to live. The funds are so low, you know, and all that."

One of them asked me soon about the expenses of living in America, especially in the large cities, and whether ladies went to the theatre in their own carriage, &c. I told them as nearly as I could, and then asked about the style and cost in different ranks in Vienna. They talked the matter over, making different statements, and finally one said: "It is very hard, Herr B., to say exactly. There are our great nobles, who are as rich as princes—but you mean the middle classes, eh? Well first, for the Professors and such people. Prof. H.,—you know him—gets about 3000 Gulden ($1500) a-year; some only 2000. The merchants and professional men live on—some of them—2000, ($1000,) up to 20,000 ($10,000.) I should think a good average income for the merchants, would be 4000 Gulden—though that would hardly keep a carriage. People are rather extravagant here in *Wien.* I have been in Berlin and Dresden, and I know it costs twice as much here. One must go to the opera, you know, and for my part, I fall sick, if I do not have a drive in the Prater. In Berlin, I could stay in the house more, over books, though it was very *langweilig,* (stupid,) was it not, *liebe Tante?*" This was addressed, very affectionately, to a *spirituelle,* dignified elderly lady, who had just joined us.

"No, liebes Kind. dear child, I did not find it so!"

"Why, aunt! you do not mean to say you like cold North Germany best?—better than *la belle Vienne?*"

"I do. I always have, in many respects. We are not so much cultivated here. Our society is not so thoughtful. It is true, it is very pleasant here in the cheerful, sunny south—but I do not find it so satisfying—and to you here I feel free to confess, it pains me, pains me every day, to see the condition of the people!"

"Ach, Tante—nichts politisch! no politics!" said the young lady. "I was not thinking of that, but are we not much the warmest hearted here, and most poetic? They are so cold and prosy in the North."

"I do not know that," replied the other. "You are more expressive here, but their feelings stand trial much better—are more lasting. Still I would never forget that many of our most beautiful souls in Germany—poets and writers, are from the South."

After farther talk of this kind, I took the liberty of asking the lady, who had defended the North, whether she was not originally from Hanover? She answered that she was, and inquired with some surprise, how I knew it. I told her it was from the purity of her accent, the Hanoverian tone and pronunciation being generally quite distinct and peculiar."

"Ach! you are noticing our accent. It is *shrecklich!* horrible!" said one of the young ladies. "Have you observed the Viennese never says *Ich* but *Ik*, and *nicht* is always *nit*, and *kann* is *kawnn* I am forever running into it before I think."

"It is not so much matter," said another, "for almost as many speak French and English now, as our own language. Your English is spoken everywhere."

In the other drawing-room, I found several gentlemen gathered, whom I was very anxious to know better. One a University professor, a keen, clear-headed man from one of the Northern universities, who, though a loyal servant of the Emperor, is doing good service also for the people—in attempting to improve the means of education. Another, a civilian who usually passed under the title of Doctor, I was very desirous to see.

When in Prussia, I had been much with his intimate friends, and they had confided to me his most adventurous history. He had reached Vienna accidentally the very day the Revolution of '48 broke out, and without a word from any one, disguised in a Tyrolese costume, he had gone out with his trusty rifle, and had fought the streets step by step, against the soldiers. I knew his friend, who was at his side through much of it. He said that the Doctor never seemed to fire, without a white coat coming down. His aim was as cool, as if shooting ducks. The students finally began to notice that the Tyrol hat was always at the head, wherever there was danger, and they at last sent an officer to him, requesting his name for the "Student Committee," that they might suitably promote him. He declined giving it—preferring to fight by himself. There came an emergency at length, in the siege of Vienna by Windisgrätz, when, if a message could be carried beyond the besieging lines, the city might be saved. Kossuth with a brave army, flushed with victory, lay within thirty or forty miles distance. If the condition of Vienna could be intelligently stated to him, it was thought he would not hesitate to deliver the city and terminate the war. But the difficulty was, to find the man. The Committee of Students met—offered rewards, made patriotic appeals—but no one would present himself to the almost certain danger, of either being shot by the sentinels or hung as a spy. Dr. ——, the moment he heard of the case, offered himself to some of the leaders, refusing still to give his name—and only demanded one companion, and two of the best horses of Vienna. A comrade was easily found, if he would lead, and two blood-horses from the Emperor's stables were brought out The Doctor presented himself, dressed in the height of the sporting fashion—red coat, white breeches, handsome top-boots, nice gloves and the et cetera, while the other followed as groom. They rode leisurely out from the gates of Vienna, and at some distance came upon the first sentinel. He demanded the "word!" and the Doctor muttered something and rode quietly on. The soldier supposing it was some country gentleman, did not fire. The two now turned by cross roads, which they knew and penetrated some distance, before the challenge startled them again. This time, bowing their heads to their horses' necks, they struck in their spurs and sprang on. There was a quick shot—without effect—and then a hot pursuit. Their horses, however, soon distanced the hussars. After this, they were not molested, the sentinels supposing them a gentleman and servant living within the lines. When nearly through, they were suddenly surprised by the sight of a knot of officers in front of an inn which they must pass. Fearing, that if they rode by, the Austrians might suspect something, the gentleman with a most characteristic coolness rode up to the door, dismounted, and called for wine, and was soon in a very social talk with the Austrian officers, even inviting them to call at his country-seat, near by. They parted amicably, and in a few hours the two were far beyond the Austrian lines. On reaching the Hungarian camps, they were conducted to Kossuth, and stated their mission. He himself, was in favor of marching directly on Vienna—how much might have been saved, had he done so!—but his officers and companions opposed it, as being a step beyond the design of the Hungarian movement—as committing them irretrievably to a war with all the arbitrary powers. The ambassador plead much, and eloquently—

out to no purpose, and he and his companion returned on their hazardous enterprise. The escapes on the way back, were as wonderful as before. At the last line of sentinels, their muttered reply was not enough. The sentinel fired, wounding the groom's horse, and in a moment the patrolling hussars were in rapid pursuit. It was a terrible run. I have often heard the Doctor relate it. He himself could easily have escaped, but, of course, he would not abandon his comrade. They were often within pistol-shot of the hussars, and once he had raised his pistol on the foremost, but without firing. He is a dead shot, and had resolved to sell his life dearly. There was no need. Just at nightfall, they came within range of the gates. A joyful shout from the walls—quickly rattling shots among their pursuers—and their jaded and bloody horses were just able to bear them safely in.

Besides this adventure, I had known of the Doctor's going down into Croatia, in the beginning of the war, and fighting on his own account on the side of the Hungarians—always at the most dangerous outposts, never accepting a commission or honor—as cool in the battle as in the drawing-room, and an unerring shot.

I had pictured to myself beforehand a real lover of the battle—a brawny, blustering, swearing blade, who would be most disagreeable anywhere, except at your side in a tough fight. I found, however, a very quiet, modest, polite gentleman, attentive to the ladies, with no especial marks of courage, except only a certain steady directness of eye in looking at you, which I have always observed in men much accustomed to shoot, and who have been tried much in scenes of danger. I saw him frequently afterwards. He never would speak of his adventures, except under great solicitation; and only occasionly alluded, in a quiet way, among his intimates to his "little ride in'48." A true *man* for these stormy times; and to be heard from again, I hope.

Luckily for him, my acquaintance with him was never suspected by the Austrian police. It was strange how well in this very company, my instincts were afterwards confirmed. There was a big blustering man, who thumped the table and often protested loud friendship for me, and cursed the government violently when I met him at his house, whom I always suspected to be a sneak; and there were others on whom unconsciously I had a most unwavering reliance. Afterwards in my imminent peril, this quiet Doctor and some others as unexpressive friends risked their lives for me, while the others either utterly disowned me to the police, or acted like children. There was a very interesting English gentleman present, who had almost forgotten his English, who stood by me, also, in a noble manner afterwards—as I should have known he would, and who was obliged to leave the capital, after his long residence there, in consequence of his interference.

Our dinner-table was set out very handsomely, with more of beautiful glass-ware than I had been accustomed to see—and with a greater variety of wine—indicating the neighborhood of wine countries.

"Have you seen everything in our beautiful Wien; and do you not like it all?" said the lady next me.

"All except the *trottoirs*," I replied, "they are execrable; it is really risking one's life to go sight-seeing on foot in Vienna!"

"But you must not leave anything," said she. "There is the People's Theatre, close by you in the Leopoldstadt. You get the best broad Viennese wit there. Then have you seen the dance-halls? travellers always go there; and we ladies, too, sometimes for curiosity. They dance till four o'clock in the morning. And you must taste all the Vienna ices, better even than the Paris; and our puddings, perhaps we can show you some to-day."

"And you should not forget, Herr B., our works of art," said the elderly lady, of whom I have before spoken. I inquired more particularly of them.

"You know the public galleries of course from your guide-books. The collection of Rubens in Prince Lichtenstein's, one of the best in Europe; and the Spanish school at Esterhazy's. The engravings you must not forget—perhaps the finest collection in the world—they are in the royal Palace. But you must see beside some of our private *ateliers*, to judge of modern Austrian art. There is Professor Rahl's studio. I think you told me you knew him."

I told her, I had been introduced to him, and had seen a large work he was preparing for a gentleman in Boston. "A rich colorist," I said, "but he seemed to me somewhat meretricious."

"Ah, you speak of that Venus *nude!* Yes; you are right. In fact, our school is not as simple as the Northern, though superior in my opinion to that finical Düsseldorf."

"But, Herr B.," said the young lady, "you should have seen the great picture of the year, here last winter. Ach! Himmel! De la Roche's 'Napoleon on the Alps!' All Vienna was *en fureur* for it!"

I had seen it, I said, in the gentleman's gallery who had owned it, in Leipsic.

I inquired, whether any of *Calam's* landscapes could be found in Vienna. I had never seen but two, but they seemed to me the finest; and, indeed, the only satisfactory landscapes I had ever met, except Turner's.

"*So!* Calam! I think there is one here. I will inquire. I see you English always speak much of *Turner.* We do not know him at all in Germany. The truth is, we cannot often afford to buy paintings from England."

"But especially," said the elder lady, or Madame Von Z——, as I found she was called, "you must see Canova's funeral group in the Church of the Augustines."

I told her I had seen it; and that I scarcely ever saw statuary which affected me more at the first impression. The white marble forms against the dark opening of the tomb which they were entering, every line so sad and drooping; nothing affected; no attempt to show features which should be concealed; the bowed matron with the urn, the tottering old man, the sorrowful maiden, the bitterly-weeping child, the crouched lion at the portal. It made an impression of *sorrow* so much on me, that I could not refrain from tears, without having really known the design intended. But the effect was exceedingly injured, when I turned to my guide-book, and found it was an "allegorical group."

"Yes; that is true. I felt it at first in the same way. I never enjoy allegorical designs."

"Ich bitte Sie, Herr B.!—pardon!" interrupted our host, "you are not doing justice to the wine. There is the Hungarian champagne by you, or the Adelsberger—an excellent wine, I can recommend it. Here, Karl! fill up a glass of Menesch—the extract, sir! I imported it from Hungary myself! *Zu Ihrer Gesundtheit*—your health!" I bowed and sipped of the little thimble-glass, filled with a dark, sweet, cordial-like wine

"Herr L. says you are going into Hungary. Is it so?" said one of the ladies to me.

"Yes."

"Why do you? What *can* you find there? There is no good theatre now in Pesth, since the Revolution, and the roads are terrible. *Ungarn* always seems *so* far off. I would rather take a trip to England, for the trouble of it. Then I should not like to see that poor people now, *die armen!*"

"But do you not like the Hungarians, here?" said I.

"Oh yes, we all like them. They are great favorites in Vienna—that is the men—we think the women a little *ungebildet*, (uncultivated,) you know. But the gentlemen are real cavaliers—very manly-looking! They have not at all your odious English custom of shaving the face. They think it girlish. Do you see what an influence we have had on Meester N.?" and she pointed to the full beard and moustache of the English gentleman.

All other conversation was now absorbed in a discussion, going on in the middle of the table, around our host. He was denouncing the financial measures of the Government, as utterly ill-judged and insufficient. This issuing of paper, he said, was only putting off the evil day. There must be thorough measures, or Austria would be bankrupt. Retrenchment! economy! that was the only thing.

"But look at this taxation!" said the Professor; "this will soon go far towards meeting the difficulty."

"*Ich bitte Sie Verzeihung*—I beg your pardon! It will do nothing. It embitters the people—that is all. We *must* retrench these expenses in armies and uniforms, and police. There is enough spent there to pay half the interest."

"Ach!" said the other, shrugging his shoulders, "that is quite another question. You know soldiers cannot be given up here."

"Leider! Alas! no!—but fewer of them! Then a better management of the public property. I agree so far with the *Lloyd*, in an entirely different system being needed by our Ministry. And this attempting to *force* commerce—it's absurd!

"There would be no difficulty," said another gentleman, "for the

Austrian Government, if there was any public confidence in .t. These foreign gentlemen here, know, that the debt of England is incomparably greater than Austria's, even in comparison with her resources. Look at our State property—it is immense. The mines of salt and iron and lead—our public forests—the monopolies of our Government—the State domains—there is security enough for the heaviest funded debt. Give us quiet and peace here a few years, and we shall have *credit.* That is all we want."

"You will find this the subject of subjects in Vienna," whispered one of the ladies to me, "especially to us who want to go to your Great Exhibition so much. A pound is worth now—how much, Herr S.? You know!"

"About 13–4;" and to me, "usually, 9 florins and 54 kreutzers."

"I fear I shall never get to the Exhibition," said she, with a sigh; "but they are going to the drawing-room again!"

Coffee was brought up—always in Vienna with iced water—and I had a long conversation, in English, with the Doctor and the Englishman. They were both confident the present state of things would not hold long in Austria. Discontent, they said, was working through every class, except the nobility. Tyranny had now reached a very tender part with the Viennese—the pocket. "They would have succeeded in '48," said the Doctor, "but there were no competent leaders. They fought well."

"A bad lot, all of them," said the Englishman; "though the students did show some pluck."

"No men ever fought braver," said the Doctor; "but it's time for the band in the Volksgarten—let's be off for a walk. Die gnädige Frau will give us a light for our cigars."

"Adieu!"

"Unterthänigster Diener!!"

"Adieu!"

APRIL, 1851.

I am much amused at the Viennese strictness in matrimonial matters. A friend of mine, Mrs. ———, an American lady residing in Vienna, was lately visited by a young German friend of hers.

"Have you heard, Mrs. ———," said the young lady, "of the great indiscretion which your American friend, Mr. S., has been guilty of in our family?"

No; she had not.

"Well, I was in our boudoir, yesterday morning, and I heard my sister in conversation in the front drawing-room with Mr. S.; at length her tones grew so loud that I feared something was the matter, and on going to the door, I could see through the rooms, that my sister was walking up and down in her riding-dress, in a terrible excitement, brandishing her little whip most violently. I rushed into the room, and found Mr. S. standing on one side, pale and in deep emotion, and my sister with a letter crushed in her hand. '*Mein Gott!* That I should be insulted so in my own house, and by one who has been treated so kindly!' she was saying. I asked what it was, and found that Mr. S. had had the presumption to write a letter to my sister, offering his hand, and had handed the letter to *her!* It was enclosed to my mother, indeed, but he had sent the letter to *her!* We had never expected such an insult from Mr. S., and certainly we had given him no pretext for it!"

Mrs. ——— could not get the point of the offence, at first, but when she did, she burst into a laugh, and told her indignant friend, that that was the custom in America; and, indeed, that a gentleman seldom even informed the mother at all, until the matter was settled. Mr. ———, too, who was present, told her that "American parents felt abundantly satisfied, if they were even invited to the wedding!" The lady was much mollified by this, and would inform her sister, who would be glad to know that Mr. S. had not *intended* to offend her.

A WEDDING.

A friend gives me the following account of a wedding lately in Vienna high life, of the daughter of Count ——, a favorite of the Emperor. "It was in the morning at the house of the pope's Nuncio, who performed the ceremony. We found the rooms filled with princesses of all high names, Metternichs, Esterhazys, Lichtensteins, &c., in full dresses and diamonds, all in bonnets, except the troops of bridesmaids. The groom was an elegant young Hungarian nobleman, in his national costume. It was of a rich blue silk, close-breasted, tight-fitting short coat, slashed with gold cords across the breast; tight blue silk breeches, joining at the knee the high, snug, polished, and spurred boots. From his shoulders, fell back the short national cloak of heavy blue watered silk, lined with white. It is only the form of the dress that is characteristic, the color is at the choice of the wearer; and the bright Mazarine blue with white lining and gold trimmings, was very becoming to the dark, brilliant, oriental beauty of the young count. Other Hungarians were there, with deep-colored velvets, trimmed with fur. The dress of the ladies is not peculiar, except of those who are of Hungarian blood; theirs is of deep black; but they are not often found at Court, unless to beg the life or liberty of some of the thousands still lying in Hungarian prisons.

" The groom was in the room all the time. Presently came in the bride, with her mother and one or two lady-friends. She went up to her father, kissed him, then kissed her step-mother, and then the father and mother of her husband, and afterwards passed about the room, kissing her intimate friends. They always kiss both cheeks; first on one side and then on the other. The bride was very pretty, and dressed like all other brides.

" After she came, the whole party crowded into the little private chapel of the Nuncio. The service was in French, and very much like that of the Episcopal Church, except that there were more ceremonies. It was finished by administering the communion to the bridal pair."

CHAPTER XLI.

AN EXCURSION—AN ARISTOCRATIC PARTY.

APRIL —.

As I awoke up this morning, the first object which caught my eye was a flowing beard, a placid countenance, turbaned head, and long smoking pipe, in the window opposite.

I could see nothing else, where I lay, and for some time, in my half-dreamy state, I puzzled myself with wondering how I had at length reached Turkey, the country I had so longed to see, and how I intended leaving it, and what strange land was next before me, when a rap with "*Ist der Herr schon auf?* (Is the gentleman up?) roused me to realities, and I remembered I was in Vienna, where Turks are plentiful enough.

The summons proved to be from a servant of my friend, the "Doctor," with an invitation to a country excursion to-day. I accepted it, and in a short time was breakfasting with him at *Daŭm's* (a celebrated coffee-house,) the breakfast consisting of two small kipfel, or bread-cakes to each, the whitest and best bread in Europe, crumbled into a tumbler of rich coffee.

We were intending to go to the valley of Briel—and accordingly walked towards the city gates to the rail-road station without the walls. VIENNA has been very well compared in its plan, to a spider's web. The den—the centre of all—the object by which the stranger everywhere guides himself through the mazes of the city, and the last which he sees at a distance in leaving it, is the Cathedral of St. Stephen, with its lofty and graceful spire. From this radiate all the streets of the "old city," until they are cut off by the ancient walls, turned now into agreeable promenades. This, though it embraces the most mouldy, interesting, and aristocratic part of the city, is only a small portion of Vienna. Beyond it, radiate out again the streets of the "Suburbs," mostly fine broad avenues, lined with handsome stuccoed houses, and only changing near the outskirts into the narrow dirty lanes of ordinary European cities. There are innumerable public gardens and parks all around and within the city, and the broad promenades of the Bastions encircling it, so that the whole has a very attractive appearance. But the glory and beauty of Vienna, in which it is equalled by no city of Europe, is in its surroundings—its environs.

Those jagged hills on one side, with their green quiet valleys, and monasteries, and castles perched along the summits, the rich plains at their base, the broad silvery stream of the Danube on the other, and the blue massive summits of the Styrian Alps in the distance, with the cheerful gardens, the walks, the towers of the city in the centre—such a scene of picturesque beauty is not in my memory.

My friend and I walked hurriedly, as every one does in Vienna, dodging the rapid vehicles, for which the pedestrian must keep the most constant look-out, as the streets are very narrow and have no sidewalks, until we came to the gate. This is a heavy arch under the Bastions, guarded by sentinels, with cannon above raking the street, a token of the martial law which still rules the city. As we came out on the broad *glacis* beyond, we stopped a moment with the crowd to look at a handsome light carriage, sweeping on rapidly towards us. Hats in the air! yes; it is—the Emperor No outriders, or carriages, or attendants, and he himself driving *four in hand*, like a Jehu! Not bad!—and I feel inclined for the first time to touch my hat to the young Nero—but do not.

"Do you see that large brick building," said the Doctor, in English, after we had walked some ways, "with a clean sweep all around it—nothing which can command it any where? That is the new Arsenal, built so that we cannot get arms as easily for another fight. Ah! such a beautiful little rifle, as I found that night in the old one! They say all the muskets of the Hungarian nation are in this. It would be devilish hard to storm!"

I took on myself the buying the tickets—as the Doctor was busy with some ladies—and bought first-class tickets for *Mödling*, where we were going. The Doctor laughed, and said *he* always took the second or third class. There were a frank, jovial set of gentlemen in this — some Hungarians, and Austrian country landlords. They passed cigars to us, and after a little while, one of them in a very good-natured, free and easy way, begged to know what country I was from? "He saw from my dress I was foreign." I told him to guess. He said from my accent, he should judge me to be from North Germany—Holstein, perhaps? "No." "Well, Denmark?" "No." Sweden, and then Russia, and finally back again to Meklenburg and Bavaria, and at last to England. Baffled in all this, he gave it up. "Where the d—l are you from, then?"

I answered vaguely, and did not gratify his curiosity till at the close of the ride,

"*Ach Himmel!* America! Who would have thought of that?"

Did any English traveller ever meet anything more completely *Yankee*, in a backwood American village?

Mödling is about nine miles from the city, full of beer-houses and restaurantes for the Viennese, who crowd the village on Sundays. We struck across into the range of hills, and after some hard climbing, were on the summit, with the wide view of the valley of the Danube beneath us. We lay a long time on the grass, enjoying the beautiful scene; my friend showed me the course of his "ride" in '48; and pointed out the various objects of old historical interest. There the green trees and occasional church-spires of Aspern, the scene of Napoleon's great battle; there again the heights of Wagram; here, below, the palace of Schönbrunn, with mathematically laid gardens, where "Napoleon II" died; and near us, along the hills, the picturesque ruins of feudal castles, yet showing the ravages of the Turks. We stopped in our ramble at various country-seats, with whose owners my friend was acquainted. These were not generally as tasteful as the other surroundings of Vienna might lead one to expect; there was something bare, unsheltered, incommodious about them. The people have the usual lively, cheerful, urbane appearance of the Viennese. The valley of the Briel is the property of Prince Lichtenstein, and contains one of his modern castles, with some interesting ruined castles, and some *artificial* ruins. A quiet, sheltered, peaceful green valley, with pretty perspectives, and excellent inns for pleasure parties. Our appetites were well sharpened, when we reached one of the best of these—the Weisse Kreutz, I believe. We found a pleasant little table under a vine-covered arbor in the garden, and ordered a good quantity of the famous Vienna dishes. The Doctor laughed when I asked the waiter for a place to wash.

"I have not heard that since I was in England!" said he. "Das thut man nie hier!" (We never do that here!)

"Good!" said he, as the first course came on; "Brod suppe mit

Ey! (Bread soup and eggs!) that is right!" "Now Kellner! the gebackenes Huhn quick, and Fogasch—and your best *Mehl-speise* (pudding)—the gute Frau knows what I like! Tell her not to make the black coffee very strong'

The *Huhn* is chicken fried in lard; *Fogasch* is a perch, much prized here.

The waiter brought in each dish, hot, as a separate course; and at length, when we had finished them, handed us our coffee, with "A good digestion! meine Herrn!"—a German salutation, especially appropriate after some of their meals.

In one corner of the garden, there were a number of workmen, rolling nine-pins, and we crossed over to look at them. The alleys were mere hard-beaten earthen tracks. The pins and balls were only about half the size of those in ordinary use with us. They played for money, and were drinking beer from large mugs, continually. A more degraded, lifeless, heavy-faced set of laboring men I scarcely ever saw, even in the worst agricultural shires of England.

"Now do you hope, Doctor, ever to raise up such creatures as these, into men for a free government?" said I.

"We shall come to it gradually," he answered. "Educate them! that is the first thing. But you must remember, these are not the men who want a Revolution. All they care for is their beer and time for a *Kegelspiel* like this, occasionally. The most discontented class now in Austria is the middle class—there is where the outbreak will begin. The mechanics and shopkeepers, and higher, the studying men—they understand Liberty, and they are galled by these restrictions."

"The merchants and nobles, then, will stand by the government?"

"Yes—*es versteht sich*—of course! They can only lose by an

overturning—though we may become so completely bankrupt, that even the merchants would be glad of any change. But see that fellow drink!—he has taken three quart mugs while we have been standing here!"

I told him it sickened me to see such a set of men as these. It was discouraging. "When I am with the better classes," said I, "I can see that they are superior in many things, to ours, and where they are not, they can improve themselves. But these brutes, will they ever be *men?* It is such a contrast to our laborers."

"Yes, it must be," he replied. "These fellows have no hope. Their place in life seems to them just as fixed as one of the laws of nature. It never enters their heads that they or their children can be any better. *Ach Gott!* is the Old World wearing out?—But it is time to be getting down the hill. *Kellner!* bring the bill!"

A pleasant walk down the hill brought us to Mödling, and we were in Vienna again, at a seasonable hour.

I was invited in the evening to the house of a gentleman, who had been quite polite to me, though he himself belonged to the ultra aristocratic party in Austria, and even to the extreme Jesuit side. I always expected to meet at his house, the most thorough conservatives of Austrian conservative society.

A servant in livery admitted me, and another conducted me to the drawing-room and announced my name.

It is singular, in the best houses of Vienna, you never find an ante-room. Even if a lady is going to a ball, there is no private room or glass. The servant merely assists the visitor in the hall.

There were only a few present here, this evening, sitting around easily, in different parts of the room, chatting with one another—

the lady on a lounge in one corner, before a small table, making tea, with two or three gentlemen talking in a lively way in French with her. The language used by the company seemed to be French, generally, though I heard English words.

I fell in at once with a stout elderly gentleman, who spoke English, and who, I believe, was a merchant or banker. We spoke of the universal subject, Austrian finances and debt. "Very much exaggerated, sir," said he, "very much. We have public property enough to meet double the amount. There will be no difficulty. A loan must be taken up, and heavier taxes laid. This *proletairiat* have cost us something, and they should pay the debt."

"But do you not fear to make the people discontented?" I asked.

"No. All the order-loving citizens will stand by the law. They see it is a question of life and death for us. We are under the necessity of sustaining a heavy taxation, in order to preserve the credit of our State."

I told him most of the impressions abroad about the Austrian moneyed difficulties were derived from the correspondent of *The Times.*

"I know it," said he. "I know the man well, Mr. ——; he has been here a long while, and he did us good service in '48; and he was even favorably noticed at court. *The Times* was on very good relations with us then. One of the proprietors came on and held a long interview with Prince Schwarzenberg, and got a very good understanding of that Hungarian matter. Since then, this Mr. ——, has taken offence at something, and gives very incorrect advices on our financial condition."

"You do not credit these stories," I inquired, "about *The Times* being paid by the Austrian Government?"

"Oh! earlier information may have sometimes been furnished it, nothing more. Our Imperial Government has not condescended yet—God be thanked!—to hire such tools!"

He went on to speak with a bitterness, singular in a staid, old commercial man, about England, and the attempts of the English to interfere in continental matters.

"The truth is," said he, "the English give us more trouble in Europe than any other people. If it was not for their own pockets, they would have had all the Continent in a blaze long ago. You Americans seem to mind your own affairs. But the English! Do you know that Lord Palmerston has done more to disturb the order of Europe, than any Revolutionist!"

I made some inquiry in regard to their future policy on the Tariff question.

"A difficult matter, sir. I have been in England, and I have studied their commercial policy; yours, I know, is very different. I must say, I like it better. We want here to push up Austrian manufactures. We do not like to be overflooded with English goods and English iron, when we can make them ourselves. There are immense resources in the empire, which have never been developed. I wish these English could be driven out of every market in the civilized world. Our tendency is to high tariffs now, but it may not last."

"Always on the money question, Herr Von T——," said our host, coming up; "excuse! let me present you, Herr B., to a lady, who much likes the Americans!"

A very pleasant, intelligent lady I found, and I had a long talk with her on America, and our cities and ladies, &c. I soon discovered that she was more liberal in opinion, than I had expected to find any one in the room. In speaking of Vienna, I told her how much impressed I had been by the Roman Catholic services in the Cathedral—how solemn they were.

"So! You were there! Yes, they were good; but, I must confess, they tire me. The best part is the lighting up the dark churches at the moment of the Resurrection. Did you see that?"

I asked her soon whether the priests came much into general society. "Ach! no. Only the Jesuits. You see there is one, that smooth, nice-looking Abbè in the corner. He is talking French with Madame ——. How bland! I never like to meet him. They say he is a secret agent of Government."

"Our friends here," said she again, "are of the *ultra-montane* (Jesuit) party, which many of us Catholics you know dislike almost as much as you Protestants."

I inquired in the conversation, what the feeling was towards the Emperor among the higher classes.

"We do not know what he may be when older," said she. "But I cannot understand, how so young a man could refuse so long any act of mercy towards those poor misguided Hungarians. We have hopes though. Persons in the court say, he is much controlled by others; and that his great ambition is to be a General. I do not know, however. But Madame —— is serving tea; let us draw nearer the table."

A haughty, brilliant-looking lady was speaking with much animation, as we came into the circle, sometimes in English and sometimes in German—each language so perfectly, that I could not tell which was native to her. She was talking of the Hungarian Revolution; after a little while she turned to me.

"We think it strange, sir, that there is so little information in foreign countries about this infamous rebellion! The English literally know nothing about it. Your countrymen seem much more enlightened, but you will pardon me, if I say, that they are not always unprejudiced."

I answered, that it was unfortunate the Austrian party had not issued more documents on the subject. All the *brochures* and histories appeared to take the opposing view.

"Yes," she replied. "It was an error. We were so confident of our cause, that we had not thought it necessary. And *Gott sei Dank!* the Austrian Empire, does not yet depend on success in pamphlet warfare!"

"But," said a gentleman, "we have documents; and if the *monsieur* is interested in the matter, I shall be pleased to furnish them to him."

I inquired what he had. He mentioned two histories of the war by Austrian *savants*, and some pamphlets. "And beside," he added, "what I had forgotten—the articles of your countryman, Monsieur Bowen, if you have not read them, in the *Nord Amerikanischer Revue!*"

I thanked him, and promised to call for them.

"Your countrymen are strangely mistaken in Kossŭth," said the lady again. "I was in Hungary in the war, with my husband, General ——, and I know him. He is a *low-born radical!*"

The rest joined in with expressions, uttered with a fervor which amused me. "Red-republican!" "vulgar agitator!" "a mere demagogue—strange that foreign nations should take such an interest in him!"

"Nothing would please me so much," said the lady of the General again, in excited tones, "*as to see Kossuth's head!*"

I looked up in surprise at such a wish; and inquired more particularly for his errors or vices, but did not gather them, except that he was a kind of a Robespierre, who desired nothing better than anarchy or revolution; and who used a certain windy popular eloquence to effect his objects with the crowd. With regard to Mr. BOWEN, I was asked,

"Is it true that he has been obliged to resign a professorship in one of your universities, on account of his views upon the Hungarian question?"

I answered, that I had heard the report through the papers; or, at least, that he was rejected as a candidate.

"Pray! why is not that *tyranny?*" said the gentleman, "as much as anything complained of here?"

I did not know the facts, I replied. I suppose the university authorities did not object to Mr. Bowen's holding what opinions he chose, but they thought those opinions indicated a tone of mind, which would unfit him to teach American youth.

"But we thought, my dear sir, you boasted for your land that it was the very place for free expression of opinion. If it is, why should monarchical views on historical subjects injure the young men Why would it not do them good to hear the other side?"

I admitted, if the facts were as they stated them, I should not consider Mr. Bowen's rejection, justifiable.

"You must confess, Mr. B.," said our host, "there is a power in your country, quite as tyrannical and troublesome as the European police-system. I mean *public opinion.* People say, you dare not move a step against it."

I admitted its power; "but the free and independent could face it, and have faced it. Besides, it comes from ourselves."

"Pardon! my dear sir, I was in England at the time of some of your slavery riots. I know how men are treated, who oppose it. For my part, I would rather be under one tyrant than twenty million; though *Gott bewahr!* (God forbid!) that I should imply, we were under a tyrant!"

I answered that this tyranny was not as great as they supposed. Our most popular journals are the most independent.

"We see many of your papers here," said the banker, "and you will pardon us, if we say that their tone seems most faulty—I should certainly hope our Austrian press would never wish such freedom."

"You must admit, Mr. B." said our host, "that there is a personality, and low abuse of a private man's character in your newspaper writing, which is not worthy of your country. It looks like the worst kind of subjection—the subjection to a vicious public opinion. Excuse our frankness, but so it seems to us!"

"Then the rioting and the bloody crimes, we hear of!" said the lady who had before spoken. "We admit your country is powerful, and is going on to a wonderful influence,—but these things! Are they not horrible!"

I admitted something of the truth of what they said, and as calmly as possible, stated at length, the causes. That our State was yet only some seventy-five years old—and, of course, there would be much which was wild and uncultivated, and even ungoverned in parts of it. But these stories, which I saw in the German press, were much exaggerated. Crime, and lawlessness, and rioting, in all the old States of our Union, were as rare, as in the best governed countries of Europe. I appealed to the value of private and public property with us, as an evidence. I spoke of the most striking fact, that with the exception of Russia, ours was the only civilized government, which was undisturbed in the convulsions of 1848. This personality of the press was an evil—perhaps a necessary evil—yet it was much worse in appearance, than reality. Nobody cared much for it. I described too, the general intelligence and happy condition of all classes. "Possibly we may fail, yet," said I; "there are many dangers before us. Still our success thus far has been beyond all expectation, and these evils are slight to the blessings."

They were softened by my admissions, and allowed in return, gloomily enough, the old, long-fastened defects and evils of their own society. "Yes, yes. Die Zukunft ist für Sie! *The Future is with you!*"

In taking leave, the lady who "wanted Kossuth's head," asked me very politely to call upon her husband, Gen. ——, and the conservative banker recommended himself *am freündlichsten*, most cordially, and my host could not repeat enough "*Unterthänigster Diener!*" I returned to my lodgings to make preparations for my approaching departure for Hungary.

"The Future is with you!"—how often have I heard it in Germany! What a sad story does it tell for the poor old World! It speaks of a Past, sown with injustices and wrongs, and contempt of human rights, and disdain of the hopes and the sufferings of multitudes of men, ripening fast into a Present of degradation, anarchy, and fierce, defying passions.

It tells the same old sad story of human Tyranny, and its curses and ills sent on to distant times; of Injustice heaped up year after year, till man can no longer bear; of the evil deeds of one age laying up retribution terrible for another. The Present so poisoned, that even the Future hath no hope!

Poor Europe! I have seen thy sufferings and experienced something of the despotism which has crushed thee; and here, at home again, in a land, uncursed by the vices and wrongs of the Past, with a youth opening before it, glorious and beautiful—save one shadow, which HE shall surely remove—as that pictured by the old Greek dreamers for their "Ideal State," I can pray from the heart, "A better Future for thee!"

May it no longer be, "The Future is with America!" but "THE FUTURE IS WITH HUMANITY!"

APPENDIX.

THE GERMAN TARIFF UNIONS.*

No. I.—The Zollverein.

The most important financial question which has ever agitated Central Europe, that of the German Tariff Unions, is scarcely known in our country, except by name. I propose, in as brief a manner as possible, to make the matter clearer to American readers, by presenting facts.

Every one of the thirty-four States of Germany, had, until 1818, considered it the first condition of its existence, to separate itself from every other State, by heavy protective duties. Even different provinces of the same kingdom, were barred by Tariffs. Every city had its Custom-houses; and the rivers seemed lines intended by nature for collecting revenue duties. The celebrated Vienna Congress, which met in 1815 to give unity and freedom to Germany, devoted one article of the Constitution, then drawn up, to this difficulty.

They premise (Art. XIX,) "at the first assembly of the League in

* For the sources of thes statistics, I refer to the following: 1. "Hübner's Jahrbuch für Volks wirthschaft, &c., 1852." 2. "Vergleichende Zusammenstellung der Grenz-Eingangs—Abgaben in Oesterreich, &c., von Reden, 1848." 3. "Für und wieder Schuz zölle, 1848." 4. "Die Seg nungen des Zollvereins. 1852." 5. "Statistiche Uebersicht, &c., von Kotelmann, 1852." 6. "Die Krisis des Zollvereins, &c., von Dr. Rau, 1852." 7. "Der September vortrag, &c., in Hanover, 1852." 8. "Zur handels politischen Frage, 1852." 9. "Dieterici's Statistische Uebersicht, 1846-1848." 10. "Die Zollconferenz zu Wien, 1852." 11. "Die Zoll conferenz zu Berlin."

Frankfort, to take into consideration, the question of commerce and traffic between the different States of the League."

This, like all the efforts of that body for the good of Germany, ended in words. At length, in 1818, Prussia passed a law removing all duties between its various provinces; promising only such protection to exports as would secure home industry and provide a revenue for the State, without burdening trade. Any foreign country granting privileges of commerce to the Prussian subjects, should be met with an equal return. The duties on foreign manufactures should never exceed *ten per cent. of their value;* and this "Freedom of Trade" should be the basis of future legislation.

The effect of the System, thus established, was so favorable to Prussia, that in 1828, the Grand Duchy of Hesse, and in 1831, the Princedom of Hesse, united with her in a Commercial Union. During the same years, a Union was formed (1828) between Bavaria and Würtemberg, and (1833) a Union, called the Thuringian, between some of the smaller States. All these associations were thus far on the basis of low duties, while Austria and other States held to the high protective system.

The Prussian Union soon surpassed all its rivals. It was found to offer a securer and larger market to those who would join it, than any other single League. Its scale of duties appeared judiciously contrived, so as to stimulate industry. It commanded all the outlets to the North Sea—and the privileges held out to the other provinces, were remarkably favorable.

In 1833, both of the last mentioned unions were merged into the Prussian, and the Treaty was formed, which is at the basis of the present German Tariff-Union, or Zollverein.

According to this treaty, there shall be a common system of trade and revenue between the States of the Union. All native productions shall pass the line of each, free of duty, with the exception of (1) certain articles, liable to a home-tax; (2) those competing with objects already patented, in other States; or (3) two monopolies specified—*salt and playing cards.* Foreign imports pass without duty. On all exports and imports, a similar tariff is laid throughout the Union; and the revenue everywhere from these sources, is divided among the different States, according to their population. A meeting of the deputies from the Union shall be held annually, and the present treaty shall be binding till 1842. If no announcement is made at least two years before this period, it shall be extended for twelve years more.

This engagement, however, shall be considered to be dissolved, if, in the mean time, the united German States, according to Art. XIX, form a commercial league, which shall fulfill all the objects of the present Union.

To this treaty various additions were made at the entry of Saxony, Brunswick, Lippe, and other provinces. In 1841, it was formally renewed for twelve years, till 1853, and various needful articles annexed. All these changes have in general tended to promote a greater freedom of trade between the several provinces. The standards for weight and measure are more carefully fixed; the taxes on home products limited to certain definite articles, as spirit and malt liquor, tobacco, and the like; and the internal commerce in foreign goods, which have entered by the custom-houses of the Union, is made free of all restraint. A separate provision is also passed, with reference to the tax on beet-sugar as a home product, and to protective duties, to be laid on foreign sugars and syrups.

The Union formed under these various treaties, embraced in 1849, the following States and population:

Prussia	16,669,153	Hesse (Princedom)	731,584
Luxemberg	189,783	Hesse (Grand Duchy)	862,917
Bavaria	4,526,650	Thuringian Union	1,014,954
Saxony	1,894,431	Brunswick	247,070
Wurtemberg	1,805,558	Nassau	425,686
Baden	1,360,599	Frankfort (on the Maine)	71,678
		Total population	29,800,063

The peaceful continuance of this Union is a thing quite unexampled in Germany. Scarce any one, among the many German Unions, for various objects, has ever lived so long and so peacefully.

The high-sounding principles, however, in which it was based, have many of them been dropped. Instead of the Free Trade, to which the German Tariff-Union should eventually lead, duties have been laid on some articles, almost prohibitive. The privileges granted by foreign countries have never been answered. And there is scarcely a foreign import, the duty on which does not exceed ten per cent. Even internal trade is much impeded by the duties on liquors, tobacco and salt.

Among the changes in the Tariff are the following:

Cotton Web (1843-5) from 2 Th. per cwt. to 3 Th., or from 5 5-19 per cent. up to about 8 per cent. duty.

Cotton Yarn from 5 per cent. up to about 8⅓ per cent. duty.

Linen Thread.—Duty raised from 1 Th. (75 cents) per cwt. up to 4 Th. ($3). Price per cwt. 60 Th. (1847).

Silk.—Duty raised from 6 Th. to 8 Th. per cwt. Price 600 Th. per cwt.

Woollen Goods.—From 30 Th. to 50 Th. per cwt., or from a duty of 33⅓ per cent. to 50 per cent.

Iron.—Till 1844 pig-iron was free, and bar-iron paid 1 Th. per cwt. Since then, pig-iron pays ⅓ Th., or 33⅓ per cent., and bar-iron from 1⅓ Th. to 2 Th.; that is, a duty of 50 to 66⅔ per cent.

Segars.—Duty raised from 11 Th. to 15 Th.

Zinc Wares.—From 3⅓ Th. to 10 Th.

Paper.—Gilt Paper, &c., from 5 Th. to 10 Th.

It will be seen from this, that the present tariff of the Zollverein is not at all, in the important articles, based on low duties. Since the years 1843 and '44, it has been a high protective system. The average of duties upon all manufactured articles would far exceed that of the American Tariff of 1846.

We propose, as a specimen of the success of the protective system of Europe, to briefly set forth the progress of the Zollverein since 1835.

The object to which the Government has especially devoted itself, in a financial respect, is the encouragement of the *beet* sugar manufacture.

For this purpose, a duty on refined Sugar was laid in 1840 of nearly 100 per cent.; and on raw Sugar of more than 100 per cent. for common use, and of about 70 per cent. for the manufactories.

On the former, the amount of revenue from the duties sank from 279,754 thalers in 1836 to 14,580 in 1850.

Raw Sugar yielded in 1837 only 5,067 thalers, and has since sunk to 1,080 thalers in its import duties.

The quantity imported has diminished of refined, from 38,888 cwt. in 1836, to 1,905 cwt. in 1851; and of raw, from 1,064,998 cwt. to 781,503. The internal production of Beet Sugar has grown from 25,000 cwt. to 736,215. Yet with all this immense tax upon the foreign article, the *consumption* of Sugar, for every purpose, during these fourteen years, has only increased from 1,032,418 cwt. up to 1,356,722 in 1851, or from an average of 4.04 lbs. to each inhabitant up to 4.52; the population having grown from twenty-five and a half millions to nearly thirty millions. A most manifest failure and loss, so far as this attempt to bolster up the home-manufacture of Beet Sugar is concerned.

As a mere question of revenue, too, it has equally proved a losing operation. The whole amount of taxes and duties on imported and domestic Sugars fell from an average of 6.26 sgr. (about 15½ cents) per head in 1838, '39 and '40, to 4.63 sgr. (about 11 cents) per head in 1851; though the tax on home Sugar, (from the beet,) had been raised to six times its original amount during those years.

The whole production of Beet Sugar in the Zollverein, from 1840 to 1850, has amounted to 3,727,480 cwt.; the taxes on this for the ten years to 3,946,495 thalers.

The established duties on the same quantity of Cane Sugar would have amounted to 18,647,400 thalers, leaving a deficit in this financial operation to the Treasury of 14,700,905 thalers, or of about $12,000,000 for ten years. This, be it remembered, not counterbalanced in any degree by the additional cheapness of Sugar to the people. As for the employment given to home-labor, it may be doubted whether more labor has been engaged in the manufacture of Beet Sugar, than was formerly in the importation and exchange of Cane Sugar; while against this must be balanced the loss of the Colonial market for German linens, which were given in exchange for the Sugar, and besides, this immense taxation for ten years, which, in some form, must come out of the pockets of the people.

Iron.—The article of Iron is a no less plain instance of the bad results of the protective system of the Zollverein. The last fifteen years have been remarkably favorable to the manufacture of Iron. Twenty-five hundred miles of railroads have been built during that time in the Tariff-Union of Prussia. There has been through the world a rapid progress in all the mechanic arts. From 1834 up to 1844, Pig Iron was admitted duty free, and the consumption of it through the whole Zollverein increased from 2,492,736 cwt. up to 6,629,736, or from 11.60 lbs. to 21.46 lbs. per head of the whole population—a gain of about 90 per cent.

After the placing a new duty on Pig Iron, and raising the duty on Bar-Iron, in 1844, the consumption, for all purposes, fell, in the first three years, to 16.37 lbs. per head, or 24 per cent; in the second, to 14.55 lbs., or about 30 per cent. There is every probability that the home manufacture of Bar-Iron would have fallen off still more, had not the Belgian Pig-Iron, by a special exception, been admitted, in 1845, on a duty of 16 per cent., when all other Pig-Iron paid nearly 100 per cent. The manufacture of both Pig-Iron and Bar-Iron reached their ultimum in 1847, and has been falling off since, Bar-Iron rising from 1,534,558 cwt., in 1834, to over 4,000,000 in 1847, and falling again to 3,429,054 in 1850. The price of Iron in the Union through all these years, despite the immense protection, have varied with the English prices, and have only in a slight degree been cheapened. The 1,000 lbs. Bar-Iron cost, in 1834, $37 50; in 1840, $41 50; in 1847, $39 25; in 1850, $34.

In the first three years of the Zollverein, English Bar-Iron cost 78 per cent. less than the Prussian; in the last triad, it cost 110 per cent. less.

So much for the economy of "Protection" for Iron in the Zollverein.

Coffee.—The duties upon this article have averaged 79 per cent., and are now about 50 per cent. Its use both for home-consumption and export, may fairly be considered one test in such a people as the German, of material prosperity. The import in the Tariff Union in 1836 was about 547,000 cwt.; in 1850, about 733,000. The export in 1836, 43,242 cwt.; in 1850, 49,129, or in all, the average per head in 1836, 1.96 lbs.; in 1850, 2.28 lbs. A poor advance, if this heavy duty be considered.

Cotton.—Raw cotton has been duty free. Cotton thread has averaged a duty of 2⅓ per cent. Cotton goods pay now from 33⅓ to 50 per cent. The importation of raw cotton has advanced from 175,377 cwt. in 1834, to 494,298 cwt. in 1850. The increase of imports over exports in cotton yarn and goods has been from 195,728 cwt. in 1834, up to 545,283 in 1845, and has then sunk to 492,640 cwt. in 1850.

Silk.—The duty upon Silk has also been small, averaging about 5⅕ per cent; though now upon Silk goods it varies from 5 to 10 per cent. The German manufacturers have had to contend not only with the great experience of the French operations, but with the protection of the French Government; an export premium of 4⅓ per cent. being offered to the French manufacturers by the State. Yet the exports of Silk goods from the Zollverein exceeded the imports in 1837 by 3,079 cwt., and in 1850, 5,540 cwt.; and the use of silks for all purposes increased from 3,890 cwt. in 1837 to 7,050 in 1850.

Woolen Goods.—Not so close estimates can be made in regard to these. The duty on Woolen Yarn has not averaged quite 2 per cent. The duties now on Woolen goods vary from 20 to 50 per cent. Coarse Wool is duty free. There has been in general an improvement under the Zollverein, though not important. The whole production of Wool in 1841 was 443,451 cwt.; in 1847, 446,933. The use of Woolen Yarn for all purposes in 1841 and '43 averaged in the Union 1.17 lbs. per head; in 1844 and '47, 1.07 lbs.—a falling off of about 8.5 per cent.

In *Linen Goods*, owing to the much greater use of Cotton Cloths, and to the loss of the colonial market, there has been a diminution. No complete statistics are to be obtained. Of rough linen, the export falls off from 25,429 cwt. in 1834 to 13,330 in 1850; of linen thread, from 6,338 cwt. to 2,188 in 1850; colored and printed linen falls from 101,720 cwt. in 1834 to 58,552 in 1850.

Nearly all other articles of consumption which indicate, in their general use, the well-being of a people, have fallen off in quantity since the beginning of the Zollverein.

In the large cities, the average consumption of *rye flour* falls from 245 lbs. per head in 1831 to 230 in 1845; while, in wheat, the average in 1836 of 93.31 lbs. is only 93.3 in 1843, and 99 lbs. in 1845.

Spices of every kind average 0.18 lbs. per head in 1837, the same in '46, and only 0.16 lbs. in 1847.

The same diminution appears in the use of luxuries—wine, tobacco, &c.

On the whole, from these statistics, one great fact must be clear—that the Zollverein, as a high protective system, has not succeeded.

Since the advance in duties in 1845, there has been a falling off in the production of almost every article of importance, and this before the disturbances from the revolutionary movements had begun. As a general fact, the Union has been most prosperous with the articles not protected by high duties; yet even in these—as, for instance, the linens—the evil effects of the burdensome duties in other articles have been felt. No more striking instance of the bad economy of high protective or rather prohibitive duties can be found, than in the most strenuous and expensive efforts made by the Prussian Union to protect their iron and sugar manufactures. An immense financial loss and disturbance, as these statistics show, have been almost the only result. One branch has been bolstered up to the weakening of another. The people have paid what was never returned to them in the cheapening of the article; the channels of business have been interrupted at the caprice of the Government, and endless dislocations and disturbances occasioned, which no one afterward could guard against or prevent. As a profitable protective system, the Zollverein must be considered a failure.

No. II.—The Steuerverein.

A neighboring and rival Union to the Prussian Zollverein has been the Import Union of Hanover. This association—the Steuerverein—dates from a Treaty in 1831 with Brunswick, by which portions of that State are included under the Hanoverian Tariff system. During the succeeding ten years, various small States were added. In 1841, Brunswick, as a whole, retired from the Union and joined the Zollverein. In 1848, the Steuerverein consisted of the following States and population :—

Hanover,	1,719,857	Provinces of Brunswick	18,295
Oldenburg and Knyphausen	225,910	Provinces of Prussia	10,281
Schaumburg Lippe	28,895		
		Total	1,997,683

This Tariff Union was based on low duties, and proved wonderfully successful. The revenue from the duties was far greater, in proportion to the population, than in the Prussian; while the average consumption of articles of luxury and comfort equally exceeded that in other parts of Germany.

We take this table of the average receipts per head from duties, from *Hubner's Jahrbuch*, p. 210. The Sgr. is a groschen, equal to about 2½ cents :

	Zollverein.	*Steuerverein.*		*Zollverein.*	*Steuerverein.*
	Sgr.	*Sgr.*		*Sgr.*	*Sgr.*
1837-38	21.4	24.9	1846-47	28.2	30.3
1841-42	24.7	31.8	1848-49	28.5	28.5
1842-43	25.3	27.9	1849-50	24.6	31.3
1844-45	28.3	30.6			

The following is a table of the average consumption per head:

	Zollverein. lbs.	Steuerverein. lbs.		Zollverein lbs.	Steuerverein. lbs.
Coffee	15.10	20.25	Wine	2.85	17.05
Rice	3.45	8.30	Sugar and Syrup	28.35	41.00
Tropical Fruits	2.75	5.30	Iron for rail-roads	37.00	42.00
Tea	.10	1.05	Iron for other objects	77.40	110.00

The following abstract will show some of the relative duties in the two Tariff Unions and in Austria. It is taken from a semi-official document called, "A Comparison of the Boundary Import Duties, &c., by Reden—Frankfort, 1848." The Thaler is worth about 75 cents:

	Austria.		Zollverein.		Steuerverein.	
	Th.	Sgr.	Th.	Sgr.	Th.	Sgr.
Cotton, per cwt.	1	1½	free.		free.	
Cotton yarn	8	8¾	8		1	
Cotton goods	72	27½	50		12	
Bar iron, per cwt.	3	22½	8		1	0¾
Steel	3	22½	1	15	0	7
Iron works, fine	37	15	10		6	4
Glass, gilded	18	¼	10		6	4
Copper wares, per cwt.	37	15	10		6	4
Leather goods	63	14¼	22		12	8
Linen, fine	187	12½	20		12	7½
Raw Sugar, per cwt.	9	10	8		3	10
Silk goods	624	8½	110		12	7½
Woolen goods, fine	114	17½	50		12	7½

To all familiar with the prosperity of Hanover under this low Tariff system, the announcement was very surprising that she had formed (September, 1851) a Treaty with Prussia, and would henceforth be a part of the Zollverein. For this movement, political much more than financial reasons were the cause. Austria was at this time pressing strongly on Prussia her demands for a universal German Tariff Union. It was to be based on her favorite system of high protective duties. If she succeded, Hanover would inevitably be forced later into the Union, and become involved in an association which might ruin her commerce. It was better for her to take the Prussian protective duties than the

Austrian prohibitive Prussia, too, offered her flattering inducements in the scale of division of the revenues.

For Prussia herself, it was a vital measure. In two years, the term of the Zollverein would expire, and if notice of a change were not now given, she was bound to the Union till 1865. The South German members were becoming more and more attached to Austria. Cassel, who ruled the connection between her provinces, was already under heavy obligations to the Viennese Ministry. They might be enabled, in the coming years, to force her to a financial Union with Austria.

In a commercial view, it was vastly more important that she should be united with Hanover, than with all South Germany together. In alliance with the Steuerverein, she would secure the connection between her Eastern and Western provinces—the great road by Magdeburg from Berlin to Cologne; she would hold possession of all the great rivers in the North, and gain a speedy outlet to the sea through the Hanoverian ports.

It will give an idea of the losses for Hanover in this measure, to compare the costs of certain articles under the two Unions.

For a ship of 700 tons, 731 cwt. of iron are reckoned, according to the Lloyd's estimate, necessary for anchors, chains, &c., in the outfit. These cost in Hanover, inclusive of freight and duty, 3,000 thalers. In Prussia, 7,000 thalers—or a difference of $3,000 which Hanover must pay under the Prussian Tariff. If imported direct, ready-made from England, they cost in the Steuerverein 260 thalers. In the Zollverein, 2,348 thalers. Iron knees cost for one such ship, in Prussia, 1,900 thalers; in Hanover, 740 thalers—a difference of 160 per cent. against the latter. Iron nails cost 100 per cent. more in the Prussian than the Hanoverian Union.

The treaty is to come into operation on Jan. 1, 1854, and shall extend to December 31, 1865.

Should the present Zollverein be dissolved by the retiring of the South German States, the new Union, in connection with Hanover, would consist of twelve different States, and 20,330,000 inhabitants.

No. III.—The Austrian Union.

Austria has always been a constant friend to high Protective Tariffs. In Maria Theresa's time, the importation of all goods, which could possibly be manufactured in the country, was forbidden. The theory of commerce being that the gold which was carried out from the Austrian States was so much loss. In consequence, even on tropical productions and "colonial wares," the highest possible duties were laid.

When the Empire was reconstructed after the fall of Napoleon, the same system was continued and extended by the Emperor Francis. Nothing prospered under this mediæval policy, and attempts were made in 1835 to reform it. They failed; and until 1848, the only changes were the removal of some prohibitive duties, to be replaced by exorbitantly high protective duties; and the lowering of the taxes on colonial goods, as it was found that the smuggling defied all the precautions of Government. In addition to this "Protective Tariff," the State enjoyed a monopoly of salt, tobacco, and gunpowder. At the close of the war with Hungary, the Austrian Government issued various "memorials" with reference to a change of their Tariff-system, and a Union with Germany.

In the memorial of December 30, 1849, the Ministry declare that they "recognize it as a need of the public administration to pass over from a prohibitive to a protective system, and to prepare thereby a nearer connection with Germany."

Various communications and negociations were entered upon with the other States of Germany for this same object—a Tariff Union—but without much success. At length, the news went over Germany of the sudden union of the Zollverein with Hanover, and of the invitations to a "Conference" at Berlin, to consider this matter of a universal German Revenue Union. Almost at the same time, (November 25,

1851,) the Austrian Government put forth a new Tariff, and an invitation to a general conference in January, 1852, at Vienna, for the same purpose. Of the Tariff, I shall have more to say hereafter. In this Assembly at Vienna, six States of the Zollverein met—Bavaria, Saxony, Würtemberg, Baden, the Hesses, and Nassau. Prussia, and the remainder, together with the Mecklenburgs and Holstein, declined all share in the proceedings.

The six States above mentioned held a separate Convention (April, 1852,) in Darmstadt, in which, after various resolves, they conclude that if Austria will pledge them their Tariff revenues in the interval, they will enter into no new relations with the Zollverein until 1853, when the negociations now in process between the Austrian Government and that Union will be terminated.

For Austria, this question of the Tariff Union is more than a financial question.

Among the pamphlets and works qnoted at the beginning of these articles is one recognized by the Prussian press, as a semi-official Austrian document—"*Die Zoll-conferenz zu Wien.*" (The Tariff Convention at Vienna. In this work the whole subject is argued with an earnestness, such as no matter of revenue would ever call forth. It is a basis-principle of the Austrian policy that Austria, as a whole, must be united with Germany. As long as Hungary and her Italian provinces are separated from her German, so long the Empire is not secure. But, incorporated in the German League, she has all Germany pledged to support her, and to put down insurrections.

SCHWARZENBERG's unceasing efforts to bring Hungary and Italy into the German Union have failed—France and England have protested and Prussia has steadily opposed.

What could not be done on the political ground, perhaps can be on the financial. The great aim of Austria now is to make the Empire and Germany one in revenue. Every motive which could reach Prussian pride, and honor, and interest, is employed in the above *Brochure.*

To the enthusiastic lovers of German unity, the picture of a united

Fatherland is presented—when Germans shall have one Tariff and one revenue; when a common scale of duties shall hold at Hamburg and at Venice; from Stralsund and Bremen to the "Iron Gate" of Hungary, and the coast of the Adriatic. The conservatives are warned of the immense unoccupied class of laborers which Free Trade shall produce—rabble—the fomentors of revolution and outbreaks. The Free Traders are told that at present their theory is only an "ideal,"—and that they will act the rational part, to promote Free Trade at home, as a preparation for Free Trade abroad. If English iron and French silks are admitted free, all the laborers in those branches in the Zollverein must become paupers, and their support be thrown on the agricultural classes.

In union with Hanover and North Germany, Prussia *must* be drawn into this destructive policy of Free Trade. The inhabitants of her northern provinces, and of the coasts of the Baltic and the German Ocean, will always have an ineradicable prejudice in favor of cheap iron and cheap manufactures from England. They will drink French wines, if they are lower than Austrian; and they can never be induced to prefer dear colonial goods for the sake of building up manufactures in Vienna.

For her manufactures, Prussia will have an almost boundless market in Hungary, while that country in return will pour forth her corn and wine into Germany. By this Union, thirty-eight millions of men will be added to the Zollverein, of which twenty millions shall be pure consumers. At present, says the *Brochure*, 30,000,000 thalers are carried away annually by the emigrants to America.

Under a universal German Tariff Union, Hungary would again revive in prosperity, and something of this great export of men and money would be turned towards her unoccupied lands to aid again in the well-being of the Fatherland.

Prussia is reminded of a recent season, when human beings were dying by the thonsands from famine in Silesia, and just over the Austrian border, corn was in plenty. If these scenes would be avoided, let there be a removal of all frontier duties, and the wheat from the Danube and Bohemia will be exchanged for the products of the weavers of the Harz, and of Eastern Prussia.

Finally, as the best guard against future "democratic outbreaks," will be the union of the German Governments,—even only for matters of finance and revenue.

On the part of Prussia, there had been three great objections to a Tariff Union with Austria:—1. The Austrian monopolies; 2. The difficulties of the united revenues; and 3. The Austrian finances.

In reply, the authors of this document promise, almost officially, that the Government will waive their monopoly in tobacco, if Prussia insists, and urge that at the worst, this and salt will only be liable to the same conditions, with the two present monopolies—salt and playing cards—of the Zollverein.

As regards the division of the Tariff revenues, the writers do not claim that it should be made according to population, whereby of course Austria would gain a great advantage. They propose to leave a "Transition-period" of four years from January 1854 to December, 1858, for the gradual change of duties, during which the average of revenues from each province may be calculated, and the division made accordingly.

In the finances, the Government for the first time abandons its old position. Hitherto the Government paper has always been considered to be at par value. Even when 33 per cent. below its exchange value, by a legal fiction, it has been given as at par for all taxes, revenues, duties, &c., &c. Soldiers have even penetrated the Exchange, and the gens d'armes have examined the books of the brokers, as if Austrian bank paper could be driven up at the point of the bayonet. In the proposed Union, the ministry admit that the Government paper shall pass at all Custom-houses and offices, for its average worth by the current month in the Exchange at Augsburg.

Of the articles which shall be free of all duties in this Union, are mentioned, the raw products of the field, garden, forest, and the mines;

certain materials for manufacture, as dye-woods, sulphur, potash, saltpetre; certain manufactures, as raw silk, rough linen yarn, pack-thread, sail-cloth, straw and basket goods of common kind; cheap wood, brick and porcelain-wares; and books, pictures and cards on paper manufactured in the Union.

Most of these articles, it should be mentioned, were already free in the Prussian Union. In addition, wine is to pay 3 thlr. ($2 25) per centner; Iron 7½ sgr. (18 cents) per cwt. These are all the propositions, thus far made by the Austrian Government.

We will now briefly compare the Austrian and Prussian Tariffs, as showing the change which the Zollverein must make to enter the Austrian Union:

PRUSSIAN TARIFF.

	Thlr.	
Cotton Goods	50	per cwt.
Linen „	1, 20, 30 and 60	„
Silk „	55 and 110	„
Woolen „	20, 30 and 50	„
Leather and Leather Goods	6, 8, 10 and 22	„
Iron Wares	1, 6, and 10	„

AUSTRIAN TARIFF.

	Thlr.	
Cotten Goods	13⅓, 33⅓ 50, 66⅔, 100 and 166⅔	per cwt.
Linen „	5, 13⅓, 50, 66⅔ and 166⅔	„
Silk „	166⅔ and 400	„
Woolen „	8⅓, 33⅓, 50, 66⅔, 100 and 166⅔	„
Leather and Leather Goods	5, 10, 16⅔, 33⅓, and 66⅔	„
Iron Wares	1⅔, 3⅓, 6⅔, 10, and 16⅔	„

The Austrian Tariff, whose rates are here given, is to come into operation in January, 1854. It is distinguished from the Prussian, by grades of duties, proportioned to the fineness of the article; so that on almost all of the commonest manufactures the Austrian duty is lower, though its average of duties is much higher.

In the event of a Union between the Zollverein and Austria, the principal exports from the latter to Prussia, will be the following: Bohemian glass, steel and iron wares, shawls, leather gloves, book binders' goods, porcelain and earthen wares, silk webs from Milan, Como and Vienna, silver, works of art, cloths and stuffs. The fine table-covers from Bohemia and Moravia would compete with those from Saxony and Westphalia. Leather, Vienna matches, white lead and fine wood wares would be in much demand in the provinces neighboring to Austria on the west. Especially would the unequalled Hungarian wines be exported to every part of Germany.

Comparison of Products in Zollverein and Austria:

	ZOLLVEREIN.	AUSTRIA.
	Thlr.	*Thlr.*
Iron Wares	35,200,000	19,200,000
Glass Manufactures	8,500,000	10,500,000
Sum of all manufacture in mineral and metallic substance, glass, copper, iron, &c., &c.	172,200,000	110,450,000
Cotton, Spinning	8,200,000	9,600,000
Wool "	29,600,000	22,200,000
Flax "	58,000,000	31,200,000
Cotton, Weaving	67,800,000	31,200,000
Wool "	64,200,000	48,000,000
Linen "	94,800,000	45,000,000
Silk	23,690,000	11,700,000
Total	250,490,000	135,900,000

	ZOLLVEREIN.	AUSTRIA.
	Thlr.	*Thlr.*
Leather and leather goods	42,400,000	27,000,000
Paper	15,700,000	4,920,000
Material for literary business of all kinds	14,750,000	4,200,000
Sum of all manufactures	642,840,000	378,060,000

STEAM ENGINES.

	For Navigation.	*Railroads.*	*Manufactures.*
Zollverein	98	430	1,519
Austria	68	240	464

	For all purposes.	*Horse power*
Zollverein	2,097	63,425
Austria	760	24,734

SPINDLES AND LOOMS.

	ZOLLVEREIN.		AUSTRIA.	
	Spindles.	*Looms.*	*Spindles.*	*Looms.*
Cotton	902,030	160,000	1,267,980	178,000
Wool	750,000	60,000	650,000	56,000
Linen	50,000	450,000	20,800	300,000
Silk	......	14,000	......	11,800
Total	1,702,030	684,200	1,938,780	545,800

In the quality and general value of her manufactures, Austria is far inferior to the Prussian Union. In the cheapness, however, of the coarsest and most common articles, as coarse cutlery, coarse linen, cotton bagging and cloths, stockings, &c., she is superior—a fact due in part to the very low rate of wages for operatives in that Empire.

In iron manufacture and machine spinning both Unions are weak.

In wool carding and flax spinning (by machine) Austria falls behind, while in cotton spinning she is superior to her rival.

In earthenware and porcelain manufacture, the Zollverein leads, while in glass manufacture she is inferior again.

In leather productions the Zollverein stands first, though in a few common articles, as ladies' gloves, gloves, &c., Austria has best succeeded.

Austria has been through Europe the great representative of the ultra, high protective school, for some thirty years. Her resources are immense, both in agriculture and in mineral wealth. She has great rivers, roads, railroads, and harbors, one of which has been the leading commercial city of the world. We propose briefly to examine the effects of this system upon her development.

The worth of the whole produce of the mines, coal, copper, iron, gold, silver, &c., &c., has fallen from 10,443,163 florins in 1823, and 13,874,213 florins in 1833, to 7,906,901 florins in 1847; showing in twenty-four years, a loss on the most important articles of production of about 33 per cent.

The use of iron for all purposes averaged before 1848, 11 pounds per head in Austria; in the Zollverein, 21.79 pounds; in England, 94; Belgium, 41; France, 34; Sardinia, 33.

An equal attempt with that of the Zollverein to bolster up Beet-Sugar manufacture has been made, and with like success. With a heavy duty laid upon foreign sugars for about twenty years, sugar is dearer than it was before the protection. And for every 200,000 cwt. produced of beet and potato sugar, 500,000 cwt. of cane sugar are imported annually. The duty on cane sugar is 7 florins, ($3 15) per cwt., and the tax on beet sugar 1 florin, (45 cents) so that as a matter of revenue merely, the State loses about a million of florins per annum.

Coffee.—In 1844, the duty on this article was put down, and the import has risen from 149,705 cwt. in 1844, to 226,275 cwt. in 1850.

In products of the soil, the total exports fell from 30,409,356, in 1844, to 26,593,500 in 1847, and to 18,924,800 in 1850.

During the last three years, the diminution in every article of export and production has been enormous. But along with the injuries to trade from high duties must be reckoned the losses and disturbances from their late revolutionary struggles. So that from the latest statistics, no conclusive result can be obtained as regards the question of "Protective Tariffs" in Europe. Still, enough has already been given, in the comparison of the high-protected manufactures and commerce of Austria, with the low-tariff system of Hanover, or the medium-protective system of Prussia, to show that no argument in favor of high protection can ever be taken from its success in Germany. Equally in the Protestant, liberal Prussia, and the despotic Austria, has the high tariff economy failed. And the States of Germany may almost measure their commercial and material success by the approach which each has made to the policy of Free Trade.

What the results of these negociations between the Austrian and Prussian Tariff Unions will be cannot yet be affirmed. My own belief is, that the Prussian King, scared by the old phantom of revolution, will yield to the demands of Austria; and that an Austrian high-protective tariff will cover Germany from one end to the other.

All the Books on this Catalogue sent by mail, to any part of the Union, free of postage, upon receipt of Price.

CATALOGUE OF BOOKS

ON

AGRICULTURE AND HORTICULTURE,

PUBLISHED BY

A. O. MOORE,

(LATE C. M. SAXTON & COMPANY,)

No. 140 FULTON STREET, NEW YORK,

SUITABLE FOR

SCHOOL, TOWN, AGRICULTURAL, AND PRIVATE LIBRARIES.

THE AMERICAN FARMER'S ENCYCLOPEDIA, - - - $4 00

EMBRACING ALL THE RECENT DISCOVERIES IN AGRICULTURAL CHEMistry, and the use of Mineral, Vegetable and Animal Manures, with Descriptions and Figures of American Insects injurious to Vegetation. Being a Complete Guide for the cultivation of every variety of Garden and Field Crops. Illustrated by numerous Engravings of Grasses, Grains, Animals, Implements, Insects, &c. By GOUVERNEUR EMERSON, of Pennsylvania, upon the basis of Johnson's Farmer's Encyclopedia.

DOWNING'S (A. J.) LANDSCAPE GARDENING. - - 3 50

A TREATISE ON THE THEORY AND PRACTI[illegible] [illegible]NDSCAPE GARdening. Adapted to North America, with a view to the im[illegible]ement of Country Residences; comprising Historical Notices and General Principles of the Art, directions for Laying out Grounds and Arranging Plantations, the Description and Cultivation of Hardy Trees, Decorative Accompaniments to the House and Grounds, the Formation of Pieces of Artificial Waters, Flower Gardens, &c., with Remarks on Rural Architecture. Elegantly Illustrated, with a Portrait of the Author. By A. J. DOWNING.

DOWNING'S (A. J.) RURAL ESSAYS, - - - - 3 00

ON HORTICULTURE, LANDSCAPE GARDENING, RURAL ARCHITECTURE, Trees, Agriculture, Fruit, with his Letters from England. Edited, with a Memoir of the Author by GEORGE WM. CURTIS, and a letter to his friends, by FREDERIKA BREMER, and an elegant steel Portrait of the Author.

DADD'S ANATOMY AND PHYSIOLOGY OF THE HORSE, Plain. 2 00

Do. Do. Do. Do. Colored Plates, 4 00

WITH ANATOMICAL AND QUESTIONAL ILLUSTRATIONS; Containing, also, a Series of Examinations on Equine Anatomy and Philosophy, with Instructions in reference to Dissection, and the mode of making Anatomical Preparations; to which is added a Glossary of Veterinary Technicalities, Toxicological Chart, and Dictionary of Veterinary Science.

DADD'S MODERN HORSE DOCTOR. - - - - 1 00

CONTAINING PRACTICAL OBSERVATIONS ON THE CAUSES, NATURE and Treatment of Disease and Lameness of Horses, embracing the most recent and approved methods, according to an enlightened system of veterinary therapeutics, for the preservation and restoration of health. With Illustrations.

DADD'S (GEO. H.) AMERICAN CATTLE DOCTOR, - - - $1 00

Containing the Necessary Information for Preserving the Health and Curing the Diseases of Oxen, Cows, Sheep, and Swine, with a great variety of Original Recipes and Valuable Information in reference to Farm and Dairy management, whereby every man can be his own Cattle Doctor. The principles taught in this work are, that all Medication shall be subservient to Nature—that all Medicines must be sanative in their operation, and administered with a view of aiding the vital powers, instead of depressing, as heretofore, with the lancet or by poison. By G. H. Dadd, M. D., Veterinary Practitioner.

THE DOG AND GUN, - - - - - - - - - 50

A Few Loose Chapters on Shooting, among which will be found some Anecdotes and Incidents; also, instructions for Dog Breaking, and interesting letters from Sportsmen. By A Bad Shot.

MORGAN HORSES, - - - - - - - - - 1 00

A Premium Essay on the Origin, History, and Characteristics of this remarkable American Breed of Horses; tracing the Pedigree from the original Justin Morgan, through the most noted of his progeny, down to the present time. With numerous portraits. To which are added hints for Breeding, Breaking, and General Use and Management of Horses, with practical Directions for training them for exhibition at Agricultural Fairs. By D. C. Linsley.

SORGHO AND IMPHEE, THE CHINESE AND AFRICAN SUGAR CANES. - - - - - - - - - 1 00

A Complete Treatise upon their Origin and Varieties, Culture and Uses, their value as a Forage Crop, and directions for making Sugar, Molasses, Alcohol, Sparkling and Still Wines, Beer, Cider, Vinegar, Paper, Starch, and Dye Stuffs. Fully Illustrated with Drawings of Approved Machinery; With an Appendix by Leonard Wray, of Caffraria, and a description of his patented process of crystallizing the juice of the Imphee; with the latest American experiments, including those of 1857, in the South. By Henry S. Olcott. To which are added translations of valuable French Pamphlets, received from the Hon. John Y. Mason, American Minister at Paris.

THE STABLE BOOK - - - - - - - - - 1 00

A Treatise on the Management of Horses, in Relation to Stabling, Groom[illegible], Watering and Working, Construction of Stables, Ventilation, Appendag[illegible] Stables. Management of the Feet, and of Diseased and Defective Horses. By John Stewart, Veterinary Surgeon. With Notes and Additions, adapting it to American Food and Climate. By A. B. Allen, Editor of the American Agriculturist.

THE HORSE'S FOOT, AND HOW TO KEEP IT SOUND, - 50

With Cuts, Illustrating the Anatomy of the Foot, and containing valuable Hints on Shoeing and Stable Management, in Health and in Disease. By William Miles.

THE FRUIT GARDEN, - - - - - - - - - 1 25

A Treatise, intended to Explain and Illustrate the Physiology of Fruit Trees, the Theory and Practice of all Operations connected with the Propagation, Transplanting, Pruning and Training of Orchard and Garden Trees, as Standards, Dwarfs, Pyramids, Espalier, &c. The Laying out and Arranging different kinds of Orchards and Gardens, the selection of suitable varieties for different purposes and localities, Gathering and Preserving Fruits, Treatment of Diseases, Destruction of Insects, Description and Uses of Implements, &c. Illustrated with upwards of 150 Figures, representing Different Parts of Trees, all Practical Operations, forms of Trees, Designs for Plantations, Implements, &c. By P. Barry, of the Mount Hope Nurseries, Rochester, N. Y.

FIELD'S PEAR CULTURE, - - - - - - - 75

The Pear Garden; or, a Treatise on the Propagation and Cultivation of the Pear Tree, with Instructions for its Management from the Seedling to the Bearing Tree. By Thomas W. Field.

BRIDGEMAN'S (THOS.) YOUNG GARDENER'S ASSISTANT, $1 50

IN THREE PARTS, Containing Catalogues of Garden and Flower Seed, with Practical Directions under each head for the Cultivation of Culinary Vegetables and Flowers. Also directions for Cultivating Fruit Trees, the Grape Vine, &c.; to which is added, a Calendar to each part, showing the work necessary to be done in the various departments each month of the year. One volume octavo.

BRIDGEMAN'S KITCHEN GARDENER'S INSTRUCTOR, ½ Cloth, 50
" " " " Cloth, 60

BRIDGEMAN'S FLORIST'S GUIDE, - - - - - ½ Cloth, 50
" " " - - - Cloth, . 60

BRIDGEMAN'S FRUIT CULTIVATOR'S MANUAL, - ½ Cloth, 50
" " " " - Cloth, 60

COLE'S AMERICAN FRUIT BOOK, - - - - - - 50

CONTAINING DIRECTIONS FOR RAISING, PROPAGATING AND MANAGing Fruit Trees, Shrubs and Plants; with a description of the Best Varieties of Fruit, including New and Valuable Kinds.

COLE'S AMERICAN VETERINARIAN, - - - - - 50

CONTAINING DISEASES OF DOMESTIC ANIMALS, THEIR CAUSES, Symptoms and Remedies; with Rules for Restoring and Preserving Health by good management; also for Training and Breeding.

SCHENCK'S GARDENER'S TEXT BOOK, - - - - - 50

CONTAINING DIRECTIONS FOR THE FORMATION AND MANAGEMENT of the Kitchen Garden, the Culture and Use of Vegetables, Fruits and Medicinal Herbs.

AMERICAN ARCHITECT, - - - - - - - - 6 00

THE AMERICAN ARCHITECT, Comprising original Designs of Cheap Country and Village Residences, with Details, Specifications, Plans and Directions, and an Estimate of the Cost of Each Design. By JOHN W. RITCH, Architect. First and Second Series, 4to, bound in 1 vol.

BUIST'S (ROBERT) AMERICAN FLOWER GARDEN DIRECTORY, 1 25

CONTAINING PRACTICAL DIRECTIONS FOR THE CULTURE OF PLANTS, in the Flower-Garden, Hot-House, Green-House, Rooms or Parlor Windows, for every Month in the Year; with a Description of the Plants most desirable in each, the nature of the Soil and Situation best adapted to their Growth, the Proper Season for Transplanting, &c.; with Instructions for Erecting a Hot-House, Green-House, and Laying out a Flower Garden; the whole adapted to either Large or Small Gardens, with Instructions for Preparing the Soil, Propagating, Planting, Pruning, Training and Fruiting the Grape Vine.

THE AMERICAN BIRD FANCIER, - - - - - -

CONSIDERED WITH REFERENCE TO THE BREEDING, REARING, FEEDing, Management and Peculiarities of Cage and House Birds. Illustrated with Engravings. By D. JAY BROWNE.

REEMELIN'S (CHAS.) VINE DRESSER'S MANUAL, - - 50

AN ILLUSTRATED TREATISE ON VINEYARDS AND WINE-MAKING, containing Full Instructions as to Location and Soil, Preparation of Ground, Selection and Propagation of Vines, the Treatment of Young Vineyards, Trimming and Training the Vines, Manures, and the Making of Wine.

DANA'S MUCK MANUAL, FOR THE USE OF FARMERS, - 1 00

A TREATISE ON THE PHYSICAL AND CHEMICAL PROPERTIES OF Soils and Chemistry of Manures; including, also, the subject of Composts, Artificial Manures and Irrigation. A new edition, with a Chapter on Bones and Superphosphates.

CHEMICAL FIELD LECTURES FOR AGRICULTURISTS, - 1 00

By Dr. JULIUS ADOLPHUS STOCKHARDT, Professor in the Royal Academy of Agriculture at Tharant. Translated from the German. Edited, with notes, by JAMES E. TESCHEMACHER.

BUIST'S (ROBERT) FAMILY KITCHEN GARDENER, - - $0 75

Containing Plain and Accurate Descriptions of all the Different Species and Varieties of Culinary Vegetables, with their Botanical, English, French and German names, alphabetically arranged, with the Best Mode of Cultivating them in the Garden or under Glass; also Descriptions and Character of the most Select Fruits, their Management, Propagation, &c. By Robert Buist, author of the "American Flower Garden Directory," &c.

DOMESTIC AND ORNAMENTAL POULTRY. Plain Plates, - 1 00

Do. Do. Do. Colored Plates, - 2 00

A Treatise on the History and Mangement of Ornamental and Domestic Poultry. By Rev. Edmund Saul Dixon, A.M., with large additions by J. J. Kerr, M.D. Illustrated with sixty-five Original Portraits, engraved expressly for this work. Fourth edition revised.

HOW TO BUILD AND VENTILATE HOT-HOUSES, - - 1 25

A Practical Treatise on the Construction, Heating and Ventilation of Hot-Houses, including Conservatories, Green-Houses, Graperies and other kinds of Horticultural Structures, with Practical Directions for their Management, in regard to Light, Heat and Air. Illustrated with numerous engravings. By P. B. Leuchars, Garden Architect.

CHORLTON'S GRAPE-GROWER'S GUIDE, - - - - 60

Intended Especially for the American Climate. Being a Practical Treatise on the Cultivation of the Grape Vine in each department of Hot House, Cold Grapery, Retarding House and Out-door Culture. With Plans for the Construction of the Requisite Buildings, and giving the best methods for Heating the same. Every department being fully illustrated. By William Chorlton.

NORTON'S (JOHN P.) ELEMENTS OF SCIENTIFIC AGRICULTURE, 60

Or, the Connection between Science and the Art of Practical Farming. Prize Essay of the New York State Agricultural Society. By John P. Norton, M.A., Professor of Scientific Agriculture in Yale College. Adapted to the use of Schools.

JOHNSTON'S (J. F. W.) CATECHISM OF AGRICULTURAL CHEMISTRY AND GEOLOGY, - - - - - - 25

By James F. W. Johnston, M.A., F.R.SS.L. and E., Honorary Member of the Royal Agricultural Society of England, and author of "Lectures on Agricultural Chemistry and Geology." With an Introduction by John Pitkin Norton, M.A., late Professor of Scientific Agriculture in Yale College. With notes and additions by the author, prepared expressly for this edition, and an Appendix compiled by the Superintendent of Education in Nova Scotia. Adapted to the use of Schools.

JOHNSTON'S (J. F. W.) ELEMENTS OF AGRICULTURAL CHEMISTRY AND GEOLOGY, - - - - - - 1 00

With a Complete Analytical and Alphabetical Index and an American Preface. By Hon. Simon Brown, Editor of the "New England Farmer."

JOHNSTON'S (JAMES F. W.) AGRICULTURAL CHEMISTRY, 1 25

Lectures on the Application of Chemistry and Geology to Agriculture. New edition, with an Appendix, containing the Author's Experiments in Practical Agriculture.

THE COMPLETE FARMER AND AMERICAN GARDENER, 1 25

Rural Economist and New American Gardener; Containing a Compendious Epitome of the most Important Branches of Agriculture and Rural Economy; with Practical Directions on the Cultivation of Fruits and Vegetables, including Landscape and Ornamental Gardening. By Thomas G. Fessenden. 2 vols. in one.

FESSENDEN'S (T. G.) AMERICAN KITCHEN GARDENER, - 50

Containing Directions for the Cultivation of Vegetables and Garden Fruits. Cloth.

NASH'S (J. A.) PROGRESSIVE FARMER, - - - - $0 60

A Scientific Treatise on Agricultural Chemistry, the Geology of Agriculture, on Plants and Animals, Manures and Soils, applied to Practical Agriculture; with a Catechism of Scientific and Practical Agriculture. By J. A. Nash

BRECK'S BOOK OF FLOWERS, - - - - - - 1 00

In which are Described all the Various Hardy Herbaceous Perennials, Annuals, Shrubs, Plants and Evergreen Trees, with Directions for their Cultivation.

SMITH'S (C. H. J.) LANDSCAPE GARDENING, PARKS AND PLEASURE GROUNDS, - - - - - - - - - - 1 25

With Practical Notes on Country Residences, Villas, Public Parks and Gardens. By Charles H. J. Smith, Landscape Gardener and Garden Architect, &c. With Notes and Additions by Lewis F. Allen, author of "Rural Architecture."

THE COTTON PLANTER'S MANUAL, - - - - - 1 00

Being a Compilation of Facts from the Best Authorities on the Culture of Cotton, its Natural History, Chemical Analysis, Trade and Consumption, and embracing a History of Cotton and the Cotton Gin. By J. A. Turner.

COBBETT'S AMERICAN GARDENER, - - - - - 50

A Treatise on the Situation, Soil, and Laying-out of Gardens, and the making and managing of Hot-Beds and Green-Houses, and on the Propagation and Cultivation of the several sorts of Vegetables, Herbs, Fruits and Flowers.

ALLEN (J. FISK) ON THE CULTURE OF THE GRAPE, - 1 00

A Practical Treatise on the Culture and Treatment of the Grape Vine, embracing its History, with Directions for its Treatment in the United States of America, in the Open Air and under Glass Structures, with and without Artificial Heat. By J. Fisk Allen.

ALLEN'S (R. L) DISEASES OF DOMESTIC ANIMALS, - 75

Being a History and Description of the Horse, Mule, Cattle, Sheep, Swine, Poultry, and Farm Dogs, with Directions for their Management, Breeding, Crossing, Rearing, Feeding, and Preparation for a Profitable Market; also, their Diseases and Remedies, together with full Directions for the Management of the Dairy, and the comparative Economy and Advantages of Working Animals, the Horse, Mule, Oxen, &c. By R. L. Allen.

ALLEN'S (R. L.) AMERICAN FARM BOOK, - - - 1 00

The American Farm Book; or, a Compend of American Agriculture, being a Practical Treatise on Soils, Manures, Draining, Irrigation, Grasses, Grain, Roots, Fruits, Cotton, Tobacco, Sugar Cane, Rice, and every Staple Product of the United States; with the Best Methods of Planting, Cultivating and Preparation for Market. Illustrated with more than 100 engravings. By R. L. Allen.

ALLEN'S (L. F.) RURAL ARCHITECTURE; - - - 1 25

Being a Complete Description of Farm Houses, Cottages, and Out Buildings, comprising Wood Houses, Workshops, Tool Houses, Carriage and Wagon Houses, Stables, Smoke and Ash Houses, Ice Houses, Apiaries or Bee Houses, Poultry Houses, Rabbitry, Dovecote, Piggery, Barns, and Sheds for Cattle, &c., &c., together with Lawns, Pleasure Grounds, and Parks; the Flower, Fruit, and Vegetable Garden; also useful and ornamental domestic Animals for the Country Resident, &c., &c. Also, the best method of conducting water into Cattle Yards and Houses. Beautifully illustrated.

WARING'S ELEMENTS OF AGRICULTURE; - - - 75

A Book for Young Farmers, with Questions for the use of Schools.

PARDEE (R. G.) ON STRAWBERRY CULTURE; - - $0 60

A COMPLETE MANUAL FOR THE CULTIVATION OF THE STRAWBERRY; with a description of the best varieties.

Also, notices of the Raspberry, Blackberry, Currant, Gooseberry, and Grape; with directions for their cultivation, and the selection of the best varieties. "Every process here recommended has been proved, the plans of others tried, and the result is here given." With a valuable appendix, containing the observations and experience of some of the most successful cultivators of these fruits in our country.

GUENON ON MILCH COWS; - - - - - - - 60

A TREATISE ON MILCH COWS, whereby the Quality and Quantity of Milk which any Cow will give may be accurately determined by observing Natural Marks or External Indications alone; the length of time she will continue to give Milk, &c., &c. By M. FRANCIS GUENON, of Libourne, France. Translated by NICHOLAS P. TRIST, Esq.; with Introduction, Remarks, and Observations on the Cow and the Dairy, by JOHN S. SKINNER. Illustrated with numerous engravings. Neatly done up in paper covers, 37 cts.

AMERICAN POULTRY YARD; - - - - - - 1 00

COMPRISING THE ORIGIN, HISTORY AND DESCRIPTION of the different Breeds of Domestic Poultry, with complete directions for their Breeding, Crossing, Rearing, Fattening, and Preparation for Market; including specific directions for Caponizing Fowls, and for the Treatment of the Principal Diseases to which they are subject, drawn from authentic sources and personal observation. Illustrated with numerous engravings. By D. J. BROWNE.

BROWNE'S (D. JAY) FIELD BOOK OF MANURES; - - 1 25

OR, AMERICAN MUCK BOOK; Treating of the Nature, Properties, Sources, History, and Operations of all the Principal Fertilizers and Manures in Common Use, with specific directions for their Preservation, and Application to the Soil and to Crops; drawn from authentic sources, actual experience, and personal observation, as combined with the Leading Principles of Practical and Scientific Agriculture. By D. JAY BROWNE.

RANDALL'S (H. S.) SHEEP HUSBANDRY; - - - 1 25

WITH AN ACCOUNT OF THE DIFFERENT BREEDS, and general directions in regard to Summer and Winter Management, Breeding, and the Treatment of Diseases, with Portraits and other Engravings. By HENRY S. RANDALL.

THE SHEPHERD'S OWN BOOK; - - - - - - 2 00

WITH AN ACCOUNT OF THE DIFFERENT BREEDS, DISEASES AND MANagement of Sheep, and General Directions in regard to Summer and Winter Management, Breeding, and the Treatment of Diseases; with Illustrative Engravings, by YOUATT & RANDALL; embracing Skinner's Notes on the Breed and Management of Sheep in the United States, and on the Culture of Fine Wool.

YOUATT ON SHEEP, - - - - - - - - - 75

THEIR BREED, MANAGEMENT AND DISEASES, with Illustrative Engravings; to which are added Remarks on the Breeds and Management of Sheep in the United States, and on the Culture of Fine Wool in Silesia. By WILLIAM YOUATT.

YOUATT AND MARTIN ON CATTLE; - - - - - 1 25

BEING A TREATISE ON THEIR BREEDS, MANAGEMENT, AND DISEASES, comprising a full History of the Various Races; their Origin, Breeding, and Merits; their capacity for Beef and Milk. By W. YOUATT and W. C. L. MARTIN. The whole forming a Complete Guide for the Farmer, the Amateur, and the Veterinary Surgeon, with 100 Illustrations. Edited by AMBROSE STEVENS.

YOUATT ON THE HORSE; - - - - - - - - 1 25

YOUATT ON THE STRUCTURE AND DISEASES OF THE HORSE, with their Remedies. Also, Practical Rules for Buyers, Breeders, Smiths, &c. Edited by W. C. SPOONER, M.R.C.V.S. With an account of the Breeds in the United States, by HENRY S. RANDALL.

YOUATT AND MARTIN ON THE HOG; - - - - - $0 75

A TREATISE ON THE BREEDS, MANAGEMENT, AND MEDICAL TREATment of Swine, with Directions for Salting Pork, and Curing Bacon and Hams. By WM. YOUATT, V.S., and W. C. L. MARTIN. Edited by AMBROSE STEVENS. Illustrated with Engravings drawn from life.

BLAKE'S (REV. JOHN L.) FARMER AT HOME; - 1 25

A FAMILY TEXT BOOK FOR THE COUNTRY; being a Cyclopedia of Agricultural Implements and Productions, and of the more important topics in Domestic Economy, Science, and Literature, adapted to Rural Life. By Rev. JOHN L. BLAKE, D.D.

MUNN'S (B.) PRACTICAL LAND DRAINER; - - - 50

BEING A TREATISE ON DRAINING LAND, in which the most approved systems of Drainage are explained, and their differences and comparative merits discussed; with full Directions for the Cutting and Making of Drains, with Remarks upon the various materials of which they may be constructed. With many illustrations. By B. MUNN, Landscape Gardener.

ELLIOTT'S AMERICAN FRUIT GROWER'S GUIDE IN ORCHARD AND GARDEN; - - - - - - - - - - 1 25

BEING A COMPEND OF THE HISTORY, MODES OF PROPAGATION, CULture, &c., of Fruit Trees and Shrubs, with descriptions of nearly all the varieties of Fruits cultivated in this country; and Notes of their adaptation to localities, soils, and a complete list of Fruits worthy of cultivation. By F. R. ELLIOTT, Pomologist.

PRACTICAL FRUIT, FLOWER, AND KITCHEN GARDENER'S COMPANION; - - - - - - - - - - 1 00

WITH A CALENDAR. BY PATRICK NEILL, LL.D., F.R.S.E., Secretary of the Royal Caledonian Horticultural Society. Adapted to the United States from the fourth edition, revised and improved by the author. Edited by G. EMERSON, M.D., Editor of "The American Farmer's Encyclopedia." With Notes and Additions by R. G. PARDEE, author of "Manual of the Strawberry Culture." With illustrations.

STEPHENS' (HENRY) BOOK OF THE FARM; - - 4 00

A COMPLETE GUIDE TO THE FARMER, STEWARD, PLOWMAN, CATtleman, Shepherd, Field Worker, and Dairy Maid. By HENRY STEPHENS. With Four Hundred and Fifty Illustrations; to which are added Explanatory Notes, Remarks, &c., by J. S. SKINNER. Really one of the best books a farmer can possess.

PEDDERS' (JAMES) FARMERS' LAND MEASURER; - - 50

OR, POCKET COMPANION; Showing at one view the Contents of any Piece of Land from Dimensions taken in Yards. With a set of Useful Agricultural Tables.

WHITE'S (W. N.) GARDENING FOR THE SOUTH; - - 1 25

OR, THE KITCHEN AND FRUIT GARDEN, with the best methods for their Cultivation; together with hints upon Landscape and Flower Gardening; containing modes of culture and descriptions of the species and varieties of the Culinary Vegetables, Fruit Trees, and Fruits, and a select list of Ornamental Trees and Plants found by trial adapted to the States of the Union south of Pennsylvania, with Gardening Calendars for the same. By WM. N. WHITE, of Athens, Georgia.

EASTWOOD (B.) ON THE CULTIVATION OF THE CRANBERRY; 50

WITH A DESCRIPTION OF THE BEST VARIETIES. BY B. EASTWOOD, "Septimus" of the New York Tribune.

AMERICAN BEE-KEEPER'S MANUAL; - - - - - 1 00

BEING A PRACTICAL TREATISE ON THE HISTORY AND DOMESTIC Economy of the Honey Bee, embracing a full illustration of the whole subject, with the most approved methods of managing this Insect, through every branch of its Culture; the result of many years' experience. Illustrated with many engravings. By T. B. MINER.

THAER'S (ALBERT D.) AGRICULTURE - - - - $2 00

THE PRINCIPLES OF AGRICULTURE, by ALBERT D. THAER; translated by WILLIAM SHAW and CUTHBERT W. JOHNSON, Esq., F.R.S. With a Memoir of the Author. 1 vol. 8vo.

This work is regarded by those who are competent to judge as one of the most beautiful works that has ever appeared on the subject of Agriculture. At the same time that it is eminently practical, it is philosophical, and, even to the general reader, remarkably entertaining.

BOUSSINGAULT'S (J. B.) RURAL ECONOMY, - - - 1 25

IN ITS RELATIONS TO CHEMISTRY, PHYSICS, AND METEOROLOGY: or, Chemistry applied to Agriculture. By J. B. BOUSSINGAULT. Translated, with notes, etc., by GEORGE LAW, Agriculturist.

"The work is the fruit of a long life of study and experiment, and its perusal will aid the farmer greatly in obtaining a practical and scientific knowledge of his profession."

MYSTERIES OF BEE-KEEPING EXPLAINED; - - - - 1 00

BEING A COMPLETE ANALYSIS OF THE WHOLE SUBJECT, consisting of the Natural History of Bees; Directions for obtaining the greatest amount of Pure Surplus Honey with the least possible expense; Remedies for losses given, and the Science of Luck fully illustrated; the result of more than twenty years' experience in extensive Apiaries. By M. QUINBY.

THE COTTAGE AND FARM BEE-KEEPER; - - - - 50

A PRACTICAL WORK, by a Country Curate.

WEEKS (JOHN M.) ON BEES.—A MANUAL; - - - - 50

OR, AN EASY METHOD OF MANAGING BEES IN THE MOST PROFITABLE manner to their owner; with infallible rules to prevent their destruction by the Moth. With an appendix, by WOOSTER A. FLANDERS.

THE ROSE; - - - - - - - - - - - 50

BEING A PRACTICAL TREATISE ON THE PROPAGATION, CULTIVATION, and Management of the Rose in all Seasons; with a list of Choice and Approved Varieties, adapted to the Climate of the United States; to which is added full directions for the Treatment of the Dahlia. Illustrated by Engravings.

MOORE'S RURAL HAND BOOKS, - - - - - - - 1 25

FIRST SERIES, containing Treatises on—

THE HORSE, THE PESTS OF THE FARM,
THE HOG, DOMESTIC FOWLS, and
THE HONEY BEE, THE COW,

SECOND SERIES, containing— - - - - - 1 25

EVERY LADY HER OWN FLOWER GARDENER, ESSAY ON MANURES,
ELEMENTS OF AGRICULTURE, AMERICAN KITCHEN GARDENER,
BIRD FANCIER, AMERICAN ROSE CULTURIST.

THIRD SERIES, containing— - - - - - - 1 25

MILES ON THE HORSE'S FOOT, VINE DRESSER'S MANUAL,
THE RABBIT FANCIER, BEE-KEEPER'S CHART,
WEEKS ON BEES, CHEMISTRY MADE EASY.

FOURTH SERIES, containing— - - - - - 1 25

PERSOZ ON THE VINE, HOOPER'S DOG AND GUN,
LIEBIG'S FAMILIAR LETTERS, SKILLFUL HOUSEWIFE,
BROWNE'S MEMOIRS OF INDIAN CORN.

RICHARDSON ON DOGS: THEIR ORIGIN AND VARIETIES. . 50

DIRECTIONS AS TO THEIR GENERAL MANAGEMENT. With numerous original anecdotes. Also, Complete Instructions as to Treatment under Disease. By H. D. RICHARDSON. Illustrated with numerous wood engravings.

This is not only a cheap work, but one of the best ever published on the Dog

LIEBIG'S (JUSTUS) FAMILIAR LECTURES ON CHEMISTRY, $0 50

AND ITS RELATION TO COMMERCE, PHYSIOLOGY, AND AGRICULTURE. Edited by JOHN GARDENER, M.D.

BEMENT'S (C. N.) RABBIT FANCIER; - - - - - 50

A TREATISE ON THE BREEDING, REARING, FEEDING, AND GENERAL Management of Rabbits, with remarks upon their diseases and remedies, to which are added full directions for the construction of Hutches, Rabbitries, &c., together with recipes for cooking and dressing for the Table. Beautifully illustrated.

THOMPSON (R. D.) ON THE FOOD OF ANIMALS - - 75

EXPERIMENTAL RESEARCHES ON THE FOOD OF ANIMALS AND THE Fattening of Cattle; with remarks on the Food of Man. Based upon Experiments undertaken by order of the British Government, by ROBERT DUNDAS THOMPSON, M.D., Lecturer on Practical Chemistry, University of Glasgow.

THE WESTERN FRUIT BOOK; - - - - - - 1 25

BEING A COMPEND OF THE HISTORY, MODES OF PROPAGATION, CULture, &c., of Fruit Trees and Shrubs, &c., &c. By F. R. ELLIOTT.

THE SKILLFUL HOUSEWIFE; - - - - - - - 50

OR COMPLETE GUIDE TO DOMESTIC COOKERY, TASTE, COMFORT, AND Economy, embracing 659 recipes pertaining to Household Duties, the care of Health, Gardening, Birds, Education of Children, &c., &c. By Mrs L. G. ABELL.

THE AMERICAN FLORIST'S GUIDE; - - - - - - 75

COMPRISING THE AMERICAN ROSE CULTURIST AND EVERY LADY HER own Flower Gardener.

EVERY LADY HER OWN FLOWER GARDENER; - - 50

ADDRESSED TO THE INDUSTRIOUS AND ECONOMICAL ONLY; containing simple and practical Directions for Cultivating Plants and Flowers; also, Hints for the Management of Flowers in Rooms, with brief Botanical Descriptions of Plants and Flowers. The whole in plain and simple language. By LOUISA JOHNSON.

FISH CULTURE; - - - - - - - - - - - 1 00

A TREATISE ON THE ARTIFICIAL PROPAGATION OF CERTAIN KINDS OF Fish, with the description and habits of such kinds as are most suitable for pisciculture. Also directions for the most successful methods of Angling, illustrated with numerous engravings By THEODATUS GARLICK, M.D., Vice President of Cleveland Academy of Natural Science.

FLINT ON GRASSES; - - - - - - - - - 1 25

A PRACTICAL TREATISE ON GRASSES AND FORAGE PLANTS, COMPRISing their natural history, comparative nutritive value, methods of cultivating, cutting, and curing, and the management of grass lands. By CHAS. L. FLINT, A.M., Secretary of Mass. State Board of Agriculture.

WARDER ON HEDGES AND EVERGREENS; - - - - 1 00

A MANUAL ON LIVE FENCES, WITH PARTICULAR DIRECTIONS FOR THEIR planting, culture and trimming, especially with regard to the Maclura hedges, and how to make it. Also an essay on Evergreens, their varieties, propagation, transplanting and culture in the United States. By JOHN A. WARDER, M.D., President of Cincinnati Horticultural Society.

THE HORSE'S FOOT AND HOW TO KEEP IT SOUND;

With Cuts, illustrating the Anatomy of the Foot, and containing valuable hints on shoeing and stable management, both in health and disease. By William Miles.

THE SKILLFUL HOUSEWIFE;

Or, Complete Guide to Domestic Cookery, Taste, Comfort, and Economy, embracing 659 recipes pertaining to Household Duties, the care of Health, Gardening, Birds, Education of Children, &c., &c. By Mrs. L. G. Abell.

THE AMERICAN KITCHEN GARDENER;

Containing Directions for the Cultivation of Vegetables and Garden Fruits. By T. G. Fessenden.

CHINESE SUGAR CANE AND SUGAR MAKING;

Its History, Culture, and Adaptation to the Soil, Climate, and Economy of the United States, with an account of various processes of Manufacturing Sugar. Drawn from authentic sources by Charles F. Stansbury, A.M., late Commissioner at the Exhibition of all Nations at London.

PERSOZ' CULTURE OF THE VINE;

A New Process for the Culture of the Vine, by Persoz, Professor to the Faculty of Sciences of Strasbourg; directing Professor of the School of Pharmacy of the same city. Translated by J. O'C. Barclay, Surgeon U. S. N.

THE BEE KEEPER'S CHART;

Being a Brief Practical Treatise on the Instinct, Habits, and Management of the Honey Bee, in all its various branches, the result of many years' practical experience, whereby the author has been enabled to divest the subject of much that has been consideed mysterious and difficult to overcome, and render it more sure, profitable, and interesting to every one, than it has heretofore been. By E. W. Phelps.

EVERY LADY HER OWN FLOWER GARDENER;

Addressed to the Industrious and Economical only; containing Simple and Practical Directions for Cultivating Plants and Flowers; also, Hints for the Management of Flowers in Rooms, with brief Botanical Descriptions of Plants and Flowers. The whole in plain and simple language. By Louisa Johnson.

THE COW; DAIRY HUSBANDRY AND CATTLE BREEDING.

By M. M. Milburn, and revised by H. D. Richardson and Ambrose Stevens. With Illustrations.

WILSON ON THE CULTURE OF FLAX;

Its Treatment, Agricultural and Technical; delivered before the New York State Agricultural Society, at the Annual Fair at Saratoga, in September last, by John Wilson, late President of the Royal Agricultural College at Cirencester, England.

WEEKS ON BEES: A MANUAL.

Or, an Easy Method of Managing Bees in the most profitable manner to their owner, with infallible rules to prevent their destruction by the Moth; with an Appendix by Wooster A. Flanders.

REEMELIN'S (CHAS.) VINE DRESSER'S MANUAL;

Containing full Instructions as to Location and Soil; Preparation of Ground; Selection and Propagation of Vines; the Treatment of a Young Vineyard; trimming and training the vines; manures and the making of wine. Every department illustrated.

HYDE'S CHINESE SUGAR CANE;

Containing its History, Mode of Culture, Manufacture of the Sugar, &c.; with Reports of its success in different parts of the United States.

BEMENT'S (C. M.) RABBIT FANCIER;

A TREATISE ON THE BREEDING, REARING, FEEDING, AND GENERAL Management of Rabbits, with remarks upon their diseases and remedies; to which are added full directions for the construction of Hutches, Rabbitries, &c., together with recipes for cooking and dressing for the table.

RICHARDSON ON DOGS: THEIR ORIGIN AND VARIETIES;

DIRECTIONS AS TO THEIR GENERAL MANAGEMENT. With numerous original anecdotes. Also Complete Instructions as to Treatment under Disease. By H. D. RICHARDSON. Illustrated with numerous wood engravings.

This is not only a cheap, but one of the best works ever published on the Dog.

LIEBIG'S (JUSTUS) FAMILIAR LETTERS ON CHEMISTRY;

AND ITS RELATION TO COMMERCE, PHYSIOLOGY, and AGRICULTURE Edited by JOHN GARDENER, M.D.

THE DOG AND GUN;

A FEW LOOSE CHAPTERS ON SHOOTING, among which will be found some anecdotes and incidents. Also instructions for Dog Breaking, and interesting letters from Sportsmen. BY A BAD SHOT.

THE PRESERVATION OF FOOD;

THE VARIOUS METHODS OF PRESERVING MEATS, FRUITS, VEGETABLES, Milk, Butter, Grain, &c., by drying, smoking, pickling, and other processes. By F. GOODRICH SMITH.

www.ingramcontent.com/pod-product-compliance
Lightning Source LLC
LaVergne TN
LVHW021123110826
845150LV00005B/926

* 9 7 8 1 4 2 5 5 5 0 8 7 5 *